The Other Pushkin

THE OTHER PUSHKIN

A Study of Alexander Pushkin's
Prose Fiction

PAUL DEBRECZENY

STANFORD UNIVERSITY PRESS 1983
Stanford, California

Title-page drawing by Alexander Pushkin, 1836

Stanford University Press
Stanford, California
© 1983 by the Board of Trustees of the
Leland Stanford Junior University
Printed in the United States of America
ISBN 0-8047-1143-7
LC 81-85449

Published with the assistance of
the National Endowment for the Humanities

To Gill, Louise, and Martin

Preface

THE PROSE WORKS OF Alexander Sergeevich Pushkin (1799–
1837) have a double claim on our attention. Some of them—
such as "The Stationmaster" and "The Queen of Spades"—can
be ranked among the highest achievements of Russian and European fiction-writing in the nineteenth century, and deserve
study in their own right. Others—completed, half-finished, or
representing mere fragments—are significant not only because
they surround and explain Pushkin's own best accomplishments in the genre, but also because they signal the beginning
of one of the richest epochs in the history of prose fiction in
any country. Pushkin's "The Undertaker," as well as other stories, paved the way for Gogol and the so-called Natural School;
Pushkin's "The Stationmaster" inspired Gogol's "The Overcoat"; and the two works together formed the thematic background for Dostoevskii's *Poor People*. Hermann of "The Queen
of Spades" served as a prototype for both Aleksei Ivanovich in
Dostoevskii's *The Gambler* and Raskolnikov in *Crime and
Punishment*; Pushkin's Belkin was the father of Goncharov's
Oblomov; and Pushkin's *The Captain's Daughter*, as a "family
chronicle," was the most useful model Tolstoi could turn to as
he experimented with the novelistic form, working on *War and
Peace*. Pushkin's artistic legacy—over and above individual
instances of influence—pervaded the whole of nineteenth-
century Russian fiction.

One difficulty for the student of his prose is that his influence on other prose writers was by no means limited to his
writings in this form. Themes in *The Gambler* can be traced

back not only to "The Queen of Spades," but also to one of Pushkin's "Little Tragedies," *The Covetous Knight*; the strongest inspiration behind Dostoevskii's *The Idiot* was not a prose work, but a single lyrical poem of Pushkin's, "The Poor Knight"; Pechorin of Lermontov's *A Hero of Our Time* and a host of other "superfluous men" of later fiction writers descended from the hero of Pushkin's "novel in verse," *Eugene Onegin*; and several of Turgenev's heroines have been shown to have originated from Tatiana of the same work. Indeed, it is not surprising that Pushkin's verse had the most profound effect on the development of later Russian fiction, for his greatest achievement was in poetry—lyrical, narrative, and dramatic. His own prose can be properly appreciated only from the perspective of his poetry; and for this reason occasional references to his poetic works could not be dispensed with in the present study.

It has been my aim to discuss all of Pushkin's fictional works in chronological order, with full documentation in the Notes. Beyond the presentation of this factual material, however, there is the broader purpose of trying to explain what prose meant to Pushkin, particularly in comparison with poetry. In the first half of Chapter One I have set up a historical framework with just that purpose in mind, hoping that the reader will find it relevant to subsequent analyses of actual stories. As for these analyses, I take it that the business of the critic and literary historian is to articulate aesthetic experience with whatever means come to hand at a particular time; like the mythical Peleus, he has to adapt his hold to the changing shape of Thetis, his subject. Therefore, though I have put most emphasis on a discussion of the literary form, I have been frankly eclectic in my critical approach. No one approach, however accurate in its methodology, is adequate, in my opinion, if it loses sight of aesthetic values. Bearing this in mind, I have not shunned value judgments even at the risk of being subjective.

I would like to thank my colleague Madeline G. Levine for reading and discussing with me each chapter of the manuscript as it was written; and I am grateful to Walter Arndt, David M. Griffiths, Walter N. Vickery, and Josephine Z. Woll for their careful reading of parts of the manuscript and for their thought-ful suggestions. Thanks are also due to the International Re-search and Exchanges Board, the Research Council of the Uni-versity of North Carolina, and the American Philosophical Society for their financial support of the project in its various stages. The research leading to this book was conducted at the Louis R. Wilson Library of the University of North Carolina, the Library of Congress, the British Library, the M. E. Saltykov-Shchedrin Public Library, the Lenin Library, and the Institute of Russian Literature (Pushkin House); I wish to express my ap-preciation to all these institutions for giving me access to their holdings. Last but not least, I am deeply grateful to my wife, Gillian, for preparing the Index.

Fragments of several chapters of this study have been pub-lished as articles in *The Slavic and East European Journal*, Vol. 18, No. 2 (1974); *Russian Literature*, Vol. 4, No. 2 (1976); *Canadian-American Slavic Studies*, Vol. 10, No. 2 (1976), and Vol. 11, No. 1 (1977); *Alexander Puškin: Symposium II*, ed. A. Kodjak, K. Pomorska, and K. Taranovsky (Columbus, Ohio: Slavica, 1980); and *Studia Slavica*, Vol. 28 (1982).

Chapel Hill, N.C.   P.D.
May 1980

Contents

The Other Pushkin

1. Pushkin's Approach to Fiction

I

When Pushkin's narrative poem *The Prisoner of the Caucasus* (1822) was first published, his friend P. A. Viazemskii reviewed it favorably in print but complained in a private letter that Pushkin had "bloodied the last verses of his tale."[1] Viazemskii was referring to the Epilogue to the poem, in which Pushkin glorified the Russian conquerors of the Caucasian region. Viazemskii's complaint was not without foundation: the preceding narrative parts of the poem had depicted the Circassians as noble, freedom-loving savages, in many ways superior to their captive, a blasé dandy from St. Petersburg; and Pushkin's sudden switch to lauding the oppressors of these attractive natives seemed, not only out of place in the context of the poem, but also inappropriate from a political point of view. The Epilogue has struck later critics, too, as incongruous. B. V. Tomashevskii has attempted to eliminate the incongruity, showing that Pushkin—like his friends in the Decembrist movement—felt little sympathy for the Caucasian peoples' national independence, and that on the contrary, one could regard Viazemskii's sensitivity to the problem as the unusual position for the time.[2] A clarification of political attitudes is not, however, sufficient to account for a poetic incongruity, if indeed there is one in this case.

Most probably, Pushkin himself saw no incongruity: what he had done was simply to replace one lyrical persona with another. If we assume, simplifying somewhat, that Parts One and Two of the poem were written in the same key, we can say that the lyrical persona standing behind these narrative parts is a

Byronic one, disillusioned with civilization and well-inclined toward uncivilized peoples, whereas the persona behind the Epilogue is a patriotic bard. Both had their places in other poems by Pushkin: variants of the Byronic attitude are found in the lyric "Napoleon" (1821), "Demon" (1823), and "To the Sea" (1824), and the voice of the bard had been heard ever since Pushkin had extolled the glory of Russian arms in "Reminiscences at Tsarskoe Selo" (1814). These two personae amounted to two different roles, either of which could be legitimately assumed by the poet, since each carried aesthetic values. What Viazemskii was demanding was that the poet assume no conflicting roles, but maintain a unified personality behind all his utterances—a demand contrary to the nature of Pushkin's art.

If the Epilogue to *The Prisoner* was "civic" poetry in the sense of commending Russia's military achievements, so were Pushkin's poems embracing liberty and castigating tyranny, only with a diametrically opposed ideology. There was poetry both in fighting native resistance in the Caucasus and in bringing down the edifice of Russian despotism, on the ruins of which the name of the poet would be inscribed ("To Chaadaev," 1818). Pushkin did not see any reason why he should limit himself to either one, to the exclusion of the other. Ernest J. Simmons seems to be correct when he states in his biography that the poems in which Pushkin advocated social reform or revolution were as much the "results of sudden inspiration" as were his poems of other moods.[3]

Contradictory as the patriotic and revolutionary stances may have been from an ideological point of view, they both committed poetry to a cause. Pushkin made this commitment explicit in a whole series of poems. In the first stanza of the ode "Liberty" (1817), he invites a martial muse to smash his effeminate lyre and help him sing of freedom. In the ironic eclogue "Village" (1819), he wishes he could awaken people's hearts to the suffering of the oppressed masses. In "Oh, Muse of Flaming Satire" (1825), he vows that his poetry will be a scourge of villainy. His most passionate statement on behalf of a *littérature engagée* is the 1826 lyric "The Prophet," in which he portrays God's chosen man (or the poet, if you will) as a man with a burning coal in his breast instead of a heart, sent out into the world "to sear people's hearts by words."* "Arion" (1827) affirms the poet's continuing commitment even after his companions (i.e., the Decembrists) have all perished in a storm. Finally, surveying his poetic achievements toward the end of his career, Pushkin predicts that he will be remembered for evoking kind feelings by his lyre, for exalting liberty in his cruel epoch, and for advocating mercy to the fallen ("I Have Reared a Monument," 1836).

This series of poems, however, was counterbalanced, all through Pushkin's creative career, by another series reflecting an entirely different image of the poet. The early "Dreamer" (1814) implies that poetry can exist only if it is removed from all earthly strife. In the verse epistle "To Zhukovskii" (1818), extolling poetry as an exquisite pleasure for the select few, Pushkin comes close to a theory of art for art's sake. "The Poet and the Crowd" (1828) is the strongest indictment of a utilitarianism that prefers a cooking utensil to Apollo Belvedere and would reduce the function of poetry to moral street-sweeping. The poem ends with the famous lines (3: 142):

> We were not born for the bustle of life,
> Nor for avarice, nor for battles:
> We are destined for inspiration,
> For sweet melodies and orisons.

This statement—supported by the lyrics "Poet" (1827) and "To a Poet" (1830), and by other affirmations of the artist's independence—would seem to represent Pushkin's poetic credo. But, as we have seen, it is sharply contradicted by works commending the civic functions of poetry. There was as much beauty in passionate commitment as in the calm of the ivory tower: Pushkin chose either one or the other, as the occasion arose. Describing "Pushkin's uncanny hospitality to ideas, however disparate or incompatible," Victor Erlich comes to the conclusion that Pushkin's conception of the poet reflected a double image.[4] This conclusion seems to be appropriate as far as the conflict between civic commitment and art for its own sake is concerned, but I would like to suggest that such a con-

---

*A. S. Pushkin, *Polnoe sobranie sochinenii*. Ed. V. D. Bonch-Bruevich et al. (Moscow: Akademiia Nauk SSSR, 1937–59), 3: 31. All the parenthetical citations in the text refer to this edition.

flict is only a part of a larger pattern, the civic poet and the withdrawn aesthete representing only two of many lyrical personae that rapidly supersede one another in Pushkin's poetry. If any one word can describe Pushkin's poetic talent, it is versatility. He can treat Napoleon with either contempt or admiration, depending on whether he speaks as a Russian patriot or as a romantic admirer of individual greatness. It was characteristic of him that he would send a copy of an ode on "Liberty" to Princess E. I. Golitsyna in 1818 in company with a note confessing that he had grown fond of vassalage since he had first beheld her. This was not just a pun on political liberty and freedom of the heart, but also a shift to a different poetic personality. In the 1818 verse epistle "To Chaadaev," he writes that delusions of love can no longer get the better of him, and that his heart's sole remaining passion is to fight tyranny; yet in the lyric to Anna Kern ("I Remember the Wondrous Moment," 1825) he describes love as his only source of inspiration. In contrast to the spirituality of this poem, other verses range from Anacreontic to downright bawdy.

It could be argued that lyrical poetry, by its very nature, records the thoughts and moods of isolated moments, which the poet is not obliged to unite in a congruous whole. But a comparison of Pushkin with other lyric poets suggests that few have ranged as far and wide as he. (One need only recall the much more limited range of, for instance, Byron.) Moreover, the same versatility that characterizes Pushkin's lyric poetry obtains also in his verse tales. If he is able to sympathize equally with the poor captive Maria, the revengeful Zarema, and the love-stricken tyrant Girei in *The Fountain at Bakhchisarai* (1823), this is due, once more, to a multifaceted lyrical persona. Even in *Eugene Onegin* (1823–31), in which the narrator is a single, defined individual, the mood nevertheless shifts so much as to accommodate both ironic and compassionate views of the characters. Pushkin tended to become completely absorbed in his subject and to grant it independent existence, creating the impression that his own personality has been surrendered. Like Garrick, he could excel equally in the roles of Richard III, Hamlet, and King Lear. But if this was so, the question then arises of just how much of Pushkin's own personality was involved in the artistic representation. Was he voicing his own opinions in the Epilogue to *The Prisoner of the Caucasus*, or was he merely giving a great performance in the role of the patriotic bard? If he was only playacting, could he be taken seriously?

Questions of this type, though applicable to other periods in the history of literature, were asked particularly frequently in the first decades of the nineteenth century. They are accorded a great deal of attention, for instance, in Jane Austen's *Mansfield Park* (1814). The main theme of this novel—Edmund's realization that Fanny Price's virtue is preferable to Mary Crawford's charm—is supported by a subtheme that amounts to a discussion of the moral functions of art.[5] Acting, mastered to perfection by the character Henry Crawford, seems to stand for art in general. Crawford, we are plainly told, is not as attractive physically as some of the other male characters, but his histrionics—both off and on the stage—wins the hearts of the two Bertram girls. It is during the rehearsals for a domestic theatrical performance that Maria becomes uncontrollably infatuated with him. Even the sober Fanny is moved by him on one occasion, when he gives a superb reading of Shakespeare. But the outward glitter of his talent does not mislead the perspicacious Fanny for long: she soon comes to understand that "whether it were dignity or pride, or tenderness or remorse, or whatever were to be expressed, he could do it with equal beauty,"[6] as though the beauty of expression alone mattered to him, while the content remained unimportant. This attitude of Henry's becomes even clearer when he says he has more than half a mind to take orders and preach just because he loves the eloquence of the pulpit—even though he obviously has no religious feelings of his own to convey. The implication is that art can become the maidservant of any moral or immoral purpose. Since it has the capacity for making vice attractive, we had better reject it altogether, as indeed the unfortunate Maria Bertram should have done.

It is characteristic of the period that Henry Crawford reads Shakespeare. The choice of the play—*Henry VIII*—further underscores the meaning Austen wishes to convey, for this play is an excellent example of Shakespearean absorption in the subject (even though it is only partially attributed to Shakespeare). The initial arrangement makes us side with Katharine, a victim of her husband's inconstancy and of Cardinal Wolsey's intrigues. Soon, however, we are forced to realign our sympathies, because Wolsey—through his own powerful speech and through Griffith's moving account of his demise—is transformed from a vicious person into a remarkable man, whose only failing was his too great ambition. And when it comes to the coronation of Henry's new wife, Anne Boleyn, the beauty of the ceremony carries the day: the folk on the streets, together with the Dukes of Norfolk and Suffolk and the Earl of Surrey—all of whom had sided with Katharine—happily participate in the joyous pageant, forgetting about the banished former Queen's sorrows. The upshot is that Katharine, Wolsey, and Anne Boleyn all have, in their turn, an equal claim on our emotions, while the dramatist himself has refused to take sides.

Pushkin was probably not familiar with Jane Austen's novels,[7] but he was keenly aware of the romantic revival of Shakespeare. Though he was hardly uncritical of the English playwright, he studied him with enthusiasm and drew much inspiration from him, especially in the second half of the 1820's. In the draft of a preface to *Boris Godunov* (1825), he openly declared that he had been trying to adapt for his tragedy "the popular rules of Shakespearean drama" (11: 141), and in a letter he wrote, "Following Shakespeare's example, I have confined my efforts to reproducing a period and some historical personalities, without theatrical effects or romantic pathos" (14: 46). Pushkin scholars have pointed out traces of Shakespeare, not only in *Boris Godunov*, but also in such works as *The Covetous Knight* (1830) and *The Stone Guest* (1830).[8] *Andzhelo* (1833) is an adaptation of *Measure for Measure*. Pushkin referred to Shakespeare in his letters, articles, and notebooks on numerous occasions, frequently placing the English playwright above Molière and Racine.

What drew Pushkin to Shakespeare was not merely a dramatic form free of the rigid rules of neoclassicism: after all, he himself was bold enough to do away with rules that hindered his art. The great attraction that the English playwright held for him was a feeling of kinship in literary attitudes. This is how he contrasted Shakespeare to Molière in his *Table Talk* (1835–36):

Shakespeare's characters, unlike Molière's, are not merely typical representatives of a certain passion or of a certain vice; on the contrary, they are living beings, complete with many passions and many vices. Their varied, many-sided personalities unfold as their circumstances reveal them to the viewer. Molière's miser is only miserly—that is all. Shakespeare's Shylock is not only miserly, but resourceful, vindictive, child-loving, and witty. Molière's hypocrite courts his benefactor's wife in a hypocritical fashion, takes on the care of an estate as a hypocrite, and asks for a glass of water hypocritically. Shakespeare's hypocrite pronounces judgment with arrogant severity,[9] but justly; he vindicates his cruelty by the profound arguments of a statesman; and he seduces innocence, not with a ridiculous mixture of piety and forwardness, but with powerful, beguiling sophistry. (12: 159–60)

What appealed to Pushkin was Shakespeare's creation of characters who lived fully and independently, not merely as a means to the author's end. In a letter to the editor of the *Moscow Herald*, he complained that "thanks to the French, we do not understand that a dramatist can completely renounce his own way of thinking in order to transfer himself entirely into the period he is describing" (11: 68).

Pushkin's admiration of Shakespeare and the romantics' revival of him sprang from the same sources. Indeed, Pushkin's opinions reflect his reading of August Schlegel's *Über dramatische Kunst und Litteratur* (1809–11), which he had in his library in a French translation. In connection with the dramatist's absorption in his subject, Schlegel spoke of Shakespeare's "capability of transporting himself so completely into every character, even the most unusual, that he is enabled, as plenipotentiary of the whole human race, without particular instructions for each separate case, to act and speak in the name of all."[10] The dramatist's involvement in the action was through the characters, while he, as a person, remained quite detached: "We may perceive in the poet himself, notwithstanding his power to excite the most profound emotions, a certain cool indifference."[11] Finally, Schlegel wrote that "Shakespeare, like an actor, always adapted himself to the quality of his material"[12]—a statement that could apply with equal validity to Henry Crawford's sermons or Pushkin's Epilogue to *The Prisoner of the Caucasus.*

In George Mead's opinion, it was the breakdown of the revolutionary movements in Europe that led to the tendency to assume roles in the early nineteenth century: the individual, awakened to his rights but disillusioned in the politics of revolution, was searching for a new identity, trying out different modes of being. "As a characteristic of the romantic attitude we find this assumption of roles," writes Mead, concluding that "the romantic attitude is the ability to project one's self upon the world, so that the world is identified in some fashion with the self."[13] Austen's strictures on Henry Crawford corroborate Mead's opinion, for she too seemed to regard the histrionic Crawford as a representative of romanticism. With romanticism she contrasted both an Augustan attitude, placing rational morality above a free play of sentiments, and a gentle sentimentalism, manifested in Fanny's fondness for stargazing and nature walks.

Yet one could not appropriate an assumption of roles for the romantic movement alone: indeed, it had been an essential part of the neoclassical theory of literature too. Outlining the properties of each genre in Cantos Two and Three of his *L'Art poétique* (1674), Nicolas Boileau-Despréaux offered fully defined sets of mental attitudes, any one of which could be assumed by a poet, in the same way as an actor could step into any role. This was, as we have seen, Pushkin's practice too, except for his most unclassical abrupt shifts from one genre to another (for example, from narrative poem to ode in *The Prisoner*).

John Keats, the most "Shakespearean" of the English romantic poets, advocated renouncing the artist's own self, not in the name of romanticism, but, on the contrary, as an adverse reaction to it. He saw a prime example of excessive romantic subjectivism (somewhat surprisingly) in the poetry of William Wordsworth. To the "wordsworthian or egotistical sublime," he opposed another poetical character that "is not itself—it has no self—it is everything and nothing—it has no character—it enjoys light and shade; it lives in gusto, be it foul or fair, high or low, rich or poor, mean or elevated—it has as much delight in conceiving an Iago as an Imogen. What shocks the virtuous philosopher, delights the camelion Poet."[14] He also objected to Coleridge on the grounds that the older poet had too much of a unified subjective world view from which he would not deviate:

I had not a dispute but a disquisition with Dilke, on various subjects; several things dovetailed in my mind, and at once it struck me what quality went to form a Man of Achievement especially in Literature and which Shakespeare possessed so enormously—I mean *Negative Capability*, that is when man is capable of being in uncertainties, Mysteries, doubts, without any irritable reaching after fact and reason—Coleridge, for instance, would let go by a fine isolated verisimilitude caught from the Penetralium of mystery, from being incapable of remaining Content with half knowledge. This pursued through volumes would perhaps take us no further than this, that with a great poet the sense of beauty overcomes every other consideration, or rather obliterates all consideration.[15]

Elsewhere he wrote that "men of Genius are great as certain ethereal Chemicals operating on the mass of neutral intellect—but they have not any individuality, any determined character."[16] All these statements were meant to deprecate romantic subjectivism, yet Keats confessed, typically for a romantic, a reliance on sentiment rather than reason: "I am certain of nothing but the holiness of the heart's affections and the truth of Imagination."[17]

The notion of "negative capability" came to the fore in an age that saw the interception of at least three major literary trends. An assumption of detached roles, part of the neoclassical tradition, was given new character by the intense emotionality of the romantic age. Since the intensity of feeling was the only measure of greatness (as Keats thought), Augustan reason no longer exercised moral control over the creatures of poetic imagination; these acquired a relatively independent existence and eventually became objects of realistic representation.

Much of Pushkin's artistic achievement was due to his "negative capability." Yet at times he felt uneasy about it. In one lyric he complained that the poet, like Echo, responded to the cry of the beast in the forest, to the shepherd's horn, to thunder, and to the singing of a maiden beyond the hill, but nothing responded to him ("Echo," 1831). In "Answer to an Anonymous

Correspondent" (1830), he bemoaned the indifference of the reading public to the poet as a human being: if he expressed his heart's most profound sorrow, they applauded him; if grievous loss, exile, or confinement befell him, they rejoiced that he would gather new thoughts and sensations to be transformed into art; and if he found personal happiness, they treated it with cold indifference. Behind both of these lyrics there was a desire to break out of assumed roles and to become simply an individual. Laura of *The Stone Guest* is exhilarated when she feels that in her performance "The words poured forth as if they had been born, / Not of slavish memory, but of the heart" (7: 144).

The problem is expressed most eloquently in the unfinished novel *Egyptian Nights* (ca. 1835), whose Italian improvisatore can create poetry on the spur of the moment and on any topic suggested, as if his heart had no inclinations of its own. At the request of his Russian patron, Charskii, he improvises a poem of outstanding beauty, ironically, on the proposition that *"a poet chooses the subjects of his songs himself: the crowd has no right to command his inspiration"* (8: 268; Pushkin's italics). His improvised poem is an ode to the freedom of inspiration, but the circumstances under which it is composed suggest that he has no freedom, as he has no personality. His predicament was, evidently, not an isolated case in Pushkin's eyes, for Pushkin once remarked in a letter that the plays of Shakespeare had been "ordered by Elizabeth" (13: 179).

2

Pushkin gave of himself to both characters in *Egyptian Nights*. Like Charskii, he considered himself an aristocrat, entitled to a place in the best of Russian society by birth, regardless of poetic achievement. He wrote to the author and critic A. A. Bestuzhev-Marlinskii in 1825: "In our country, writers come from the upper class. Their aristocratic pride is mingled with their self-esteem as authors. We do not want to be patronized by our own equals" (13: 179). Later the same year, however, he made an important qualification, writing about the same question to the poet K. F. Ryleev: "How can you fail to see that the genius of our literature depends, at least in part, on the writers' status? We cannot lay our works at the feet of some grandees, because we consider ourselves their peers by birth. Hence our pride, etc. One must not view Russian writers in the same light as those abroad. There writing is done for money, here with us (except for me) from vanity" (13: 219). The qualification "except for me" recorded the fact that Pushkin was increasingly relying on his literary income for his livelihood. In other letters he compared himself variously to a cobbler, a baker, and a tailor who sell their products for so much a piece (13: 59, 86, 89). Although he insisted that he still wrote for himself, obeying the whims of inspiration (13: 89, 95) and thinking of profit only when the product was finished, he could not help dreading the predicament of the Italian improvisatore. If not to a Maecenas, he had to pander to the taste of the reading public, which he sometimes openly admitted, but other times denied (11: 66, 142). Eventually he waved the problem aside with an epigram about the author who "wrote for money and drank for glory" (3: 145).

Although Pushkin's narrative poems of the early 1820's fetched handsome royalties, it was clear even at the time that, in the literary market, the future belonged to prose fiction. In England, for example, several thousand pounds had been paid for some narrative poems—notably Thomas Moore's *Lalla Rookh* (1817) and Byron's *Don Juan* (1819–24)—but during the 1820's poetry was losing its popular appeal, while novels, particularly those of Walter Scott, were selling in large numbers of copies. Pushkin, always keenly interested in developments abroad, could not help noticing this new trend in the West. In any event, in Russia, too, such critics as Bestuzhev and O. M. Somov were calling for increased attention to prose fiction by this time.[18] At the end of the decade F. V. Bulgarin, an astute judge of the temper of the time, was making quite a fortune with his popular novel *Ivan Vyzhigin* (1829). In this connection, Pushkin recommended that critics should analyze the social reasons for a literary work's success, not just comment on its inherent qualities (11: 89). The demands of readers were brought home to him even more forcefully by the publisher

A. F. Smirdin, who informed Pushkin in 1832 that he had committed himself to publishing novels, for "tragedies were not selling" (15: 27). By 1836 we even find Pushkin pondering whether "poetry had not always been the pastime of the select few, while stories and novels were read by everybody everywhere" (12: 98). It would of course be an oversimplification to claim that Pushkin turned to prose writing merely out of market considerations. Although the state of the literary market was not lost on him, he also had an unselfish concern for the development of Russian literature, and it pained him to see prose fiction coming under the domination of cheap, second-rate writers. "By turning to prose," writes the Soviet scholar V. F. Pereverzev, "Pushkin was solving not so much a neutral problem of artistic creation as a polemical task: he wished to counter the crude fiction, written for the lower gentry and the *petite bourgeoisie,* with a more refined imaginative prose, befitting the taste of the upper echelons of a nobility that had attained the highest standards of European culture."[19] Moreover, Russian literature was developing toward prose by its own logic. As the ideas writers wished to convey grew in complexity, poetry began to prove too limited in scope, insufficiently expandable as a form. Bestuzhev wrote in 1823 that poetry was to prose as an infant's rattle was to a youth's compass, and it was time for Russian writers to reach for this more advanced tool.[20] The language of poetry itself had come to a crisis: brought close to the vernacular by Pushkin, it was becoming more fit for prose.[21]

All these factors considered, Pushkin would still not have turned to prose writing had it not been demanded by his personal artistic development.

At the beginning of his career, he did not regard prose as a genre that called for a special literary attitude. Some of the entries in his Lyceum diary, for instance, though in prose, are very close to his epigrams, love lyrics, and verse satires written at the same period. As L. S. Sidiakov shows in his excellent brief survey of the prose writings, Pushkin's character sketch of A. N. Ikonnikov, one of the tutors at the Lyceum, is a particularly striking example of poetic prose—of the kind the sentimentalists N. M. Karamzin and K. N. Batiushkov had cultivated.[22] But past this early stage, from the end of the 1810's, prose seemed to acquire a new character in Pushkin's eyes: it seemed to offer a way out of the assumption of literary roles, roles that he fondly indulged in at times but found tiresome at others.

In the spring of 1825, during his banishment to his mother's estate in Mikhailovskoe, he worked out a scheme to get out of Russia, with the aid of friends, on the pretext of seeking a cure for his aneurism. When V. A. Zhukovskii and Viazemskii mildly reproached him for his scheme, he protested that his friends "deprive me of my right to complain (not in verse, but in prose—a devil of a difference)" (13: 226). This implied that if he had poured his anger into an elegy or metrical satire, his friends would have rejoiced in the birth of a beautiful new poem (like the public in "Answer to an Anonymous Correspondent") but would not have taken his plea seriously. He would have simply been performing a poetic role. But since he had chosen to complain in prose, it was clear that he meant what he said, and his friends had to respond. In other words, poetry was an amusement, whereas prose was the language of practical business, admitting no role playing at all. A similar view of prose is expressed in the 1828 lyrical fragment "Alas, the Language of Garrulous Love": the lady he loves, the poet claims, would have read a letter in amorous verse with pleasure, but she tore up a confession of love in prose (because, it is implied, it had to be taken seriously).

In both of these cases, prose clearly meant epistolary, rather than imaginative, writing. At other times Pushkin used the term with reference to expository prose. On two separate occasions, urging Viazemskii to write "prose," he spoke of the need to develop a "metaphysical" Russian language, that is, a "language of ideas" (13: 44, 187). The same terms occur in his article "M. Lemontey's Preface to a Translation of I. A. Krylov's Fables" (1825): "Scholarship, politics, and philosophy have not yet found expression in Russian; we have no metaphysical language at all. Our prose is so little cultivated that even in simple correspondence we are obliged *to invent* new phrases in order to convey the most ordinary concepts" (11: 34). One of the most important characteristics of Pushkin's fiction—as it eventually emerged in the last decade of his life—was that it had developed primarily from nonfictional prose.

It is true, nevertheless, that he maintained at least a peripheral interest in fiction from the very start of his creative career. He is known to have worked on two novels during his first two years at the Lyceum (which he had entered in 1811).[23] For one of these, we have no more than the title—*The Gypsy*. Tomashevskii has hypothesized that the novel must have been conceived under the influence of Voltaire's *L'Ingénu* (1767) and must have presented an uncivilized man's baffled reactions to civilization.[24] The other novel was entitled *Fatam, or Human Reason* and was, once more, probably inspired by Voltaire, notably by "Memnon, ou La Sagesse humaine" (1747), by *Candide* (1759), and by dramas with Eastern themes such as *Zaïre* (1732) and *Le Fatalisme, ou Mahomet le Prophète* (1741).[25] Pushkin mentions in his Lyceum diary that he is working on the novel's third chapter, which he has entitled "Natural Law" (12: 298)—a title that further attests to the project's connection with the eighteenth-century Enlightenment. Some of Pushkin's Lyceum friends remembered the novel even after many years: it was from their words that the nineteenth-century scholar V. P. Gaevskii and Pushkin's first biographer, P. V. Annenkov, wrote down summaries of the plot.[26] Although the two scholars' summaries are not identical, they both confirm that Fatam would have been born with the wisdom of a sage and would have regressed into an infantile stage of mental development by the end of the novel—a denouement suggesting that Nature will revenge herself on those who transgress her laws. Unfortunately, not even a fragment of the manuscript has survived, though we do have four lines of a poem, written down by the hand of a Lyceum friend, which was probably to have been incorporated in the novel (17: 15).[27]

In 1819 Pushkin jotted down the beginning of a short story under the title "Nadenka." This half-page fragment anticipates the introductory scene of "The Queen of Spades" (1834), presenting several young aristocrats who are finishing a card game at two o'clock in the morning and preparing to pay a visit to the charming Nadenka. An even smaller fragment, indeed just an outline that begins in mid-sentence with the words "cards;

sold," written in the same year, seems also to suggest a fictional
project.

Further, Pushkin's friend I. P. Liprandi has recorded that in
the early 1820's Pushkin attempted to write two stories based
on Moldavian oral tradition.[28] Pushkin was dissatisfied with
the two drafts he had written and asked Liprandi to find out
more about the events they recorded. Apparently unclaimed by
Pushkin, the drafts remained in Liprandi's possession until the
1860's, when he gave them to P. I. Bartenev, a collector of
Pushkiniana. Bartenev did not publish them, possibly because
he thought Pushkin had simply recorded the words of his infor-
mants, adding little of his own, and possibly because of censorship difficulties.[29] Subsequently the manuscripts were lost, and
we know only the titles as quoted by Liprandi: "Dafna and
Dabija, a Moldavian Legend of 1663" and "Duca, a Moldavian
Legend of the 17th Century." Interestingly, Moldavian ethnographers published legends by almost the same titles in 1830
and 1838, respectively.[30] If Pushkin used the same sources as
the ethnographers, then the first of his stories was presumably
about Duca's scheme to gain the hand of Dafna, daughter of the
Moldavian Prince Dabija (Duca would secretly set Dabija's palace on fire in order to conspicuously "save" Dafna, compelling
her father's gratitude), and the second story related to Duca's
disastrous reign after he had succeeded his father-in-law as
ruler of the principality.[31]

Finally, sometime in the years 1821–23 Pushkin jotted down
the outline of a fantastic tale, whose title—"A Devil in
Love"—must have been inspired by Jacques Cazotte's Le Diable amoureux (1772).[32] According to the outline, the Devil in
disguise, while leading a young man down the path of dissipation, meets and falls in love with a widow's younger daughter,
but it is her elder sister who responds to him and is eventually
driven insane by him. Apparently, Pushkin hesitated over the
treatment of the story, debating whether to write it in straight
prose or to make a verse tale or even a drama out of it; he took
up the project several times over the years and made a number
of drawings relating to it, but eventually decided to drop it.[33] It
came back to his mind only in 1828, when he was passing the
evening at the Karamzins' house and felt inspired to tell a tale

to a number of guests.[34] A young man called V. P. Titov, who was among the guests, was fascinated by Pushkin's story, wrote it down from memory afterwards, showed it to Pushkin, and published it, incorporating some corrections suggested by the poet, under the title "The Lonely Cottage on Vasilev Island."[35]

Some changes in this story, as against the original outline of "The Devil in Love," might have been made by Pushkin himself; others may reflect Titov's taste.[36] The story's best feature is that its supernatural elements can be interpreted as reflections of the characters' inner drives: although it is the Devil who lures the hero, Pavel, away from the innocent Vera, introducing him to the enchanting Countess, it is clear that Pavel's own inclinations also drew him in that direction. Vera, in her turn, is wary of the Devil's advances and eventually rejects him, yet she dies of remorse, indicating that she too was not beyond the reach of demonic temptation. These elements must have been Pushkin's, for nothing of comparable quality can be found in the only other work of fiction Titov published.[37] One unmistakably Pushkinian element, anticipating *The Stone Guest*, is the following sentence: "Varfolomei [the Devil in disguise] entered with the coolness of marble, just as the statue of the Commander would come to Don Juan for supper."[38] Moreover, just as Pavel is about to win the Countess's favor, a mysterious messenger—a symbolic representative of evil and death—comes to call him away, which is not unlike the Commander's fatal appearance in *The Stone Guest* or Silvio's ill-timed arrival in "The Shot" (1830). Further, the story is set in the same milieu as the verse tale *The Little House in Kolomna* (1830); the flowers sprinkled with poison, which Pavel dreams of, remind one of Pushkin's lyric "Anchar" (1828); the ride in the blizzard anticipates both the story "The Blizzard" (1830) and the lyric "Devils" (1830); and the cabman who turns out to be a skeleton is clearly a predecessor of one of Adrian Prokhorov's guests in "The Undertaker" (1830).[39] Finally, as critics have pointed out, some details of the story unmistakably reproduce Pushkin's life.[40] On the other hand, there has been disagreement about the stylistic qualities of the story as recorded by Titov: although Pushkin's speaking style (as distinct from his written style) may indeed be reflected in about two-thirds of the text,[41] we must heed the poet Anna Akhmatova's warning that "the version in front of us is Titov's, carved by an ax."[42]

Pushkin undertook, and abandoned, quite a few fictional projects in his career, but all the projects undertaken up to the late 1820's seem to represent only an occasional spurt of inspiration. "With prose—I have trouble," he said to Liprandi in 1824, with reference to his Moldavian stories.[43] The problem may well have been that though he was looking to prose for new modes of expression, he failed to find the kind of fictional design that would answer his quest. What did seem to answer it, and what he did write, with much interest and evidently in great volume, was autobiographical prose.

Between 1821 and 1825 alone, in fact, Pushkin filled several copybooks with sketches of his life and times.[44] Since these sketches contained politically incriminating details, both about him and about his friends, he destroyed most of them after the Decembrist uprising, but a few survived, either in the possession of friends or salvaged by Pushkin himself. Among these we find a fragment about Karamzin and about the public's reaction to the first eight volumes of his *History of the Russian State*, published in 1818 ("From the Autobiographical Sketches"; 12: 305–7); an account of the adolescent Pushkin's triumphant reading of "Reminiscences at Tsarskoe Selo" before the celebrated poet G. R. Derzhavin ("Derzhavin," extant in a later variant; see 12: 158); and a recollection of the poet's journey from the Caucasus to the Crimea in 1820, which was to be published in 1826 as "A Fragment of a Letter to D." (8: 435–39). The Soviet scholar I. Feinberg, the person responsible for collecting all the material available on these copybooks, suggests that some of Pushkin's letters written during his southern exile—addressed to individuals but intended for circulation among several friends in St. Petersburg—also should be regarded as autobiographical sketches.[45] A notable example is his letter of September 24, 1820, to his brother, partially overlapping in content with "A Fragment of a Letter to D."

Some of these sketches contain narrative elements; others, such as "Notes on Eighteenth-Century Russian History" (11: 14–17), represent purely expository prose. Those containing narrative elements offer themselves readily as antecedents of

Pushkin's later fiction. But—significantly for the development of Pushkin's prose—these narrative passages differ very little from the discursive parts in mode of presentation. For example, this is how Pushkin recounts his impressions of the Caucasus in the above-mentioned letter to his brother:

I spent two months in the Caucasus; I needed the waters badly, and they helped me to a great extent, especially the hot sulfur water. I did, actually, take baths in warm acidulous sulfur waters, iron water, and cold acidulous waters as well. These healing springs are all located not far apart, in the last spurs of the Caucasian Mountains. I am sorry, my dear, that you were not with me to see this magnificent range of mountains, with their ice-covered peaks, which look like strange multicolored and immobile clouds from a distance, in the clear twilight. I wish you had climbed with me the sharp summits of five-ridged Beshtu, of Mashuk, and of Iron, Stone, and Serpent mountains. The Caucasian region, this sweltering borderland of Asia, is interesting in all respects. Ermolov has spread his name and beneficent genius over it. The wild Circassians are frightened; their ancient audacity is disappearing. The roads are getting less dangerous by the hour, and the numerous convoys are becoming unnecessary. Let us hope that this conquered land, which has yielded no substantial gain to Russia so far, will soon bring us closer to the Persians through safe trade and will no longer be an impediment to our wars. Perhaps Napoleon's chimerical plan of conquering India will become feasible for us. I have seen the banks of the Kuban and the border-guard villages; I admired our Cossacks. They are ever on horseback, ever ready to fight, ever vigilant. I rode within sight of the hostile fields of the free mountain peoples. Sixty Cossacks were convoying us; and a loaded cannon, with a slow fuse at the ready, was dragged along behind us. Although the Circassians are quite peaceful right now, you cannot depend on them: they are always ready to fall on a prominent Russian general in the hope of a large ransom. Where the indigent officer can safely gallop through on post horses, His Excellency may easily be caught on a Circassian's lasso. You can understand how much this smack of danger appeals to the romantic imagination. (13: 17–18)

Although close to *The Prisoner of the Caucasus* chronologically and thematically, this passage vastly differs from its poetic counterpart in mode of presentation. Personal experiences, geographical data, nature descriptions, and information about the behavior of the natives are all given in an even tone, from the point of view of the average Russian traveler. The remarks about Ermolov and about danger's appeal to the imagination hint at poetic possibilities, but no attempt is made to develop these in prose. They were left undeveloped, for the time being, to be taken up later in *The Prisoner*. And as the narrative poem was born, the poet's immediate experiences became transformed and stylized; different lyrical personae stood behind the changing moods; a compositional key ordered the presentation, creating a distance between the poet and the work.

Prose, as Pushkin perceived it in the 1820's, would require no changes in authorial personality, no performing of roles. It would convey the thoughts of the writer directly. Such a mode of writing, of course, might mean a return to a Coleridgean "irritable reaching" after unity, a Wordsworthian subjectivity—the qualities that had evoked the necessity of performing roles. Naturally, such a return to subjectivity was not Pushkin's purpose. What he strove for was the elimination of an obvious assumption of roles; and the medium that seemed to answer his purpose best was prose. Prose meant an eschewal of conspicuous poetic gestures. He began to cultivate the genre by writing autobiography and expository prose. Given this fact, it is not surprising that the fiction he was to write later was to be closest—at least in the use of vocabulary, as R. M. Frumkina has shown—to his essays.[46]

Letter writing likewise provided practice for the later fiction, particularly for the fashioning of dialogues. Letters meant to Pushkin, as N. L. Stepanov says, "oral dialogues, face-to-face conversations, studded with the unmotivated digressions and interruptions of live speech."[47] Indeed, Pushkin's *A Novel in Letters* (1829), as one critic has suggested, grew out of his personal correspondence.[48]

It must be borne in mind, however, that Pushkin's letters do not constitute a homogeneous body of literary output: epistolary discussions of literature and politics, official correspondence, and letters to friends about personal matters belong to altogether different kinds of prose. The first of these categories, as we have seen, can be regarded as part of Pushkin's account of his life and times. Letters of an official nature offer little of interest to the student of Pushkin's development as a fiction writer. And the last category—personal correspondence—proves to be very close to poetry.

One of the main conclusions Frumkina draws from her statistical analysis of Pushkin's vocabulary is that "the correlation between the fiction and the letters is no greater than that between the poems and the letters. It would seem that the letters—a 'school' for prose—should have been much more closely related to the fictional texts. Just as unexpected is the fact that the correlation between texts of a journalistic nature and the letters is no greater than that between the poems and the letters."[49] Even without the aid of statistical data, critics have tended to agree on the closeness of Pushkin's personal letters to his lyrics. They are, in the words of J. Thomas Shaw, "like the lyrics in their saturation, their succinctness, and the immediacy of their presentation of thought and feeling."[50] V. F. Khodasevich has shown how frequently Pushkin transferred themes from letters to poems and vice versa.[51] But the most interesting comment on Pushkin's letters, from the point of view of our investigation, was made by V. V. Sipovskii at the turn of the century:

> The distinguishing feature of these letters is that the image the poet presents in them changes according to the *person addressed*. It changes to the point of becoming unrecognizable, to the point of merging into the addressee's image: with a man of letters, Pushkin is exclusively a man of letters; with a politician, he is a politician; with a gossip, a gossip; with an idler, an idler and nothing else. Like a good actor, unrecognizable as he dons his various roles, Pushkin merges with the images he presents. . . . If we compare these images with those shining through his lyric poems, we see a complete identity.[52]

Plainly, then, Pushkin's personal letters employ as varied an array of literary devices and conceal the author behind as colorful a set of assumed masks as do the poems. This does not necessarily mean, of course, that they could not have provided good exercise for fictional dialogue. On the contrary: the more varied the letters, the more varied the dialogues that could evolve from them. Nor does it necessarily mean that they should not be regarded as an "apprenticeship" for the later fiction in general. What limits their role in the development of Pushkin's fiction is that in the 1820's he saw prose as the opposite pole of poetry, and therefore tended to put greater emphasis on those kinds of prose furthest removed from poetry.

In this connection one must bear in mind what has been emphasized by some historians of literature:[53] that before the late 1820's few Russian authors paid much attention to the distinction between imaginative and other kinds of prose. Pushkin was obviously aware of the distinction—for example, he chided those critics who had expected Karamzin to write a "novel" instead of scholarly history (13: 306)—but the distinction was not of any practical importance to him until he came to treat one and the same subject in both a fictional and a scholarly way (as he was to treat the Pugachev Rebellion in the 1830's).

In the 1820's, while he was only approaching fiction, he tended to describe prose in terms that seem more applicable to discursive than to imaginative writing. "One's years incline him to stern prose, / One's years drive mischievous rhymes away" (6: 135), he wrote in Onegin, implying that the direct manner of prose was more suitable for a mature writer. Interestingly, in a draft version of these lines the object driven away by years was not only rifma (rhyme), but also vymysel (6: 408, note 4), which could be rendered in English as "invention," "fiction," or in this context, even the "plot" of a work of imaginative literature. Feinberg interprets the use of this word in the draft as indicating that Pushkin, in referring to prose, did not have fiction in mind.[54]

A similar view of prose writing was reflected in the contrasting metaphors that Pushkin used to characterize the youthful enthusiast, Lenskii, and the experienced Onegin: "Wave and rock, / Verse and prose, ice and flame / Could not be more different" (6: 37). Prose was "humble" (6: 57; 8: 131) compared with the contentious, turbulent world of poetry. There was an unbridgeable gap between the two—"a devil of a difference" (13: 73, 226). If poetry was all ornament and pleasant form (11: 60), prose represented pure content, tolerating no decorative frills and demanding "thoughts and thoughts, without which magniloquent phrases serve no purpose" (11: 19).

As has been amply documented in scholarly literature, before Pushkin's time the Russian terms poeziia and proza were used almost exclusively as technical terms of literary criticism, and it was not until the 1820's that their secondary, figurative meanings—"worlds of the ideal and of the real"—came into use.[55] Pushkin played no small part in establishing these new meanings. For example, a deliberate interchanging of the primary and secondary meanings of the word prose (and of its synonyms) explains some of the irony we find in *Onegin*, whose subtitle—a "Novel in Verse"—is itself a play on these meanings. When Pushkin says Olga's portrait can be found in any novel (6: 41), he obviously means a work of fiction written in prose, but not in the kind of prose that deserves the name. He means prose still only in a technical sense when he speaks of the "deceptions" of Richardson and Rousseau and the "seductive deceit" of novels (6: 44, 55). The switch from primary to secondary meaning occurs in Stanzas Nine to Fourteen of Chapter Three, where he first gives a list of the books Tatiana has read—all novels of a sentimental hue—then discusses a number of romantic prose writers, connecting them with Byron, and finally says (6: 56–57):

> My friends, what sense is there in all this?
> Maybe, if Heaven so wills,
> I will cease to be a poet:
> A new demon will possess me
> And, braving the anger of Phoebus,
> I will stoop to humble prose.

"Ceasing to be a poet" meant, at the most obvious semantic level, that Pushkin would no longer write verse, but it also implied a rejection of authors like Jean Jacques Rousseau, Madame de Staël, Samuel Richardson, and Charles Maturin, as if *Julie, ou La Nouvelle Héloïse* (1761), *Delphine* (1802), *Clarissa* (1747–48), and *Melmoth the Wanderer* (1820) had all belonged to poetry. It is interesting that Stanza Nineteen of Chapter Two, the first passage that mentions some of Tatiana's readings, originally contained the names Chateaubriand and Rousseau (6: 568), which were changed to Richardson and Rousseau in the final version (6: 44). The change shows how carefully Pushkin considered "prose" in a merely technical sense and what qualified for both meanings of the word: Chateaubriand's *René* (1802) was more fit for Onegin's bookshelf, which contained some true prose. (Tatiana was to find it there, at least in the first draft of Stanza Twenty-two, Chapter Seven; 6: 438.) One might note that Pushkin praised the "poetry" of I. I. Lazhechnikov's novels (16: 62) and of N. V. Gogol's short stories (11:

216), using the figurative meaning of that word too.[56] There was, of course, no reason why prose should be regarded exclusively as an austere, unadorned mode of writing. All those whom Pushkin refused to admit to his select club of prose writers would actually belong there by any broader critical standards. But Pushkin, as he approached prose, assigned it a specific role: that of "counterbalancing" poetry.[57]

The calm maturity of prose lacked the lively, youthful beauty of poetry. In a fragment of "Onegin's Travels" (1830), Pushkin says that in his earlier days he had regarded wilderness, rocks, a roaring sea, the ideal of a proud maiden, and nameless sufferings indispensable, but in his maturity he has grown to love the farmhouse on a sandy slope, the rowan trees, the garden gate, the broken fence, the heaps of straw before the barn, the pond with its willows and ducks, the balalaika, the dance of drunken peasants in front of the pothouse, and—instead of the proud maiden—a housewife. In the next stanza he launches into a description of the farmyard but breaks off the sentence, calling all this "prosaic nightmares" and "the motley trash of the Flemish School." Overcome by nostalgia for youth and poetry, he exclaims, "Tell me, fountain of Bakhchisarai, / Was this what I was like in my burgeoning spring?" (6: 201). Endowed with this most flat-footed personality, prose emerged as the very antithesis of poetry. It is no surprise to find that two lines from this passage, which in the final version read "I have mixed much water / Into my poetic goblet," appear in a draft as "I have mixed much prose / Into my poetic goblet" (6: 200, 489). Over the years, Pushkin showered unflattering epithets—such as "slovenly" (3: 10) and "contemptible" (5: 3; 11: 67)—on prose writing. Having begun his first serious attempt at fiction, he reported to a friend that, lacking inspiration, he was writing prose (13: 334); and his Belkin of Goriukhino, acting on the recommendation of Onegin's narrator, "stoops" to prose (8: 131).

Most of the Pushkin statements on prose that I have quoted so far were made in the 1820's, either before he tried his hand at fiction with any seriousness or when he was just beginning to. They reflect the fact that he proceeded to fiction after an apprenticeship primarily in essays and autobiography. In my opinion, A. Z. Lezhnev is wrong when he applies these statements to all of Pushkin's prose works, with the assumption that Pushkin had an unchanging attitude to the genre all through his life.[58] On the contrary, not only did Pushkin come to differentiate more and more with the passage of years between fiction and other kinds of prose, but there was to be considerable variety of theme and style within his eventual fictional output itself.

Even in the preparatory stages, as Pushkin was just approaching fiction, he began to realize that prose writing offered opportunities for more than just one kind of unassuming attitude. His reference to the Flemish School in "Onegin's Travels" presaged the Russian school of Naturalism of the 1840's. His promise, in Chapter Three of *Onegin*, to write an old-fashioned novel about a Russian family's traditions was fulfilled in *The Captain's Daughter* (1836)—a work far removed from the Flemish School. The "two or three novels" Tatiana read from among Onegin's books represented, once more, an entirely different kind of prose fiction: the kind in which "Contemporary man / With his immoral soul / Was depicted quite faithfully" (6: 22).

Prose writing, Pushkin realized as he became a practitioner of the art, was not limited to a single set of characteristics, but possessed as great a potential for varied applications as poetry. This realization was a gradual and painful one, paid for by several failures and false starts. And although he modified his original concept of prose over the years, the idea of a mode of writing requiring no assumption of literary roles remained attractive to him. His development as a fiction writer was greatly influenced by the tension between his original concept of prose and its later modifications.

II. Experiments with Narrative Modes

I

Pushkin made his first serious attempt at writing fiction in the summer of 1827, when he completed six chapters of a proposed historical novel, now known to us as *The Blackamoor of Peter the Great*. The prototype for its central character, Ibrahim, was Pushkin's maternal great-grandfather, Abram Hannibal, an African who had been brought to Russia as a child during the reign of Peter I. Having been raised by Peter, Ibrahim (like the actual Hannibal) was sent to Paris to study military engineering. When we meet him in the opening chapter of the novel, he has already finished his training and distinguished himself in French military service, and would be ready to return to Russia if he were not involved in an adulterous affair with an elegant French lady, the Countess D. Their union even produces a baby—a black one, whom the Countess's attendants surreptitiously exchange for a white one in order to conceal the father's identity from her husband—but Ibrahim eventually returns to Russia, driven both by a sense of indebtedness to Peter and by a fear that the Countess will grow tired of him. He participates in Peter's efforts to build the new Russian empire and is treated kindly by his foster father: Peter even decides to find a bride for him. His choice falls on young Natalia Rzhevskaia, whose father is a high-ranking nobleman of the old school, opposed to Peter's reforms. Precisely because he has been in opposition, the old Rzhevskii dares not refuse his daughter's hand to the Tsar's favorite. When Natalia learns of her father's decision she falls ill, not so much because Ibrahim's unfamiliar appearance frightens her as because she is in love with a young man, Valerian, who had been brought up as an orphan at her father's house and lately joined the military. When we last see her, she has finally come around from a coma of two weeks' duration but is still unwell.

At this point in the narrative Pushkin's work on the novel came to a halt. He took up the project again in the spring of 1828, but this time succeeded in writing only one more page—showing Valerian's return to the Rzhevskii household—which is all that remains of Chapter Seven. Having given up hope of finishing the novel, he published two fragments from it, in 1829 and 1830.[1] The assembled text of all the extant parts (with a few minor omissions) was published posthumously by the editors of the journal *The Contemporary*, who also gave it its title.[2]

How much Pushkin identified with his great-grandfather can be seen from his verse epistle "To Iurev" (1820), in which he described himself as a descendant of Negroes. Fascinated by his ancestor, he had attempted to write about him several times before he set to work on the novel. As early as 1824 he wrote a fragment of a poem beginning with the line "As the Tsar's Blackamoor Thought of Marrying," and he also appended a footnote to the first edition of Chapter One of *Onegin* (6: 654–55) describing his ancestry in order to explain why he called the skies of Africa his own. This footnote, amounting to a brief biography of Hannibal (based on family tradition), might have been taken from Pushkin's autobiographical sketches.[3] Thus the material that was to lie at the foundation of Pushkin's historical novel had already been treated by him in a nonfictional way.

During 1825 and 1826 Pushkin had an opportunity to expand his knowledge—hitherto confined to family tradition—about Hannibal and his times. Not only did he acquire, from a great-uncle, a handwritten biography of Hannibal,[4] but he was also able to read I. I. Golikov's *The Deeds of Peter the Great* (1788–97), which his neighbors, the Osipovs, had in their library.[5] Furthermore, the text of *The Blackamoor* clearly shows that he had familiarized himself with A. O. Kornilovich's four sketches of Russian mores under Peter I, published in 1824.[6] In pursuing these sources, Pushkin probably had a historical essay, rather than fiction, in mind. Some of the material he had gathered for a historical study never became "fictionalized" as he worked on the novel: for example, the description of the Regency after the death of Louis XIV, given in Chapter One, is very close both stylistically and conceptually to Pushkin's purely essay-like "Notes on Eighteenth-Century Russian History."[7] It is not clear why Pushkin decided in the end to switch to fiction. Possibly he simply came across some unflattering details about Hannibal and thought he could handle them more easily in fiction than in a conscientious historical account.[8] In any case, having turned to fiction, he did not strictly adhere to facts: for instance, he made Peter propose to the Rzhevskiis on Ibrahim's behalf, though the real Hannibal did not marry until well after Peter's death; he made Ibrahim's bride a member of the ancient nobility in order to sharpen the social contrast with Peter's black officer; and he brought together such historical personalities as I. F. Kopievich and Feofan Prokopovich, who could not have been at Peter's Court at the same time.[9]

The most noticeable trace of Pushkin's original nonfictional approach to the story is the novel's detached mode of narration. In the text Pushkin left us, the author-narrator steps directly before the reader only twice: he begins Chapter Four with the words "I must now acquaint my gracious reader with Gavrila Afanasevich Rzhevskii" (8: 19); and toward the end of the same chapter he tells us that he is making an aside. Both of these first-person appearances of the author, however, are motivated purely by technical convenience, and no attempt is made to create a narrator with a personality of his own. Beyond this, there are a few occasions when the author's hand is revealed indirectly. Sometimes he introduces generalizations that are not attributable to any particular character in the novel and so must belong to him. He says, for instance, "Whatever you say, love without aspirations and demands touches the feminine heart more surely than all the wiles of seduction," and that "to follow the thoughts of a great man is a most engrossing mental exercise" (8: 5, 13).[10] At other times he attaches emotionally colored epithets to characters—"unfortunate" Ibrahim, "poor" Natasha (8: 9, 32)—or asks rhetorical questions—"What sensations filled Ibrahim's heart? Jealousy? Rage? Despair?" (8: 15)—

both of which imply the presence of a sympathizing or interested author. But his presence is nowhere obtrusive; nor does he ever enter into a dialogue with the reader.

Such a detached mode of narration, as we have seen, was a reaction on Pushkin's part to the conspicuous assumption of roles characteristic of his poetry. True, the author's own personality seemed to be hidden, as the contrasting lyrical personae—the Byronic poet and the patriotic bard—voiced their respective points of view in *The Prisoner of the Caucasus* and its Epilogue, but it was nevertheless obvious that the author was manipulating these lyrical personae. What was needed was not histrionics, but a detached narrator, rather like Father Pimen of *Boris Godunov*, who would simply record events as a "witness of many years" (7: 17). The narrator of *The Blackamoor* emerges as just such a chronicler.

The mode of narration Pushkin adopted for his novel was most unusual for the 1820's. Jane Austen had developed a similar authorial stance in the preceding decades, but Pushkin—as we have seen—was probably not familiar with her novels. Balzac and Stendhal had not yet published the novels that were to make their fame. In the fiction that Pushkin is known to have read before 1827, the convention was that the reader be initiated into the secrets of authorship, and that the author emerge as a distinct personality. As Washington Irving put it, "The public is apt to be curious about the sources from whence the author draws his stories, doubtless that it may know how far to put faith in them."[11]

Voltaire, whose prose Pushkin professed to admire the most (11: 18), attributed his *Candide* (1759) to a certain Doctor Ralph and claimed to have acquired additions to the manuscript from among the papers found in the doctor's pockets after his death. Horace Walpole, father of an altogether different tradition— that of the Gothic novel—whose writings were well known to Pushkin, claimed that he had found the manuscript of *The Castle of Otranto* (1764), written by a sixteenth-century monk, in the library of an ancient English family.[12] The manuscript of Benjamin Constant's *Adolphe* (1816)—much closer to Pushkin, both in time and in spirit—had been sent to the author by mistake.

Most interesting from the point of view of our investigation are the attitudes of the most popular novelist of the time, Sir Walter Scott, whom Pushkin praised for presenting history "in a domestic manner" (12: 195). Scott's *Tales of My Landlord*, a series that contained *The Black Dwarf* (1816), *Old Mortality* (1816), *The Heart of Midlothian* (1818), *A Legend of Montrose* (1819), and *The Bride of Lammermoor* (1819), was attributed to a whole set of fictitious narrators: the stories were supposed to have been told by the landlord of a public house in the town of Gandercleugh, written down by Peter Pattieson, the town's assistant schoolmaster, and published by Jedediah Cleishbotham, the schoolmaster, to whom the late Pattieson had bequeathed them. In addition, each tale was furnished with an introduction in which Cleishbotham gave particulars about the people from whom the landlord had heard the tale or who had at least contributed some details to it. Finally, two other fashionable writers of the day whose books Pushkin read—Washington Irving and E. T. A. Hoffmann—were notorious for their fictitious narrators, for their framed tales, and for the teasing relationship they created between the narrator and the reader.[13]

Russian writers contemporary to Pushkin or preceding him followed the dominant trend. N. M. Karamzin, whom Pushkin grudgingly acknowledged to have been the best Russian prose writer of the period (11: 19), had heard the story of "Poor Liza" (1792) from the heroine's repentant seducer, Erast. V. T. Narezhnyi's *Russian Gil Blas* (1814)—in keeping with the picaresque tradition—was characterized by a shifting narrative point of view and by the presence of inserted tales. And A. A. Bestuzhev-Marlinskii, whom Pushkin once admonished not to write in the manner of Scott (13: 80), claimed either to have derived his tales from historical sources (e.g. "Roman and Olga"; 1823) or to have gathered them by the campfire ("An Evening on Bivouac" and "A Second Evening on Bivouac"; 1823).

A frame for a tale or a fictitious narrator was, in itself, merely a technical device that authors sometimes dropped after a point; what made these devices important was that they were symptomatic of an overbearing authorial presence. Scott, for instance, could not leave it to the reader to simply follow the fate of his characters: as he said in his 1829 Preface to *Waverley*

(1814), he liked to revert to first-person discourse with the reader even in a novel narrated in the third person:

The author can only promise to be as little of an egotist as the situation will permit. It is perhaps an indifferent sign of a disposition to keep his word, that having introduced himself in the third person singular, he proceeds in the second paragraph to make use of the first. But it appears to him that the seeming modesty connected with the former mode of writing, is overbalanced by the inconvenience of stiffness and affectation which attends it during a narrative of some length, and which may be observed less or more in every work in which the third person is used, from the Commentaries of Caesar, to the Autobiography of Alexander the Corrector.[14]

In order to avoid the "stiffness" inherent in objective, third-person narration, Scott plays games with his reader. In Chapter Five of *Waverley*, for instance, he claims not to know whether it was "the merest accident in the world" that Cecilia Stubbs, daughter of the local squire, had taken up walking through Waverley-Chase—a place frequented by the dashing young Edward. The reader, of course, does know; he can see that the author is teasing him; and, as a result, a special author-reader relationship is formed. In Chapter Fifty-four of the same novel, when Edward is ready to fall in love with Rose Bradwardine, Scott reports how the young man suddenly discovers that Rose's manner is "most engaging," that "she has a more correct ear than Flora," and that "she has more feeling, too." Edward, so slow to realize the inclinations of his heart, appears to be somewhat on the silly side, but the reader, of course, is not so slow to perceive what is going on. A private joke has passed between author and reader, behind the character's back.

Given the conventions of the period—when the most popular novelist regarded a neutral, impersonal narrative as both stiff and affected—it was a bold undertaking on the part of Pushkin to begin his career as a prose writer with just such a narrative. In doing so, he anticipated a later trend in the development of nineteenth-century fiction, which was to be formulated in Flaubert's famous statement: "It is one of my principles that one must not be his own subject. The artist must be in his work like God in His creation: invisible and omnipotent; he should be everywhere felt, but nowhere seen."[15] Although this trend was not an exclusive one (authors have never abdicated their right to experiment with different narrative modes), its powerful influence on Russian literature is witnessed by such masterpieces—otherwise vastly different—as *Fathers and Sons* (1862), *Crime and Punishment* (1866), and *Anna Karenina* (1875–77).

What mattered most, as Pushkin sought a new manner of writing, was not just the question of whether the author was hidden from the reader or revealed to him, of whether he spoke in the first person or the third, but the question of whether he would be courageous enough to write as an intelligent chronicler, whose attitudes would be subtle and implicit, without clownish masks and false assumptions. In *The Blackamoor of Peter the Great* Pushkin projects the image of an author who does not have to pretend—for the sake of a joke with the reader or for any other reason—that he possesses only half of the truth about his characters. Unencumbered by a play-acting narrator's jocular or sentimental postures, he can reveal his characters' feelings in their full complexity. His narrator knows that human affairs are beset with both passion and compromise, and he does not feel obliged to apologize for this knowledge.

Stating that many a Parisian beauty looked at his black hero "with feelings more flattering than mere curiosity" (8: 5), he quite naturally assumes that members of different races can be attracted to each other.[16] But even as he depicts the Countess D.'s genuine love for Ibrahim, he does not attempt to conceal Ibrahim's own feelings of insecurity and fear of prejudice. Ibrahim's decision to return to Russia is motivated not only by his sense of duty and by his attachment to Peter I, but also by the anticipation of a break with the Countess, which would hurt him much more if he were not to initiate it himself.[17] After he leaves Paris, his burning passion fades into a cherished memory—a bold development indeed for an early-nineteenth-century novel. The news that his old friend Korsakov brings of the Countess—that she has taken a new lover—shocks him, but not enough to make him reject Peter's plan to find him a bride. He suspects that he will be unable to kindle the same feelings in Natalia Rzhevskaia as those he had kindled in the Countess, but he is willing to compromise in the hope of achieving, if not happiness, at least a respectable family life. Natalia, on her part, seems to be prepared to submit to her fate, which is also a compromise in the context of early-nineteenth-century literature: many an earlier heroine not only had hoped to pine away under the weight of sorrow, but had actually succeeded in doing so. How Pushkin would have treated the further events of his story, we do not know: all we have is a bare outline of a plan—calling for Ibrahim's unfaithful wife to deliver a white baby—which was recorded by Pushkin's friend A. N. Vulf in September 1827, just after Pushkin had completed the second chapter of the novel.[18]

Pushkin's attempt to present affairs of the heart in all their complexity was not entirely without precedent: he could borrow at least a few elements from a favorite novel of his younger days, Benjamin Constant's *Adolphe*. Pushkin's Countess D. (whose first name is Léonore) and Constant's Ellénore are both characterized as beautiful women though no longer in the first bloom of youth; they both fall in love with younger men, whose main attraction is their seemingly undemanding devotion; and they both have to face losing their young men.[19] Some of the very phrases Pushkin uses to describe Ibrahim's relations with the Countess are demonstrably taken from *Adolphe*. Constant's novel reveals the inner contradictions of his characters with a ruthlessness that, one feels, sometimes goes beyond his own intentions. Not only does Adolphe's love for Ellénore turn sour in the course of the narrative, but he and his mistress lacerate each other in a compulsive manner that anticipates Dostoevskii's heroes and heroines.

Although *Adolphe*, with its frank revelations, is a forerunner of the psychological novel, it seems that Constant was wary of the possible effect of such a narrative, and consequently clothed it in the most conventional style. Adolphe recounts his story with as much contrition as Karamzin's Erast; he moralizes; he bestrews the novel with high-flown rhetoric. Such a style— with its "Charme de l'amour, qui pourrait vous peindre?" and similar phrases—was obviously of no use to Pushkin, who strove for simplicity in prose. It is not surprising that Pushkin wrote "nonsense" in the margin of his copy of *Adolphe* where Constant has his hero throwing himself on the ground and wishing to be swallowed up by the earth (Chapter Three).[20] The ending of *Adolphe*—Ellénore's death on learning that her lover intends to desert her—must have also seemed nonsensical to Pushkin, for in *The Blackamoor* he depicted a passionate affair that terminated without fatal consequences and a maiden who tried to, but—at least according to the plan recorded by Vulf— could not die of grief.

Pushkin's attempt to develop an omniscient mode of narration was a pioneering venture, but it involved—because of its very novelty—enormous technical difficulties. These difficulties may well have contributed to his decision to abandon his novel, though there may have been other factors as well. Some scholars explain his failure to complete the work by the fact that Bulgarin published a lampoon claiming that Pushkin's ancestor Hannibal had been bought for a bottle of rum.[21] After the appearance of this lampoon, they suggest, it may well have been impossible for Pushkin to continue his novel without exposing himself to public ridicule. Yet against this is the fact that the lampoon did not appear until 1830, which is to say, two or three years after Pushkin had stopped working on the novel.[22] Other scholars argue that Pushkin had designed his novel as a lesson in good statesmanship to Nicholas I (Peter I being offered as a model) but grew more and more disillusioned with Nicholas, and seeing the futility of trying to influence him, simply lost interest in the novel.[23] Even if Pushkin's feelings toward Nicholas were changing, however, this explanation ascribes a much too narrowly utilitarian purpose to a work of art whose scope extends far beyond a didactic lesson to a tyrant. Although Peter I looms large in the novel, its protagonist is nevertheless his black officer, with whom Pushkin identified to a great extent. It has been shown that there is much in common between Ibrahim, wondering if he could win at least the respect and fidelity of Natalia, and Hannibal's great-grandson, who pondered the question of matrimony in very similar terms in his letter of December 1, 1826, to V. P. Zubkov.[24] This link between Pushkin's personal worries and Ibrahim's courtship problems by no means elucidates all aspects of the novel, but it is at least as important as the writer's attitude toward Nicholas.

Whatever the contribution of biographical factors to the interruption of the novel may have been, the difficulties that Pushkin encountered in the creative process itself must be taken into consideration.[25] Problems of the craft of prose writing were certainly on Pushkin's mind at the time. We have seen how he had complained to Liprandi about the difficulties of prose earlier in the decade. The same complaint—implying technical problems—is echoed in the confession he made to the writer and scholar V. I. Dal in 1833: "You wouldn't believe how much I long to write a novel, yet I cannot. I have begun three of them. I start off perfectly well, but then I run out of patience and cannot manage."[26] Among the problems of the creative process, the advantages and disadvantages of the narrative point of view Pushkin had chosen for *The Blackamoor* appear to be the crucial ones.

We may be able to get closer to the problem through a comparison of *The Blackamoor* with *Poltava*—the narrative poem in whose favor Pushkin abandoned his novel in the spring of 1828. The most obvious similarity between the two works is that they are both set in the epoch of Peter I, who himself plays an important role in each. Less obvious but equally important is the similarity between Ibrahim and Mazepa as incarnations of a certain side of Pushkin's personality. Both characters represent explorations of how disadvantaged men might fare in love—one disadvantaged by the color of his skin, the other by his age. The close link between the two characters was clearly revealed by Pushkin when he wrote—in answer to the critic N. I. Nadezhdin's objection to Maria's love for an old man[27]— that the ways of love are inscrutable: think of young Desdemona falling in love with the "old Negro," Othello (11: 164). Moreover, a sentence from *Othello*—"Transported . . . to the gross clasps of a lascivious Moor" (Act 1, Scene 1, line 137)—is paraphrased in *The Blackamoor* as "Don't throw Natashenka into the clutches of that black devil" (8: 25), which in turn reminds one of the image of Mazepa as an old kite preying on a young dove (5: 26). A further similarity, at least between *Poltava* and *Othello*, is that Maria's heart is touched by Mazepa's tales of vicissitudes just as Desdemona's is by Othello's tales. Othello, black and no longer young, was an inspiration to Pushkin in creating both Ibrahim and Mazepa.

Both heroes appear to enjoy success at first—Ibrahim with the Countess and Mazepa with Maria—only to encounter failure later, one in marriage, the other in his political career. In both cases, the germs of failure are hidden in the initial situations of seeming success. If Ibrahim leaves the Countess because he fears that prejudice against his color may awaken in her heart, it is also his fear of prejudice that drives him toward an unpropitious marriage, for it makes him blind to the possibility that some other woman might love him better than Natalia. If Mazepa wins Maria's heart with a passion belying his age, it is also a youthful overconfidence that leads him to his political error. Errors of judgment, springing from psychological causes, underlie the actions of both characters. A further parallel between the two works is that both Natalia and Maria are excluded from their relatives' discussion of the respective marriage proposals; both faint on hearing the decision; and though Maria does not fall quite as ill as Natalia, she too refuses to eat and sleep, staggering around pale as a shadow for two days after her parents' decision. Thus, even though Pushkin switched from prose to poetry, he evidently retained some of his original ideas. And at least one of the reasons for this switch was that, innovative as his detached mode of narration might have been, Pushkin had failed to find the right compositional key for his novel.

For *Poltava* it was easier to find a compositional key, since poetry was familiar territory to Pushkin. One might say that he wrote the poem in a double key, much as he had *The Prisoner* and its Epilogue. On the one hand, Mazepa is attractive, able to fire the young Maria's imagination, has an air of somber dignity about him; he leads "sorrowful Little Russia" against "hated Moscow" (5: 24) at the urging of his fellow countrymen, and in this sense he appears to be, at least at first, the hero of a national liberation movement. What the objective narrator says about him is contradicted, however, by another narrative voice, that of a patriotic bard singing the praises of Peter I while heaping adjectives like "base," "cunning," and "deceitful" (5: 25) on Mazepa. This bard-author seems to enter into a contest with the author-narrator, who in turn strives to give out as much information, often favorable to Mazepa, as he can under the barrage of the bard's hostile epithets. We get two perspectives on reality, neither of which has absolute validity: Pushkin has risen to a height of detachment where he does not feel compelled to present one comprehensive, morally unified view of the world. But the image of Peter I, as presented by the bard, is entirely stylized. The contest between him and Mazepa, transcending the feud of two political leaders, becomes a contest between the forces of history and an individual, between idealized greatness and fallible humanity. With this double perspective, Pushkin anticipates his *Bronze Horseman* (1833).

Such a conspicuous use of contrasting authorial personalities—highly successful in *Poltava*—would have been incompatible with the mode of narration Pushkin had chosen for *The Blackamoor*. A detached chronicler writing in prose could not poeticize Peter the way a patriotic bard could. Pushkin's praise of Sir Walter Scott for showing history "in a domestic manner" and for presenting historical personalities "in the ordinary circumstances of life" (12: 195) suggests that he had hoped to make Peter a heroic figure without recourse to poetic stylization in his novel. The result of the experiment was that, in the six completed chapters of the novel, Peter emerged neither fully heroic nor entirely human. Pushkin must have felt that the "domestic" scenes he had chosen—Peter having a nap after lunch, playing chess with an English sailor, finding a bride for his young officer—were not adding up to the image he had had in mind. They were endearing scenes, but they did not suggest the gigantic figure of the hero of Poltava. It must have been for this reason that he made some attempts to aggrandize Peter even at the price of sacrificing some of his principles of prose writing. For instance, the sentence "With every day he [Ibrahim] became more and more attached to the Emperor, more able to comprehend his lofty mind" (8: 13) had been written without the word "lofty" in the first draft (8: 525, note 5). It is not clear in the final version whether this word, carrying a value judgment, is a narrated thought of Ibrahim's or belongs to the author himself. We are left with the impression that the author is as much involved in the value judgment as his hero, which goes against the grain of a detached, neutral mode of narration.

Brought down to a domestic level as he is, Peter nevertheless fails to impress us as a real person. If Pushkin had truly wanted to portray him without idealization, he would have had to show the Tsar's savage cruelty along with his monumental achievements. As he appears in the novel, he is too good, too considerate, too moderate, to be convincing. Pushkin himself must have felt he was erring in this direction, for he proceeded to introduce some less flattering details about the Tsar. For example, the sentence "'And now,' he continued, shaking his cudgel, 'walk with me to that scoundrel Danilych's house; I must talk to him about his latest pranks'" (8: 28) had been written without the words "shaking his cudgel" even in the second draft (8: 517). The word cudgel has such far-reaching implications for the image of Peter that its introduction into the text signals an entirely new departure.

A few years later Pushkin said to Dal with reference to Peter: "I am not yet able to comprehend, to grasp the whole of this giant at once: he is too large for us shortsighted people; we are still standing too close to him."[28] As is well known, Pushkin was soon to engage in a thorough historical study in order to come to a balanced understanding of the great Tsar, but at the time he was writing *The Blackamoor* he still stood too close to Peter to be able to portray him as a hero, yet too far to be able to depict him as an ordinary human being.

If Peter had emerged as a gigantic statue in the novel—as he was to do in *Poltava* and in *The Bronze Horseman*—the proportions of Ibrahim would have shrunk: his love affair in Paris, his ill-starred engagement to Natalia, and other personal concerns would have appeared dwarfed alongside the Tsar. This would have established a perspective on Ibrahim and could have served as the compositional key to the whole novel. As it turned out, Pushkin was not able to find the right angle from which to view his central character, any more than he was able to establish the right approach to Peter.

Having deliberately put the expressive means of poetry aside, Pushkin was unable to replace them with new ones appropriate to prose. He adopted a colorless narrator, as impersonal as the author of a historical treatise, but failed to develop the characters whose function it should have been to provide the color lacking in the narrator. Those independent attitudes that were expressed through contrasting lyrical personae in poetry should have been allowed to emerge as contrasting characters in prose. For this, however, Pushkin lacked the technique at this time.

What was needed was a new set of representational devices suited to prose fiction. As one such device, the heroes could have been endowed with speech characteristics that would have set them apart both from each other and from the author, creating a distance across which the reader could look with amusement, sympathy, or any other sentiment. One indication that Pushkin did not have the "feel" of his character is that he hardly ever made Ibrahim speak anywhere in the six chapters. The Regent speaks to him, Peter speaks to him, Korsakov pours out long tirades at him, but when the time comes for him to open his mouth, either he utters the tersest of sentences or Pushkin reports his statements for him. There are two exceptions to this rule: he gives full answers both to Peter, who offers to propose to Natalia for him, and to Korsakov, who counsels against his marriage. In the first case, he says he likes Natalia, and he mentions his appearance with anxiety—both of which details are revealing—but otherwise he speaks in the impersonal style of a courtier ("Your Majesty, I am blessed with Your Highest protection and favor"; 8: 27). In the second case, he responds to Korsakov with a Russian proverb ("It's not your duty to rock other people's babies"; 8: 30), a wholly unconvincing turn of phrase, coming as it does from the mouth of a foreign-born person who had spent only the years between his early childhood and his young manhood in Russia. One has the impression that Pushkin used this phrase, not in order to characterize Ibrahim, but in order to be able to include Korsakov's prophetic repartee to it: "Take care not to let it happen that you should illustrate this proverb in a literal sense." Two other passages that should reveal Ibrahim's character through his individual style are his letter to the Countess and his internal monologue about getting married, but both are abstract and impersonal. Thus Ibrahim does not emerge as a separate entity in a stylistic sense.

In addition to dialogues, letters, and internal monologues, the omniscient narrator of realistic fiction has at his disposal the opinions of the characters about each other. Pushkin made use of this device—for instance, Korsakov's comments on both Ibrahim and Peter provide amusing side views of these characters—but not with sufficient consistency. A case in point is the description of how Ibrahim's relations with the Countess develop. In the seventh paragraph of Chapter One (from line 10, p. 5, on), the point of view shifts from Ibrahim to the Countess, then to other people, then back to Ibrahim; in the eighth, from Ibrahim to the Countess, to the narrator, to the Countess's reputed former lover Merville, once more to the narrator, then back to Ibrahim, and finally to the Countess; in the ninth, from the narrator to other people, then to both Ibrahim and the Countess together, then to Ibrahim alone, then to the Countess alone, and so forth, with the result that no character's point of view is sufficiently established. There emerges a mosaic with no consistent perspective.

The best parts of the novel are those in which Pushkin succeeds in maintaining a consistent point of view. One of these is the description of the assembly at Peter's Court, which is seen mostly through Korsakov's eyes. "Korsakov was dumbfounded," says Pushkin at the opening of the scene, as if to emphasize the point of view, and the following two pages abound in phrases like "Korsakov could not regain his presence of mind," "Korsakov was struck by an unexpected sight," "Korsakov . . . stared wide-eyed," "Korsakov rejoiced," and "Korsakov grew more and more astonished" (8: 16, 17). The point of view is well chosen because Korsakov, a westernized fop, assumes he knows all about behavior in the best society, yet he discovers that his behavior is ridiculous by the standards of the recently westernized Russian Court. Another highly successful passage in the novel is the depiction of a dinner at Rzhevskii's house. Here the characters, voicing their opinions in detail, come fully alive.[29] It is not surprising that these were the two passages Pushkin decided to publish. Unfortunately, however, neither of them helped solve what seems to have been the main problem: the characterization of Ibrahim.

The lack of perspective is apparent also in the narrator's own descriptions of Ibrahim's feelings. This is, for instance, what Pushkin tells us about Ibrahim's thoughts concerning the Countess:

It was more difficult to dismiss from his mind another, dear recollection: he often thought of the Countess D., imagined her just indignation, tears, and grief... At times a dreadful thought took his breath away: the distractions of high society, a new liaison, another lucky man—he shuddered. Jealousy began to seethe in his African blood, and burning tears were ready to course down his black face. (8: 13–14)

Are we to pity the man who worries about the possible infidelity of a former mistress he has abruptly deserted and may never see again? Some of the words chosen—such as "a dreadful thought took his breath away," "he shuddered," "jealousy began to seethe in his African blood," and "burning tears"— seem to indicate that the narrator expected as much. But barely two pages further on we are introduced to Korsakov's view that the Countess's infidelity was the most natural thing in the world, and Ibrahim's own tears seem to dry up fast as he hurries off to the assembly. Once more, the cause of the difficulty seems to lie in the difference between poetry and prose. A lyrical passage in a narrative poem or in a novel in verse can stand on its own, regardless of an ironic statement that may follow a few stanzas further on, for in poetry the presence of several lyrical personae facilitates quick transitions in mood; but a "novel in prose"—with a consistent, neutral, detached narrator—demands a steadier atmosphere. The quick transitions in mood inconsistent with the narrator's personality—added to the other problems—prevented Pushkin from getting a firm grip on Ibrahim's character. The outline of the character—strong passions yet weak compromises—was excellent, and the mode of narration augured the future development of the novel, but the technical difficulties of an entirely new way of writing were so enormous that Pushkin could not flesh out the well-conceived idea with appropriate details.

As he became conscious of his difficulties, he returned to his native element—poetry—and as a homecoming present to himself, he indulged in eight similes in a row in the second verse paragraph of *Poltava*—a practice he would never have allowed himself in "stern prose."

2

Far from being discouraged by his experience with *The Blackamoor of Peter the Great*, in the following years Pushkin endeavored to apply an omniscient mode of narration to a psychological study of "Contemporary man / With his immoral soul"—an even more formidable task. Two fragments, each in several drafts, and a number of plot outlines have remained of his efforts.

The first fragment is known by its opening words, as "The Guests Were Arriving at the Dacha." It consists of three chapters, written sometime between the fall of 1828 and the beginning of 1830.[30] Chapter One contains a conversation about Russian mores between a Spanish visitor and a young Russian called Minskii; introduces a restless young married woman by the name of Zinaida Volskaia; and hints at an incipient romance between her and Minskii. The other two chapters are fragmentary: Chapter Two shows Minskii reading a note from Zinaida, which makes it clear that she is in love with him; and in Chapter Three the discussion between the Spaniard and Minskii is resumed.

The author-narrator of this fragment is as uncompromisingly intelligent as that of *The Blackamoor* was. He manages to reveal the complexity of his heroine in a mere few pages. Motherless since age five and left to the care of nurses and tutors by an indifferent father, she writes love letters to her dance teacher at age fourteen, which is enough to persuade her father to "bring her out" in society immediately. She soon marries the rich young Volskii, enjoys entertaining the whole town at her house, and develops a taste for shocking the best society with her pranks. Intent on taking a lover, she discusses prospective candidates with her confidant Minskii and ends up, predictably, in his arms. Unloved, she resorts to promiscuity as a means of drawing attention to herself, yet all the while "remained a fourteen-year-old at heart" (8: 39). This behavior is accompanied by a sense of guilt and inadequacy—the aspect of her character Pushkin emphasizes most. When she enters the drawing room at the dacha, she fails to take notice of anything; she refuses to engage in small talk; she sulks; her face is "changeable as a cloud" (8: 38); her general distractedness seems to indicate that she is engrossed in her inner problems. She awakens from her thoughts with a shudder (8: 38) and proceeds to the balcony to spend the rest of the evening alone with Minskii, which shocks the hostess and her other guests. One gets the feeling that she has sought her hostess's disapprobation as much as Minskii's company. Her anxious sense of inadequacy is revealed also in her note to Minskii, as she declares him vastly superior to herself, and complains and entreats (8: 41).

In the second draft (already corrected and copied out but not yet final) Pushkin had emphasized Zinaida's emotional problems even more openly. What was to become "her lively movements" had been "her restless movements" (8: 38, 536); the phrase "she got up" had been qualified by the adverb "impatiently" (8: 38, 536); and the gentleman conversing with Princess G. had said about her, "I look on her as if she were a sleepwalker, asleep yet walking on the roof: one would like to wake her but dares not" (8: 537; deleted from the final version). It is possible that Pushkin toned down the references to Zinaida's emotional problems because he feared that she might appear too far out of the range of normal to remain an attractive heroine. It is even more likely that he felt he could soften the tone of his description because he had found a subtler way to convey his meaning. In the drafts, Zinaida had entered the drawing room looking for Minskii, and her disquietude resulted from his absence. Deleting this detail from the final version proved to be a great gain, for the immediate cause of Zinaida's anxiety was now removed, and an impression of the general uneasiness of her mind was created. The change made it possible to put the rest of the characterization in a lower key.

Whether these were the considerations guiding Pushkin's hand or not, it is significant that he made such painstaking efforts to create a character of great psychological complexity. What we know of his further plans for the novel confirms that he wanted to continue it in the same vein: Zinaida's tragedy was to have been that, having lost Minskii to a young debutante, she would throw herself into a scandalous affair with a man she did not love (8: 554).

A second surviving fragment of a psychological novel begins with the words "In the Corner of a Small Square." It consists of one complete chapter and part of a second, both written sometime between November 1830 and March 1831. Chapter One consists of a dialogue between the heroine, once more called

Zinaida, and her lover, Valerian Volodskii. It becomes clear from the dialogue that, having taken up with Volodskii, she has left her husband and set herself up in a remote quarter of the city, where Volodskii comes to visit her, though he is getting bored with her. The incomplete second chapter briefly summarizes how she left her husband and how Volodskii reacted to this unexpected development.

Most critics have regarded this fragment as a continuation of "The Guests Were Arriving at the Dacha," since it is set against a similar social background and treats the same theme of adultery.[31] Moreover, the respective plot outlines associated with the two fragments both call for the heroine's lover to abandon her for the sake of an unmarried girl. However, as A. V. Chicherin, the critic who has studied these fragments most thoroughly, points out, the differences between the two fragments are greater than the similarities.[32] Indeed, the meek, submissive, pathetic Zinaida of the second fragment does not resemble her predecessor, even if we take into consideration a lapse of several years. She is older than her lover (an influence of *Adolphe*), which rules out the possibility that her Volodskii is a reincarnation of Minskii under a different name. Furthermore, although the first plot outline mentions Zinaida's confession to her husband, nowhere does it refer to her decision to leave him and to set up house on her own. One has to conclude that the second fragment represents, not a direct continuation of the first one, but a new attempt at handling the same theme.

In "The Guests" Pushkin concentrated most of his attention on his heroine, since it was she who had to make the decisions that were vital to the development of the plot. "In the Corner" presents the heroine at a stage in her life where her decisions have already been made: her fate now depends on what her lover decides to do. For this reason, Pushkin's attention here shifts to the hero; and the full range of Volodskii's feelings—from love through remorse to a desire for freedom and uncomplicated comfort—is at least sketched in, if not entirely developed.

The intricacy of characterization in these two fragments contradicts A. Z. Lezhnev's claim that Pushkin's prose in general concentrates "on actions rather than emotional experiences."[33] Nor does Lezhnev's monolithic view of Pushkin's style as always terse, austere, and simple hold true. Far from gravitating toward the barest subject-predicate-object structure, Pushkin's syntax is often complicated in these fragments, matching the nature of the material. Volskii's reasons for falling in love with Zinaida, for instance, are described in this sentence: "Volskii, a wealthy young man who usually let his feelings be governed by the opinions of others, fell head over heels in love with her because the Sovereign had once met her on the English Embankment and talked with her a full hour" (8: 39). Rather than whittling his phrase down to one precise, carefully chosen word, Pushkin tends in these fragments to pile synonym on synonym for cumulative effect, as in this sentence: "Volskaia reproached him for his coldness, his distrust, and the like; she complained and entreated, not knowing herself what about; showered on him a profusion of tender, affectionate assurances—and made an assignation to meet him in her box at the theater that evening" (8: 41). By no means anxious to avoid a profusion of qualifying epithets, Pushkin writes sentences like this one: "A pale lady, no longer in the first bloom of youth but still beautiful, dressed with great refinement, lay on a sofa strewn with cushions, in a room appointed with taste and luxury" (8: 143). Moreover, as Chicherin points out, in the unfinished works "the place of honor is occupied by the kind of epithet that denotes changeable, dynamic, relative qualities."[34] As an example, Chicherin cites the adjective "funny" (smeshna; 8: 39), applied to Zinaida, which has none of the fixed, absolute qualities that we find, for instance, in the word "haughty" (nadmennyi; 8: 162), applied to Troekurov in Dubrovskii. One might add that Pushkin, augmenting his epithets, compares Zinaida's face to a changeable cloud, aristocrats to Egyptian mummies, high society to a herd, and Volodskii to a restless schoolboy (8: 38, 41, 42, 144). All this testifies to a rich, varied style, by no means shorn of ornament.

Perceptive as Chicherin's comments on the early fragments are, he makes the error of referring to their stylistic features as "new" in comparison with those of the finished works, as if all the experimental pieces had been written after the publication of the main body of Pushkin's prose.[35] As Chicherin would have it, Pushkin first wrote a number of relatively uncomplicated works for publication and then began experimenting with more complex matters. This is a neat enough scheme—one would normally expect a writer to develop in this way—but it does not prove true in the case of Pushkin, who had already reached his full maturity in poetry when he turned to prose. Indeed it was "In the Corner of a Small Square," conceived before *The Tales of Belkin*, that was to inspire Tolstoi in writing *Anna Karenina*;[36] and it was Zinaida of "The Guests Were Arriving at the Dacha" who foreshadowed many a heroine in the novels of Turgenev and Dostoevskii. In fiction, Pushkin began with the complex, and then—temporarily, never abandoning the hope of incarnating the complex—he descended to the simple.

The question arises once again: if the creation of significant new characters was within Pushkin's grasp, why did he stop working on his psychological novel? There are several possible answers: he may have lacked the settled circumstances and spiritual calm indispensable for a sustained effort in prose;[37] he may have anticipated difficulties with the censor;[38] he may even have been embarrassed by the closeness of Zinaida to her real-life model, A. F. Zakrevskaia;[39] but it must not be overlooked that in these fragments, as in *The Blackamoor of Peter the Great*, the highly original design involved formidable difficulties of craftsmanship.

In "The Guests" Pushkin makes an earnest effort to endow his heroes with speech characteristics. He is most successful with Zinaida's letter to Minskii, which reveals her desire to impress him with a style more "bookish" than her education would lead one to expect. Phrases like "[this] proves that you're invariably superior to me," as they are put in the Russian original (*eto dokazyvaet tvoe vsegdashnee prevoskhodstvo nado mnoiu*; 8: 41), do not sound like the words of a flighty society lady. How deliberately Pushkin was aiming at an awkward effect is witnessed by a change he made in the text. In the first draft of the letter, we read, "Your sophisms don't convince me" (*tvoi sofizmy ne ubezhdaiut menia*; 8: 539), which is a perfectly clear and natural phrase. In the final text, however, Pushkin changed this to "your sophisms don't convince my suspicions" (*tvoi sofizmy ne ubezhdaiut moikh podozrenii*; 8: 41), which makes little sense and in translation has to be rendered as something like "your sophisms don't allay my suspicions." One has the impression that Zinaida had conversed at parties with members of some of the intellectual groups of the day, such as the Archival Youths or the Lovers of Wisdom, and had learned some of their bookish phrases, without, however, understanding them.

Unfortunately, Pushkin cuts Zinaida's letter short and tells us about the rest of it in his own words, as if he had run out of breath trying to imitate her. As for dialogue, we hear her utter only two phrases: "I'd like to fall in love with R." and "How about the Baron W.?" (8: 40). The second of these is purely functional, with no marked speech characteristics. At first glance the other seems to reveal her character, but if we compare it with the style that is used by both Minskii and the author-narrator, we realize that it carries class, rather than individual, characteristics.

What strikes one most about Minskii's manner is his flippancy. The Spanish visitor's earnest praise of the northern night, for example, is not to his taste: he twists it into a comparison of northern and southern beauties, with a banal reference to "the old controversy between *la brune et la blonde*" (8: 37). Further, he cracks a joke about the purity of Petersburg morals, ascribed by a foreigner to the fact that "our winter nights are too cold and our summer nights too bright for amorous adventures" (8: 37). The Spaniard interposes with another earnest remark about Russian beauty, amicability, and purity, only to elicit the answer that amicability is "not in vogue" (8: 37). Later, in his conversation with Zinaida, Minskii counsels her not to get involved with R. because the man's "insufferable wife is in love with him" (8: 40). He recommends, instead, having an affair with L., *un homme à grands sentiments*, adding: "He'll be jealous and passionate; he'll torment you and amuse you: what more would you wish?" (8: 40). Finally, what makes him love Zinaida so sincerely, he says, is that she is "excruciatingly funny" (8: 39).

One might assume that Zinaida's phrase "I'd like to fall in love" is adapted to Minskii's flippant style, which would not be surprising since she clearly wants to impress him. What confounds the matter is that the narrator also resorts to the same style time and again. His statement, for instance, that Zinaida married Volskii because the man "was not repugnant to her" (8: 39), might just as well have been made by Minskii. In connection with rumors about Zinaida's love affairs, the narrator says: "According to the code of high society, plausibility equals verity, and to be the target of slander lowers us in our own estimation" (8: 39). This sentence reminds one of J.-F. Marmontel's phrase, "Les soupçons, dans le monde, valent des certitudes"; [40] and it shows the dandy's penchant for borrowing aphorisms in order to shine at a social gathering. Further, explaining why Minskii was temporarily absent from society in his youth, the narrator says: "For a while passions muted the anguish of his wounded pride" (8: 40). The assumption is made that affairs of the heart are the transient aberrations of youth, but social vanities endure.

The attitudes of Minskii and Zinaida were obviously not Pushkin's own. A desire to expose the cynicism of a certain segment of Russian society is apparent in the fragment. Also, everything indicates that the emotional experiences of the characters were to be studied objectively, at a distance from the author. Yet instead of limiting the flippant tone of fashionable society to his characters, Pushkin allowed it to seep into the style of his narrator too. This failure to separate the narrator from the characters in a stylistic sense seems to have been the greatest problem Pushkin encountered in working on the novel.

This problem is most painfully obvious in Chapter Three of "The Guests," where the Russian Minskii and the Spanish visitor discuss the characteristics of the Russian aristocracy. The opinions they voice can be found in Pushkin's 1830 lyric "My Genealogy" and in his "Attempt to Rebut Some Non-Literary Charges" (1830), as well as in other fictional fragments. They are plainly Pushkin's own; they were provoked by searing social experiences and have an air of petulance about them. Voicing them, Minskii and the Spaniard lose their identity, not only in a stylistic, but also in an ideological sense. Their conversation resembles Nadezhdin's critical essays written in the form of dialogues.

We must bear in mind that before Pushkin's time no Russian prose writer had attempted to use dialogue for characterization.

To most writers, dialogue meant allowing the characters to say what the author himself would otherwise have said. It simply varied the form, enlivened the pace. In the eighteenth century Russian prose writers considered the use of numerous dialogues not only an unnecessary touch, but a positive flaw in craftsmanship.[41] Dialogue came into its own with the emergence of the detached, third-person narrative form. Pioneering this form, Pushkin also had to pioneer characterization through dialogue. In both, he encountered difficulties.

His great success in dialogue, in this early experimental period, was Chapter One of "In the Corner of a Small Square." Written about the same time as the last chapter of "The Guests," this fragment also treats the theme of the Russian aristocracy, but infinitely more successfully. Here both speakers, descendants of ancient nobility, have personal reasons to resent those aristocrats of more recent vintage who set the tone in contemporary society. Zinaida has been ostracized for her adulterous affair. Volodskii, though not, as a man, formally excluded from society, has nevertheless been piqued by a Prince Goretskii who—obviously because of Volodskii's notorious affair—did not invite him to a party. Since both characters have perfect motivations for their irritability, we no longer feel that they are voicing Pushkin's own grievances. The argument about aristocracy is thus well motivated. But in addition, it has a well-designed place in the plot. While Zinaida bitterly reminds her lover that she has not frequented *his* aristocratic circles for quite some time, she is giving information to the reader about her situation. Her jealousy of his role in society reveals not only her hatred of that society, but also her premonition about his involvement with a younger society girl. Volodskii, in turn, not only vents his anger over the snub he received from Prince Goretskii, but seems to use this opportunity to discharge a great deal of accumulated hatred—hatred whose proper target should be Zinaida, since she is the one who has put him in an awkward social position. This perfectly constructed dialogue, then, characterizes the heroes, provides information about their past and present, hints at their incipient conflict, and at the same time conveys the author's social ideas in an unobtrusive way. It shows a situation, as one critic has aptly remarked, in which

Tatiana might have found herself, had she yielded to Onegin's entreaties.[42] No wonder Tolstoi was so much impressed by it. Still, since this dialogue remained an isolated fragment of two and a half pages, one has to conclude that Pushkin was not yet able to sustain such a high level of writing throughout a novel. In the second chapter of "In the Corner" he turns to an extremely fast-moving narrative, with no dialogue.

This great speed of narration is another problem Pushkin encountered in his first attempts at prose. Chapter Two of "In the Corner" begins with the sentence "X. soon found out that his wife was unfaithful to him" (8: 145), which summarizes an experience that could have been expanded into several chapters. Tolstoi's Karenin, for instance, first notices that other people find Anna's behavior improper; he lectures her; his suspicions increase gradually; and he is not fully convinced of her infidelity until she tells him about it herself. The scene of confession itself, whose dramatic potentials are so skillfully exploited by Tolstoi, is summed up in one single sentence by Pushkin. Finally, Volodskii's reaction to Zinaida's precipitate action, described by Pushkin in one paragraph, could have occupied a whole volume, or more, as indeed the changes in Vronskii's attitudes were to do in *Anna Karenina*.

V. V. Vinogradov, in his monumental study of Pushkin's style, has likened Pushkin's prose to Russian chronicles, in which only essential events—like the pillars of a structure—were visible, nevertheless creating the impression of great latent wealth.[43] Another critic has drawn attention to the similarity between Pushkin's prose and the notes he jotted down while planning narrative poems.[44] In such notes—in those on Tatiana's letter, for instance—the barest essentials of the outline provide guideposts for the poetic development of the theme. These critical observations are valid at least in relation to those parts of the early fragments where the narration is rapid. With reference to these parts, one could say that Tolstoi's novel, realizing the potentials of Pushkin's sketch, filled out the space between the "pillars." What complicates the issue, however, is that other parts of the fragments—Chapter One of "In the Corner," for instance—present fully developed details rather than rapid outlines. This fact shows, once more, how difficult it is to characterize Pushkin's prose in general. He obviously tried to fill out his outlines with details—to transcend a merely essay-like presentation—but he did not always succeed, finding out in the process what a "devil of a difference" there was not only between the poetic development of a theme and its development in prose, but also between essay and fiction.

In order to examine the difference between poetry and prose once more, let us see how Pushkin introduces Tatiana in *Eugene Onegin*. She is first mentioned at the end of Stanza 23, Chapter Two, where the narrator asks the reader's permission to turn his attention to Olga's elder sister. In Stanza 24 Tatiana's name is given, and a digression about Russian girls' names follows. In the next stanza, six lines tell us what Tatiana was like (6: 42):

> Timid, sad, taciturn,
> Shy as a woodland fawn,
> She seemed to be a stranger
> In her own family.
> . . .
> Often she sat alone all day
> Silently by the window.

The remaining eight lines of the stanza detail what she was *not* like: she did not have her sister's beauty and fresh complexion, she did not like to cuddle up to her parents, and even as a little girl, she would not run and play with other children. The following two stanzas contain a total of four and a half lines characterizing her directly—describing her pensive ways and her fondness for horror tales—with all the remaining lines again devoted to negative characterization, bringing to life everything she was not and did not do. Stanza 28 records that she loved to watch the sunrise from the balcony, which gives Pushkin an opportunity for a lyrical description of night and dawn. Finally, the first four lines of Stanza 29 contain the information that Tatiana loved novels, especially those of Richardson and Rousseau. With this, Pushkin considers her introduction and first characterization complete, and enters into the courtship and marriage of her parents. Put in prose, her description would amount to little more than an outline, but since a great wealth of poetry—witty digressions, lyrical descriptions, the charm of all the childish things Tatiana did not do (and which nevertheless remain associated with her in our minds)—fills out the gaps between the supporting pillars of design, we come away with the impression that she has been fully characterized.

What works in poetry, however, does not necessarily succeed in prose, at least not in the kind of prose Pushkin cultivated. Almost as much information is provided about the Zinaida(s) of the two prose fragments as about Tatiana, yet the novel fails to get off the ground because Pushkin's concept of prose did not allow the kind of "padding" he used in poetry. All that the narrator of the fragments knows about his characters is revealed to the reader immediately; instead of saving some of his material for later, gradual release, he sets it all off in a single dazzling display of fireworks. This is connected with the fact that his narrator—even when he slips into the characters' style—is invariably an intelligent person who does not play games with the reader, but speaks directly to the point (as if writing an essay). Pushkin was soon to find that the manner of a somewhat dull-witted, semi-educated narrator—a "prosaic persona," so to speak—would be easier to handle.

3

The dull-witted narrator was shortly to be employed in *The Tales of Belkin*. But before Pushkin set himself to that task, he experimented with another narrative mode in the hope of overcoming the difficulties of detached, third-person narration. This was the epistolary form, which he put to use in the unfinished *A Novel in Letters*, written in the fall of 1829. As far as the letters take us, we become acquainted with Liza, an orphan brought up in a rich family, whose head was indebted to her late father. Although she has always been treated as an equal, she feels her inferiority, especially next to her foster mother's niece, the wealthy young Princess Olga. Tormented by a sense of her inferior social status, she has decided to retire to the country, where her grandmother, though reduced to modest circumstances, has received her with open arms. As her letters to her girl friend Sasha unfold, however, we realize that she had another reason for leaving St. Petersburg: she had fallen in love with a wealthy young man called Vladimir and feared that though he was obviously attracted to her, he would not marry her because of her poverty. Vladimir, missing her in the city, arrives at the house of a relative whose estate is adjacent to her grandmother's; the romance is renewed, but when the plot line breaks off we do not know what to expect because the relative at whose house Vladimir is staying has an attractive daughter, Masha.

Taking up the epistolary form marked a retreat: instead of pioneering an entirely new mode of writing, Pushkin was both drawing on his own experience as a correspondent and making use of existing literary models. Liza of *A Novel in Letters* says, of some eighteenth-century novels she has just been reading, that the action is entertaining but the characters speak in an unnatural language. "A clever man," she continues, "could adopt these ready-made plots and characters, amend the style, eliminate the absurdities, supply the missing links—and the result would be a splendid original novel" (8: 50). This seems to be precisely what Pushkin set out to do in his epistolary novel; and he was to take his heroine's advice not only on this, but on other occasions.

In this particular case his chief models were *Julie, ou La Nouvelle Héloïse* (1761) by Jean Jacques Rousseau, which he had mentioned several times in *Onegin*; *Les Liaisons dangereuses* (1782), by Pierre Choderlos de Laclos,[45] to which he made an unflattering reference in "The Guests"; and *Clarissa* (1747–48) by Samuel Richardson. The last is discussed in *A Novel in Letters* itself: Liza reports to her friend that she has borrowed it from her neighbors and decided to plod her way through it despite the dullness of the first six parts, because the Preface to the translation promised that the last six would reward the industrious reader. "I bravely set about the task," she continues. "I read the first, the second, the third volumes... at last I reached the sixth one: dull beyond endurance. Well, thought I, now I shall be rewarded for my pains. And what happened? I read about the deaths of Clarissa and Lovelace, and that was the end of it. Each volume contained two parts, and I did not notice the transition from the six boring to the six entertaining ones" (8: 47).[46]

Despite this anecdote, Pushkin was making use of Richardson's technique. The choice was between it and that of Rousseau; each had its advantages and drawbacks. Unlike Julie and Saint-Preux, Pushkin's lovers do not correspond with each other, describing to each other how they kissed the day before. Their correspondents are friends, relatively uninvolved in their relationship and therefore needing information about it. This allows the reader to be initiated into the proceedings more naturally. On the other hand, describing events to friends—as Clarissa Harlowe does to Miss Howe, and Lovelace does to Belford—lacks the dramatic potential inherent in a correspondence between the lovers themselves. Pushkin might have objected to the behavior of Rousseau's lovers—arguing their sexual impulses as minutely and rigorously as if they were legal matters—but eliminating their direct exchange of letters meant depriving the novel of some lively moments. As used by Richardson and Pushkin, the letters quoted were not themselves the events: they were merely descriptions of events. The Richardsonian epistolary form came close to the first-person narrative of a journal or memoir, except for its more varied point of view.

It was perhaps the use of this form, lacking in dramatic opportunity, that hindered Pushkin in developing an otherwise promising plan. Liza of *A Novel in Letters* is potentially as interesting a person as Ibrahim or Zinaida. Her most characteristic trait is a morbid sensitivity, caused by her social position. When her friend the Princess refuses to wear expensive pearls, not wishing to outshine her, Liza resents this, just as Dostoevskii's Underground Man will resent Zverkov for refusing to be rude to him. When she desires her Vladimir to fall in love with Masha, she appears to be an early Nastasia Filippovna telling Myshkin to marry Aglaia (*The Idiot*; 1868–69). Her ambivalent feelings are matched by the ambiguous situation Pushkin places her in. It never becomes clear, at least not in the existing letters, whether she is right in her judgment of Vladimir as a flighty young man who is only leading her on. His behavior with Masha seems to indicate the correctness of this judgment, but Liza's friend Sasha implies that events might have taken a different turn if Liza had been bold enough to seize her opportunity earlier. Sasha's assessment of the situation may be simply a function of her vulgar mind—which is amply revealed in Letter 4—yet there is a prophetic ring to her words in Letter 7: "You're asking for misfortune: take care not to bring it on yourself" (8: 52). We cannot tell whether adversity coins Liza's character or her character generates adversity. The poet Valerii Briusov has aptly characterized her as another Tatiana, for whom "happiness is ever 'possible,' ever 'close at hand,' but never actually attainable."[47]

Her very style gives Sasha away as an empty-headed society girl, but Liza and Vladimir—perhaps because they lack the opportunity for dramatic confrontation—never develop a style of their own. It is noteworthy that Liza's description of Masha's family in Letter 3 was lifted, at least partially, from another fragment of Pushkin's, "In the Beginning of 1812" (1829), where the describer was a young officer. Liza's literary judgments are clearly Pushkin's own; her indignation over critical reviews in the *European Herald* anticipates Pushkin's "Letter to the Editor of the *Literary Gazette*" (1830); her claim that society ladies are not as prudish as some critics imagine them to be is a thought Pushkin expounds in "An Attempt to Rebut Some Non-Literary Charges"; and both her and Vladimir's discussions of the Russian nobility represent yet another attempt to convey Pushkin's own ideas on the topic.

In *A Novel in Letters*, Pushkin had given up the omniscient narrator of his other fragments, but he was still having difficulty with the narrative point of view. Having endowed his characters with his own lucid mind and critical judgments, he found it difficult to separate them from himself. This is why the letters of Liza and Vladimir appear to be Pushkin's own letters or essays, in spite of the individual and highly interesting psychological features that he intended to give to these characters. The stock of experience he had built up in writing his own letters was not, by itself, enough for fiction.

The same problem arose in connection with two more unfinished works: "My Fate Is Sealed: I Am Getting Married" and a short piece, known simply as "A Fragment" (both dated 1830), containing a discussion of the poet's place in society. Both are close to autobiography, written in the first person and illuminated by the insights of an intelligent mind. But neither gets off the ground as fiction. The second, in particular, comes quite close in style to an essay.

Pushkin's difficulty in the early fragments was that he insisted on treating complex material, though he had not found the right key, the right narrative point of view, the right technique for the new genres he was experimenting with. In order to find a solution, he had to lower his sights.

III. 'Belkin' and 'Goriukhino'

I

The difficulties Pushkin encountered in the early fragments drove him toward simpler subject matter, to be presented by simpler narrators.

The idea of concealing himself behind an assumed personality—that of a poorly educated country squire—came to his mind first in the course of altercations with literary critics. Back in 1820 A. Glagolev, a critic of neoclassical persuasion, had launched an attack on Pushkin's *Ruslan and Liudmila* (1820) in the form of a "letter" to the editor of the *European Herald* from a certain Citizen of the Village of Butyrki.[1] By way of introduction he described himself as a simple old man with a traditional education who was, nevertheless, interested in recent achievements in literature. He welcomed the greater freedom and versatility of the new generation of writers on the whole, he said, but when he came cross Canto 3 of Pushkin's poem and a ballad by P. A. Pletnev in *Son of the Fatherland*,[2] he concluded that liberty was being carried to the utter limits of unruliness, and he could not help raising his voice in protest. This citizen from Butyrki was not the only simple old man whose common sense was being applied to the fanciful works of the young generation: we come across letters from Averian the Curious to the Old Man of Luzhnitsk, statements by the Citizen of Galley Docks, critical reviews by the Sedulous Reader of Journals, and the like.[3] The tradition of employing simple old men as literary oracles became so widespread that P. A. Viazemskii decided to satirize it in his Preface to the first edition of *The Fountain at Bakhchisarai*, directing his argument against a fatuous Classicist from the Vyborg District or from Vasilev Island (pseudonyms used in the journal *The Stead-fast*). Despite Viazemskii's satirical treatment, however, the tradition continued all through the 1820's, culminating in the essays of N. I. Nadezhdin. That critic reviewed both *Poltava* and Chapter Seven of *Onegin* disguised as a person "from the Patriarch's Ponds," whose old friend Pakhom Silich, the retired proofreader of a printing house, pronounced the most sagacious literary judgments.[4]

Pushkin, astounded by the stupidity of some of his critics, once remarked that his best revenge on them would be simply to reprint their reviews without comment (11: 157–58); and he carried this idea out, at least partially, in his Preface to the sec-ond edition of *Ruslan and Liudmila* (1828). The Fatuous Critic grew into a social type in his eyes. Once he wondered—as if he were collecting material for a fictional portrait—where he could observe the speech habits of some of these prim and proper reviewers, especially as they conversed with ladies (11: 155). His fragment "If the Appellation 'Lover of Native Litera-ture'" (1827) is an attempt to represent the literary attitudes of one of these denizens of Butyrki from an ironic "inside." He writes in first person:

If the appellation "lover of native literature" is in itself sufficient to command respect and does indeed carry meaning, then I, the paucity of my talents notwithstanding, also have a right to expect some atten-tion from the public. Born of honest though indigent parents in 1761, I could not make use of those resources of enlightenment that in later years were to become so abundant; I had to content myself with les-sons from the parish clerk—a man who was, incidentally, remarkably well educated for his humble station. It is to this worthy man that I owe gratitude for my devotion to the sublime in general and to Rus-sian literature in particular. Mr. Kurganov's *Handbook of Composi-tion*, entrusted to me, was ever in my hands, and I knew it by heart at the age of eight years. Since that time, I dare say, not one Russian com-position, not one translation, not one Russian journal (including works on economics, cookbooks, and calendars) has come off the press with-out my reading it or at least acquiring sufficient information about it. Old men are generally accused of blind attachment to the past and of turning away from the present. I do not deserve such reproach. The achievements of our literature have always warmed my heart, and I could not read without indignation those demented and unjust as-saults that some have made in our journals on writers who are the pride, not only of Russia but of the whole of mankind, and generally on the state of enlightenment in our dearest fatherland. Are not these journals themselves eloquent proof of the gigantic strides our enlightenment has made? (11: 62).

There follows a list of practically all of the major Russian journals, and the writer avows that his purpose in coming out of obscurity is to defend them. The passage concludes with an invocation to the Parcae who weave the thread of his life. In all, good-natured as he may be, this "lover of native literature" is just about to launch an attack on those writers who stood ready to criticize Russian culture, among whom Pushkin no doubt numbered himself.

Pushkin represented the simpletons of literary life in a similarly ironic manner in another fragment, "Some Moscow Men of Letters" (1829). His highest achievements in this manner of writing were to be his two articles under the pseudonym of Feofilakt Kosichkin (1831). What is interesting to us, however, is that by 1829 the comic personality whom Pushkin had originally endowed with critical ambitions had acquired the aspirations of a fiction writer. In the fall of that year, around the same time as he was working on *A Novel in Letters*, Pushkin jotted down the first draft of what was to become the Introduction to *The Tales of Belkin*. The second draft followed a year later.[5] The provincial simpleton, who had at first intended to enter the lists only in a critical tournament, had now written down five tales, supposedly heard from four different narrators. These tales (dating from the fall of 1830), together with the final version of the Publisher's Introduction written in the summer of 1831, were published in October of that year under the title *The Tales of the Late Ivan Petrovich Belkin*.

The tales were essentially anonymous; Pushkin's authorship could be guessed only from his initials, A.P., which he had appended to the Publisher's Introduction. Originally he had not planned to reveal even that much of his connection with the tales because, as he wrote to Pletnev, he was afraid that F. V. Bulgarin would attack them (14: 133). But as the time of publication drew closer, he decided to give the public at least a hint, and eventually he even instructed Pletnev to whisper his name to the publisher A. F. Smirdin, who in turn was to pass the word to customers in his bookstore (14: 209).

Like his predecessor in the 1827 sketch, Belkin comes from a humble, though respectable, family; he too acquired his education from a parish clerk, to whom, it is stated, he owes "his fondness for reading and for exercising his pen in the realm of Russian letters" (8: 60). It is a noteworthy change, however, that Belkin was born some thirty-seven years later than his predecessor, and that his biography is given, not by himself, but by his neighbor, the squire of Nenaradovo, a much older man. Appropriately, this older man writes in the same cumbersome style as the persona of the 1827 sketch: we must remember that this is not Belkin's own style. We come across sentences like "On the twenty-third of this month I had the honor of receiving your esteemed letter of the fifteenth in which you express your wish to obtain detailed information concerning the dates of birth and death, army service, family circumstances, and occupations, as well as the moral character, of the late Ivan Petrovich Belkin, my erstwhile sincere friend and owner of an estate neighboring mine" (8: 59); and "The young landowner at first followed my investigations with the greatest possible attention and assiduity; but as soon as it became evident from the accounts that in the last two years the number of peasants had increased while that of the poultry and cattle belonging to the estate had noticeably decreased, Ivan Petrovich contented himself with these preliminary reckonings and would not listen to me anymore; and at the very moment when I had thrown that rogue of an elder into utter confusion by my investigation and stern questioning and had reduced him to total silence, I caught, to my great irritation, the sound of Ivan Petrovich vigorously snoring in his chair" (8: 60). The only precedent for this unwieldy style in Pushkin's prose is the 1827 sketch. It is a complex enough style that does not shun involuted periods; but its complexity does not arise from the complicated nature of the subject matter. It is, rather, the result of the writer's lack of skill in expressing himself.

This lack of skill is the main source of humor in the squire's letter. It shows not only in the clumsiness of style, but also in a lack of logic. To begin with, he says he received "on the twenty-third of this month" the Publisher's "esteemed letter of the fifteenth"; yet he is answering on the sixteenth of the same month.[6] Further, he says he is sending the Publisher "everything" he can remember from his conversations with Belkin and from his own observations. The meager information that follows reveals either that the good squire has a very poor memory or that there is not much to remember about the late Ivan Petrovich. Yet the squire, not realizing how parsimonious he has been with his information, proudly declares at the end of his letter that he has told all he can remember about "the way of life, occupations, moral character, and appearance" of his friend (8: 62). Instead of concentrating on Ivan Petrovich, he digresses to censure young landowners for neglecting their estates, and peasants for their perpetual discontent—apparently two of his hobbyhorses. He cannot keep his mind on the subject matter at hand even when he relates the saddest part of his narrative, Belkin's early death: even here he digresses about the excellent qualities of the physician who, though he failed to save Belkin's life, was nevertheless very skillful in curing "such deep-rooted ailments as corns and the like" (8: 61). This digression about the physician contains the kernel of Gogol's future style; it is based on the same principle as the description of Ivan Ivanovich, who was an excellent man because he loved watermelons.

The squire's style is notoriously inappropriate to his subject. His avowed purpose is to paint an attractive portrait of a man he liked and respected, but in the simpleness of his mind, he makes Belkin appear as a backward child, helpless in matters of practical life and bashful as a maiden—a prototype for Gogol's Ivan Fedorovich Shponka. To be sure, there is something endearing about Belkin, but to make him the paragon of guileless native existence, as some critics have done, is clearly an exaggeration.[7] Like the man of the 1827 sketch, Belkin was created as part of a satirical design; he is a literary adversary of Pushkin's.[8] His meekness, and whatever other agreeable qualities he may possess, only serve to heighten the comic effect.

If Belkin and his neighbor were born of literary controversies, so was the Publisher of the tales. Since he appears under the initials A.P., and since he seems to have selected ironic epigraphs for the whole volume as well as for each tale, it might be assumed that he is Pushkin himself. In fact, however, he is as much a tool of satire in Pushkin's hands as the other two characters. It would indeed be surprising if Pushkin agreed with the Publisher that the squire of Nenaradovo's letter about Belkin was both "a precious document testifying to a noble frame of mind and to a touching bond of friendship" and "a perfectly adequate biographical sketch" (8: 59). Nor is it likely that Pushkin would have stated that he was publishing the squire's letter "without any change or annotations" (8: 59) and then deleted an anecdote about Belkin's bashfulness, with only a footnote to the effect that the anecdote contained nothing injurious to the good man's memory.

The epigraph to the volume, taken from Act 4, Scene 8, of D. I. Fonvizin's comedy *The Young Hopeful* (1782), reads as follows:

> *Mme. Prostakova*: Aye, truly, my dear sir, he's been fond of histories ever since he was little.
> *Skotinin*: Mitrofan takes after me.

The irony of this dialogue results from the characters' understanding of the word history (*istoriia*). Prostakova has been trying to show off her son Mitrofan's learnedness in front of three guests, but with little success: he has betrayed his lack of familiarity even with the simplest grammatical concepts. Seeing the boy's total ignorance of grammar, one of the guests ironically suggests that Mitrofan must be equally strong in "history"—a word that Prostakova and her brother Skotinin proceed to interpret as "story" or "anecdote."

The choice of such an epigraph for Belkin's stories is enough to suggest that they are not to be taken seriously. Moreover, if the stories contained in the volume are of the kind the uncouth Mitrofan would love, the reader is not likely to have much curiosity about their author. Yet the earnest Publisher—whose style, incidentally, is as clumsy as that of Belkin's neighbor—writes that he is trying to satisfy "the legitimate curiosity of lovers of our native literature" (8: 59) about the identity of Belkin. The irony of the epigraph is, then, unintentional as far as the Publisher is concerned: he probably selected it simply because the distinction between "story" and "history" was as hazy to him as it was to Prostakova.[9]

The phrase "lovers of our native literature," as used by the Publisher, is borrowed from the 1827 sketch, which seems to indicate that Pushkin had divided the satirical personality of that sketch into three characters—Belkin, the squire of Nenaradovo, and the Publisher—for the Introduction to *The Tales*. One might add that the Publisher's tone is equally close to that of the satirical fragment "Some Moscow Men of Letters," these being described as "the pride of our epoch both by their creations and by their moral conduct" (11: 85). His prim and proper attitude toward the anecdote about Belkin's bashfulness also makes him akin to the people satirized in that fragment. Finally, it is characteristic of the Publisher's absentminded, slightly senile ways that he does not reveal how he got hold of the tales he is publishing.[10] In the first draft Pushkin indicated that the squire of Nenaradovo had sent the manuscript to the Publisher (8: 581), but he deleted this detail from the subsequent versions, in order, presumably, to increase the comic ambiguity of the Introduction.

The tales presented by Belkin appear to be in keeping with the introductory description of their author. They were collected from people more or less on the same educational level as Belkin himself. As the Publisher informs us in a footnote, "The Stationmaster" had been narrated by Titular Councillor A.G.N., "The Shot" by Lieutenant Colonel I.L.P., "The Undertaker" by the steward B.V., and both "The Blizzard" and "The Squire's Daughter" by the maiden K.I.T. Scanty as this information is, it seems to hint that "The Stationmaster" will involve matters interesting to the lower ranks of civil servants, "The Shot" will present a story in the taste of the military, "The Undertaker" will have a lower-middle-class appeal, and the two stories told by the maiden K.I.T. will probably reflect the point of view of a provincial Miss. We do not learn much about these narrators, but the little we do learn does not inspire confidence in their literary taste.

Pushkin's original intention, as witnessed by his "Lover of Native Literature" sketch, was to caricature literary critics.

Broadening his design, he arrived at the figure of Belkin and ended up caricaturing fiction writers. This meant assuming the roles, ironically, of the very writers whose style he had been carefully avoiding in his experimental fragments. We have seen, for instance, that in *The Blackamoor of Peter the Great* he had shunned all the jugglery with fictitious narrators that was fashionable in the 1820's. That novel's omniscient mode of narration had signaled an entirely new departure in Russian fiction, eliminating the projection of an elaborate, separate, individualized authorial personality. However, since the simplicity of such a mode of narration, its closeness to the essay, presented formidable technical difficulties, Pushkin eventually reverted to the assumption of roles. This meant giving up some of his original principles of prose and retreating, in a way, toward poetry; but it proved to be a useful compromise.

In creating his imaginary narrators, Pushkin used Sir Walter Scott's *Tales of My Landlord* as his chief model.[11] Given Scott's popularity in Russia in the 1820's, it is obvious that Pushkin intended to make no secret of the connection between his Introduction and Scott. As for the experimental nature of the tales, he could have said with Scott: "The work is unto me as a child is to a parent; in the which child, if it proveth worthy, the parent hath honour and praise; but, if otherwise, the disgrace will deservedly attach to itself alone."[12]

Although Scott's influence on *The Tales of Belkin* is important, one difference between the two authors' use of narrators must be noted. Scott needed narrators to disguise himself (quite genuinely, for many years) and to establish a familiar relationship with the reader. Once this relationship was established, however, the personality of the original narrator often became blurred, and only an occasional learned footnote by Cleishbotham reminded the reader of the framework of *The Tales of My Landlord*. Indeed, it would have been a tedious task for Scott to write long novels in the stylized manner of poorly educated narrators; as long as the familiarity with the reader could be maintained, the narrator's individual characteristics played no further role. Scott would even interrupt the narrative in order to address the reader in his own name, from an educated point of view, with no pretense at maintaining the original narrator's identity. For instance, before describing the appearance of blind Alice's ghost in Chapter Twenty-three of *The Bride of Lammermoor*, he disclaims the authorship of this episode and justifies its inclusion by the need for a tinge of Scottish superstition in a Scottish story. At the end of Chapter Thirty-four he refers to the popular appetite for the horrible in connection with Lucy's stabbing of Bucklaw, once more opening up an educated perspective on the elements of the plot. And he concludes the novel (the last one in the cycle) with the following words: "Reader! *The Tales of My Landlord* are now finally closed, and it was my purpose to have addressed thee in the vein of Jedediah Cleishbotham; but, like Horam the son of Asmar, and all other imaginary story-tellers, Jedediah has melted into thin air."[13] Whatever stylistic differences there are among the tales of the Landlord are due to varying subjects, but still within one author's range. From this point of view, Pushkin did not follow Scott's example: the personalities of his narrators are definitely reflected in his tales, which is of course much more easily achieved in shorter than in longer forms of fiction.

In the shortness of his pieces and in the pervasive use of his narrators, Pushkin was more akin to Washington Irving than to Scott. Irving would take care to mark the difference between, say, "Rip van Winkle," taken from among the posthumous writings of Diedrich Knickerbocker, and "The Stout Gentleman: A Stage-Coach Romance," narrated by the "thin, pale, weazen-faced, extremely nervous man." In both of these tales— as in many others by Irving—the narrator's role is not limited to creating an air of familiarity while at the same time camouflaging the author: they each satirize a particular literary trend. Likewise, Pushkin's Belkin does not serve merely to avert Bulgarin's eyes from the real author, but stands as a satirical portrait of a fiction writer whose personality, together with his narrators' personalities, pervades the whole volume. It is not surprising that the reviewer of the *Moscow Telegraph* immediately recognized the affinity of *The Tales* to Irving's stories.[14]

Taking on satirical roles in *The Tales of Belkin* seems to have helped Pushkin's development as a prose writer in two ways. First, he "settled accounts," so to speak, not only with Scott and Irving, but with contemporary fiction in general. The set of tales taken together amount to a parodic anthology of early-nineteenth-century prose writing, both Russian and Western. The themes carry with them a range of style, from the Karamzinite early sentimental through the Byronic to the Hoffmannesque. Never had Pushkin ventured into roles quite so far removed from his own personality.

But writing in this satirical vein was not merely Pushkin's vengeance on contemporary prose writing, whose standards he had not succeeded in surpassing; it was not limited to a demonstration of "how you all write." Parodying contemporary trends gave him an opportunity to practice different styles. He must have had his own plans at least at the back of his mind when he commented, in connection with one of Nikolai Polevoi's parodies earlier in 1830: "This kind of drollery requires an exceptionally flexible style: the good parodist has all styles at his command" (6: 118). With his characteristic penchant for total absorption in his subject, the deeper Pushkin delved into his stylistic exercises, the more interest he developed in them; and in one or two of the tales—certainly in "The Stationmaster" and to a lesser degree in "The Shot"—he succeeded in transcending parody to create original masterpieces.

2

The personality of Belkin-as-narrator is further revealed in another piece of writing attributed to him, *A History of the Village of Goriukhino*. The last of *The Tales*, "The Blizzard," was completed on October 20, 1830, and Pushkin must have set to work on *Goriukhino* immediately afterwards, for the manuscript bears the dates October 31 and November 1.[15] It begins with Belkin's introduction, in which he gives a short autobiography and explains how he became a historian, and continues with two fragments of the actual *History*: a general description of the village of Goriukhino, followed by an account of how the village, originally prosperous while enjoying its owners' benevolent neglect, became impoverished after the arrival of a new steward. At this point the narrative breaks off, but a set of notes Pushkin left indicates that he intended to continue the story to include a rebellion by the Goriukhino peasants (8: 719). It is obvious that such a topic would not have gone down well with the censors, which must have been the main reason why he abandoned the project. Another reason might have been that a bloody revolt would not have fitted in with the humorous stylistic context, already strained to include serious matters. However that may be, the unfinished *Goriukhino* was published only after Pushkin's death, and then in mutilated form; [16] the full text was to be restored, from Pushkin's manuscripts, only in much later editions.

Although technically unfinished, *Goriukhino* can be regarded as a completed work in the sense that it conveys an impression to which little could be added within the given framework. Straddling the fence between the humorous and the pathetic in a way that is achieved only in a masterpiece, it represents one of Pushkin's highest achievements in the use of a fictitious narrator.

It is hard to say whether Pushkin intended the Belkin of *Goriukhino* to replace the Belkin of *The Tales* or saw the two as complementary and mutually reconcilable figures. By the time he put the finishing touches to the Introduction to *The Tales* in July or August 1831, he must have known that he was not going to finish *Goriukhino*, and therefore we do not know how he would have coordinated the two Belkin images had he used both in published works. In any case, there is no direct contradiction between the two. One indication that Pushkin probably regarded the two figures as essentially one is this passage in *Goriukhino* referring to Belkin's first literary efforts: "I began writing tales, but because of my lack of experience I did not know how to string fictitious events together, and therefore chose some remarkable anecdotes I had heard in the past from various people. I tried to embellish the truth by lively narration and sometimes even by the flowering of my own imagination. Composing these tales, I gradually formed my style, until I had learned to express myself correctly, pleasantly, and fluently" (8: 132). Presumably, Belkin had already arrived at this stage of development by the time he was writing his introduction to *Goriukhino*; but his real tour de force, the exemplar of "correct, pleasant, and fluent" style is, of course, his history itself. We must remember, when we come to discuss *The Tales*, that the Belkin who wrote them had not yet acquired his stylistic expertise.

The biography of Belkin that the squire of Nenaradovo provided for the Introduction to *The Tales* and the one that Belkin himself gives in his introduction to *Goriukhino* agree on most points (except that the Belkin of *Goriukhino* is three years younger). We read about the same social background, the same educational experience under the guidance of the parish clerk, the same service in the army, the same boredom after settling down in a village, and the same housekeeper famous for her tales. Yet there is this difference between the two biographies, that Belkin's own version—without contradicting that of his neighbor—is much more detailed, and the added details make him look even more ludicrous. In this version, he not only states that he was educated by the parish clerk, but adds: "Although my progress was slow, it was not without promise, for by the age of ten I had already acquired almost all the knowledge that I was going to retain, to this day, in memory" (8: 127). The description of how he loved Kurganov's *Latest Handbook of Composition* (omitted by his neighbor) is transferred here from the "Lover of Native Literature" sketch.[17] Here also he explains why he did not return to school after the Napoleonic War ("I persuaded my dear mother to let me stay in the country, because my state of health did not allow me to get up at seven in the morning, the usual time of rising in boarding schools") (8: 128); recalls his most enjoyable experience while in the army (the winning of 245 rubles); and adds a host of other laughable details.[18]

We have seen that some of Pushkin's experimental fragments anticipated Tolstoi, Turgenev, and Dostoevskii. The writings of Belkin, in turn, anticipate Gogol.[19] We have already noted some Gogolesque features in the Introduction to *The Tales*; similar features are even more pronounced in *Goriukhino*.[20] For example, Belkin speaks of how much he admired Kurganov, of how diligently he tried to learn something about this favorite author of his, and of how he failed to acquire any information. Since he thought Kurganov was second only to General Plemiannikov, his father's erstwhile commander, and since he compared Kurganov to an "ancient demiurge" (8: 127), one would expect him to have formed a heroic image of the man. In the end, however, he says: "[I] finally decided that he [Kurganov] must have looked like the assessor of the district court, Koriuchkin—a small old man with a red nose and flashing eyes" (8: 127–28). The reader's expectations are frustrated by this description just as they are in Gogol's account of why Bashmachkin was christened Akakii Akakievich: after an elaborate description of the decision making, the anticlimactic information comes that he was simply named after his father. Frustrated expectations and a deliberate lack of logic were to be as characteristic of Gogol's art of writing as the personification of lifeless objects and the reification of animate beings—hallmarks of the technique of the grotesque. An example of this grotesque technique is Belkin's account of how he chased after a pea-colored coat in St. Petersburg (the coat of an author, but in the course of the description the coat replaces the man). One is reminded of the two fur coats that converse in Gogol's short play *Leaving the Theater After the First Performance of a New Comedy* (1842). Pushkin seems to have carried in his brain the beginnings of most of the major trends of nineteenth-century Russian literature.

All of these Gogolesque stylistic features have a common source: the author's feigned absentmindedness. Anticlimax comes when he "forgets" to satisfy the reader's expectations; lack of logic results when his mind jumps from one idea to another, oblivious to the absence of connection; the effect is grotesque when he fails to realize the difference between animate beings and inanimate objects, between the sad and the gay, the real and the chimerical. This "forgetful" style is the ideal medium of literary parody.

The parodist writes in the same vein as the author parodied, forgetting that his subject matter is inappropriate. Belkin has the air of a nation's profound historian—of "a judge, observer, and prophet of centuries" (8: 132), reminding one of Pimen—as if it had slipped his mind that he was in fact writing the history of only one village. In his pretentiousness he calls a bundle of old calendars "precious" documents (*dragotsennye*; 8: 133, the same word that the Publisher applied to the letter of Belkin's neighbor); he describes rabbit-hunting as "martial exercise," finds "profundity of thought and extraordinary magniloquence" in the sexton's notes, and believes in the "sensual delights" of drunkenness (8: 134, 135). His pretentious words perpetually tumble over descriptions of trivial objects: a legend about a demon-haunted swamp arose because a shepherdess was unable to account for her pregnancy; the proof of the peasant women's valor is that they dare defy the village elder, and the expressive gesture they use to repulse men bears witness to their chastity; a two-headed eagle—symbol of the Russian state—decorates the alehouse. The available variants show that Pushkin, working on the manuscript, consistently amplified its absurdity. In an earlier version, Belkin had chased after the author rather than his pea-colored coat, and the clerk had not yet acquired his grandiloquence (8: 701, 706).

Closest to Belkin in social background and manner of writing, and therefore the most obvious targets of Pushkin's parody, were the amateurs who wrote the histories of their localities.[21] But professional historians—even the renowned N. M. Karamzin, for whom Pushkin had great respect—were parodied just as much as the amateurs.[22] The first volume of Karamzin's *History of the Russian State*, just like *A History of the Village of Goriukhino*, lists all the source material used before beginning the narrative; and its first chapters, describing Russia's geographical features and original inhabitants, contain many details that must have influenced Belkin. For instance, Karamzin's phrase "This extensive part of Europe and Asia, today called Russia,"[23] finds its echo in Belkin's reference to the "recreational building (called pothouse in the vernacular)" (8: 138). The similarity of phrasing is striking in Russian, because both authors use the participle *imenuemyi* ("called," or "named")— a stylistically marked bookish form. Karamzin describes the ancient Slavs as having a swarthy complexion and blond hair; Belkin mentions that the inhabitants of Goriukhino have gray eyes and either blond or red hair. Like Karamzin, Belkin proceeds from geographical, ethnographical, horticultural, and commercial details to a description of mores, culture, language, poetry, and religious rites. Karamzin usually introduces new topics by phrases like "Having summarized the ancient Slavs' historical characteristics, let us now say a few words about their language,"[24] to which the following sentence of Belkin's corresponds: "Having thus acquainted my reader with the ethnographical and statistical state of affairs in Goriukhino and with the mores and customs of its inhabitants, I will now begin the narrative proper" (8: 137). Belkin's pedantic scrupulousness in describing trivial things may also be traced to passages in Karamzin, such as the following: "The heartfelt pleasure evoked by music makes people express this said pleasure by various movements of the body: *dancing*, the favorite pastime even of the most primitive peoples, has come into existence."[25]

These minor similarities in the presentation of material might not, by themselves, be convincing indications of parody if there were not other, more important correspondences. Karamzin writes: "The bagpipe, the horn, and the fife were also known to our ancestors, for they are, to this day, much favored by all the Slavic nations. Not only in peacetime, at home, but also during campaigns, in the face of the multitudinous enemy, did the Slavs make merry, sing, and forget danger. Procopius, describing a night attack on them by the Greek commander in 592, says that they had lulled their senses with songs and had taken no precautionary measures."[26] The inhabitants of Goriukhino, too, lulled their senses with songs (not to mention other intoxicants) on the fatal day before the steward's arrival, and they, too, made merry in the face of the dangerous enemy. "This people," writes Karamzin elsewhere, "like all other peoples at the beginning of their civic existence, did not know the advantages of well-regulated government, did not tolerate either lords or slaves on its land, and considered wild, unlimited freedom man's greatest treasure."[27] In Goriukhino, too, such wild, unlimited freedom had been the ideal during the "fabulous times" before the steward's arrival. "With the passage of time," continues Karamzin, "this wild simplicity of mores had to be replaced. The Slavs, plundering the Empire where luxury reigned, became acquainted with new pleasures and developed new demands, which curbed their independence but at the same time secured civic ties among them."[28] Belkin, too, connects the curbing of freedoms in Goriukhino with the landowners' luxurious ways. Finally, it is quite possible that Push-kin intended the forcible introduction of firm rule into Goriu-khino as an ironic contrast with Karamzin's famous lines: "The dawn of Russian history presents us with an astonishing event, probably unprecedented in the annals of nations: the Slavs voluntarily destroy their ancient popular form of government and request rulers from the Varangians, who had been their enemies."[29]

The researcher's attention is drawn to another source of par-ody by the fact that the copybook containing the manuscript of *Goriukhino* includes some notes of Pushkin's on the second volume of Polevoi's *History of the Russian Nation* (in six vol-umes, 1829–33).[30] The second volume itself was probably no target of parody, since it covered the period 1055–1157, which bore little resemblance to happenings in Goriukhino. But read-ing it, Pushkin must have been reminded of the first volume, which he had reviewed scathingly for the *Literary Gazette* ear-lier in 1830.[31]

In his review of the first volume Pushkin had ridiculed Pol-evoi's obsequious dedication to the renowned historian B. G. Niebuhr, objected to his slighting of Karamzin, and chided him for his clumsy style. "Mr. Polevoi," he wrote, "displays an all too obvious desire to be different from Karamzin; but just as the title of his book is no more than a frivolous parody of *A History of the Russian State*, so his recital of events rarely amounts to more than a parody of Karamzin's narrative" (11: 121). Pushkin, evidently, had parody very much on his mind in connection with Polevoi's book. Curiously, however, when he criticized Polevoi's style he singled out features that were also part and parcel of Karamzin's *History*. He objected, for in-stance, to Polevoi's introduction of new topics with the aid of phrases like "having outlined in a few strokes the main feature of this great panorama, we shall now turn to"—just the kind of phrase Polevoi must have learned from Karamzin. Also, mockingly imitating Polevoi's bookish style in his review, Push-kin used the participle *imenuemyi* (11: 122), as if it was a spe-cial attribute of Polevoi's clumsiness. All this seems to indi-cate that the difference, at least from a stylistic point of view, between the two histories was somewhat blurred in Pushkin's mind, and he might not have been aware that in parodying Polevoi he also parodied Karamzin. Indeed, in some instances it is difficult to say which historian Pushkin had in mind. Polevoi's book is structured in much the same way as Karamzin's: an introduction expounding his philosophy of history is followed by a listing of source materials; the narrative is preceded by geographical, ethnographical, and cultural characterizations; obvious things are given the same pedantic treatment. There are, however, a few passages in *Goriukhino* that seem to be aimed specifically at Polevoi. For instance, describing the inhabitants of the Scandinavian peninsula, Polevoi says: "The farther we go to the North, the less we see of natural life; people become weaker and weaker, both physically and mentally; and in that region where the ice and the snow cover the ground most of the year, we find man to be small of stature, with his mind dulled and his feelings blunted."[32] This seems to be echoed in one of Belkin's sentences: "To the north it borders on the territory of the villages of Deriukhovo and Perkukhovo, whose inhabitants are poor, thin, and small of stature" (8: 134). Belkin's officious indictment of all belief in a golden age originates from Polevoi's Preface,[33] and his comparison of Goriukhino peasants, in their river crossings, to the ancient Scandinavians seems also to hint at Polevoi, who devoted much attention to Scandinavian seafaring. Similes and metaphors in general, such as "my old nurse met me—much enduring Odysseus—with cries and sobs" and "a dark cloud hung over Goriukhino" (8: 129, 138), meaning impending danger, are closer in style to Polevoi than Karamzin. Polevoi was given to writing sentences like the following: "In the southern and central parts of the peninsula, the inhabitants are as powerful, robust, and rugged as the surrounding nature; they are wild as the forests that they inhabit; untamed in their passions as the streams carrying the thawed snow, swelling the lakes and rivers in the spring; untamed as the hot short Scandinavian summer in whose season the sun hardly ever sets."[34]

It may seem unlikely that Belkin, whose education was supposed to have stopped at age ten, would mention Odysseus, as well as "the well-known Virgil" (8: 137), but he could have taken these names from Kurganov's *Handbook* (which does in fact refer to both Homer and Virgil on p. 392 of Part One). It is extremely unlikely, however, that Belkin would be aware of Niebuhr's critical approach to history and would appeal to his authority twice (8: 127, 135). This feature, though absurd in the light of Belkin's personality, accords well with the many other absurdities in *Goriukhino*. If Belkin has heard of Niebuhr, Pushkin seems to be saying, then it is not surprising that Polevoi has too; even a man whose education stopped short at age ten can make references to the German historian—or, for that matter, dedicate his book to him.

In writing *Goriukhino*, Pushkin aligned himself with a long tradition of parody, both Russian and foreign. Ever since François Rabelais' satire on the University of Paris in *Pantagruel* (1532), pedantic pseudo-science had been a favorite target for satirists. Miguel de Cervantes mocked scholarly pretensions in his Prologue to *Don Quixote* (1614).[35] Laurence Sterne followed the same tradition in *The Life and Opinions of Tristram Shandy, Gentleman* (1760–67) when he introduced scholarly debates on two quibbling questions, namely, would the baptism of an unborn child in the womb, with the aid of a syringe, be acceptable to the Church; and was a nose as large as the one the traveler wore in Slawkenbergius's tale scientifically possible.

One way of ridiculing authorship—whether scholarly or fictional—was to show how little a manuscript meant to an ordinary, uninitiated person. Volume Seven, Chapter Thirty-nine, of *Tristram Shandy* contains a description of how Tristram, traveling in France, had lost and subsequently found his manuscripts. He kept them in his carriage, but forgot to remove them when he sold it; he had to return to the chaise-vamper's house in search of them; when he got there, he saw that the man's wife had used them as curl-papers; and in order to regain possession of them, he had to persuade her to untwist every one of them. This motif was to be used by several writers following Sterne. For example, the Sedulous Reader of Journals wrote in the *European Herald*: "Yesterday, as I was visiting a lady of my acquaintance, I noticed, under a jar of rouge on her dressing-table, a booklet, half of which had already been torn up for curl-papers."[36] The squire of Nenaradovo similarly writes that Belkin's housekeeper has used the first half of her late master's novel for sealing the windows in a wing of the house (8: 61); and in *Goriukhino* the village priest's children make a kite out of some of the sexton's "precious" chronicles (8: 134). Using this motif, which had already become somewhat hackneyed in the journals (and which Gogol was also to use on more than one occasion), Pushkin clearly wanted to indicate that he was adhering to a tradition. (It is ironic that some of Pushkin's own manuscripts were to be discovered in 1917, after a housekeeper had put them to domestic use.)[37]

There are other motifs in *Goriukhino* that can be traced to authors preceding Pushkin or contemporary to him. Like Belkin, Jedediah Cleishbotham is proud to have rubbed shoulders with the sophisticated in great cities. "I have seen states and men also," he writes, "for I have visited the famous cities of Edinburgh and Glasgow, the former twice, and the latter three times, in the course of my earthly pilgrimage. And, moreover, I had the honour to sit in the General Assembly (meaning, as an auditor, in the galleries thereof) and have heard as much goodly speaking on the law of patronage, as, with the fructification thereof in mine own understanding, hath made me be considered as an oracle upon that doctrine ever since my safe and happy return to Gandercleugh."[38] (Cleishbotham clearly was a worthy rival to Belkin in expressing himself "correctly, pleasantly, and fluently.") If Cleishbotham could not forget the General Assembly in Edinburgh, Belkin's memorable experience in St. Petersburg was that he almost made the acquaintance of an author.

This experience also can be connected with Irving's "The Stout Gentleman." The narrator of that story tells how he was laid up, sick, at an inn in Derby. Dying of boredom, he scrutinized everyone else staying at the inn. His attention was caught by a guest who was known to all only as the Stout Gentleman, and who did such remarkable things as impatiently ring for his breakfast, speak rudely to the maid, and pace up and down in his room. All the narrator's efforts to see the man were frustrated until the next morning, when at last he managed to get a glimpse of him: "The mysterious stranger then was on the point of setting off. This was the only chance I should ever have of knowing him. I sprang out of bed, scrambled to the window, snatched aside the curtains, and just caught a glimpse of the rear of a person getting in the coach-door. The skirts of a brown coat parted behind, and gave me a full view of a broad disk of a pair of drab breeches."³⁹ The Stout Gentleman, as contemporaries immediately recognized, was Walter Scott, who had made a great mystery of his person.

The author B., whom Belkin had the honor of meeting in St. Petersburg, was presumably Bulgarin. (His name, abbreviated as "Bulg.," is indicated in Pushkin's preliminary notes for *Goriukhino*; 8: 718. However, the year 1820, which Belkin mentions as the date of his visit to St. Petersburg, was just a little after Bulgarin's first arrival in Russia, when he was not yet known as an author. This is just another of *Goriukhino*'s absurdities.) Bulgarin, as Belkin meets him in the confectioner's shop, behaves as remarkably as the Stout Gentleman: he eats, reads a paper, scolds the waiter, and leaves. Belkin sets out after him with the same intense curiosity that characterized Irving's narrator; his efforts to meet the man are just as frustrated; the same atmosphere of pseudo-adventure pervades both episodes; and people are replaced by their clothes in both. Belkin's admiration for Bulgarin is further proof that he belongs with the denizens of a Russian Grub Street.

Belkin's decision to take up writing from nothing better to do also has its parallel in a work by Irving. In the Preface to *Tales of a Traveller* (1824) the narrator (similarly to the narrator of "The Stout Gentleman") tells how he was once obliged to linger in an inn because of sickness and, since there were no books to be had, was terribly bored: " 'Well then,' said I at length in despair, 'if I cannot read a book, I will write one.' Never was there a more lucky idea; it at once gave me occupation and amusement."⁴⁰ But the most striking parallel, not only in minor details but in general tone and design, is between Irving's *A History of New York* (1809) and *Goriukhino*.⁴¹ *A History of New York* too was written under a pseudonym (Diedrich Knickerbocker); it too was at least begun as parody (on S. L. Mitchill's *The Picture of New York*, 1807); and it too proceeds from general descriptive material to a narration of events.

Moreover, its historical narrative is divided into chapters according to the "reigns" of the various governors (the "Golden Reign of Wouter van Twiller," in particular, corresponding to the "Fabulous Times" under the village elder Trifon); and it is studded with pretentious pedantry, such as the explanation of the name Van Zandt, "that is to say, from the sand,"[42] which might have inspired Belkin's pompous "my grandfather, Ivan Andreevich Belkin, and . . . my grandmother, that is, his wife, Evpraksiia Alekseevna" (8: 134).

Once Pushkin had cast away his detached impersonal narrator and donned the clownish mask of Belkin, he had no qualms about either parodying or imitating any kind of writer he could lay his hands on. The responsibility was not his; it was Belkin's. It is for this reason that so many sources for Belkin's writings can be identified.[43]

Hilarious as *Goriukhino* may be, its emotional range is by no means limited to lighthearted parody. Here, as in one or two other writings that we shall be discussing, Pushkin succeeded in transcending parody, creating a work whose emotional impact is as ambivalent as his own attitude to the Russian feudal serf.

Up to 1830, Pushkin had been a member of a landowning family but had not himself owned any land or serfs. At Mikhailovskoe he had simply been the proprietress's son, not responsible for what was happening on the estate. But in 1830, after his engagement to Natalia Goncharova, his father gave him Kistenevo, which was part of the Pushkins' Boldino estate in the vicinity of Nizhnii Novgorod. Pushkin went there early in the fall of 1830, in order to have Kistenevo, with its two hundred serfs, officially transferred to his name. Belkin's description of his dealings with local officialdom is obviously autobiographical: "Some three weeks passed in toil and trouble: I had to fuss with assessors, marshals of the nobility, and all manner of provincial civil servants. At last I received my inheritance and was installed as proprietor of my ancestral estate" (8: 129).

Meanwhile, a cholera epidemic spread through the country, and the quarantines imposed prevented Pushkin from returning to his fiancée in Moscow. He stayed in Boldino until the beginning of December, working on *The Tales of Belkin, A*

History of the Village of Goriukhino, Chapter Eight of *Eugene Onegin,* the so-called Little Tragedies, and a number of other famous works of this remarkably fertile period. He desperately needed money in order to comply with his future mother-in-law's preposterous demand that he provide Natalia's trousseau. Sympathetic as he may have felt toward his newly acquired serfs, he mortgaged them all for 40,000 rubles. For the first time in his life he was not a carefree man-about-town, or an exile driven from place to place by an irate Tsar, or exclusively a professional writer living on royalties; he was now a feudal lord whose interest it was to squeeze as much out of his peasants as he could. According to an anecdote, he preached to the peasants in the Boldino church that God had sent the cholera on them because they had not been paying their quitrent.[44] (One is reminded of Belkin, who sat chewing his pen over his notebook, attempting to compose a sermon to his villagers, 8: 132; and of Pushkin's own letter of September 29, 1830, to Pletnev: "I wanted to send you a copy of my sermon to the local peasants; you would have died of laughter, but you don't deserve a gift like that," 14: 113.) The sermon might have been a mere joke, but it is certain that Pushkin held some of the views, or at least impulses, of the landowner, and these were reflected in his writings.

Goriukhino was modeled after Boldino, which had yielded very little but had been left alone by its owners until 1825, when Pushkin's father appointed a new steward, Mikhailo Ivanovich Kalashnikov. This man, himself a serf at Mikhailovskoe, performed his new duties at Boldino zealously, extracting over 13,000 rubles from the peasants in 1826 alone. Like Goriukhino, the village of Boldino became destitute within three years. In 1829 it yielded only 1,639 rubles. Part of the problem was that Kalashnikov, while driving the villagers to utter penury, stole as much as he could for himself. When Pushkin took over part of the estate, the peasants lodged a complaint against their steward (14: 114), and Pushkin would have "thrown that rogue of an elder into utter confusion by his investigation and stern questioning" but for a special circumstance. Kalashnikov's daughter Olga, while still living in Mikhailovskoe, had become pregnant by Pushkin. First he sent her to Moscow, asking Viazemskii to take care of her (13: 274), but eventually she joined her father in Boldino.[45] She must have been there during Pushkin's stay, because he formally released her from serfdom on October 4, 1830.[46] Pushkin's dramatic poem *The Water-Nymph* (begun in 1829), which concerns the seduction and abandonment of a miller's daughter by a gentleman, has been interpreted as reflecting Pushkin's guilty conscience about Olga.[47] Presumably, then, Pushkin felt obliged to leave her father alone, but he resented his unscrupulousness and, it seems, he took his revenge on him by depicting him as the steward in *Goriukhino*.[48]

All this shows how complicated Pushkin's feelings were toward his peasants. On the one hand, Belkin describes the peasants of Goriukhino as prone to plunge into the "sensual delights of drunkenness" (8: 135) on all occasions, even church holy days and funerals; he shows that the village commune, if left to itself, will send only "sly excuses and humble complaints" (8: 138) to the landowner instead of payments; and cites a poem about the ruses of a village elder. Belkin, of course, is not Pushkin, but it should still be noted that the landowners and their stewards are not the only people satirized in *Goriukhino*.

On the other hand, many passages show warm sympathy for the oppressed Russian serf. In the manuscript the name of the village is spelled Gorokhino in five places (8: 698, 711, 712), which implies that in the original "fabulous times," when it was a "large prosperous village," where all the inhabitants were wealthy and "even shepherds wore boots while tending their herds" (8: 137), this community belonged to the kingdom of a fairy-tale Tsar Gorokh (King Pea). The change to Goriukhino, derived from *gore* (sorrow), amounts to a reproach to the masters who had destroyed the opulence of the past.[49] Their refusal to give up their luxurious living is presented as the chief cause of their serfs' poverty. The word citizens (*grazhdane*; 8: 139), applied to the villagers by the high-sounding Belkin so inappropriately, is a painful reminder that these people, too, might have possessed civil liberties under different circumstances. Belkin's mirthful description of how peasant husbands, who at the age of fourteen marry women of twenty and are beaten for four or five years by their wives, then redress the balance by beating their wives for the rest of their lives, reminds the reader of Tatiana's old nurse whose marriage was anything but mirthful. When the steward promises the peasants that he will "beat the nonsense out of your heads" (8: 139), one can take his word for it, since even Belkin—even the meek, good, harmless Belkin—thrashed the back of the coachman on his way home.

The closer we get to the end of the fragment, the more lyrical force attaches to the description of the peasants: the melancholy village, with its deserted marketplace, seems to be falling out of the framework of satire; the document about the "accursed steward's" tyrannical actions (8: 140) is no longer funny; and the steward's political theory—about keeping the peasants poor in order to be able to control them—explains the workings of an autocratic regime in a way that would be worthy of a better historian than Belkin. In the original version of the manuscript, Trishka the house servant was beaten three times for drunkenness (8: 705); in the final version only Senka is thrashed for that offense, but Trishka is beaten once for rudeness and once "on account of the weather" (8: 133)—an indication that Pushkin wanted to heighten the impression of senseless cruelty. Polevoi's history of the *nation* contrasted with Karamzin's history of the *state*: Pushkin's *Goriukhino* is a lesson in the history of the *people*.

As the narrative drew closer to the peasant revolt, it became more and more difficult for Pushkin to maintain the humorous atmosphere, and it must have been his sense of style—in addition to a fear of censorship—that made him stop where he did.[50] Even in the parts he completed, the ludicrous and the pathetic are pulling so powerfully in different directions that at times the effect is grotesque—a case in point is the scene with the sneezing corpse over which a drunken revelry is held for three days (8: 136). A degree of ambivalence in the emotions expressed can be a sign, not necessarily of a lack of skill on the part of the author, but often of the complexity of the experience that is being transformed into art. Since it successfully unites the disparate trends that comprise it, *A History of the Village of Goriukhino* is a lasting achievement of Pushkin the prose writer.

3

The five stories published as *The Tales of Belkin* strike one, first of all, as uneven in quality. The outstanding achievement of the cycle, "The Stationmaster," is in immediate juxtaposition with "The Squire's Daughter"—a story described by Pushkin's younger contemporary, V. G. Belinskii, as "pitiful," "lacking in truth," and "close to a vaudeville."[51] Although a naïve mode of narration serves as a common denominator for all five tales, the discrepancies in achievement are nevertheless so great that one wonders what made Pushkin enclose all five in one volume, arranging them in the particular order in which they appear.

Pushkin put the date of completion on the manuscript of each tale as he produced them in rapid-fire fashion. The first one to be finished, "The Undertaker," bears the date of September 9, 1830; "The Stationmaster" was completed on September 14, "The Squire's Daughter" on September 20, "The Shot" on October 14, and "The Blizzard" on October 20 (8: 1052). This was, evidently, the order in which he intended to publish them—at least this is the sequence in which he listed the projected volume's table of contents as late as the summer of 1831—but just before sending the manuscript to the printers, he moved the last two tales to the front of the volume.[52] The Publisher's footnote about the narrators lists the tales in still another sequence: "The Stationmaster," "The Shot," "The Undertaker," "The Blizzard," and "The Squire's Daughter" (8: 61). Given the differences in the quality of the tales, it will be best, for our purposes, to ignore their sequence and examine them from the point of view of the one feature that unites them: the naïve mode of narration. We shall begin with its simplest application and proceed to the tales in which its function becomes highly complex.

The two tales that amount to scarcely more than playful anecdotes—"The Blizzard" and "The Squire's Daughter"—are both supposed to have been narrated by the maiden K.I.T. Her primary role is to provide plots that are preposterous to begin with, and to make them even less believable through her presentation. Not only does she fail to notice, in the innocence of her heart, that they are incredible in their basic conception, but she adds a number of details that reveal holes in the plot to the point of absurdity.

The heroine of "The Blizzard," Maria Gavrilovna, is the daughter of a wealthy landowner, and since her parents object to her love for an impecunious young officer, Vladimir, she decides to elope with him. On the appointed night his coachman takes her from her home in Nenaradovo to the church of a neighboring village, Zhadrino, but Vladimir himself fails to arrive there because, riding in a separate sleigh, he loses his way in a blizzard. It is not described what happens to the disappointed bride in the church; all we are told is that the next morning she was back home as if nothing had happened. She falls ill, however, and in a delirious state talks about Vladimir. Her parents, thinking that love is the cause of her illness, decide to let the young man marry her; but he responds in an incomprehensible way, declaring that he will never set foot in their house again. The time is 1812: Vladimir returns to his regiment to fight against Napoleon and dies in battle. In the meanwhile Maria loses her father and settles with her mother on a different estate. She is unreceptive to the advances of all young men, until a war hero, Burmin, arrives in the neighborhood. They are mutually disposed to each other, but he fails to declare his feelings, until at last he confesses that one dark night before the war, riding through a village, he was mistaken for the bridegroom at a church and, as a joke, let the priest marry him to a total stranger, who did not realize the mistake until after the ceremony was over. "So it was you!" exclaims Maria (8: 86).

If Vladimir had been held up by some circumstance—not finding a priest, for instance—and had been forced to send his coachman for Maria, the situation might have seemed credible; but in fact Vladimir goes home in good time, and there is no reason why he should not see to the elopement himself. If Burmin had been riding in a one-horse sleigh like the one in which Vladimir was known to have set out, Vladimir's associates might have made a believable mistake in stopping him and urging him to hurry in; but we are plainly told that Burmin was riding in a larger sleigh, driven by a coachman whose presence alone should have been enough to show that this was not the bridegroom arriving. If the narrator had been content to state that the church was too dimly lit for people to be able to recognize each other, this would have been hard enough to believe; but she makes Burmin add that he could see he was marrying a pretty girl. And finally, if Burmin had at least come back to the same region where he had been married (even if the exact location was not known to him), there might have been some chance of his meeting his unknown wife; but in fact Maria and her mother have moved away to live on another estate, and it is entirely by accident that he comes across them.

The situations in "The Squire's Daughter" are equally contrived. Two landowners living in the same region, Berestov and Muromskii, are enemies, and therefore Muromskii's daughter, Liza, cannot meet Berestov's son, Aleksei, when he comes home after completing his education. She learns through her maid that, though he puts on airs with young ladies, he is free and easy with village wenches, which persuades her to dress up as a peasant, assume the name Akulina, and walk out to the wood where he is known to go hunting. The pair meet, converse, agree to meet again, and eventually fall in love. In the meanwhile the two fathers make up their quarrel, and Muromskii invites both Berestov and his son to dinner. In order to disguise herself, Liza heavily powders her face, and indeed, Aleksei fails to recognize his Akulina—a twist that, to say the least, requires a high degree of credulity from the reader. The two fathers decide that it would be mutually advantageous to unite their children, and Berestov tries to force his son into an unwanted marriage. At last Aleksei decides to marry Akulina even at the risk of being disinherited; he writes a letter to her about it; and the next day sets out to explain to Muromskii that he does not wish to marry his daughter. Muromskii is out, but Liza is in, this time undisguised: Aleksei surprises her in her living room just as she is reading his letter.

Many of the ludicrous details—innocently presented by Miss K.I.T., although deliberately planted by Pushkin's invisible hand—indicate either literary parody or imitation. The plot of "The Blizzard," for example, could have been drawn from any number of fictional works popular at the time. In *St. Ronan's*

Well (1823) by Scott, Valentine, hoping to gain a large fortune through Clara Mowbray, treacherously replaces his half-brother Francis by her side at the altar and is not recognized by her until after the ceremony. In "The Spectre Bridegroom" (1819) by Irving, Hermann von Starkenfaust has no chance to explain that he is not the bridegroom whose arrival the Katzenellenbogens have been expecting, and he ends up (after some complications) marrying the bride, to her and his mutual satisfaction.[53] In Letter 1 of A. A. Bestuzhev-Marlinskii's "A Journey to Revel" (1821), Evgenii Kron and Baron Erens, who had once exchanged swords swearing eternal friendship, meet later, quarrel, and do not recognize each other until they bare their swords at a duel.[54] In Karamzin's "Natalia the Boyar's Daughter" (1792), the hero and heroine, eloping, express the hope that her father will forgive them when they eventually throw themselves at his feet—a hope reiterated by Pushkin's Maria and Vladimir. (Only, ironically, in Pushkin's story it is Burmin who throws himself at Maria's feet at the end.)[55]

The epigraph to "The Blizzard," in turn, seems to suggest that the story is a prose version of V. A. Zhukovskii's *Svetlana* (1812), for in that poem, too, there is a bride who rides to a nightmarish wedding in a blizzard, though in this case everything works out happily in the end.[56] Miss K.I.T. herself refers to *Julie, ou La Nouvelle Héloïse*, implying that her characters might have been fashioned after those of Julie and Saint-Preux. Maria Gavrilovna's illness after her would-be elopement and her murmuring her lover's name in an unconscious state were inspired by Cordelia's story in Charles Nodier's *Le Peintre de Saltzbourg*.[57] Furthermore, the story's device of *quid pro quo* has been traced through the ages, all the way back to the ancient Greeks,[58] and it has been shown that Miss K.I.T. had at least six alternative denouements to choose from, as she toyed with the conventional plots of the genre.[59]

No less deeply rooted in tradition is "The Squire's Daughter." The following passage from *St. Ronan's Well*, for instance, may have supplied the basic idea:

Francis, happy dog, became the companion of the damsels . . . through the following incident. Miss Mowbray had dressed herself and her companion like country wenches with a view to surprise the family of one of their better sort of farmers. They had accomplished their purpose greatly to their satisfaction, and were hying home after sunset, when they were encountered by a country fellow ... who, being equipped with a glass or two of whisky, saw not the nobility of blood through her disguise, and accosted the daughter of a hundred sires as he would have done a ewe-milker. Miss Mowbray remonstrated—her companion screamed—up came cousin Francis with a fowling-piece on his shoulder, and soon put the sylvan to flight.[60]

Another Scott novel, The Bride of Lammermoor, and Shakespeare's Romeo and Juliet may have served as sources for the theme of family feuds. The remark that Liza's maid Nastia was "a personage of considerably greater importance in the village of Priluchino than the confidante in a French tragedy" (8: 111) hints that the story may have been derived from French dramatic literature, and when Aleksei claims to be his own valet, we are reminded of Le Jeu de l'amour et du hasard (1730) by P. C. de Chamblain de Marivaux, in which Dorante and his valet, as well as Silvia and her maid, change clothes with deception in mind.[61] (The twist on the theme in "The Squire's Daughter" is that Aleksei does not succeed in deceiving Liza, and the incognito remains unilateral.) Belinskii had good reason to compare the story to a vaudeville, for it relies almost exclusively on makeup (Liza's powdered face), on funny situations (the proud rider Muromskii falling off his horse, which elicits his neighbor's help and leads to their reconciliation), and, above all, on clothes (Liza/Akulina's blue nankeen sarafan with brass buttons is fit for a folksy operetta).

Other literary allusions planted in the story lead us to Karamzin: Liza (as Akulina) reads "Natalia the Boyar's Daughter," which hints that a wedding without parental approval might take place; and the name Liza itself ironically alludes to the (unrealized) possibility of a carnal affair between a nobleman and a peasant girl. Richardson's Pamela (1741) is mentioned with sarcasm as a work cherished by Liza's prim and proper governess, Miss Jackson, yet its subject—a girl of humble origin defending her virtue to profit—is clearly relevant to Liza's own designs. The name of Aleksei's dog, Sbogar (Lara in the original manuscript; 8: 674) comes from Nodier's novel Jean Sbogar (1818); the line "But Russian grain won't grow after a foreign fashion" (8: 109) is taken from a satire by A. Shakhov-skoi;[62] and the name of Skotinin, casually mentioned, provides a link with the epigraph to the volume. In addition to the titles already mentioned, critics have proposed quite a few others that might have served as models for "The Squire's Daughter."[63] The less ambitious Pushkin's design, the more scope he seems to give to the comparativist.

"The Blizzard" and "The Squire's Daughter" reveal what a provincial maiden read in the Russia of the 1820's. Telling her stories to Belkin, the good Miss K.I.T. draws on all the literary conventions of her epoch: sometimes she simply imitates, neither improving on her model nor playing havoc with it; and sometimes—presumably involuntarily—she travesties the works that have inspired her. With her poor taste, she becomes just as much the target of Pushkin's satire as the models she draws on. Like Belkin, she is a literary adversary of Pushkin's, which becomes particularly clear when we consider how she treats the theme of *Onegin* in her two stories.

An acquaintance of Pushkin's, A. P. Novosiltseva, recorded a conversation she and some other young ladies had with him sometime after the publication of Chapter Six of *Onegin* (which contained the hero's duel with Lenskii):

My album lay before him; we were talking about *Eugene Onegin*. Pushkin silently drew something on a page. I asked him:
"Why did you kill Lenskii? Varia wept over him all day yesterday!" Varvara Petrovna at this time was sixteen years old and quite attractive.
"Well, Varvara Petrovna, how would you have concluded the duel?"
"I would have only wounded Lenskii's arm or shoulder; then Olga could have looked after him and dressed his wound, and they would have grown even fonder of each other."
"You know where he was killed? Right here." He held up his drawing and pointed at a spot, showing a clearing in a forest. He turned to me: "And how would you have finished the duel?"
"I would have wounded Onegin, so that Tatiana could have looked after him; he would have learned to value her and would have fallen in love with her."
"Oh, no. He is not worthy of Tatiana," he answered.[64]

As Pushkin was finishing Chapter Eight of *Onegin*, simultaneously with *The Tales of Belkin* in the fall of 1830, such conversations with impressionable ladies must have been on his mind, all the more so since Chapter Eight did not present a happy ending. Miss K.I.T. appears to be something of a reincarnation of his real-life interlocutresses; and her two stories show how she would have concluded *Onegin*.[65] The connection between *Onegin* and the tales narrated by Miss K.I.T. has been emphasized by several critics.[66] Maria Gavrilovna of "The Blizzard" is just as "slender and pale" as Tatiana; she too "had been brought up on French novels and was consequently in love" (8: 77); and she has a prophetic nightmare that parallels Tatiana's.[67] The two male characters are counterpoised somewhat similarly to Lenskii and Onegin: Vladimir, a hotheaded young man, lacking in circumspection, gets himself killed, and his beloved does not stay faithful to his memory any longer than Olga does to Lenskii's; and Burmin is reported to have been "a frightful rake" (8: 84) in his earlier days and quite a favorite with women, not unlike Onegin. The parallels, of course, are only superficial; but it is significant that Miss K.I.T. is determined to give her story a happy ending in the teeth of all reason and probability.

The squire's daughter does not have the outward appearance of Tatiana, but inwardly she belongs to the same stereotype:

Brought up in fresh air, in the shade of the apple trees in their orchards, they [provincial misses] acquire all their knowledge of the world and life from books. Solitude, freedom, and reading early develop in them feelings and passions that are unknown to our scatterbrained debutantes. For the provincial miss the jingling of a coach bell is an adventure; she considers a trip to the nearest town a milestone in history; and the visit of a guest leaves behind a lingering, sometimes everlasting memory. (8: 110)

One cannot help recalling how Tatiana "Loved novels at an early age / And found in them a substitute for everything else; / She fell in love with the deceits / Of both Richardson and Rousseau" (6: 44); how strong an impression one single visit by Onegin made on her; how she went afterwards "To wander in the silence of the woods / In company of a dangerous book" (6: 55); how genuine were the feelings nurtured in her solitude; and how long the memory of her love for Onegin stayed with her.

Aleksei, in turn, arrives in the country an interesting stranger, just like Onegin; he scorns the charms of the provincial misses; affects an air of boredom and satiety; seeks the kind of "youthful, fresh kiss of a dark-eyed fair maid" that Onegin enjoyed (6: 89); and, when scheduled to meet a squire's daughter for the first time, "ponders what role he should assume in [her] presence" (8: 119). Miss K.I.T., who might have been one of the neighbors, cannot tolerate such behavior. Realizing Aleksei's fondness for a "fresh kiss," she dresses her heroine as a country wench, but only to mislead Aleksei: as soon as he tries to embrace her, she answers with all the dignity of her station that "If you wish us to remain friends, be good enough not to forget yourself" (8: 114)—a phrase not exactly in the style of a country wench. Aleksei, by an act of Miss K.I.T.'s will, decides not to mind Liza's squeamishness, swallows the bait, and ends up marrying one of the provincial misses he was determined to ignore in the first place. A happy ending, as Miss K.I.T. saw it, had been secured.

Miss K.I.T.'s two tales represent, then, two possible variants of *Eugene Onegin*, tailored to suit the taste of a lady of sentimental disposition.[68] In *Onegin*, though the characters are complex and surrounded by an aura of poetry, the plot—two people failing to understand each other at the right time—is kept at the simple level of ordinary life. By contrast, the characters in "The Blizzard" and "The Squire's Daughter" are shallow and lacking in poetry, and the action goes through contrived convolutions in order to arrive at an artificially happy ending. In order to emphasize that the stories reflect Miss K.I.T.'s ideas, Pushkin makes her authorial presence felt at every step.

We have seen that in *The Blackamoor of Peter the Great*, which is longer than "The Blizzard" and "The Squire's Daughter" put together, the narrator steps before the reader only twice. By contrast, Miss K.I.T.'s narratives are liberally sprinkled with phrases like these: "But let us entrust the young lady to her lucky stars and to the skill of Tereshka the coachman, while we turn our attention to our young paramour"; "What news awaited him!"; "Moral maxims are surprisingly useful on occasions when we can invent little else to justify our actions"; "Can one determine with precision what is on the mind of a seventeen-year-old miss when she is by herself in a grove before six o'clock on a spring morning?"; "I am aware that the majority of my readers would not share my enjoyment of such details"; "My readers will no doubt excuse me from the unnecessary chore of relating the denouement" (8: 79, 81, 82, 114, 117, 124). The most conspicuous intrusion of the narrator occurs in "The Blizzard" at the point where the reader is denied knowledge of what horrendous news awaited Vladimir at the church. Instead of communicating the news (an all-too-obvious device to create suspense), the author says:

> But let us return to the good proprietors of Nenaradovo and take a look: what might be happening at their house?
> Well, nothing. (8: 81)

The phrase "Well, nothing" (A nichego), set off to form a paragraph by itself, approaches in its jocularity what Sterne called Shandeism.

Such devices emphasize the presence of a narrator, though not necessarily Miss K.I.T.: for all we know, they may have been inserted by Belkin, who wrote the narrative down. There are, however, attitudes and phrases that unmistakably reveal the personality of a lady author as perceived by Pushkin for satirical purposes. Of all things that could have made the end of the Napoleonic War memorable, she remembers that "the bands were playing songs captured in the war: 'Vive Henri Quatre,' Tyrolean waltzes, and arias from *Joconde*," and that "arriving in one of these villages was a veritable triumph for an officer; ... a lover in a frock coat fared poorly in his vicinity" (8: 83). In characterizing her male heroes, she cannot hide the inclinations of her own heart: though she has little sympathy for Vladimir, she praises Burmin for having "the kind of mind women like," and she is willing, along with Maria, to forgive him for "mischiefs that revealed a daring and ardent nature" (8: 84). Analyzing her biased comments, one critic shrewdly observes that she seems to have been attracted to Burmin herself.[69] As for Aleksei of "A Squire's Daughter," Miss K.I.T. does not fail to notice his slim waist; she praises him for being "capable of enjoying innocent pleasures" (8: 116); and she finds it natural that, in the innocence of his male heart, he does not even notice how heavily Liza is made up. Her two stories are both centered on love and women.

Occasionally—though only occasionally—linguistic elements also point to her authorial presence. Her vocabulary is derived partly from Karamzinite sentimentalism, partly from a romanticism à la Marlinskii. Her Vladimir is "aflame with . . . passion"; his witnesses "swore they would sacrifice their lives for him"; when he realizes how far he still is from Zhadrino in the middle of the night he feels "like a man condemned to die"; and in severing his ties with Maria's family, he asks them "to forget the unhappy man for whom death was the only remaining hope" (8: 77, 79, 80, 82). Maria is driven by "the irresistible force of her passion"; "two flaming hearts" are engraved on her seal; as she is eloping, the wind seems to be trying to stop "the young malefactress"; and she is driven to "the brink of the grave" (8: 78, 79, 81). As for Burmin, he vows that the memory of Maria will remain "both the torment and the joy of [his] life"; he feels obliged to reveal his "horrible secret" and begs her not to deprive him, "the most unhappy creature," of his "last solace" (8: 85). A good match for Maria's seal, a "black ring engraved with a death's head" turns up on Aleksei's hand in "The Squire's Daughter" (8: 111).

A sentimental style is mirrored less frequently in the syntax, but there is at least one passage in each of the two stories that betrays Miss K.I.T.'s presence even syntactically. Describing the end of the war in "The Blizzard," she bursts into a series of exclamations characterized by anaphora and an emotional gradation that culminates in a contemplation of the feelings of the Tsar: "Unforgettable time! A time of glory and ecstacy! How mightily beat the Russian heart at the word Fatherland! How sweet were the tears of reunion! How unanimously did we ally our feeling of national pride with our love for the Emperor! And what a moment it was for him!" (8: 83). Depicting Liza's early morning walk in "The Squire's Daughter," on the other hand, Miss K.I.T. uses a long, loose compound sentence, a large number of epithets, a simile, and a metaphor, all of which are unusual for a Belkin tale: "The dawn was radiant in the east, and the golden ranks of clouds seemed to be awaiting the sun like courtiers their sovereign; the clear sky, the morning freshness, the dew, the light breeze, and the singing of the birds filled Liza's heart with childlike joy; afraid of meeting somebody she knew, she seemed not to walk, but to fly" (8: 113–14).[70] Finally, another syntactic feature is Miss K.I.T.'s occasional use of gallicisms: bearing in mind Pushkin's comment in *Onegin* on the Russian women's poor knowledge of their native tongue, we could ascribe these also to a "feminine" style.[71]

All these "feminine" elements notwithstanding, however, the presence of Miss K.I.T. in the two stories is neither ubiquitous nor consistent. One typical departure from the norm is upward: her quotation of a line from Petrarch in the Italian, her use of a Latin phrase, and her reference to Jean Paul all seem to be incompatible with the level of education we ascribe to her on the basis of the general texture of the tales.[72] The absurdity is as striking as it is when Belkin discusses Niebuhr in *Goriukhino*; and we have to conclude that at times it is not the narrator, but Pushkin himself, speaking.[73]

It has been suggested that Miss K.I.T. must have been getting on in years at the time she narrated her stories because of a certain condescension in her attitude toward her young heroines.[74] In "The Blizzard," when she tells us that Maria had been brought up on French novels and was "consequently in love" (8: 77), she perhaps means to indicate that she knows only too well the follies of youth, which are behind her. Her statements that "it goes without saying that the young man was aflame with an equal passion," that the young lovers' decision to elope was "quite natural," and that "it is easy to guess" (8: 77) that this felicitous idea had occurred to Vladimir first are all in the same vein. But it seems that her age by itself is not sufficient to explain her attitudes. If she is laughing at the banal stories she is relating, why did she choose them in the first place? If she is looking at the events from such a height of sophistication, why will she not tell us more sophisticated tales? Is she, or is she not, a sentimental maiden herself, and if she is, why does she poke fun at Maria's "romantic imagination" (8: 77) and why does she mention, tongue in cheek, that Maria wrote a farewell letter to "a sentimental young lady" (8: 78)?

As a result of these remarks, Miss K.I.T.'s identity becomes confused. It does not help to clarify the matter, either, when she praises the charm of the provincial miss and compares her favorably to "our scatterbrained debutantes." In the original manuscript, this latter phrase read "our high society dolls" (8: 666), which makes it even clearer that she had in mind the belles of Moscow and St. Petersburg. But who is she herself? Is she a society lady, and if so, where did she meet the simple-hearted Belkin, who had only paid one fleeting visit to St. Petersburg in his life?

It is revealing from this point of view that "The Squire's Daughter" was not the first prose tale by Pushkin to contain a discussion of the merits of provincial misses. Liza of *A Novel in Letters* had portrayed the daughter of a neighbor in the country as "a slender melancholy girl of seventeen, brought up on novels in fresh air [who was] in the garden or in the fields with book in hand all day" (8: 47). As we have seen, the idea did not even originate with this Liza: an even earlier fragment, "In the Beginning of 1812," had at least hinted at it already. In that fragment, the narrative voice and the narrator might have been in harmony (as far as one could tell from half a page), since a young officer was describing a provincial town new to him. The same theme, recurring in *A Novel in Letters*, did not help much in characterizing Liza, but at least there was no glaring inconsistency: after all, Liza had just arrived from St. Petersburg and had an outsider's view of provincial misses. The "maiden K.I.T.," however, seems to be a provincial miss herself. Giving herself airs, she becomes absurd. Here, as in *Goriukhino*, Pushkin appears to be deliberately subverting consistency in order to heighten the comedy.

The other type of deviation from Miss K.I.T.'s style points downward, to social and educational levels lower than what we can assume from the stories to be her own. The technique is very similar to what we have seen in *Goriukhino*: literary pretensions tumble over crude reality; elevated style becomes nonsensical when placed side by side with the racy vernacular of the people of the province. Vladimir may feel like "a man condemned to die," but his personal plight appears insignificant when compared to the plight of the old peasant who is astonished at Vladimir's even thinking that he might have some horses for hire. Maria Gavrilovna may have had horrifying adventures during the night of her elopement, but the valid perspective on life is from the living room in her house, where her parents take their morning tea, "Gavrila Gavrilovich [in his] nightcap and a flannel jacket, Praskovia Petrovna . . . in her quilted dressing gown." Her mother attributes all Maria's problems to "the fumes from the stove" (8: 81). It is noteworthy, in this connection, that Pushkin's contemporaries were struck, above all, by the abundance of little details about everyday life in Belkin's tales: at least this was the aspect O. I. Senkovskii focused on when he parodied the tales in the 1830's.[75]

Details of quotidian life may represent lapses in Miss K.I.T.'s own style—she may simply not be able to live up to her own pretensions—but they are more likely to belong to Belkin the editor. In at least one passage in "The Squire's Daughter," where he says "Were I to follow my own inclinations, I would describe in full detail the young people's meetings" (8: 117), Belkin unmistakably reveals his hand, for the phrase he uses (esli by slushalsia ia) indicates masculine gender.[76] Although there is no sure way to tell Belkin from K.I.T., one can suppose that the plots belong to her, whereas the style—apart from the markedly sentimental phrases and passages—is Belkin's.

If Miss K.I.T. is able to quote Jean-Paul in French translation and Petrarch in the Italian original, she is not likely to be the person who identifies Miss Jackson as Liza's "madam" (meaning her governess; 8: 111). This is more likely to be Belkin's language. He may also be the person who considers Muromskii "not altogether stupid because he was the first landowner in the guberniia to think of taking out a mortgage on his estate" (8: 109). And, above all, he may have been the one who introduces a quotation from A. S. Griboedov's comedy Woe from Wit (1824) into the text of "The Blizzard," which is one of the funniest details. The quotation—"And tossed their caps into the air" (8: 83)—follows immediately after the exclamations about the end of the war that we have already discussed; and it is supposed to accentuate the enthusiasm of Russia's patriotic women as they welcomed their heroes home. The very image—girls, like hussars, shouting "hurray" and tossing their caps high—is not in keeping with the elevated style of the passage. But the irony of the quotation can be fully appreciated only if one considers its context in Griboedov's play (which

Belkin could only have heard cited or read in manuscript, since Act 2, Scene 5, from which he took the quotation, was not published until 1834). In the comedy the words belong to Chatskii who, far from extolling the military, is berating Russian women for their stupidity in falling for uniforms. Belkin—if it is indeed he who inserted the quotation—appears to be as unaware of its implications as the Publisher was oblivious to those of the epigraph he had chosen for the volume.

The Belkin of *Goriukhino*, as we have seen, said he had had rather a poor style until he managed to perfect it by writing down a number of tales. Consequently, his *Tales* amount to an exercise book mirroring his trials and tribulations as a stylist. No wonder, then, that he falls down on choosing an appropriate citation for a pathetic passage. Nor can he be trusted to match a tragic moment with appropriate syntax. By the time he wrote *Goriukhino*, he had developed a studied enough style; but in his *Tales* the mode that came to him most naturally was sweet simplicity—not always appropriate to the topic. For example, the first half of "The Blizzard" focuses on Vladimir's courtship of Maria—Vladimir appearing to be the hero of the tale—but after the elopement founders, the narrator's further references to Vladimir become exceedingly terse, as if he had receded from the center of interest. All we read about him is this: that Maria fainted "a few months later, when she saw his name on the list of those who had distinguished themselves and had been severely wounded at Borodino, and it was feared that her fever might return, but, thank God, her fainting had no consequences" (8: 82). There is nothing else to be said about Vladimir, except, two paragraphs farther down, when we learn that he was "not among the living." A more conscientious stylist— perhaps even Miss K.I.T., despite her preference for Burmin— would have introduced a pathetic tirade about the plight of the patriot fallen on the battlefield in defense of his fatherland; but Belkin is just not in possession of eloquence yet. As a result, not only does the style of the passage appear crippled, but the reader comes away with a sense of moral dissatisfaction: the memory of the patriot only "seemed to be sacred" (8: 83) to Masha. In Belkin's narration, a full development of sentimental details is often replaced by key phrases that only telegraphically indicate what kind of stereotyped situations we are dealing with.[77]

It may well be that the brevity and simplicity some critics have assigned to Pushkin's prose style in general should more appropriately be assigned to Belkin (or to similar imaginary authors). Most of the stylistic characteristics A. Z. Lezhnev enumerates—a sparing use of epithets, similes, and metaphors; a great reliance on verbs; brevity; an exact material frame of reference; laconic concluding scenes; and an emphasis on actions rather than feelings[78]—apply to Belkin, without necessarily being applicable to all other prose works by Pushkin. It has been shown that 70 percent of the sentences in "The Blizzard" are simple sentences (if we include simple segments of compound sentences set off by semicolons, without conjunctions). This compares with 41 percent in Karamzin's "Poor Liza," just over 38 percent in Bestuzhev-Marlinskii's "Raids" (1831), and 37 percent in M. Iu. Lermontov's "Princess Mary" (1840). Out of a total of 238 sentences, only in 20 to 25 is the basic subject-predicate-object order of words reversed to any marked degree. There is only one simile in the whole story. Epithets usually stand alone, rarely come in pairs, never in clusters of three or more. Close to a third of the vocabulary consists of verbs; the share of adjectives is less than 10 percent.[79]

Belkin's terse tales have often been contrasted with the works of the most flowery stylist of the time, Bestuzhev-Marlinskii. The contrast is indeed striking if we compare, for example, how Bestuzhev introduces his heroine, Minna, in "A Journey to Revel" (1821) with Belkin's introduction of his Liza in "A Squire's Daughter." Bestuzhev's passage reads:

Nature, as her father was fond of saying, had filled the beautiful frame with appropriate content. Some quality—"what exactly, I don't know, but endearing"—animated her features, lent majesty to her gait, ease to her manners, and sweetness to her speech. From her blue eyes, from behind her long eyelashes, glances darted... But what glances? They would have set ice on fire. In short, Minna was one of those beauties endowed with both striking appearance and captivating charm.[80]

Belkin, by contrast, tells us that Liza "was seventeen years old. Dark eyes animated her dusky, very attractive face" (8: 111).

Alongside Bestuzhev, Belkin seems preferable, especially to the modern reader. And there can be no doubt that an element of Pushkin's own taste—a tendency to bring fiction close to expository prose with no embellishments—contributed to Belkin's style. Yet on the whole Belkin is not Pushkin: his simplicity springs from his unambitious subject matter; he writes tersely primarily because he does not have much to say and because he does not know how to say it more colorfully.

Let us consider, for example, the following paragraph describing the blizzard:

At last Vladimir realized he was going in the wrong direction. He stopped, began to think, to recollect, to consider, and became convinced that he should have turned to the right. He started off to the right. His horse could hardly move. He had already been on the road for over an hour. Zhadrino should not have been very far. Yet though he rode on and on, there was no end to the open country. Snowdrifts and gullies at every step; the sleigh kept turning over; he had to lift it upright every minute. The time was passing; he began to worry in earnest. (8: 80)

What a difference, when compared with Pushkin's lyric "Devils," written on the same subject a few weeks before! The little momentum gained in the second sentence of the paragraph is lost in the following ones, which are chopped up, jerky, lacking rhythm. The style, like the content, seems to be a joke: Miss K.I.T. tells romantic tales for which the appropriate garb would be an ornate style, but Belkin cannot achieve it, try as he might.

4

In "The Undertaker," as in the other two stories so far discussed, the subject is in full conformity with the conventions of the 1820's. The central character, Adrian Prokhorov, is invited with his daughters to his neighbor Schulz's silver wedding anniversary. The assembled guests, mostly artisans of one kind or another, propose toasts to the health of their customers in the course of the party, and the police guard Iurko, also present, suggests that Adrian should drink to the health of his "clients" too. Adrian goes home drunk and offended, and issues an invitation to all the corpses he has ever buried. They all come, ready to enjoy themselves, but when Adrian pushes away a skeleton that is trying to embrace him, the others advance on him threateningly—and he wakes up.

At least two allusions are made in the text to the story's literary sources. In the second paragraph we read: "The enlightened reader knows that both Shakespeare and Walter Scott presented their gravediggers as merry and jocular people, in order to strike our imagination all the more by this contrast" (8: 89). Apart from the obvious allusion to *Hamlet*, which was also Scott's source, this sentence hints at Chapter Twenty-four of *The Bride of Lammermoor*, where Mortsheugh, the sexton of the old cemetery of Armitage, is portrayed.[81] Mortsheugh is not exactly cheerful in his conversation, but he is both a gravedigger and a fiddler at weddings, which presents a symbolic contrast. His image conjures up the atmosphere of *The Bride of Lammermoor* in general: its dark portents (Lucy's first encounter with Edgar by the haunted well), its apparitions (the ghost of blind Alice), and its macabre outcome (Lucy going mad and Edgar disappearing in the quicksand). Another literary reference—to "Pogorelskii's mailman" (8: 91)—also evokes associations with tales of the macabre and preternatural. The reference is to "The Poppy-Seed-Cake Woman of the Lafertovo Quarter" by A. Pogorelskii (A. A. Perovskii; 1825), a story reflecting the influence of E. T. A. Hoffmann, particularly of his "Der goldene Topf" (1814).[82] "The Poppy-Seed-Cake Woman" is close to "The Undertaker" not only in its general use of the miraculous—eerie little lights, like ghosts, come dancing toward the Poppy-Seed-Cake Woman's house after her death, and a cat dressed like a civil servant appears as a suitor for Masha—but also in its lower-middle-class social setting and in the particular detail that after the mailman and his family move into a new house, strange things begin to happen in it.

Still another work in the same tradition, with which "The Undertaker" is closely connected—though Pushkin makes no overt reference to it—is Bestuzhev-Marlinskii's "An Evening at a Caucasian Watering Place in 1824" (1830). In one of the tales in this work, a dragoon captain tells of what happened when his brother made a wager with friends that he had no fear of the dead: "They decided that my brother must go outside the city, to the place of execution, where they had seen the corpse of a robber, hanged on the previous day. He was to take the corpse by the hand and ask him as politely as he could to do him the honor of coming to the inn in order to feast with them till the cock crows."[83] As the captain's brother does what he was told, the corpse seizes his hand and does not let go of it until he promises to perform a service for him.

All these works belong to the same tradition from which Pushkin's earlier plan, "A Devil in Love," and the tale he lent V. P. Titov, "The Lonely Cottage on Vasilev Island," had sprung. The fact that "The Undertaker" does not present the marvelous in a serious manner—that the corpses' visit turns out to have been a mere nightmare—does not distinguish it significantly from the prevalent tradition, for a jocular attitude toward the grisly was common to many stories. Few writers would unflinchingly declare—as did Horace Walpole—that a statue was bleeding at the nose. Some would try to explain away unusual phenomena by a reference to magnetism, fuming powders, and the like—as did Ann Radcliffe. Others would present them as a function of the character's psychology—as did both Hoffmann and Scott. Still others would treat the supernatural in a frankly mocking way, aware that the chief gain was not that the reader believed the unbelievable, but that his imagination was titillated by it. In its humorous treatment of the miraculous, "The Undertaker" is perhaps closest to Irving's fantastic tales, such as "The Adventure of the German Student" and "The Bold Dragoon: or The Adventure of My Grandfather" (both in *Tales of a Traveller*). The first describes a beautiful pale woman making love all night, though her head— guillotined the day before—is only held on to her neck by a black brocade band. In the second an Irish captain of dragoons concocts a tale about the furniture dancing in his room in order to account for the noise he made prowling after the innkeeper's buxom daughter.

"The Undertaker" is as much inspired by literary tradition as "The Blizzard" and "The Squire's Daughter," though the tradition it draws on is somewhat different, since it has a different narrator, with different tastes. The person who told the story to Belkin is listed in the Publisher's Introduction as the "*pri-*

kazchik B.V." (8: 61). The word *prikazchik* could mean either the steward of an estate, or a shop assistant, or a salesman. Whatever B.V.'s own profession was, it is interesting that we meet with a *prikazchik* in the story itself: he is the steward of the newly deceased old widow, Triukhina, with whom Adrian "exchanged meaningful glances" (8: 93) as he swore not to charge a kopeck too much for the widow's funeral. Although this steward is not necessarily B.V. himself, he could be: what Pushkin wants to convey is that the narrator belongs to the same social class as his characters. This is also underscored by the fact that whereas all the other narrators of Belkin's tales— all belonging to the gentry—are given three initials to stand for their given name, patronymic, and surname, the steward is endowed with only two. Since he is a commoner, Belkin treats him in a familiar way and neglects to make note of his surname. (Adrian Prokhorov has no surname either.)[84] All this indicates that B.V. is probably a man of little education and of low-brow literary taste, which is confirmed by his choice of a gleefully macabre theme.

V. V. Vinogradov points out that a certain "professional" attitude also makes B.V.'s presence felt.[85] All the details he chooses to describe are connected with the world of business. If Adrian is sad, there is a business reason for it: he is remembering that rain has ruined some of the cloaks and hats he rents out for funerals. When his new neighbor comes by to introduce himself, the conversation soon turns to "How's Your Honor's business?" (8: 90). The police guard Iurko is cultivated because he might sooner or later prove to be useful, and, as we have seen, Schulz's dinner party culminates in toasts to the tradesmen's clients. Even Adrian's dream is a mirror of his business-oriented waking hours: in his unearthly guests he recognizes the brigadier who was buried in pouring rain and thus caused him damage, the poor man who took his coffin for nothing, and the retired sergeant of the Guards for whom he sold a pinewood coffin pretending it was oak. The tradesman's inside view of trade saves "The Undertaker" from the sentimental condescension and moralizing that characterized most of the stories about the lower classes by Pushkin's contemporaries.

B.V.'s choices of subject matter and "professional" vantage point, then, are what mark him as an individual, distinct from the other narrators. Stylistically, however, he is very difficult to distinguish from Belkin. In the two stories narrated by Miss K.I.T., the sentimentality could be safely assumed to belong to her, and the naïveté to Belkin; but in "The Undertaker" it is hard to tell whether Belkin or B.V. is the simpler, the more naïve, the less educated. To be sure, colloquialisms characteristic of merchants and their servants occur in the dialogues, but these could have been recorded by Belkin just as well as by B.V. Pushkin was careful not to overload his stories with class patterns of speech, mostly preferring a "middle register" of linguistic usage and only occasionally resorting to substandard phrases.[86] B.V. and Belkin seem to reinforce each other's efforts in creating a simple style, thereby deviating from "the manner adopted by today's novelists" (8: 91). "The Undertaker" is like "The Blizzard" and "The Squire's Daughter" in that a tension is created between this simple style and the subject matter.

The effect of this tension, however, is not wholly comic in "The Undertaker." Prokhorov's "kitchen and living room were filled with the master's wares—coffins of all colors and sizes as well as cupboards full of mourning hats and cloaks and torches" (8: 89). The epigraph for this story—"Do we not daily gaze on coffins, / The silver thatch of earth decaying?," from G. R. Derzhavin's poem "Waterfall" (1794)—was obviously chosen with the same innocence as the one for the volume: the author thought of it simply because in Adrian's house, too, we behold coffins every day. But in fact the epigraph serves, not as a fitting introduction to the subject, but as a sharp contrast to it, for Derzhavin's meaning is symbolic whereas B.V.'s use is entirely literal.[87] The practical B.V., just like Adrian himself, fails to realize that the coffins and mourning hats stand for death. They are simply what the undertaker makes his living by.

This is most obvious from B.V.'s recollection of the sign over Adrian's gate: "Plain and Colored Coffins Sold and Upholstered; Available for Rent; Used Ones Repaired" (8: 89). B.V. must have remembered a sign over a tailor's or carpenter's door, rather than over an undertaker's, which shows that to him there is no important difference between making sofas and making coffins. Adrian himself must be totally indifferent to the symbolic meaning of the implements of his trade if he can have them stacked up in his kitchen and drawing room. Forgetting that his clients are dead, he regards the wealthier ones as his "benefactors" (8: 92) and resents a poor man for "taking" (*beret*; 8: 90) a coffin free of charge, implying active participation on the dead man's part. It seems to him as if death applies to his clients only in a limited, business sense—one that could not apply to him. In this light the earlier reference to Shakespeare's and Scott's gravediggers acquires even greater poignancy, for the dialogue from Act 4, Scene 1, of *Hamlet*, which Scott used as an epigraph for Chapter Twenty-four of *The Bride of Lammermoor*, contains Hamlet's puzzled question: "Has this fellow no feeling of his business, that he sings at grave-making?"[88]

The peripeteia occurs in the story at the moment when, following Iurko's suggestion that Adrian drink to the health of his corpses (8: 92), the symbolic meaning of his profession is visited on the undertaker. The dream that follows may simply be funny to B.V., but its implication—when associated with the epigraph—is that the idea of his mortality has been brought home to Adrian. Anticipating Tolstoi's Ivan Ilich, Adrian has labored all his life under the assumption that death applied only to others; but now, just when he has moved into a new house at the peak of his career, a Stone Guest has responded to his careless invitation, a man in a dark suit has come to him to order a Requiem, a long-forgotten adversary has arrived to point a gun at him.

The links connecting "The Undertaker" with Pushkin's serious works are many. His letter of November 4, 1830, to his fiancée reveals that Adrian was modeled on a real-life undertaker, who lived close to the Goncharovs in Moscow and was on Pushkin's mind because he worried that Natalia might fall victim to the cholera epidemic. Partly because of the epidemic and partly because—soon to be married—he saw himself at a turning point in his life, he was preoccupied with the meaning of his past and present, and with worry over the future. Several

of his lyrical poems written during the Boldino autumn—
"Farewell," "An Invocation," "For the Shores of Your Distant
Homeland"—summon the dead from the grave. In the poem
"My Ruddy-Faced Critic, Paunchy Joker," the only living being
the poet can descry in the desolate countryside is a little peasant carrying the coffin of his dead child under his arm. But closest to "The Undertaker" in theme are the dramatic works written in the same period: [89] not only *The Stone Guest* and *Mozart
and Salieri*, but also *The Feast During the Plague*, with its
lurid contrasts, and *The Covetous Knight*, in which the miser's
victims arise in his imagination in much the same way as
Adrian's clients come back to haunt him. [90]

Closely linked as it may be with serious works, "The Undertaker" is nevertheless told by the artless B.V., and its basic tenor
remains comic. Like the sparkling wine drunk at Schulz's party,
a Belkin tale, when compared with the Little Tragedies, is only
"almost like champagne" (8: 91). There is, however, enough
of a serious element in "The Undertaker" to make it different from the wholly comic tales told by Miss K.I.T.; there is
enough of an incongruity between the comic and the serious to
puzzle the reader and to make him experience what Wacław
Lednicki has aptly described as a grotesque effect. [91]

From the point of view of its grotesquerie, "The Undertaker"
foreshadows the Gogolesque trend of Russian naturalism. The
"chubby Cupid" (8: 89) that appears on Adrian's sign outshines
even the lathered face accompanied by an offer of bloodletting
that hangs above the barber's door in Gogol's "The Nose"
(1836). The sentence "A dead man can't live without a coffin" (8: 90) anticipates the last part of Gogol's "The Overcoat"
(1841), in which an order is given to catch the ghost "alive or
dead." [92] The statements that "the only *Russian* official there
was a police guard, a *Finn* called Iurko" (8: 91; my italics) and
that from among the dead "only those stayed at home who are
by now really incapacitated" are joined with expressions like
"his skull smiled affably," "the bones of his legs rattled in his
jackboots like pestles in mortars," and "osseous embrace" (8:
93, 94). "The Undertaker," despite its comic spirit, ranges beyond the limits of sheer comedy.

5

The tale in which Pushkin manipulates the narrative point of view most elaborately is "The Shot." The narrator, recalling his youthful days, describes the life of an officer stationed in a small provincial town. The only person among his acquaintances there who is not in military service is a strange man called Silvio. This man, a former hussar, is an exceptionally good shot, yet when an officer hurls a heavy candleholder at him during a card game, he fails to challenge the man to a duel, which lowers him in the eyes of the other young officers. He nevertheless lives on in their midst as a friend until he receives a letter one day and announces that he must leave for Moscow. That same day he gives a farewell dinner party, and afterwards, when all the other guests are gone, he explains to the narrator why he failed to challenge his offender to a duel. All this framework, emphasizing the narrator's own role, occupies three-fourths of the first chapter—a unique structure for a Belkin tale.[93]

Another peculiarity of the story's structure is that the narrator, after setting the stage, yields it to his hero. The rest of Chapter One is given over to Silvio's account. As a young officer he was popular with his comrades until the arrival in his regiment of a brilliant young aristocrat, who upstaged him with his money, good looks, high spirit, and daring. Silvio picked a quarrel with his rival, and this led to a duel. His rival fired the first shot, sending his bullet through Silvio's hat, an inch above his forehead. It was Silvio's turn, but when his adversary showed so little concern that he stood there eating cherries from his cap while awaiting the shot, Silvio thought there was no point in depriving him of his life if he himself did not cherish it. He asked him if he could postpone his shot. His adversary agreed, and ever since that day Silvio has lived in retirement, daily practicing his marksmanship and impatiently waiting for a better opportunity to conclude his duel. This is the reason he could not risk his life in any other duel. Now, at last, he has received news that his rival is engaged to be married: this is the time, thinks Silvio, when the man will at last cherish his life. He sets out to resume the duel.

Of Chapter Two the narrative frame occupies two-thirds. At first the narrator tells us about his uneventful life in the country after his retirement from the service; then he relates that a wealthy young neighbor, the Countess B., married several years before, has come to spend the summer on her estate. He sets out to visit his aristocratic neighbors soon after their arrival. We soon learn that Count B. was Silvio's adversary; and the narrator once more yields the stage to his hero, this time the Count, for the conclusion of the story. The Count relates that he and his wife spent their honeymoon on this estate, and once, when he returned from an outing ahead of his wife, he found Silvio in his study. He was ready to face Silvio's pistol, but Silvio did not wish to shoot at an unarmed man and insisted that they draw lots for the first shot. The Count drew the lucky number and fired, missing Silvio and hitting a painting on the wall. It was Silvio's turn, but just as he took aim the Countess arrived, and when she understood the situation, she threw herself at Silvio's feet. This satisfied Silvio, and he left, but not before firing a bullet exactly above the Count's. At the end of the story the narrator reports the rumor that Silvio joined the Greek freedom fighters led by Alexander Ypsilanti, and died in the battle near Skuliany.

A further interesting feature of the structure is the parallelism between the two central heroes' gallantry about each other's actions: when Silvio describes the first stage of their duel, he frankly disparages his own motives and presents his adversary in a favorable light; just so, the Count, in his story of the second confrontation, detracts from his own worth and lays stress on his adversary's courage.

The story, then, has three "authors" in addition to Belkin. On closer examination, however, we find that the events of "The Shot" are viewed, not from three vantage points, but from six, for each speaker recounts the past when he was younger and put different values on his own and others' actions. I.L.P., who told the story to Belkin, says that he and his comrades regarded the thirty-five-year-old Silvio as an old man; and that Silvio's strange ways "made a strong impression on our young minds" (8: 65); he generalizes about the young, observing that "they consider valor the height of human virtue and an excuse for all possible vices" (8: 67); he emphasizes his "romantic imagination" (8: 67); and in the closing paragraph he remarks, "This was how I came to know the end of the story whose beginning had at one time made such a deep impression on me" (8: 74), implying that it was only "at one time," in the past, that he could have been impressed by Silvio's adventure. Yet though there is an unmistakable ironic distance between I.L.P.'s erzählenden Ich and erzählten Ich,[94] Chapter One conveys, by and large, his impressions as a young man; and thus a dual perception emerges. Similarly, Silvio remarks in the course of his narrative that his general disposition to take the lead had been a "passion" with him in his youth (8: 69), which implies a more sedate mind in later years; yet this more distant, cooler view does not prevent us from seeing the first stage of his duel essentially through his eyes as a young man. Finally, the Count's statement that "I haven't had a pistol in my hand for some four years now" (8: 72)—among other details—suggests that he too has changed since the time of the second stage of the duel; yet that duel is recounted with the vividness of an immediate experience.

A shifting point of view, opening unconventional perspectives on conventional situations, is a favorite tool of the parodist. "The Shot," like the other three Belkin stories so far discussed, is a parody above all else. Its primary target is the literary hero whose mind is spellbound by a traumatic event of the past, to the exclusion of all interest in the present. A classical example of such a hero is Byron's Giaour: after his beloved Leila's death his mind is set on the single purpose of taking vengeance on her murderer Hassan; that accomplished, he is left with "The leafless desert of the mind, / The waste of feelings unemploy'd";[95] and he spends the rest of his life in a monastery, brooding on the past and inspiring awe in the monks by the sheer look of horror in his eyes. Several other Byronic characters—Conrad of The Corsair (1814), Alp of The Siege of Corinth (1816), Manfred of the dramatic poem bearing his name (1817)—incarnate similar mental qualities. The same type found its way also into Russian narrative poems of the 1820's. The hero of I. I. Kozlov's The Monk (1825), for instance, loses his wife and child through the intrigues of a "villain"; he spends seven years in the wilderness carrying the burden of this memory; eventually he murders the malefactor and retires to a monastery to dedicate himself to sullen repentance.

Pushkin's first epigraph for the story—"We exchanged shots"—derives from this type of narrative poem. It comes from E. A. Baratynskii's *The Ball* (1828), whose hero Arsenii is portrayed at first as a Byronic character:[96]

> Traces of tormenting passions,
> Traces of melancholy thoughts
> Were writ on his brow; from his eyes
> A gloomy recklessness radiated.

He is aloof, respected, and feared for his sharp tongue; the beautiful Nina's love cannot warm his heart; he speaks of "The compulsive gloom of my soul— / A vestige of erstwhile pitiful errors / And of erstwhile destructive passions."[97] As we eventually learn, the experience that left such a deep wound on his psyche was that his beloved, Olga, seemed to show preference for a friend he had introduced to her. Arsenii "swears to take revenge on his rival" and does everything in his power to provoke a quarrel:[98]

> I teased and tormented him
> With caustic remarks all the time,
> And at my instigation
> A quarrel erupted between us:
> We exchanged shots.

It must have been these elements—rivalry, a duel provoked deliberately, and a psychological (as well as physical) wound received by the hero—that Pushkin was alluding to by his choice of the epigraph.[99]

The monomaniac as hero emerged, naturally, in the prose fiction of the time too. It has been established that one of Pushkin's main sources for Silvio was the mysterious Hungarian nobleman depicted in Bestuzhev-Marlinskii's "An Evening at a Caucasian Watering Place in 1824."[100] Here are some excerpts showing the characterization of that hero:

No one knew either his social status or his country of origin, though in his passport he was identified as a Hungarian nobleman. They say he was the most strange and incomprehensible being. . . . He lived exceedingly modestly, yet at the same time scattered gold among the poor. He dressed simply, but each of the stones in his rings was worth tens of thousands. He was unsociable and taciturn as a rule, befriending no one and bowing to no one. Yet some persons of consequence spoke with him and about him with the greatest reverence.

. . .

At night the Hungarian would sit for long periods, intent on some books, which he would then proceed to lock away carefully. . . . He groaned piteously in his sleep, as if his conscience had been burdened by some crime; and his usual appearance, the sepulchral pallor of his face, his deep-set, glassy eyes, and his abrupt, distracted speech—all betrayed spiritual torment, much more than physical decline.[101]

The Hungarian, like Silvio, is dedicated to a secret mission that has some connection with a traumatic experience in his past. Another Bestuzhev story relevant to "The Shot" is "An Evening on Bivouac," from which Pushkin took his second epigraph. Its hero, Mechin, fights a duel with a rival and is badly wounded by his adversary, who has the first shot; when he recovers he plans to claim his turn, but—thanks to the good offices of a friend—he is sent away on an urgent mission by the Minister of War. Interestingly, Pushkin at first did not realize that the line he wanted to use as an epigraph—"I swore I'd shoot him by the rules of dueling (I still had my turn coming)"—came from this story.[102] Sending the manuscript of the *Tales* to Pletnev on August 15, 1831, he appended this postscript to his covering letter: "By the way, about the epigraphs. For 'The Shot' we'll have to find another one, from A. Bestuzhev's 'A Novel in Seven Letters,' published in the *Northern Star*: 'I still had my turn coming, I swore,' etc. Please find it, there's a dear friend" (14: 209). Pletnev, of course, could not find the line in "A Novel in Seven Letters" (1824) and suggested another one, but Pushkin persisted with his original idea because of its relevance to the theme of a delayed shot. Even so, it is revealing that he had originally thought of "A Novel in Seven Letters," one of Bestuzhev's weakest stories.[103] Its hero falls in love with a society girl and fancies she is not indifferent to him, but he cannot be sure, for he has only formal social contact with her; when he realizes that she favors another man, he challenges his rival to a duel and kills him. This story corresponded to Pushkin's purposes even more than "An Evening on

Bivouac," because its hero had even less right to kill his rival than Mechin did; Mechin at least had found the lady of his choice receptive until his rival came along. Still another Bestuzhev story from which Pushkin seems to have borrowed is "A Journey to Revel," in which Evgenii Kron describes his youthful days in the following terms: "There was not one duel . . . in which I did not play either an active or a secondary role; and all my friends allowed me to take the lead at all times."[104]

One possible model for the character of Silvio that has, curiously, not been mentioned in critical literature is Professor Androni in Pogorelskii's "The Baleful Consequences of Unbridled Imagination," narrated on the third evening in *The Double* (1828). Androni has a grudge against the father of the hero, Alceste; in order to settle this old account, he constructs a lifelike doll, which he manages to marry off to Alceste; and the young man, on discovering the hoax, commits suicide. Androni's elaborate and time-consuming stratagem may well have been the model for Silvio's singleminded dedication to marksmanship; and the idea of making one's revenge more cruel by involving the adversary's family in it may have also been inspired by Pogorelskii's tale.

Finally, at least two dramatic works have been mentioned by critics as possible sources for "The Shot." The phrase "If he had expressed a wish to shoot a pear off the top of somebody's cap, no one in our regiment would have hesitated to offer his head" (8: 65) evokes an association with Friedrich Schiller's *Wilhelm Tell* (1804), and the association is reinforced by the shot through Silvio's cap and by the selection of a Swiss landscape as the subject of the bullet-riddled painting in Chapter Two.[105] Victor Hugo's *Hernani* (1830), on the other hand, may have given Pushkin the idea of one hero's long-standing right to kill another. After Don Ruy Gomez de Silva saves Hernani's life, despite his recent discovery that Hernani is his rival, Hernani gives him his horn and swears he will kill himself whenever de Silva decides to blow it. De Silva, like Pushkin's Silvio, arrives to blow the horn at the moment of his adversary's greatest happiness.[106]

Parodying these, and possibly other romantic works, Pushkin makes skillful use of his narrators with their shifting point of view. A related device, noticeable from the very beginning of "The Shot," is a contrasting method of presentation, much like Bestuzhev's introduction of his Hungarian. The latter is supposed to be poor, yet there are signs betraying his wealth; he is supposed to be indifferent to local society, yet he manages to win its respect; he is supposed to shun human contact, yet he befriends a young Russian staying in Kislovodsk. In each pair of contrasting statements, the second seems to cancel the validity of the first: the hero in fact emerges as rich, jealous of his reputation, and capable of close friendship.

As if impressed by Bestuzhev's ability to pique the reader's curiosity, I.L.P. employs this technique *à toute outrance*. His first paragraph bemoans the drabness of an army officer's life and the lack of acquaintances other than those wearing the same uniform. The reader assumes that the story will present a slice of uneventful provincial life. But the next paragraph introduces a man in civilian clothes, surrounded by an air of mystery, most unlike the run-of-the-mill army officer. Like Bestuzhev's Hungarian, Silvio appears to be poor, but obviously has money. He avoids discussions of duels, as if he had less interest in them than the young officers, who discuss them frequently; yet he soon turns out to have more interest in them than anybody else. We are told that he "hardly ever" (8: 66) plays cards, yet the first time we behold him he is doing just that; and I.L.P., having forgotten that Silvio hardly ever plays, proceeds to tell us that all the officers knew how Silvio always played. Not only this: as soon as we are told that no one ever interferes with Silvio's silent way of correcting the other players' occasional mistakes, we are presented with an occasion that negates the rule. The general seems to be given only to be negated by the individual in every single case.

This pattern is followed throughout Chapter One. Silvio is withdrawn, yet he seeks I.L.P.'s friendship; everyone forgives Silvio his apparent cowardice except I.L.P., yet he is the only one Silvio seems to trust; the statement that their "frank conversations came to an end" (8: 67) is followed by the only frank conversation in the story; Silvio says he has "little regard for other people's opinions" (8: 68), yet he proceeds to tell I.L.P. his story for the sole purpose of improving the young man's opin-

ion of him. The most important of these contradictory statements occurs at the beginning of Silvio's story: "You are familiar with my character: I am accustomed to taking the lead; in
my youth this was a passion with me" (8: 69). The story that
follows is an example of how he was *unable* to take the lead;
considered alongside all the other statements that have been
negated, Silvio's claim of leadership (phrased, as we have seen,
à la Marlinskii) loses all credibility.

M. Petrovskii sees this technique as evidence of Pushkin's
mastery of composition.[107] To be sure, in small doses such a
technique might serve as a stimulant to the reader's interest;
but Pushkin belabors it in an unmerciful manner that leaves no
doubt about his mocking attitude. Used by I.L.P. and Silvio,
this technique demonstrates, not so much Pushkin's mastery
of composition as his mastery of parody.

An individual example that contradicts the preceding general
statement frustrates the reader's expectations. They are also
frustrated if allusions to the hero's likely behavior or to the
outcome of the plot are not followed up.[108] (We have seen something similar in *Goriukhino*.) At the beginning of "The Shot,"
Silvio's habitual sullenness, acrimonious temper, and sharp
tongue are emphasized. If questioned about his past involvement in duels, he responds so unwillingly that "it was obvious"
to the narrator "that he found such questions unpleasant" (8:
66). The young officers conjecture that his conscience must be
burdened by the death of "some hapless victim of his terrifying
skill" (8: 66). His expertise at shooting seems to guarantee that
he is a formidable duelist, and his very appearance forbids any
suspicion of cowardice. All this conforms with the characterization of the Byronic hero. Lara, for instance, had a "brow in
furrowed lines" that "spake of passions, but of passions past";
he was known for his "sarcastic levity of tongue"; "not much
he loved long question of the past," and if "still more prying
such enquiry grew, / His brow fell darker and his words more
few"; finally, his appearance was so forbidding that "things
more timid that beheld him near, / In silence gazed or whis-
pered mutual fear."[109] The reader of "The Shot" is led to believe
that Silvio, if challenged, would answer "To-morrow!—ay, to-
morrow!" as did Lara at Otho's hall. Ominous signs point to

the likely outcome of Silvio's quarrel with the young officer over the card table: he rises, "pale with anger, his eyes flashing" (8: 66); the other young officers have "no doubt about the consequences" and regard their comrade as "a dead man"; they talk of the vacancy in the regiment that will be created by Silvio's bullet; and the next morning they wonder whether "the poor lieutenant was still alive" (8: 66). Yet nothing happens. Either because I.L.P. has tamed his "romantic imagination" by the time he tells the story or simply because he is not skillful enough to maintain the narrative at the level on which he began it, he lets the reader down.

No sooner are the first expectations frustrated, however, than new ones begin to build up. Silvio is still a mysterious character, which is emphasized by phrases like "his life was an enigma" and "he himself had struck me as the hero of some mysterious story" (8: 67). He tears the seal from the letter he receives "with a look of utmost impatience"; he displays "feverish gaiety" during the farewell party, then grows exceedingly "preoccupied" (8: 67, 68). The "grim pallor" (8: 68) of his face is emphasized once more, his flashing eyes are mentioned twice, and he is compared to the Devil—which stands out particularly strikingly in a narrative generally scant of metaphors. Some great passion—usually associated with an air of nobility—is suspected in him, but he turns out to be most unheroic and unappealing as he declares: "If I had been able to punish R. without the slightest risk to my own life, nothing could have persuaded me to let him get away" (8: 68). This sentence is strange in the sense that it speaks the truth plainly yet has a romantic ring to it: the phrase "nothing could have" overstates Silvio's emotions and is incongruous with the matter-of-fact message of the sentence as a whole. Such incongruity is characteristic of the texture of "The Shot" in general.

Silvio's unromantic statement may be disappointing, but the reader's interest is not allowed to flag for long. The narrator's astonishment and embarrassment—states of mind that occur frequently in the tale—are emphasized in order to keep the emotional pitch high; expectations are raised even further when Silvio declares, "Six years ago I received a slap on the face, and my enemy is still alive" (8: 68); and to delay satisfying the reader's curiosity, Pushkin has the narrator talk about his own curiosity instead. His questions—"Didn't you fight him?," "Circumstances, I suppose, must have separated you?" (8: 68)— establish a parallel with "An Evening on Bivouac": in that story, Mechin does not succeed in avenging himself, at first because he is wounded, and later because he is sent on a mission by the Minister of War. The reader of "The Shot" expects that similar circumstances prevented Silvio from receiving satisfaction. The tension mounts when Silvio shows his bullet-pierced hat as he talks about his hatred and despair, and as he describes how ladies "fainted one after the other" during his public quarrel with his adversary (8: 69). But it turns out that he postponed his shot merely because he was irritated by his opponent's nonchalant way of eating cherries and spitting the stones while waiting for him to fire.

The end of the first encounter between Silvio and his adversary would seem ludicrous enough to demolish all further expectations, yet I.L.P. manages to raise some new ones even past that point. To Silvio, obviously, the outcome of the duel was no laughing matter, for he retired from the hussars in order to spend the next six years practicing his pistol shooting. "Since then," he says, "not one day has gone by without my thinking of revenge. And now my time has come" (8: 70). (The same phrases, repeated almost verbatim by the Water-Nymph in Pushkin's poem, arouse forebodings that prove to be fully justified.) Silvio is compared to a tiger pacing up and down in his cage, which reinforces his image as a beast of prey ready to pounce on his victim—even though the mention of the cage at a time when Silvio is just about to set off, free, seems to be inappropriate. Despite this disturbing resonance, however, the impression is created that Silvio, like Pogorelskii's Androni, has at last hatched his plan of revenge and, given his mastery with the pistol, will kill his adversary, who has at last learned the value of life. Chapter One ends on this supposition, none too subtly enticing the reader into Chapter Two. I.L.P. has succeeded in raising expectations once more.

In the manuscript, Pushkin put the date October 12 after Chapter One and wrote: "The ending has been lost" (8: 597). But then he decided to proceed and completed Chapter Two in another two days. If he had abandoned the story after the first chapter, it would have had an entirely different meaning, for in that case the reader would assume that Silvio's adversary could not escape his fate.[110] Indeed in that case the last of the expectations raised would not have been unmistakably frustrated, which would have spoiled Pushkin's design. One reason he decided to continue the story must have been that he wanted to bring frustrated expectations full circle.

D. D. Blagoi has attempted to show that the two chapters are constructed symmetrically.[111] They contain an almost equal number of pages. They both begin with descriptions of uneventful provincial existence as backgrounds against which the contours of interesting heroes (Silvio and the Count) are seen. The poor furnishings of Silvio's apartment, where the expensive guns constitute the only luxury, are contrasted with the luxury of the Count's mansion (the word used in both cases for "luxury" is *roskosh'*, 8: 65, 71). Silvio's room with its bullet-riddled walls is paralleled by the Count's bullet-punctured painting. Silvio's hat, as a symbol of offense, reappears in Chapter Two; planting his bullet on top of the Count's, Silvio only repeats his feat of planting bullet on bullet through an ace, which we saw him do in Chapter One; to remind the Count of the cherries he ate in the first encounter, Silvio mentions in the second that the bullet in his pistol is heavier than cherry stones; in taking his revenge he recounts the slap he received six years previously; and he reproaches the Count for his devilish good fortune in drawing the lucky number on both occasions.

Moreover, the technique of frustrating the reader's expectations is continued in Chapter Two. In the first chapter it was Silvio's more mature age that disposed I.L.P. to create a hero out of him; in the second, it is the Count's superior social position that fills him with awe. The respect inspired by the two characters is ironically overstated in each case. In the first chapter Silvio proves disappointing; so now is the Count. Contrary to his previous favorable characterization, he loses his head when caught off balance, agrees to fire a second shot to which he has no right, and allows his wife to plead with Silvio. It is true that the reader's expectations about the Count are not built up as deliberately as they are for Silvio, which distorts the symmetry of the two chapters somewhat, but then the Count is not the central character of the tale.[112] Another thing that distinguishes the second chapter from the first is that its conclusion frustrates expectations doubly; this time the reader is disenchanted not with just one, but with both characters. Not only does the Count fall short of the narrator's expectations, but Silvio fails to fire the shot we have been waiting for all through the story. This Lara has not slain his Otho; this Androni has not driven his enemy's son (or wife, as the case may be) to suicide.

Some critics see the denouement of "The Shot," not as a final debunking of Silvio, but as an indication that he has "conquered himself," has transcended his former murderous ways.[113] Yet when all is said and done, Silvio does not let the Count off lightly: as the Count himself clearly states, Silvio has succeeded in taking revenge on him, persuading him to act against his conscience and humiliating him so much, both in his own eyes and before his wife, that he still blushes as he recounts the events four years later.[114] But the chief question is, not how far Silvio has succeeded with his revenge, but what sort of a man he is in the final analysis.

The one undisputable fact is that Silvio loses his romantic halo by the end of the story. The same technique we saw in "The Blizzard" is at work here: when viewed from the perspective of a provincial squire's dining-room window, romantic notions become ludicrous. One important reason Pushkin proceeded to Chapter Two must have been that it gave him an opportunity to establish this perspective. As Thomas Shaw says, "The Shot" is not just an account of Silvio's three failures to fire a shot, but also the story of I.L.P.'s discovery of the meaning of these events.[115] Also, the fact that the Count is a married man, ready to settle down to an unadventurous life at the time Silvio seeks him out, helps provide a new perspective on Silvio: his plan to fire his shot, conceived as a romantic notion of vengeance six years before, is simply murder by the standards of ordinary life. Exposing a false sense of honor and courage, parodying the preposterous idea that a man might spend his life plotting revenge for a slight he received in his youth, and altogether debunking the Byronic hero—these must

have indeed been the tasks Pushkin set himself and successfully accomplished with the aid of fictitious narrators and related devices. But Silvio's strange character seems to involve
more than mere parody.

One excellent guide to an understanding of Silvio is the interpretation Dostoevskii put on him—not in a critical essay,
but in fiction. Just as Silvio's futile death at Skuliany was an
inspiration to Turgenev for the conclusion of *Rudin* (1855),
so the character of Pushkin's hero influenced Dostoevskii in
creating his Underground Man. With his insight into the workings of Pushkin's mind, demonstrated on so many occasions,
Dostoevskii hinted at a connection between Silvio and Albert
of *The Covetous Knight*. From that drama he took Albert's
phrase, "To keep me like a son, not like a mouse, / Born under
ground" (7: 109), and turned it into a metaphor for the existence of the Russian intellectual of the nineteenth century.[116]
Silvio, on the other hand, is referred to in that part of *Notes
from Underground* (1864) where the hero, as he is riding to the
brothel, plots revenge on Zverkov and his comrades:

"We will duel at daybreak, it's all settled..."
"I'll say, 'Look, you monster, look at my sunken cheeks and my
rags! I've lost everything—career, happiness, art, science, the *woman
I loved*—and all because of you. Here are the pistols. I have come to
fire my pistol and... and I forgive you!' At this point I'll fire into the
air and vanish without a trace."
I was even on the point of bursting into tears, though I knew at that
same precise moment that all this came from Silvio and from Lermontov's *Masquerade*. And suddenly I felt so terribly ashamed that I
stopped the horse, got out of the sled, and stood in the snow in the
middle of the street.[117]

The phrase "I have come to fire my pistol" is quoted verbatim from "The Shot" (8: 73). Silvio did not come to the Count
in "rags," but his appearance—"covered with dust and un-
shaven" (8: 73)—was at least disheveled. Planting a bullet on
top of the Count's showed a mastery of the pistol, but it was
just as harmless in its effects as firing in the air. The clearest
indication of the influence of "The Shot," however, is an earlier
episode in *Notes from Underground*: the one describing the
hero's feud with the large officer, who picks him up by the
shoulders and moves him out of the way in a billiard room

without even noticing who he is. Like Silvio, the Underground Man spends years plotting revenge on an enemy—who has long since forgotten the whole squabble.

The Underground Man is of course different from Silvio in many ways, but it is significant that Dostoevskii could find, at least in an embryonic state, some elements in Pushkin's character that suited his design. Indeed, if we cast away the romantic mask—which Pushkin himself was busy doing—Silvio emerges as not so much an awe-inspiring maniac as a pitiable wretch. After all, it was only stated and not shown that the young officers held him in great respect; the one incident actually shown revealed that he was unable to defend his honor. In the light of that incident, his sullen nature, his malicious tongue, and his secretiveness appear merely as an incapacity for simple friendship; and his efforts to excel with the gun can be interpreted as an attempt to acquire a self-assurance he otherwise lacks. It is hard to believe he had had the habit of "taking the lead" even six years earlier, before the Count joined his hussar regiment. If he was so gay and happy and popular, how could the appearance of one rival knock him so completely off his balance that he would give up his career and comrades, and retire to a gloomy corner of Russia, alone with his pistols?

It has been remarked that Pushkin, parodying the conventional tale of duels, underplayed the element most crucial to that type of tale, namely, rivalry over a woman.[118] To be sure, Silvio does resent the Count's success with a Polish landowner's wife with whom Silvio was having an affair, but this is only one of the grudges he bears the Count. Mainly what he resents is the newcomer's "youth, intelligence, good looks," his "frenzied vivacity" and "lighthearted courage," his "exalted name," and his "money, more than he could count" (8: 69); the Count's most offensive act is that, his friendly approaches to Silvio having been repulsed, "he withdrew without the slightest regret" (8: 69); and Silvio's most maddening defeat comes when the Count responds to his malicious epigrams with good-natured jests. Pushkin's primary purpose may have been parody, but having demolished the romantic hero's contrived characteristics, he substituted some true-to-life features.

The cherry stones the young Count keeps spitting out while

Silvio is aiming at him convey the same meaning as the
Count's good-natured jests: they indicate that he will just not
be ruffled by a bully. They become symbols of Silvio's blind
rage over not being noticed and feared. He refuses to shoot because he realizes that his adversary would remain indifferent to
him even if he shot him; what he wants is, not that the Count
should die, but that he should—as the Underground Man
hoped Zverkov would—"beg for his friendship on his knees,
clutching his legs."[119] Like Liza of *A Novel in Letters*, Silvio
has a morbid sensitivity to offenses, real or imagined: although
he himself provokes the Count to slap him; although this incident gives him a convenient opportunity to fight the Count;
and although the duel, by all codes of honor, should wipe clean
the shame of the slap—he simply cannot forgive or forget it. A
slap on the face is as central to the symbolic structure of "The
Shot" as it is to that of *Notes from Underground*. It seems to be
the work, not of one man's arm, but of life in general, of fate:
the Count is only a scapegoat for the perversity of the Parcae in
not providing Silvio with the same money, name, good looks,
and happy temperament that are his. "A brilliant child of fortune" (8: 69) is what Silvio calls the Count at the beginning of
his story; he sees the Count as "ever favored by fortune" (8: 69)
when he draws the lucky number in the first stage of their
duel; and when the same thing happens at their last meeting,
he congratulates the Count on being "devilishly lucky" (8: 74)
with a leer that the latter would never forget. In this context
the image of Silvio as a tiger, not on the run but in a cage, becomes more understandable: he is locked up in a blind rage
that he is unable to vent. He is an Albert, mistreated, if not by a
cruel father, at least by an indifferent fate.

It seems certain that Pushkin added Chapter Two to the
story in order not only to complete the cycle of frustrations and
to underscore I.L.P.'s prosaic point of view, but also to shed
more light on Silvio's character. As soon as the Count's tale
gets under way, a new emphasis is put, for instance, on Silvio's
indecisiveness. We saw him hesitate before: he turned pale
with anger when the young officer hurled the candlestick at
him, and he must have considered the possibility of challeng-
ing him; he was to fire the first shot during his duel with the

Count, but tells us, "I was so incensed that I did not trust the steadiness of my hand, and in order to give myself time to cool off, I yielded the first shot to him" (8: 69); and even when the Count has already put a hole through his hat, he still does not shoot back, doubting whether he would get as thorough a revenge as he thirsted for. But it is in Chapter Two that his character is finally stamped with infirmity of purpose. He had set out for Moscow hastily enough as soon as news of the Count's engagement had reached him—he had actually threatened to shoot the Count before his wedding (8: 70)—yet he failed to seek out his victim until after the newlyweds had gone to the country for their honeymoon. One suggestion is that this inconsistency was a residue of the original plan to finish the tale at the end of Chapter One, and that Pushkin simply overlooked it as he continued the narrative.[120] It is true that Pushkin—or, rather, his narrator—fails to explain this delay, but his failure to explain it does not necessarily mean that he overlooked it. Conceivably, something could have delayed Silvio—a carriage breaking down, an illness, or the like—but then why not say what this was? Left unexplained, on the other hand, the delay ties in with Silvio's hesitating nature, of which we have already seen evidence. He had, after all, embarked on a mission of doubtful correctness, not only from the moralist's, but even from the duelist's point of view. Elegant self-assurance, if Silvio had had it, would have demanded that he simply forget his shot. To claim it after six years, when his adversary had long forgotten the quarrel, is "a dirty trick."[121] On his way to the Count's estate he would have had every reason to stop the horses, get out of the carriage, and stand in the middle of the road, ashamed of himself—much as the Underground Man was to do. The confrontation that follows is made dramatic by the twists and turns of his irresolution.

Thanks to the details added to his characterization in Chapter Two, Silvio emerges as a man tormented by self-doubt and driven by a compulsion to put himself in humiliating situations. If he wishes to assert his superiority, can he have chosen a worse way to do it? What kind of honor does he hope to regain by renewing a duel in a way that is contrary to all codes of conduct? To begin with, no duel could be regarded as correct without seconds to oversee its fairness. Further, if the duel was indeed to be resumed, a time and place should have been appointed for it: going into a man's study on the spur of the moment and threatening to shoot him cannot pass under the name of a duel. Finally, and most important, no gentleman would insist on continuing a duel after a lady has entered the room. By doing all these things, Silvio, anticipating Dostoevskii's compulsive buffoons, succeeds only in making the Count and Countess despise him. Brandishing his pistol, he manages to frighten them all right, making the Countess throw herself at his feet,[122] but though he relishes their fright, he must at the same time be aware of how despicable his own behavior is. Revenge over the Count he may have, but at the cost of turning the knife in his own wounded self-esteem.

Critics have mentioned several real-life persons, above all Pushkin's friend I. P. Liprandi, who might have served as the prototype for Silvio.[123] Some of his superficial characteristics may indeed have been copied from friends, but in this connection one may legitimately ask, what share of Pushkin's own personality was given to each of the characters. At first sight it may seem that Pushkin identified only with the Count, and not at all with Silvio. Eating cherries while being shot at is a well-known incident of Pushkin's own youth.[124] Pushkin, like the Count when Silvio set out to kill him, was soon to be married. He was a happy child of fortune who had acquired fame effortlessly: if Silvio is to the Count what Salieri is to Mozart, then it is obvious where Pushkin's sympathies lie.[125] And finally, just as Don Juan, visited by the Statue of the Commander at the very moment he thought he had found happiness, is an alter ego of Pushkin's,[126] so also is the Count, confronted with Silvio's pistol during his honeymoon.

Other touches, however, indicate that Pushkin identified even more fully with Silvio. For example, though it is true that Pushkin had acquired easy fame in his youth, by the time he was working on *The Tales of Belkin*, his popularity had declined. Moreover, he had been viciously attacked in the press [127] and, as one would expect, had become highly sensitive to criticism. Bulgarin's lampoon on his ancestor was a particularly painful memory, and thoughts of revenge could not fail to enter his mind. As is clear in connection with *A Novel in Letters*, the fragment "The Guests Were Arriving at the Dacha," and the lyric "My Genealogy," the late 1820's had seen a sharpening in Pushkin's mind of the contrast between his aristocratic ancestry (on his father's side) and his family's relatively low social standing under the reign of Nicholas. In his 1829 travel notes, to be collected later as "A Journey to Arzrum" (1835), he recorded how, when he was dining at a general's table, the waiters had neglected to serve him because of his low rank. Quarantined in Boldino in the fall of 1830, he was tormented by the thought that he could not make ends meet, what with his impending marriage and the demands his future wife's family was putting on him. All these circumstances added incentive to making more of Silvio than just a ludicrous Professor Androni, and Pushkin ended up, as was his wont, dividing himself between his characters.

This does not mean that Silvio is a portrait of Pushkin; but Pushkin's own awakening to certain sensitivities undoubtedly helped add the psychological dimension to Silvio's character that was to arouse Dostoevskii's interest. Nor can "The Shot" be regarded as a psychological study; but Dostoevskii's use of Silvio indicates that in that character—despite the overall parodic design—there was the kernel of a type that was to occupy a central place in nineteenth-century Russian fiction.

6

"The Stationmaster," by far the most successful of Belkin's tales, is narrated by Titular Councillor A.G.N. Older than Belkin, he claims to have, "in the course of twenty years, traversed Russia in all directions" (8: 97) at the time of the telling—a claim incongruous with other information given on the same page. He informs us that in 1816—the time of his first meeting with the stationmaster—he was of low rank and was "young and hotheaded," which implies that he had just begun his career. We know, on the other hand, that Belkin retired in 1823, and that the *Tales* represented his first literary efforts, written probably no later than 1824 or 1825. A.G.N., therefore, could not have been traveling around on business for more than seven or eight years before he told his tale.[128] By this incongruity—in line with the many others in *The Tales of Belkin*—Pushkin may have wished to remind the reader that his narrators are playful fabrications, not to be taken too seriously.

Making A.G.N. older than Belkin was a device for parodying someone of old-fashioned style and literary taste. Whereas all of Belkin's other narrators seem to represent literary trends fashionable in the 1820's (which is another incongruity, for Belkin appears to have already written down his tales by the time some of the literary works he parodied in them appeared in print), A.G.N. stands for eighteenth-century and early-nineteenth-century sentimentalism. His Karamzinite stance shows, first of all, in the prologue he provides—the only prologue we find in any of the five tales. In style and spirit it conforms to such well-known introductions as A. N. Radishchev's contemplation of the human capacity for compassion in the opening chapter of *Journey from Petersburg to Moscow* (1789); Karamzin's admonition to the reader to love Russian antiquity at the beginning of "Natalia the Boyar's Daughter"; and his nostalgic prelude to "Poor Liza," culminating in the exclamation: "Oh, I love to dwell on subjects that touch my heart and make me shed tears of gentle sorrow!"[129] A.G.N.'s appeal to the conscience of his readers in connection with the physical abuse stationmasters are occasionally subjected to has been interpreted as a reference to the third chapter of Radishchev's *Journey*, where the author contemplates thrashing an indolent and deceitful stationmaster.[130] The prologue to A.G.N.'s tale is also close to some later imitations of the early sentimentalists, such as M. P. Pogodin's story "The Beggar" (1826), which begins with a philanthropic discussion of the need to understand those whom fate has driven to the streets.[131] But the most telling indication of A.G.N.'s literary attitudes is his disapproving reference to Viazemskii's poem "The Station" (1828)—the poem that also provided the epigraph to the tale.[132] Viazemskii's playful tone—he calls stationmasters despots and wishes a tumor on their tongue when they say there are no horses—does not appeal to the earnest A.G.N. He, along with Belkin's other narrators, is an adversary not just of Viazemskii, but also of Viazemskii's friend and literary ally Pushkin.

The discord between A.G.N. and Pushkin is most apparent from the following passage:

> Of low rank at the time, I traveled by post, hiring two horses at each stage. As a result, stationmasters treated me with little ceremony, and I often had to take by force what I thought should have been given me by right. Being young and hotheaded, I felt indignant over the baseness and pusillanimity of the stationmaster who gave away to some high-ranking nobleman the team of horses that had been prepared for me. It also took me a long time to get used to being passed over by a snobbish flunkey at the table of a governor. Nowadays both the one and the other seem to me to be in the order of things. Indeed what would become of us if the rule convenient to all, "Let rank yield to rank," were to be replaced by some other, such as "Let mind yield to mind"? What arguments would arise? And whom would the butler serve first?
> (8: 98)

This passage contains two details that Pushkin used elsewhere in entirely different stylistic contexts. One is the comment on being passed over at a high-ranking official's table, which is mentioned with indignation, as we have seen, in "A Journey to Arzrum." The other is the discussion of the relative merits of rank and mind—a topic given serious consideration in Pushkin's "On Public Education" (1826), a memorandum he prepared at the request of Nicholas I.[133] To A.G.N., indignation over being snubbed in society and a preference for intelligence over rank are the follies of a "hotheaded youth," something that he has outgrown in his mature wisdom. The hotheaded youth was close to Radishchev in his ideas—the reference to losing one's horses to a high-ranking official could be taken as an allusion to the "Zavidovo" chapter of Radishchev's *Journey*, in which this almost happens—whereas the mature A.G.N. is a follower of V. A. Zhukovskii, who advocated in his 1808 essay "The Writer in Society" that those who were not born into good society should not try to fight for a place in it, but enjoy peace in the humble bosoms of their loving families. A.G.N. may be speaking ironically of course, as some critics have assumed,[134] and his sudden switch from earnestness to irony may be just another of the inconsistencies characteristic of *The Tales of Belkin*, but it is more likely that the ironic presence is Pushkin's, and A.G.N. should be read literally.

The tale that follows is, at least at first glance, in keeping with the prologue. When A.G.N. first visits the hero of the tale, the stationmaster Samson Vyrin, he meets a hale and hearty man, the doting father of a fourteen-year-old daughter, Dunia, a pretty and coquettish girl, who willingly gives A.G.N. a farewell kiss when he asks for it. When A.G.N. visits Vyrin again some years later, the stationmaster is alone, depressed, and old-looking. He tells A.G.N. the story of his daughter. Dunia had always been good at calming travelers who were angry because of a lack of horses. On one occasion a young hussar officer named Minskii came to the station, demanded horses, and was ready to raise his whip when he heard there were none; but Dunia's appearance on the scene produced its usual effect. Minskii enjoyed waiting in Dunia's company, and when horses became available, he declared that he was ill. He was put to bed and stayed at Vyrin's house for a couple of days.

It was a Sunday when Minskii was at last able to continue his journey; he offered to drive Dunia as far as the village church. Dunia never came back; her father learned from the coach driver that she had gone on with Minskii. Vyrin fell sick with grief, and when he recovered he went to St. Petersburg, aware that this had been Minskii's destination. There he found Minskii; the young man assured him that Dunia was happy and gave him some money. But this encounter with Minskii did not satisfy the old man: he wished to see Dunia in person just once more. He succeeded in finding her apartment, forced his way in past a protesting maid, and saw her sitting close to Minskii, who was visiting with her. When she caught sight of her father she fainted, and Minskii angrily pushed the old man out of the apartment. Vyrin returned home and had been living by himself ever since, obviously drinking a great deal. It is clear to A.G.N. that he expects Dunia to be abandoned by Minskii and to end up on the street.

Some more years pass, and A.G.N. comes to visit Vyrin's station once more. The post had been abolished; A.G.N. is told that Vyrin is dead. He visits his grave and hears from a village boy that an elegant lady, traveling in a coach-and-six with three children, had also been seeking Vyrin; and when she heard of his death she went to the cemetery and lay prostrate on his grave for a long time.

Some of the sentimental imagery introduced in the prologue is carried over into the narrative. The image of a station-master's "poor abode" (8: 97), mentioned in the first paragraph, recurs in connection with Vyrin, who lives in a "humble but neat dwelling" (8: 98–99). This image is, once more, borrowed from Zhukovskii, who advised that "the whole universe, with all its joys, should be contained in the unpretentious dwelling where one loves and reflects."[135] Vyrin and his daughter create the impression of domestic bliss, of the kind depicted by V. Karlgof in his sentimental idyll "The Stationmaster" (1826)—another target of Pushkin's parody.[136] It is this tranquil family happiness that the cruel young hussar sets out to destroy.

A.G.N. strives to touch the reader's heart at every step. On his second visit, not only does he exclaim about how much Samson had aged (the "laconic" Belkin, one would suppose, would be content with that much), but he enters into detail about the man's "gray hair, the deep furrows lining his face, which had not been shaven for a long time, [and] his hunched back." Not satisfied even with this forceful image, A.G.N. repeats what he has already stated in other words, that Vyrin had become a "feeble old man" (8: 100). Further, Vyrin does not simply put up the sick Minskii (for which there should have been facilities at a wayside station), but yields him his very own bed, which makes the young man's ingratitude appear even more heinous. A civil servant, low-ranking as he may have been, should have nevertheless been able to go to the city by coach, but A.G.N. makes Vyrin take to the road on foot, in order, presumably, to make even more of a martyr of him. Phrases like "his heart began to ache and ache," he was "more dead than alive," "tears welled up in his eyes," "tears welled up in his eyes once more," "with an inexpressible leap of the heart," and "a few seconds of painful anticipation" (8: 102–4) put added emphasis on emotions that should already be clear from the situation. When the sorrowful old man goes to religious services, it is, naturally, to the Church of All the Afflicted

(Tserkov' Vsekh Skorbiashchikh; 8: 104). A.G.N., like Karamzin, often addresses the reader, asks rhetorical questions, bursts into exclamations, uses anaphora to achieve poetic effects, and—what brings him even nearer to the early sentimentalists—favors archaic forms such as *tokmo* ("only"), *stol'* ("so"), *sii* ("these"), and *koi* ("which," 8: 97, 98). Miss K.I.T. succeeded in stamping her sentimental style on "The Blizzard" and on "The Squire's Daughter" only occasionally; A.G.N.'s stylistic presence, though not exclusive, is felt throughout "The Stationmaster."

Like Burmin in "The Blizzard" and Silvio and the Count in "The Shot," Samson Vyrin is given an opportunity to tell his own story up to a point. His speech abounds in colloquialisms, often substandard. But, as we have seen, Pushkin did not like to burden his prose with class speech: after a dozen or so sentences the stationmaster ceases to speak in first person, letting A.G.N. tell the rest of the story for him. He takes over again only after the conclusion of the St. Petersburg episode, in order to lament his daughter's fate. Consequently his narrative, except for dialogues quoted directly, is not given in his style. But often where his style is not maintained, his point of view is. For example, when Minskii slips "something" (8: 103) into the cuff of Samson's sleeve, this is clearly his own, and not an omniscient narrator's, perception of what happened.[137] His point of view is all the more easily maintained because A.G.N. is fully in sympathy with Samson, describing him as his "friend" (8: 105), as the "warmhearted stationmaster" (8: 101), and as "the poor stationmaster" (8: 102). Minskii is no less of a "deceiver" (8: 102) in A.G.N.'s eyes than he is in Vyrin's. And, what also emphasizes his closeness to the indigent stationmaster, A.G.N. worries about the seven rubles it cost him to make a detour in order to accomplish his last visit.

As we have seen, in "The Shot" Pushkin fully exploited the technique of frustrating expectations to great effect. At first sight exactly the opposite seems to be happening in "The Stationmaster": A.G.N. seems to fulfill each and every expectation he raises. The theme of the beating of stationmasters, introduced in the prologue, is taken up by Vyrin as he describes how Dunia used to calm angry gentlemen; and Minskii raises his whip at Vyrin, only to lower it again as he beholds Dunia. The general rule is that gentlemen pretend they want a meal in order to stay with Dunia a little longer; the individual scene presented to us shows Minskii pretending to be ill with the same purpose in mind. We see Dunia sewing a dress before Minskii's arrival; it is her physical attractiveness that will make a lasting impression on the young hussar. She sees A.G.N. to his carriage and gives him a kiss, which prepares the reader for the second occasion she walks to a carriage—this time in order to get in and ride away for good. When ladies give kerchiefs and earrings to Dunia, she is placed dangerously within the reach of all the wealth that passes by the station; and indeed we shall see her in St. Petersburg, decked out in the latest finery, with her fingers glittering with rings (8: 104). "The pots of balsam" (8: 99) are sketched in as symbols of a cheerful household in the first scene, only to be mentioned for their conspicuous absence in the second.[138] Minskii's generous payment for his room and board is a prelude to the scene in which he gives money to the old man in an attempt to compensate him for his daughter. The bed that Vyrin yields to the seducer is the same bed he himself takes to later, sick in earnest. If the story begins with a spring shower, a big storm will play havoc with the lives of the characters; if Vyrin feels instinctively restless after his daughter has gone to church, there is good reason for it; and if A.G.N. is full of forebodings while approaching the station for his second visit, we can safely predict some tragic development in the plot. There is no detail given in this story that does not fit into a pattern or is not followed up in some way.

If A.G.N. is such a trustworthy fulfiller of expectations, can we believe that he would place a set of images in the center of the story's symbolic structure without assigning those images prognostic function? Yet this is precisely what happens. These central images are a set of pictures on the stationmaster's wall depicting the parable of the Prodigal Son; their function is to reverse the pattern of fulfilled expectations.[139]

The first quality that strikes us as we read the description of these pictures is their divergence from the Biblical text. Here are the relevant passages from Luke 15 and "The Stationmaster"; expressions in the tale that conspicuously deviate from the Biblical text are italicized:

Luke 15	"The Stationmaster"
11 And he said, There was a man who had two sons;	
12 And the younger of them said to his father, Father, give me the share of property that falls to me. And he divided his living between them.	In the first [picture], a *venerable* old man, in *nightcap and dressing gown*, was bidding farewell to a *restless* youth who was *hastily* accepting his blessing and a *bag of money*.
13 Not many days later, the younger son gathered all he had and took his journey into a far country, and there he squandered his property in loose living.	
14 And when he had spent everything, a great famine arose in that country, and he began to be in want.	The second one depicted the young man's lewd behavior in *vivid colors*: he was seated at a table, surrounded by *false friends* and *shameless women*.
15 So he went and joined himself to one of the citizens of that country, who sent him into his fields to feed swine.	
16 And he would gladly have fed on the pods that the swine ate; and no one gave him anything.	Farther on, the ruined youth, in rags and with *a three-cornered hat* on his head, was tending swine and sharing their meal; *deep sorrow* and *repentance* were reflected in his features.
17 But when he came to himself he said, How many of my father's hired servants have bread enough and to spare, but I perish here with hunger!	
18 I will arise and go to my father, and I will say to him, Father, I have sinned against heaven and before you;	
19 I am no longer worthy to be called your son; treat me as one of your hired servants.	
20 And he arose and came to his father. But while he was yet at a distance, his father saw him and had compassion, and ran and embraced him and kissed him.	The last picture showed his return to his father: the *warmhearted* old man, in the same *nightcap* and *dressing gown*, was running forward to meet him; the Prodigal Son was on his knees; in the background the
21 And the son said to him: Father, I have sinned against	

heaven and before you; I am no longer worthy to be called your son.

22 But the father said to his servants, Bring quickly the best robe, and put it on him; and put a ring on his hand, and shoes on his feet;

23 And bring the fatted calf and kill it, and let us eat and make merry;

24 For this my son was dead, and is alive again; he was lost, and is found. And they began to make merry.

25 Now his elder son was in the field; and as he came and drew near to the house, he heard music and dancing.

26 And he called one of the servants and asked what this meant.

cook was killing the fatted calf, and the elder brother was asking the servants about the cause of all the rejoicing. (8: 99)

(The Biblical parable continues through six more verses, detailing the ensuing discussion between the father and his other, obedient son, but they are unimportant to an understanding of the stationmaster's pictures.)

A.G.N. concludes his description with the words: "Under each picture I read appropriate verses in German." "Appropriate" translates the Russian word *prilichnyi*, which can also mean "decent" or "proper"—associated meanings that emphasize the didactic nature of the verses. The fact that they are in German is important for two reasons. In the first place, it suggests that the prints were prepared by some German publisher for mass consumption and peddled through the Russian countryside.[140] In an early draft—included in a fragment called "Notes of a Young Man" (1829 or 1830)—Pushkin himself had implied that the pictures catered to a lowbrow taste. There the illustrations to the parable of the Prodigal Son were placed among pictures of "the burying of the cat, a dispute between the red nose and the mighty frost, and the like" (8: 404)—all representing cheap popular prints. Having decided to make use of the parable illustrations in "The Stationmaster," Pushkin eliminated the reference to these other popular prints, probably because in this new context he did not want to risk a farcical effect. Wishing to create an appropriate ambience for the illustrations, he proceeded to place them in the company of "a portrait of General Kulnev and a view of the Khutynskii Monastery" (8: 645), but in the end he decided to make them the only pictures on the stationmaster's wall—presumably because he did not want the reader's attention to stray from their symbolic significance. To emphasize their importance even further, he made his narrator remark that "all this has remained in my memory to this day" (8: 99).

The German language of the verses is also important because Germany was the chief route by which sentimentalism had traveled to Russia. The anachronistic features—the nightcap and dressing gown, the three-cornered hat of the Napoleonic era, and a bag of money instead of the natural goods the original Prodigal Son took with him—reflect a world far removed from the ancient Jews or the early Christians. They reflect the morality of the German burgher of the eighteenth or early nineteenth century.

This is the morality that suits A.G.N.'s sentimental attitudes best. He clearly is very favorably impressed by the pictures, for he attempts to heighten their effect by the epithets he chooses in describing them. The simple Biblical phrase "there was a man" is transformed into a "venerable old man"; the Prodigal Son, instead of simply asking for his share, is "restless" and receives his money "hastily"; later "deep sorrow and repentance" are reflected on his face, which is the same kind of overstatement of emotions that we have seen A.G.N. make elsewhere in the story; the Biblical father, just like Vyrin, is a "warmhearted old man"; and all this is depicted in "vivid colors."

Indeed, at times the reader cannot be sure just what was in pictures and what was read into them by A.G.N.: one can credit a painter's brush with suggesting the looseness of women, but how can the falseness of friends, sitting by a table, be indicated in a picture? The most amusing detail, however, is the image of the Prodigal Son sharing the swine's meal, which in the original is rendered as "partaking of their table" (*razdeliaet s nimi trapezu*). The word *trapeza* (archaic "table") is, of course, used metonymically, signifying "food"; but the original association of table and food breaks down, and the Old Church Slavic flavor of the expression becomes grossly inappropriate in the context of the trough from which swine eat their slop. A.G.N. clearly wants his choice of words to match the great reverence he felt for the moral message of the pictures; and the same kind of incongruity between high style and low subject emerges that we saw in *Goriukhino*.

As he arrives for his second visit, A.G.N. emphasizes that he "immediately recognized the pictures illustrating the parable of the Prodigal Son" (8: 100). This repeated emphasis lends the pictures the kind of premonitory meaning that the reader of romantic literature was used to. One is reminded, for example, of the carving of the black bull's head, with the legend "I bide my time," that portends the downfall of Sir William Ashton's family in *The Bride of Lammermoor*. A.G.N.'s general trustworthiness is a further enticement to the reader to accept the pictures as portentous. So many signs have been followed up, so many expectations have been fulfilled in the story, that the reader cannot doubt the outcome of the plot: it is only too natural that Dunia, the Prodigal Daughter, should come on hard times in St. Petersburg and return to her father, repentant.

Several details, in accord with the pictures themselves, seem to point to such a denouement. Encouraging his daughter to take a ride with Minskii, Vyrin says, "His Honor's not a wolf; he won't eat you" (8: 102), which prepares us for the old man's later declaration, "I shall bring my lost sheep home" (8: 103).[141] This detail refers the reader back to Luke 15, for the parable of the Prodigal Son immediately follows—indeed elucidates—that of the lost sheep. In both parables, the dear ones that have been lost are found. Further, when Samson Vyrin begs Minskii, "You have had your fun with her; do not ruin her needlessly" (8: 103), we are reminded of the false friends and shameless lovers of the parable and do not doubt for a moment that Dunia will indeed end up on the street. Indeed, the old man explicitly says as much. "Anything can happen," he predicts. "She is not the first, nor will she be the last, to be seduced by some rake passing through, to be kept for a while and then discarded. There are many of them in Petersburg, of these foolish young ones: today attired in satin and velvet, but tomorrow, verily I say, sweeping the streets with the riffraff of the alehouse" (8: 105). Sweeping the streets with the riffraff, Dunia would of course remember her aging father and come home.

In sympathy with Vyrin and sharing his view of the world, A.G.N. also accepts his friend's interpretation of the pictures. This is evident from some other literary references that he ties to the parable of the Prodigal Son. The most obvious reference, as we have seen from the prologue, is to Karamzin's "Poor Liza."[142] Not only is it another tale about a child who betrays a parent and comes on hard times, but even some of its minor details are reproduced in "The Stationmaster." Liza, for instance, notices her unfaithful Erast riding along a street in an elegant carriage, just as Vyrin notices Minskii. Erast puts a hundred rubles in her pocket in much the same way as Minskii thrusts money in the stationmaster's cuff. Both Liza and Vyrin are shown the door by servants; both Liza and Dunia faint after a fateful meeting. The Russian reader of the 1820's would notice these parallels and expect Dunia's downfall. So sure is A.G.N. himself of the analogous fates of the two heroines that he keeps calling Dunia "poor Dunia" (8: 103, 105).

Indeed convention—not only of sentimentalism, but eventually also of romanticism—demanded that the victim of seduction perish. Baratynskii's Eda, in the verse tale bearing her name (1826), pines away after her hussar leaves, and even Pushkin's own Water-Nymph throws herself in the Dnieper after her Prince tells her he is marrying someone else. The stationmaster's exclamation "Oh, Dunia, Dunia!" (8: 100) echoes both Karamzin's "Oh, Liza, Liza!" and Baratynskii's "Oh, Eda, Eda!"

But in this instance A.G.N. lets his reader down. In all likelihood he does not do this by design: rather, his own expectations have been frustrated. Try as he might, he cannot fit life into the mold of *petit bourgeois* morality. The analogy between the parable of the Prodigal Son (as perceived by a Philistine) and Dunia's fate proves to be false. In fact the parallels only serve to draw attention to the contrasts: unlike the Biblical father, the stationmaster himself encourages his daughter to ride away with Minskii; Dunia takes no bag of money from her father; she runs away from poverty rather than recklessly abandoning a life of contentment; the father, rather than the child, appears to sue for favors at another man's doorstep; and Dunia, even if she wished to return, would have no home to come back to, for it is her father, rather than she, who ends up in dissipation. The details that reverse the parable in the most subtle manner are items of clothing: in the picture it is the father who is in night-cap and dressing gown—that is, wearing the symbols of domestic comfort and stability—but in the story we see Minskii receiving the stationmaster in just such garments. Moreover, in the parable (though, admittedly, this is not mentioned in the description of the pictures) the father orders his servants to put a ring on his repentant son's hand, but in the story it is through Minskii's generosity that Dunia's fingers glitter with rings.

Pushkin's manipulation of his narrator is most successful in "The Stationmaster" because A.G.N.'s narrow point of view is never ostensibly abandoned, yet vistas open to a broader understanding of life. This creates a dual perspective, reminiscent of that in *Poltava*. Like Mazepa, the characters in "The Station-master" are susceptible of different interpretations: some critics see Vyrin as a poor old man, a victim of corrupting social forces that have taken away his last comfort in life, his beloved daughter; [143] others see Dunia as a justified and successful rebel against social and moral stagnation. [144]

Despite the narrator's naïve overstatement of his case, a sympathetic appraisal of Samson Vyrin is indeed achieved, for he is undoubtedly the victim of a cruel personal and social destiny. Yet this sympathetic view is at times obstructed by a ludicrous presentation. Just as Miss K.I.T. (or Belkin) thought a quotation from *Woe from Wit* would enhance the beauty of her description of the end of the war, so A.G.N. seeks to embellish his narrative with literary references—with the same results. This is, for instance, the comment he makes after Vyrin has just finished his tale of misfortune: "Such was the story of my friend, the old stationmaster—a story often interrupted by tears, which he wiped away with the skirt of his coat in a graphic gesture, like the zealous Terentich in Dmitriev's beautiful ballad" (8: 105). The reference is to I. I. Dmitriev's humorous poem "A Caricature" (1791), which relates the return of a soldier to his homestead after twenty years of army service. He finds his house deserted, except for one old serf, Terentich, who tells him that his wife kept bad company, was arrested, and has not been heard of for five years. This is how Terentich concludes his tale: [145]

> "Woe's me! Alackaday! My Lord!,"
> The old man answered.
> "Woe's me!," and, mopping and mowing, he
> Wiped his tears away with the sleeve of his coat.

The soldier, seeing no point in grieving over his lost wife, re-marries and lives happily ever after. A.G.N., one has to assume, forgot the context of Terentich's picturesque gesture; other-wise he would not have tried to arouse sympathy for Vyrin by this reference.

In certain passages the same down-to-earth unromantic view of life that we saw in the other Belkin tales intrudes into "The Stationmaster." Remarks like "These tears were partly induced by the five glasses of rum punch that he had swilled down" (8: 105) are presumably the work of Belkin; as in the other tales, they tend to destroy the romantic atmosphere. Most charac-teristic from this point of view is the description of how Vyrin went back to try and pick up the money Minskii gave him after first throwing it to the ground and trampling on it in anger. Such notes, discordant with the general sentimental tenor of the tale, alert the reader to the possibility of a more realistic appraisal of the stationmaster.

Indeed, should our sympathies be undivided? Does Dunia de-serve no pity at all? There is certainly no direct indication that she was mistreated by her father: she does her chores around the house, but there is nothing unusual about that, considering her social station; she seems perfectly happy when we see her at home. Yet two little remarks Vyrin drops incidentally—that she was "just like her late mother," and that "the whole house-hold rested on her" (8: 98, 100)—imply that Vyrin expected her to act as a substitute for his wife. Jan van der Eng suggests that at times—especially when Vyrin pursues Dunia to St. Peters-burg and comments on her beauty—the stationmaster behaves more like a jealous husband than a worried father. [146] The sym-bolic role of Vyrin's bed, on which we see Dunia seated twice (first alone, sewing, and later with Minskii, while nursing him), seems to point in the same direction. Finally, Vyrin's complicity in raising her to be flirtatious—to please men on his account—also introduces a discordant note into a relationship that is supposed to be one of father to daughter. However that may be, a father-daughter relationship in which the physical and psychological welfare of the father depends exclusively on the presence of the daughter can certainly be suffocating. It is interesting, from this point of view, to take a look at the sources Pushkin used and the stages of planning he went through in shaping the Vyrin-Dunia relationship.

According to Viazemskii, one day when he and A. A. Delvig, Pushkin's closest friend, were traveling together to a Petersburg suburb, Delvig told him the outline of a story he was planning to write (but never actually wrote).[147] The narrator of the story, Delvig said, had to pass by a certain house on his way home day after day, and he was struck by the changes he could see in the house through the window. At first only one middle-aged man, who looked like a retired officer, lived there; then the house was redecorated and a pretty young woman, obviously the officer's bride, moved in; the couple seemed to live happily for a while, but then a young man started frequenting the house; all the wife's attention seemed to be fastened on the visitor; and finally, some months later, the wife could no longer be seen, the husband had visibly aged, and a wet nurse was carrying around a baby whom the man did not seem to cherish much. Viazemskii says he does not remember for sure how Delvig was planning to conclude the story, but he has a vague recollection that the young woman was to die under some circumstances.

Although Viazemskii does not mention Pushkin's presence in their carriage, he was probably there, for his "Fragment of Recollections About Delvig" (n.d.) seems to refer to this occasion.[148] In this fragment Pushkin relates that he and Viazemskii set out from St. Petersburg for Moscow on August 10, 1830, and Delvig decided to accompany them for the first stages of the journey. At first Delvig was quiet because he was not used to early rising, but after they had stopped for breakfast at an inn, he grew lively. "The breakfast at the inn," Pushkin notes, "reminded him of a story he was planning to write. He had the

habit of turning his works over in his head for long periods
even if they were to be only short pieces. He loved to develop
his poetical projects in conversation; we usually knew about
his splendid creations several years before he wrote them
down" (12: 338).

Since Pushkin's ride with Viazemskii and Delvig took place
only a month before he wrote "The Stationmaster," it is likely
that he was influenced to some extent by Delvig's project.[149]
One is led to this conclusion also by the outline Pushkin jotted
down prior to writing his story:

A discourse on stationmasters. Unfortunate and warmhearted people
as a rule. My friend, the widowed stationmaster. His daughter. That
route has been abolished. I rode by it recently. I did not find the daughter. The story of the daughter. A clerk in love with her. The clerk goes
after her to Petersburg. Sees her during holiday festivities. When he
returns, he finds the father dead. The grave outside the village. I ride
by. The clerk is dead. The coach driver tells me about the daughter.
(8: 661)

We do not know exactly what role Pushkin planned to assign
to the clerk—whether he was to be the woman's husband or
merely her admirer—but it is significant that her desertion
would have broken up a man-woman relationship. If there is a
shade of just such a relationship between Dunia and her father
in the final version of "The Stationmaster," it originates from
Delvig's project and Pushkin's own first outline.

This seems to support the view that Dunia is running away
from a suffocatingly close relationship with her father as well
as from the boredom and poverty of provincial life. The description in the epigraph—"Despot of the posting station"—
may well imply, as one critic suggests, Vyrin's emotional tyranny over his daughter.[150] Moreover, the fact that Pushkin
insisted on restoring Vyrin's original first name, "Samson,"
after it had been misprinted as "Simeon" in the first edition
(8: 660, note 3), indicates that he wanted Vyrin to be associated
with a Biblical hero who had been deprived of his power by
a woman. Finally, Dostoevskii's interpretation of the Vyrin-
Dunia relationship is also instructive: Makar Devushkin of
Poor Folk (1846) fully identifies with Pushkin's character and
threatens to drink himself to death if Varvara deserts him (see

his letter of July 1). The irony of the situation in Dostoevskii's novel is that Varvara, who is no relative of Makar's, insists on being treated like a daughter every time Makar makes a feeble attempt to establish himself as a man; it testifies to Dostoevskii's sharp eye that he discerned the kernel of such an ambiguous relationship in Pushkin's story. With this in mind, we are not so surprised to hear that Vyrin would sooner see his daughter in the grave than in Minskii's arms.

Whether or not Dunia's elopement can be justified, she certainly feels guilty about it: although she is going voluntarily, she cries all through the first two stages of the journey; she faints when she beholds her father in her apartment; and she lies prostrate on his grave for a long time. All these details make us judge her conduct less harshly. Besides, there is something attractive in her daring. Against all odds, she makes a dash for a better life. What she takes is a calculated risk: she might very well end up as her father expects—as Katia Maslova was to do in Tolstoi's *Resurrection* (1899)—but she throws a challenge to fate. In his 1829 lyric "Reminiscences of Tsarskoe Selo" Pushkin had likened himself to a Prodigal Son; there is no doubt he felt kinship with Vyrin's Prodigal Daughter.

But it is not only the author's divided sympathies that leave the story open to various interpretations. If the parable of the Prodigal Son were fully reversed—if we saw Dunia happily married at the end—the issues would be much clearer. In that case we could simply say that the stationmaster and his friend A.G.N. applied the wrong set of moral standards to life and were deceived. But in fact the final outcome is not the exact opposite to A.G.N.'s expectations: it is neither their confirmation nor their full reversal, for we are not told whether Dunia is married or not.

This is a story, as we have seen, in which most questions are answered and most details conscientiously followed up—either in a straight line or reversed—but there is one question that is asked twice, yet left conspicuously unanswered to the very end. Approaching Vyrin's house for the second time, A.G.N. says: "I remembered the old stationmaster's daughter, and the thought of seeing her again gave me joy. I told myself that the old stationmaster might well have been replaced, and that Dunia was likely to have married" (8: 99). Having roused Vyrin from sleep and asked how his daughter was doing, A.G.N. receives an uncertain answer, to which he rejoins: "So she's married, is she?" (8: 100). If A.G.N. were true to himself, he would answer this question in no uncertain terms; but in the end all the information we are given is this: "'A wonderful lady,' replied the urchin; 'she was traveling in a coach-and-six with three little masters, a nurse, and a black pug'" (8: 106). Is Dunia married, then, or not? Some critics have assumed she is, despite the scarce evidence of the text.[151] Yet she could equally well still be a kept woman. If she is, she is certainly kept well; and the fact that she has had three children indicates that her position must be fairly secure. But it was by no means unusual for nineteenth-century noblemen to refuse to marry mistresses who were not of their own social status: one has only to recall the legally ambiguous position of A. I. Herzen's mother. And an unmarried woman could be cast away, "little masters" and all, at any time; Anna Karenina would probably have felt less insecure if she had been able to get a divorce and marry Vronskii. Thus in my own view Dunia's fate is still in the balance. She is not sweeping the street with the alehouse riffraff; nor has she come back, as the Prodigal Daughter, to sue at her father's door. But her future is uncertain: otherwise, as a married woman, she would have come to make it up with her father much sooner.

The critics' contradictory interpretations of Dunia remind one of the opposing views Belinskii and Dostoevskii took of Tatiana; the one condemned her for accepting the morals of her society and rejecting Onegin; the other extolled her as a paragon of conjugal virtue.[152] Such divergent interpretations are possible because Chapter Eight of *Onegin* is not without a certain moral ambiguity: each endowed with independent existence and each commanding the author's affection, Onegin and Tatiana act as they are compelled to do by their own natures; to judge them each for cherishing the other at the wrong time is as pedantic as deprecating Chekhov's characters for their unhappiness. Ambiguity—a result of the author's identification with all sides—is a concomitant of Pushkin's highest artistic achievements. It is a quality particularly pronounced in the works of the Boldino autumn of 1830. One can no more say for sure whether Onegin is drawn to Tatiana in the last chapter by her prominent social position—as she suspects—or has merely grown mature enough to be able to genuinely appreciate her, than one can decide whether Don Juan has genuinely "learned the value of transient life" (8: 157) since he fell in love with Doña Anna or is just saying this as a seductive ploy.[153] "The Stationmaster," with its complexities and ambiguities, rises above the other tales of Belkin, to the level of *Onegin* and *The Stone Guest.*

Having experienced difficulties with an omniscient mode of narration, Pushkin turned to the use of imaginary narrators chiefly with parody and stylistic experiment in mind. Four of Belkin's five tales reflect—to varying degrees—his parodic design. But in the fifth he transcended parody and, putting a conventional technique to a novel use, created one of the masterpieces of nineteenth-century Russian prose.

IV. 'Roslavlev' and 'Dubrovskii'

I

The Tales of Belkin were not "stern prose," nor did they convey "thoughts and thoughts" in a "metaphysical language" without decorative frills. If the demands Pushkin had put on prose in the 1820's are anything to judge by, he had failed to achieve his purpose. Far from being a detached observer of the scene, he had actively participated in a masquerade with pretty misses disguised as country wenches. Although his assumed roles had resulted in some considerable accomplishments—such as "The Shot" and, even more so, "The Stationmaster"—they involved him in the same histrionic gestures that he had sought to cast off in turning to prose.

The next time Pushkin decided to engage in similar play-acting he reverted to his original disguise as an obtuse literary critic. His two articles "The Triumph of Friendship, or Aleksandr Anfimovich Orlov Justified" and "A Few Words About Mr. Bulgarin's Pinkie and Other Matters," both published in 1831 under the pseudonym Feofilakt Kosichkin,[1] were very close in manner to the Publisher's Introduction to *The Tales of Belkin* and to the prologue to *A History of the Village of Goriukhino.* Their connection with Pushkin's earlier, unpublished critical sketches is even more obvious: for instance, Feofilakt Kosichkin echoes the persona of the fragment "If the Appellation 'Lover of Native Literature'" when he boasts, imagining himself at the zenith of enlightenment, that he has not missed one of the "profound and brilliant compositions on politics, the exact sciences, and pure literature" (11: 212) that have come off the press in Russia during the past decade. This technique of hiding the author behind a simpleton suited the purposes of satirical journalism very well indeed; but it had obvious limitations in the fictional genres.

In the summer of 1831, while he was readying *The Tales of Belkin* for publication, Pushkin wrote a few chapters of a projected historical novel under the title *Roslavlev*. These chapters were also told by a fictitious narrator, but this time the use of such a narrator led to a contradiction that Pushkin could never resolve.[2]

An openly polemical piece of writing, *Roslavlev* is directed against M. N. Zagoskin's novel by the same title, published in June 1831. Zagoskin says in the Preface to his novel that the kernel of his story—Polina's engagement to Roslavlev, her unpatriotic marriage to the Frenchman Sénicour during the Napoleonic invasion, and her eventual demise—were all taken from real life.[3] Pushkin's narrator, in her turn, claims to be Roslavlev's sister, writing her own memoirs in order to defend Polina's "shade" (8: 149). She does indeed make an effort, on the first few pages, to accomplish this task. Instead of an indifferent, cosmopolitan Polina, she presents us with a high-minded young lady, at first indignant over her compatriots' gallomania and later adamantly opposed to the ostentatious show of nationalism that becomes the fashion in her social circles with the onset of the Napoleonic War.[4] These pages have persuaded some critics that Pushkin's purpose was to contrast a more broad-minded patriotism to Zagoskin's primitive nationalism.[5]

On the following pages, however, Pushkin's narrator seems to lose sight of her avowed intention, and the portrait of Polina that eventually emerges is no more flattering than that painted by Zagoskin. Zagoskin's Polina meets and falls in love with Sénicour before the war, but since he is already married she has no hope of ever being united with him. Back in Russia but still in love with Sénicour, she tries to discourage Roslavlev's attentions, and even after agreeing to be engaged to him, contrives to postpone their wedding several times. When Sénicour, by this time widowed, turns up at her house as a wounded prisoner of war, she marries him and eventually deserts to the French side with him. Although she betrays Roslavlev and she lacks patriotic feeling, her heart, at least, is constant.

Pushkin's Polina, by contrast, does not meet Sénicour before the war; her engagement to Roslavlev is as much her own doing as it is his; and it is only after her engagement, while Roslavlev is sacrificing his life on the battlefield, that she develops an interest in Sénicour. The implication may be that her patriotism is compatible with a sense of universal humanity that transcends a narrow-minded nationalism: despite her hatred of Napoleonic aggression, she is capable of valuing the qualities of an individual Frenchman. Yet within the moral context of the story—given her own passionate avowals of patriotic fervor—her infidelity to the Russian soldier Roslavlev is as unsatisfactory as was the conduct of Maria of "The Blizzard," to whom the memory of her Vladimir only "seemed" to be sacred. Further, the news (presumably false) of Roslavlev's death might have been viewed by the narrator as an excuse for Polina's conduct, since it made her think her hand was free. But the moral implications of this reaction are questionable: after all, Roslavlev's death is hardly the kind of news that could be expected to put a patriotic girl in the mood to marry her betrothed's enemy and desert with him to the other side. (That is, obviously, the plot development the narrator has in mind: otherwise she would not call Polina "unfortunate," would not mention her death, and would not identify her with Zagoskin's heroine.) Pushkin's narrator, as it turns out, has not been able to vindicate the fickle heart of her friend. What diverted her from her original purpose?

We are supposed to be reading her first-person recollections, but since she is only a passive participant in the events she recollects, the narrative appears almost as impersonal as if it were told in the third person. At the beginning a few token efforts are made to set her apart as a lady narrator: she apologizes for the "feebleness of her pen" and mentions how she was brought out in society, exchanging the schoolroom and tutors for endless balls, immersing herself in a "whirl of gaiety." But she adds in the same breath that at this early stage in her life she was "not yet a thinking person," implying that she was later to become one (8: 149). The recollections she writes witness that she is a thinking person with insight into the motives of other people's actions. Her perceptive mind draws her close to Pushkin himself, and when it comes to expressing literary opinions, she appears as much Pushkin's mouthpiece as Liza of *A Novel in Letters* was. As the difference between her and Pushkin becomes obliterated, the singleness of her purpose is also lost. Instead of defending her friend's "shade" one-sidedly, she offers a many-sided representation of a full-blooded person.

In undertaking *Roslavlev*, we may note, Pushkin was not initiating a duel of wits with Zagoskin: on the contrary, it was Zagoskin who had challenged him by thinly veiled allusions to *Onegin* in his *Roslavlev*.[6] Not only did Zagoskin borrow the names Lenskii and Zaretskii from *Onegin*; he also gave his Polina a younger sister by the name of Olga. His withdrawn, mysterious Polina parallels Tatiana; but her sister, with her open, simple, cheerful nature, represents an improved copy of Pushkin's Olga. Pushkin's Lenskii falls in love with the simple Olga; Roslavlev chooses the complicated Polina. Lenskii's friend Onegin tells him he should have chosen Tatiana; Roslavlev's friend Zaretskii says: "What a pity it is not Olga you are marrying."[7] Eventually, Polina proves to have been the wrong choice, and Roslavlev ends up marrying Olga. Zagoskin's message seems to be that the simple Olgas are preferable to the complicated Tatianas and Polinas. What is unfair about his presentation is that, though he insists on Polina's complexity (see, for instance, Roslavlev's tirade about her extraordinary capacity for self-sacrifice in Chapter One, Volume Four), he leaves her character undeveloped and unexplained. The need to elucidate her character must have captivated Pushkin, and he ended up doing just that, instead of letting his narrator whitewash her friend's conduct.[8]

In Pushkin's description, Polina is as defiant of social opinion as Zinaida Volskaia. As the narrator says, quoting from Chateaubriand's *René*, she could never be happy because happiness can only be found along the trodden path.[9] Endowed with a "masculine loftiness" of mind (8: 154), she cannot accept the role assigned to women in her society. She makes friends with Madame de Staël, and her idols are women like

Charlotte Corday, the assassin of the French Terrorist Marat; Marfa Boretskaia, the fifteenth-century mayoress of Novgorod; and Princess Ekaterina Dashkova, famous not only as an author, scholar, and memoirist, but also as one of the engineers of the palace revolution of 1762. She toys with the idea of assassinating Napoleon by her own hand.

But her unhappiness with her feminine identity involves more than an independent mind and a strong character. If these alone motivated her, she would find it sufficient to say to Roslavlev: "To some people, honor and fatherland are mere trifles. While their brothers are dying on the battlefields, they play the fool in drawing rooms." With this, one would think, she has made her point; but she continues, translating the question of patriotic honor into terms of a man-woman relationship: "I wonder if any woman would sink so low as to allow such a buffoon to pretend to be in love with her" (8: 154). The narrator imagines that Roslavlev's impertinent answer— making it plain that he does not feel obliged to speak seriously with a woman—will enrage Polina. "I thought," she writes, "they had quarreled forever, but I was wrong: my brother's insolence appealed to Polina" (8: 154). Further, the narrator explains that Polina forgave Roslavlev because she saw his true patriotism behind the façade of pleasantries; yet the impression had already been created that she likes to challenge her men boldly and be boldly challenged by them, anticipating Dostoevskii's heroines. (One is reminded, for instance, of the initial stages of Katerina Ivanovna's relationship with Dmitrii Karamazov.)

In this connection, Polina's engagement to Roslavlev may imply more than her respect for a man who has volunteered for the army: she is, in a way, exacting the sacrifice of his life as a price of her love, just as Cleopatra of *Egyptian Nights* was to do with her men. When Roslavlev, far from feeling like a sacrificial lamb, writes humorous letters from the front, she is angered. "You must admit," she says to his sister, "your Aleksei is the most trivial man. Even under the present circumstances, from the very fields of battle, he manages to write letters totally lacking in meaning. What sort of conversation will he have for me in the course of quiet family life?" (8: 156). The phrase "quiet family life," missing from the first draft (8: 737), seems to have been added by Pushkin in order to emphasize her revulsion at the thought of a marital relationship that promised to lack the intense emotional give-and-take of her engagement. Polina loses interest in Roslavlev and turns her attention to Sénicour for very good reasons: on the one hand, the Frenchman's reserve and personal dignity impress her; on the other, she can insult him with impunity since he is a prisoner of war. When the news comes, for instance, that Moscow is burning, she vents her anger on him. The narrator's playful description—"Captured by the enemy, the wounded knight falls in love with the castle's noble proprietress" (8: 157)—further underscores Polina's superior position. Although the story is not continued beyond the time when word of Roslavlev's death is received, it is clear that a complicated relationship—better suited to Polina's psychological needs than her previous engagement—is to develop between her and Sénicour.

The basic contradiction in the structure of Pushkin's *Roslavlev* is, then, that the narrator and the narrative are not integrated. At first the narrator speaks in her own voice, pursuing her own goals, but then Pushkin replaces her altogether and draws a complex character inconsistent with the narrator's original intentions. All this showed how much he was longing to throw off the constraints inherent in a stylized narrative voice.

Another reason for abandoning fictitious narrators was that *The Tales of Belkin*, published later in 1831, were not received in the press as well as Pushkin might have hoped. Not only were the critics unanimous in calling the tales trifling though entertaining, but the reviewer of the *Moscow Telegraph* poked fun at the very technique of literary disguise, comparing it to the trick of a child who imagined he would not be recognized if he covered his face with his hands.[10]

2

One attempt to develop an omniscient narrative stance involved a novel that Pushkin worked on in September 1831. All that survives of this project, which became known post-humously as *A Novel at a Caucasian Spa*, is one fragment, running to two pages—probably the very beginning of the novel—and three different plot outlines, each accompanied by notes amplifying the themes.[11]

Although Sir Walter Scott's *St. Ronan's Well* and A. A. Bestuzhev-Marlinskii's "An Evening at a Caucasian Watering Place in 1824" might have served as literary models for this novel, it was based on real-life people and events, and was probably conceived by Pushkin while he was traveling through the Caucasus in 1829. It was common knowledge in those regions that a Moscow lady, M. I. Rimskaia-Korsakova, whom Pushkin knew quite well, had been ambushed and robbed by natives as she had journeyed in a convoy from one Caucasian spa to another in the summer of 1828, and that an attempt had been made to kidnap her daughter Aleksandra, the object of Pushkin's passion at one time.[12] Pushkin's plot outlines, though they differ somewhat in detail, all seem to be centered on this kidnaping episode.

As far as one can make out, the novel would have begun with the departure of the Korsakov (or in the two-page fragment, Tomskii) family from Moscow, an episode to be followed by a satirical description of society at the watering places. The plot line was then intended to run something like this: a notorious cardsharp and daredevil by the name of Iakubovich (Pushkin obviously had in mind the Decembrist A. I. Iakubovich as he had known him in his pre-1825 days) falls in love with Korsakova's daughter (whose fictional name was sometimes Masha, sometimes Alina); rejected by her, he arranges to kidnap her with the aid of his Circassian friends; another young Russian, called Granev in some of the outlines, saves her and eventually kills Iakubovich in a duel. What must have been a very unpleasant and degrading experience for the Korsakovs had thus been turned into a romantic plot by Pushkin. However, the one fragment of the novel that he actually wrote is far from romantic.

One of the interesting features of this short fragment is its mode of narration. An omniscient narrator describes the Tomskii household, in a state of disarray prior to the family's departure for the Caucasus, and proceeds to introduce the mother in the following way:

The head of the household herself, a forty-five-year-old lady, sat in her bedroom, going over the accounts brought to her by her corpulent steward, who was now standing in front of her with his hands behind his back and with his right foot thrust forward. Katerina Petrovna pretended to be fully conversant with all the ins and outs of the management of her estate, but her questions and suggestions revealed the ignorance of a noblewoman about such affairs: they occasionally brought a barely perceptible smile to the steward's dignified face, though he nonetheless went into the details of all the required explanations with great indulgence. (8: 412)

This passage is very like Chapter Three of Tolstoi's *Childhood* (1852), though one could not have influenced the other, since Pushkin's fragment was not published until 1881. In Tolstoi's description, too, the steward Iakov is respectful and indulgent with his master, but clearly knows more about the estate than he, and can steer him in any direction he wishes. There is, however, a great difference between the two scenes in technique. Tolstoi's is observed by little Nikolai, the first-person narrator of the autobiographical novel: it is he who notices that the more excited his father gets as he argues with the steward, the faster Iakov twirls his fingers behind his back; the scene is given entirely as it was imprinted on the child's mind.[13] Pushkin's passage, by contrast, seems to give first Tomskaia's view of her steward (she must be the one who sees his corpulence and his posture); then the steward's impression of his mistress (it is he to whom her questions and suggestions reveal ignorance); and finally returns again to her vantage point (for who notices his barely perceptible smile if it is not she?).

Following this scene, the arrival of a certain Praskovia Ivanovna is announced. Tomskaia tells her about her plan to seek a cure for her and her daughter's ailments in the hot springs of the Caucasus, and then offers to show her visitor the newfangled carriage, loaded with every sort of amenity, that she has just bought. "The coachmen pulled the carriage out of the shed," the narrator continues. "Katerina Petrovna told them to open the doors; she got in and rummaged through everything, turning up all the cushions, pulling out all the drawers, revealing all the secrets and conveniences, letting up all the blinds, displaying all the mirrors, and turning all the pouches inside out—in other words, she acted very nimbly and energetically for a sick woman" (8: 413). The question arises: who makes this last observation?

One would think it is Praskovia Ivanovna, but in other ways the impressions of the scene are not filtered through her mind. The point of view seems to be shifting as fast here as it was in *The Blackamoor of Peter the Great*. In fact, however, the technique is not quite the same, for though the narrator here is as faceless a personality as the one in *The Blackamoor*, he is far more colorful. The impression gained by the reader is not that of disorientation: rather, it is a feeling that an omnipercipient eye—a very mobile movie camera—keeps changing its direction and focus, and that an omniscient mind is putting its interpretation on the scene. This new narrator-figure—all-encompassing yet lacking personal identity—anticipates the one to be used in *Dubrovskii*.

Using different narrative voices in *The Tales of Belkin* meant endowing each narrator with characteristic speech habits, which almost amounted to creating characters. In that sense the *Tales* provided Pushkin with excellent practice in characterization. In subsequent works all he had to do was to transfer the characteristic speech habits from narrators to heroes, at the same time creating a new, impersonal narrator whose task would be simply to set the stage for the action.

The matrons who step before us in *A Novel at a Caucasian Spa* could have been narrators of some Belkin tales. The dialogue between them reveals each as an individual. We soon learn about Praskovia Ivanovna, for instance, that she is privy to all the small and large secrets of Moscow social life: what brought her over to Katerina Petrovna's house were rumors about the Tomskii family's plans to go to the Caucasus. It must have been no small curiosity that made her, as she says, "drag herself" (8: 413) all the way from Basmannaia to Arbat (two districts of Moscow), for she is a great enemy of stirring abroad, as witnessed by her exclamations against the Tomskiis' traveling plans. She betrays both a blunt old woman's lack of tact when she urges the sickly young Masha to find herself a husband in the Caucasus and a seasoned Muscovite's common sense when she remarks, in answer to Katerina Petrovna, that though a good man may take a girl without a dowry it is still better to have a dowry.

Katerina Petrovna herself emerges as a person given to fussing about her health and fond of pious commonplaces. Short as this fragment is, it reflects great care on Pushkin's part. The manuscript shows, for example, that originally Tomskaia was to lament her daughter's poor health (8: 963), but subsequently Pushkin made her complain about her own (8: 412). Similarly, the conversation about finding a husband in the Caucasus was originally to take place between just Masha and Praskovia Ivanovna (8: 964), but subsequently Pushkin made Tomskaia answer for her daughter (8: 413). Both changes show Pushkin's effort to sharpen her features. What is even more obvious from the manuscript is that Pushkin was adding new idiomatic expressions at every step, using the middle and upper gentry's vernacular.

The tiny fragment of *Caucasian Spa* was clearly a new achievement for Pushkin the prose stylist, but it is difficult to see how he could have reconciled it with the romantic plot that was to follow. The contradiction between the two probably explains why he never got seriously involved in the project.

Sometime in the early 1830's Pushkin also jotted down the following few lines, which probably reflect an idea for a satirical story about Petersburg society: "N. chooses Nevskii Avenue as his confidant—he confides all his domestic troubles and family grievances to it.—They pity him.—He is satisfied" (8: 429). But this project never developed any further either, and Pushkin did not make another serious attempt at writing fiction until October 1832, when he began *Dubrovskii*.

3

The beginning of the 1830's was a turbulent period in both Russia and Western Europe. News of the French and Polish revolutions intruded on Pushkin's interest, so much so that, looking for the origins of social unrest, he was contemplating writing a history of the Great French Revolution. The inner provinces of Russia, too, saw the outbreak of rebellion following a widespread cholera epidemic. As we have seen, the epidemic and riots were very much on Pushkin's mind while he was quarantined in Boldino in the fall of 1830, and inspired him to begin *A History of the Village of Goriukhino*. These topics received considerable attention in his diaries and letters as well.

Several scenes of rebellion he recorded show that he was interested both in what triggered such events and in the human element in them. The following account, which he jotted down on July 26, 1831, is characteristic of his concern. It deals with Nicholas I's personal involvement in putting down a mutiny at a military settlement in Novgorod Province.

Several officers and physicians had been killed by the mutineers. Their deputies came to Izhora seeking pardon and showing a statement, extracted from one of the officers by force before his death, according to which he and the physicians had been poisoning people. The Emperor spoke with the deputies and sent them back, telling them to obey the orders of Count Orlov, who had been sent to the settlement as soon as the first news of the mutiny was received. The Emperor also promised the deputies to come to their settlement in person, adding: "I will pardon you then." The mutiny has been put down, it seems, or if it has not, it soon will be, thanks to the Emperor's presence.

Such extreme measures as the Emperor's personal appearance, however, must not be taken at just any provocation. The simple people must not get accustomed to the Emperor as if he were an ordinary person. It is the duty of the police to quell the riots of the rabble: the Emperor's voice should not threaten with grapeshot or the whip. He must not be in personal contact with the people. The mob would soon cease fearing his mysterious power and would become presumptuous in its intercourse with him. It would soon start demanding his appearance as an obligatory ritual in any riot. Until now the Emperor, who is endowed with eloquence, has been the one and only orator; but it might happen that a voice from the crowd would answer back. Such exchanges would be indecent: debates on street corners soon turn into the howl and the roar of the hungry beast. (12: 199)

The scene was rife with possibilities for fictional treatment. One can sense Pushkin mentally coining the phrases that would ring out in the middle of the crowd.

The troubles were not confined to the provinces: even before the disturbances in Novgorod Province, the cholera epidemic had spread to St. Petersburg as well. In times like these it was difficult for Pushkin to keep his mind on purely literary matters. He wrote to P. A. Viazemskii in August 1831: "When such tragedies take place under your eyes, you have no time to think about the comic dog show of our literature" (14: 205). This was said with particular reference to "Mr. Bulgarin's Pinkie," on which Pushkin's work had proceeded slowly; but the broader implication was a general mood against writing merely for entertainment. The real stuff of literature, Pushkin intimated, was to be found at the military settlements and in the cholera-ravaged regions where the riots were taking place.

In order to understand the social processes behind these events, one needed, above all, facts—both contemporary and historical. "I must confess," wrote Viazemskii, reflecting the yearning of Pushkin's circle for factual information, "that I would gladly give away the greater part of our belles-lettres in exchange for a few volumes of *Memoirs*, for a few *Nestor Chronicles* about events, mores, and people neglected by history."[14] Pushkin, following the same impulse, became more and more involved in historical research during the 1830's. In the summer of 1831 Nicholas agreed to take him back into government service as a historian, with permission to use official archives in his studies for a history of Peter the Great. *Dubrovskii*, the next fictional work he attempted to write, was born of this hunger for verifiable facts.

In the middle of September 1832 Pushkin went to Moscow for a brief stay. At the end of that month he reported to his wife: "An idea for a novel has come to my mind; I shall probably set to work on it" (15: 33). What had happened was that his friend P. V. Nashchokin had told him a true story that he thought suitable for a novel. Nashchokin's role in suggesting the theme was subsequently recorded by P. I. Bartenev:

The novel *Dubrovskii* was inspired by Nashchokin. He told Pushkin about an impecunious Belorussian nobleman by the name of Ostrovskii (which was also to be the title of the novel originally) who had lost his land to a neighbor in a lawsuit. Left with nothing but his serfs, he began to rob people, at first only court clerks, but later others as well. Nashchokin has seen this Ostrovskii in jail.[15]

In search of further information about dispossessed landowners, Pushkin and Nashchokin hit on the idea of acquiring the transcript of court proceedings in a similar case.[16] Thus *Dubrovskii*, just like Stendhal's *Le Rouge et le noir* (1830), which Pushkin had been avidly reading, was to be based on a genuine court case.

The document Pushkin had acquired was a copy of the actual trial record of a case heard in the Kozlov District Court in October 1832, bearing the title "On the adverse possession by Lieutenant Ivan Iakovlevich Muratov of the village Novopanskoe in Kozlov District of Tambov Guberniia, which properly belongs to Colonel of the Guards Semen Petrovich Kriukov" (8: 764). Pushkin took the document as it was and inserted it into the manuscript of his novel as he worked on it, without even recopying it. All he changed were names and dates, but even some of those were left as they stood in the original. The story reflected in the transcript went a long way toward providing the plot of Volume One of the novel.

The name Dubrovskii, which Pushkin eventually decided to give to his dispossessed landowner, may have come from historical sources as well. A serf of a certain Aprelev in Pskov Guberniia had escaped to Poland in 1737, reportedly with the aid of two serfs of a neighbor called Dubrovskii. Acting on Aprelev's complaint, the local authorities made several attempts to arrest Dubrovskii's two serfs, but their fellow villagers hid them and put up strong resistance to the authorities, apparently with Dubrovskii's encouragement.[17] Pushkin may have known of this case, as well as of the case of another Dubrovskii, of Nizhnii Novgorod Guberniia, whose supposedly legitimate inheritance had been taken away through litigation by the wife of the *guberniia* prosecutor, Iudin, in 1802.[18] Finally, the narrator of Pushkin's "Journey from Moscow to Petersburg" (1833–34) tells a story about an acquaintance who had been murdered by peasants at the time of a fire (11: 267)— another real-life detail that found its way into *Dubrovskii*.[19]

Although the skeleton of the plot for Volume One was supplied by actual court cases, the characterization of the parties involved was entirely Pushkin's own. Andrei Dubrovskii is a proud and independent man, though his estate consists only of one small village. He is friendly with a rich, powerful neighbor, Kirila Petrovich Troekurov, who in his arrogance rarely stoops to friendship, but makes an exception for Dubrovskii. Their friendship, however, is disrupted when Dubrovskii once remarks, as he and other guests are being shown Troekurov's magnificently appointed kennels, that his host's hunting dogs probably live better than his servants. One of Troekurov's serfs answers Dubrovskii rudely; Dubrovskii goes home offended; and thereafter the relations between the two neighbors rapidly deteriorate. Dubrovskii catches Troekurov's peasants stealing timber in his woods, punishes them, and confiscates their horses. The angry Troekurov is inclined to gather all his men and fall on Kistenevka (as Dubrovskii's village is called), but eventually changes his mind and instead commissions the court assessor Shabashkin to find some excuse for taking away Dubrovskii's property. Shabashkin exploits the fact that all of the Dubrovskii family's legal documents, including the act of sale showing that they had bought Kistenevka from the Troekurovs, were burned in a fire. The court challenges Dubrovskii to prove his legal possession of the estate and, receiving no satisfactory answer, finds against him. Both he and Troekurov are summoned to town to hear a reading of the court's decision, after which they are invited to sign it, indicating either their concurrence or their exception. The only detail in which Pushkin departs from the actual case is that Muratov had signed the document, reserving his exception to the court's decision, and only lost the case because he failed to appeal in time (8: 767); Pushkin has the hot-tempered Dubrovskii hurl the inkpot at the assessor instead of signing the document, and then take no further action.

After the incident at the court Dubrovskii becomes seriously ill. His son Vladimir, who has been serving in a regiment of the Foot Guards, is summoned home; but he is unable to find out what exactly happened. Meanwhile, the deadline for an appeal passes, and Kistenevka becomes Troekurov's. At this point, he feels remorseful and decides to make up with his old friend, restoring his property to him; he rides to Kistenevka with this purpose in mind; but Andrei Dubrovskii, catching sight of him through the window, has a stroke, and Vladimir orders Troekurov from the premises. The old Dubrovskii dies. Just after his funeral, representatives of the court, including Shabashkin, arrive to take possesion of Kistenevka in the name of Troekurov; the Dubrovskii peasants riot; the officials retreat into the house; at night Dubrovskii and his men set the house on fire; Arkhip the blacksmith, without Vladimir's knowing it, locks the door, and the officials perish inside. Dubrovskii is thereupon branded an outlaw.

On October 10, 1832, Pushkin left Moscow for St. Petersburg, and by October 25 he was already at work on the first chapter of his freshly conceived novel. Work went fast: as the dates on the manuscript witness, the first eight chapters—what he called Volume One—were completed by November 11 (8: 832).

Here was an opportunity to demonstrate the causes of rebellion in a fictional work. In *A History of the Village of Goriukhino*—from which, incidentally, Pushkin transferred a passage to *Dubrovskii* almost intact [20]—he suggested that a deterioration of living conditions could easily lead to riot. The message of *Dubrovskii* is similar. In *Goriukhino* it is the arrival of the new, overbearing steward that upsets the peasants; in *Dubrovskii* it is the prospect of falling into the overbearing Troekurov's clutches. The legal document and the assassination through arson, the two focal points of the first volume of the novel, are presented as cause and effect. With this novel, Pushkin was joining the tradition of Radishchev, whose *A Journey from Petersburg to Moscow* contained a description of a wicked landowner's death at the hands of his serfs (see the chapter "Zaitsovo"). Much as Pushkin was on the side of the nobility, he was putting responsibility squarely on its shoulders. Alerting his peers to the dangers they were creating by their lawless behavior was no "comic dog show": this time Pushkin was saying something serious, something that was important for his tragic time, and he was saying it in a straightforward manner.

But if the project was so promising—just as *The Blackamoor* and others had been—why did he not carry it through? After November 11, 1832, he stopped working on the novel for a while; and on December 2 he wrote to Nashchokin:

I have the honor to report to you that the first volume of *Ostrovskii* is finished: within the next few days it will be sent to Moscow for your perusal and for Mr. Korotkii's critical comments. I wrote it in two weeks, but then I stopped because of a cruel bout of rheumatism that has been tormenting me for the last two weeks, so much so that I could not take pen in hand and could not connect two thoughts in my head. (15: 36–37)

But the curious fact is that Pushkin had been suffering from rheumatism ever since he had left Moscow.[21] To be sure, his discomfort might have intensified after November 11, but it is reasonable to suppose that other factors contributed to his sudden reluctance to continue his novel.

One important stumbling block was that with Volume One he had actually exhausted his topic. What had interested him was the question of how rebellions were engendered, and for all practical purposes he had answered that question in the first six chapters of his novel. Chapters Seven and Eight were already leading into a love story that had very little to do with his original interest.

We learn, to begin with, that after the fire at Kistenevka, robberies began to spread throughout the neighborhood and the young Dubrovskii is suspected of being the robber chief. We are also told that Troekurov's illegitimate son, Sasha, who is being brought up as a legitimate child, needs a new tutor. A Frenchman named Desforges is brought in. Sasha's older half-sister Maria pays little attention to the new tutor at first, but a remarkable incident piques her curiosity: like many of Troekurov's acquaintances, Desforges is thrown into an empty room in which a hungry bear is chained to the wall, able to reach every point in the room except for one corner; but instead of cowering in that corner, as most of the other victims of the practical joke have done, Desforges pulls out a pistol and kills the bear. After this incident Maria begins to take singing lessons from him, and a romance blossoms.

Volume Two begins on the day of the patron saint of Pokrovskoe (as Troekurov's village is called), when the landowner gives a big party. Tales about Dubrovskii's robberies are bandied about. Among the guests is Spitsyn, a rich fat man who gave false testimony in Troekurov's suit against the elder Dubrovskii and is therefore particularly fearful of the vengeful son. Since he carries his fortune in a pouch under his shirt, tied around his neck, he is anxious to spend the night in a safe place, and asks Desforges, known for his courage, if he can share his room. The Frenchman agrees—and robs him during the night, telling him he is Dubrovskii. At this point the narrator explains to the reader that Dubrovskii had accidentally met the real Desforges at a wayside station and, learning where he was going, bribed him to give him his passport and letters of recommendation. Desforges, with his large payoff, headed back to France, allowing Dubrovskii to present himself at Troekurov's house as the tutor. The reason for this action is that, while prowling around Troekurov's house with the intention of setting it on fire, he had caught sight of the lovely Maria and fallen in love with her. After robbing Spitsyn, however, he soon has to leave the house. Departing, he asks Maria to meet him alone in the garden, reveals his identity to her, and makes her promise that if ever she needs help she will turn to him.

A rich fifty-year-old landowner, Prince Vereiskii—Troekurov's only equal in the neighborhood—arrives on his estate, comes to Pokrovskoe for a visit, and soon asks for Maria's hand. Her father finds the proposal advantageous, but Maria is horrified: she begs her father not to force her to marry a man she does not love, but he remains adamant. Maria eventually asks for Dubrovskii's help, agreeing to become his wife if there is no other way to escape Vereiskii. She expects Dubrovskii to kidnap her on the way to the church, but Dubrovskii fails to come; she is married to Vereiskii against her will; and Dubrovskii arrives to rescue her only on the way from the church to Vereiskii's house. Vereiskii wounds Dubrovskii in the melee but is soon disarmed by the robber's men; Maria would be free to go, but she declares that she is already Vereiskii's wife and cannot desert him. In the last scene the convalescent Dubrovskii repels an attack by government troops on his woodland hideout and afterwards dismisses his men, giving up brigandage.

Pushkin's study of rebellion, contained in the first six chapters, was highly original, springing from the deepest artistic urge. So why, then, did he tack onto a serious study of social processes a love plot as unoriginal as the story lines of "The Blizzard" and "The Squire's Daughter"? There can be no doubt that he had great respect for the kind of art that did not sacrifice its serious purpose for the sake of popular appeal. For example, this is what he wrote in praise of E. A. Baratynskii at the beginning of the 1830's: "He never made a fainthearted attempt to cater to the dominant trend or to the demands of momentary fashion; he never resorted to counterfeit art or to exaggeration for the sake of greater effect; he never scorned the thankless, rarely appreciated labor of fine finish and precision; and he never followed on the heels of the epoch-making genius in order to pick up the accidentally dropped ear of grain. He went his own way, alone and independently" (11: 186). Similarly, he had great praise for M. P. Pogodin's *The Mayoress Marfa* (1830) because he felt the author had written his tragedy, "not out of the calculations of vanity that thirsts for ephemeral success, or in order to play up to the general mass of readers that not only is unprepared to accept a romantic drama, but is positively hostile to it; he wrote his tragedy as a result of strong inner conviction, fully devoting himself to his independent inspiration and shutting himself off in the seclusion of his work" (11: 180–81). A little later the poet P. A. Katenin was also to earn Pushkin's approbation for a similar attitude to art (11: 220). All this, of course, applied to Pushkin's own creative career to a great extent. Indeed he wrote in connection with his own *Boris Godunov* that he was no longer courting "the appreciative smile of vogue" (11: 142).

Yet as we have seen earlier, Pushkin was not altogether indifferent to the reading public's appreciative smile. In the same fragment where he praised Pogodin for his independence, he also advocated a return to the popular, "Shakespearean" drama, fully aware that "the populace, like children, demands diversion, action" (11: 178). He was hoping that it would be possible, without falling into the Italian improvisatore's predicament, to make serious art entertaining. He liked M. N. Zagoskin's *Iurii Miloslavskii* (1829), for instance, precisely because Zagoskin had managed "to introduce a romantic plot into the framework of broad historical action without strain" (11: 92). Although he "corrected" *Roslavlev* in his own parodic version, and although he agreed with Viazemskii's critical comments on it, he added the following praise for it in a letter to Viazemskii: *"The situations, though contrived, are entertaining; the dialogues, though false, are lively; and it is possible to read through the whole thing with pleasure"* (14: 221; Pushkin's italics). At times Pushkin thought that in order to captivate, and eventually to educate the taste of, the broad masses, one first had to stoop to commercial tricks. It is most characteristic that he should have pondered, in September 1831, whether to have a fashions department in a journal if he was to launch one. He wrote to Viazemskii, in the same letter:

You mention a journal. Yes, goddamn it! Who ever will give us permission for it? Fon-Fok has died; just watch it, N. I. Grech will end up in his place.[22] That will be something! There is no point even in thinking about a political newspaper. As for a monthly, quarterly, or triquarterly journal, that we could try, but there is one trouble: *without fashions* it will get nowhere; *with fashions* we would be standing on the same level as Shalikov, Polevoi, and others of their kind: it would be a shame.[23] What do you think? With or without? (14: 220; Pushkin's italics)

Pushkin may well have been asking himself the same question with regard to *Dubrovskii*: with or without fashions? Without, it would be a serious novel of manners, but how many people would be interested in it? With fashions, it would have to have an entertaining plot with a love intrigue. Pushkin chose to take the second course, evidently hoping to combine quality and popular appeal. But this combination presented great problems, which may well have been what made him lay the project aside for over a month.

In any event, it was not until December 14, 1832, that he took up pen once more. He worked at the manuscript more or less continually until January 22, 1833; on February 6 he added one more paragraph to the last chapter; but with that he abandoned his novel, never to show any further interest in it. To take this unfinished piece of writing (the existing material was only published posthumously)[24] and analyze it as if it had been fully intended for publication is unfair to the author.[25] He himself was obviously unsatisfied with it: his attempt to combine the serious with the entertaining had failed; his introduction of "fashions" had led to an incongruity in the structure that his sensitivity to artistic form could not allow to stand.

Apart from Pushkin's unwillingness to publish the text, several facts point to its incomplete nature. To begin with, a few plot outlines were left among his papers, and these indicate that he was planning to write a third volume, evidently not considering the action complete with Dubrovskii's failure to kidnap Maria in good time and with his dismissal of his band of robbers. As far as it is possible to tell from the sketchy outlines, Prince Vereiskii would have died, and Dubrovskii would have met the widowed Maria again, but betrayed by one of his servants, would eventually have been arrested (8: 830–32).

Further, the two volumes contain some loose ends that Pushkin would have had to tie up if he were to prepare the manuscript for publication. For example, the Frenchman Desforges meets Dubrovskii at a post station not far from Pokrovskoe (he says he would have got there the same day if he had been given horses); after he yields his identification papers to Dubrovskii, he goes to a nearby town (arriving there the same night), where, in accordance with Dubrovskii's instructions, he is supposed to declare that he has been robbed by the famous robber; yet— despite the town's closeness and everybody's great interest in Dubrovskii's affairs—news of the Frenchman's adventure never reaches Troekurov.[26] Also, the opening words of the novel, "A few years back" (8: 161), indicate that the time of the action is the 1820's; a reference to a decree issued in 1818 (8: 169) and still in effect at the time of the two neighbors' lawsuit seems to point to the same; it is mentioned several times that Vladimir Dubrovskii is in his twenty-third year; yet his mother's letters, written "during the Turkish campaign" (8: 182), express joy over early signs of his abilities. If he was a child during the Turkish campaign (1787–91), he would have to be thirty-odd years old in the 1820's.[27]

Incompleteness is felt even in Pushkin's interpretation of the revolt of the Dubrovskii serfs, although this was the event he paid most attention to. Certain passages suggest that the fear of Troekurov is the chief reason for mutiny. For example, Anton the coachman says: "To pass into Kirila Petrovich's possession!

The Lord save and preserve us from that! His own people have a rough enough deal at times: if he gets his hands on strangers, he'll not only skin them, but tear their very flesh off" (8: 174). It is characteristic from this point of view that in two of the plot outlines Pushkin jotted down before writing the novel, the serfs would have killed the court clerks without Vladimir's prior knowledge (8: 830). Without Vladimir's active participation the riot could have appeared as a protest against the whole feudal system, the change of masters being only the last drop that made the cup of resentment run over. But in order to conform with the active role of a robber chieftain, Vladimir had to become the leader of the revolt, and this obscured its social coloring. With him actively engaged in the affair, it is not clear whether the serfs are rebelling or whether they are simply "good peasants" who are taking up arms in defense of their master.[28]

Vladimir's active role in the revolt, however, was difficult to reconcile with his other function as romantic lover. In an effort to overcome this difficulty, Pushkin resorted to borrowing a literary device from *Iurii Miloslavskii*. In Part Three, Chapter Three, of that novel Kirsha, at the head of a Cossack troop, frees Iurii from a vault under a chapel where he has been kept by Shalonskii and Turenin, and in revenge locks them up in the same dungeon; but knowing that Iurii is in love with Shalonskii's daughter, he does not really want them to perish. He calculates that Shalonskii's men will come looking for their master and, noticing that the slab of iron normally covering the vault's secret entrance has been moved, will find their way to the prisoners. For this reason he tells the Cossacks not to put the iron slab back in place; but the Cossacks, after he is gone, replace it with the intention of starving the two men. Shalonskii and Turenin do get released later (because Zagoskin needs them for other purposes), but the scene nevertheless represents a clever device for punishing evil characters without directly implicating the hero in the act. This is precisely what happens in Chapter Six of *Dubrovskii*, when Vladimir, just before setting his house on fire, tells the blacksmith Arkhip to go and check if the doors are open so that the court clerks can get out;

Arkhip goes to check as told, but on finding that the doors are indeed open, he promptly locks them.

The ambiguity of Vladimir's relationship to his peasants and their rebellion is also revealed at the end of Chapter Nineteen when, as he dismisses his men, he advises them to start a new life within the bounds of the law, and adds: "But you are all ruffians and will probably not want to give up your trade" (8: 223). Considering that his peasants revolted in his defense (if that is what they revolted for), always obeyed him, helped him, and nursed him back to life after he had been wounded, his calling them ruffians can hardly be justified.[29] It is clear that Pushkin did not coordinate all the details as he put a nobleman at the head of a peasant revolt. The inconsistencies of the text might have been eliminated quite easily if Pushkin had revised his manuscript for publication, but the fundamental incongruity—that between the basic social theme and the superimposed romance—would have been very difficult to reconcile.

At the beginning of Chapter Three Vladimir is sketched in as a careless and carefree young rake, "prodigal and ambitious" (8: 172), who pegs his future hopes on an advantageous marriage. After he has received his old nurse's letter about his father's poor state of health, his filial affections are described in the following terms: "He had lost his mother in infancy and, scarcely knowing his father, had been sent to Petersburg in his eighth year. Nevertheless he had a romantic attachment to him, and he loved family life all the more for having never enjoyed its quiet pleasures" (8: 173). This tongue-in-cheek statement established an ironic distance between narrator and hero, and we anticipate that Vladimir will be treated with the same objectivity as Troekurov, but in fact all irony is soon eliminated from his characterization. What follows is the unhumorous stock in trade of romantic literature.

All the sentimental passages are thrown into the text of the novel with utmost crudity, indicating how little interest Pushkin had in them. Vladimir's relations to Maria are not much different from Burmin's to his Maria in "The Blizzard" or from the other Vladimir's to Liza in "The Squire's Daughter." In those Belkin tales, however, the crudities served the purpose of parody. Here, the tone is completely serious at the outset, and if it turns farcical the change can hardly be intentional. When Burmin was taken for another man in the teeth of all probability, this was clearly intended as a joke, but what do we make of some of the contrived scenes in *Dubrovskii*, which had at least begun as a serious novel of manners?

In the first six chapters, for example, the reader is told about all the aspects of the action directly, but in Chapter Eight a mysterious Frenchman arrives, and the reader is left in the dark about his identity until the all-too-calculated punch line at the end of Chapter Ten reveals him to be Dubrovskii—a cheap trick of the popular novelist unworthy of Pushkin. Further, since there had been no indication up to the time of Vladimir's departure from the Troekurov house (in Chapter Twelve) that Troekurov might force his daughter to marry against her wishes, and since Prince Vereiskii has not even arrived on the scene, why is Vladimir so presumptuous as to make Maria promise to turn to him for help in case she should be in distress? Clearly, a link is missing from the carelessly constructed chain of events. Likewise, with regard to Chapter Fourteen, even if Vladimir somehow guessed that Vereiskii was going to propose, how did he know that Maria would reject the proposal? He passes her a note at the beginning of the chapter, before Maria herself has even heard that the Prince has asked for her hand. Again this is presumptuous of him, considering that he has never had any firm indication of Maria's love for him or any sign that she disliked Vereiskii. It is unlikely that Pushkin endowed him with this presumptuousness intentionally: in fact in other scenes he is extremely modest, even self-effacing. More likely, Pushkin had so little interest in Vladimir's love life that he did not bother to put the story line together convincingly, probably leaving it till a later date to straighten it out.

As we have seen before, the less ambitious Pushkin's design, the wider the scope for the comparativist. Tacking a romantic plot onto his novel, Pushkin made no effort to be original: over the years critics have found literary models for virtually every aspect of Vladimir's role as a robber and of his relationship to Maria. To begin with the first, in Western European literature the robber theme originates with picaresque stories and tales of chivalry. The connection with the latter is particularly obvious in Friedrich Schiller's drama *Die Räuber* (1781), one of the works that made the theme fashionable toward the end of the eighteenth century.[30] Its hero Karl Moor, anticipating Vladimir Dubrovskii, is driven to become an outlaw by the wickedness of another person (his brother Franz); he visits with his family incognito, unrecognized even by his beloved Amalia (which is similar to Vladimir's stay at the Troekurovs' disguised as Desforges); his rival Herrmann tries to prove his death to Amalia by showing her Karl's ring (in Maria's case a note to Vladimir would do just as well, but a ring is used for its symbolic meaning); since he has become the robbers' chieftain, Karl no longer thinks himself worthy of his Amalia (just as Dubrovskii thinks himself unworthy of Maria and begs her to do everything in her power to avoid having to elope with him); and finally, as in most works of robber romanticism, *Die Räuber* presents the scene of a siege of the robbers' woodland camp by government troops.

Victor Hugo's outlaw Hernani—in the drama that was much more a focus of Pushkin's attention than the older Schiller play—is even more of a noble character. He has become a robber not because he himself has been wronged, but because of the murder of his father—a moving circumstance that Pushkin was to exploit in *Dubrovskii*. There are some other similarities between Hugo's drama and Pushkin's novel—the old man de Silva tries to force his young niece to marry him as Vereiskii forces Maria; attempts at elopement are thwarted in both works; Hernani, like Dubrovskii, enters the house of his beloved in disguise—but *Hernani* must have been important to Pushkin, above all, as an indication of the popularity of the robber theme even as late as 1830.[31]

The prose work that had made this theme fashionable all over Europe, that indeed generated an enormous number of imitations, was Christian August Vulpius's novel *Rinaldo Rinaldini, der Räuber-Hauptmann* (1798), to which Pushkin himself refers in *Dubrovskii* (8: 208).[32] Its hero, less chivalrous than Karl Moor or Hernani, is not significant as an antecedent for Dubrovskii, but a number of situations and narrative devices—

for example, the failure of Rinaldo to kidnap his Aurelia before her wedding with the Count Rovezzo, the importance of rings, the scene of the robbers being surrounded by government troops, the use of disguises, the device of the hero's listening to a discussion of his exploits by people who do not realize the famous robber is sitting in their midst, conflicting stories about Rinaldo's physical appearance, his habit of reading for pleasure (untypical for a brigand)—may well have influenced Pushkin either directly or through imitative works.

There can be no doubt that Sir Walter Scott's *Rob Roy* (1818), the most popular robber novel of Pushkin's own epoch, was on his mind as he worked on *Dubrovskii*. Macgregor, alias Rob Roy, alias Campbell—a man as skillful at disguises as Dubrovskii—was a prosperous cattle dealer until the actions of his enemies, including a raid on his hamlet, drove him to become an outlaw. Even as an outlaw, he retains his nobility of heart, was "still remembered in his country as the Robin Hood of Scotland, the dread of the wealthy, but the friend of the poor, and possessed as many qualities, both of head and heart, which would have graced a less equivocal profession than that to which his fate condemned him."[33] This characterization—though by no means unique in endowing a robber with chivalrous traits—may have inspired Pushkin to write about Dubrovskii that "the band's chief gained a reputation for intelligence, daring, and a certain magnanimity" (8: 186). Further, Spitsyn's night encounter with Dubrovskii is very similar to Mr. Morris's encounter with Rob Roy: Morris, terribly afraid of robbers, seeks the protection of Rob Roy, who is traveling in disguise, and ends up being robbed.[34]

Although the robber theme could be fused with the theme of social or political protest, in Pushkin's novel it does not serve to shed light on, or further elaborate, the problem of peasant rebellion. On the contrary: it in fact detracts from the interest of Pushkin's study of social processes. Its only function is to somehow bring a romance into relation with a revolt—subjects that do not naturally hold together. For depicting the romance itself, Pushkin did not necessarily have to use works of robber romanticism as models; indeed in several instances he went beyond the limits of that genre.

The main question arising in connection with the Vladimir-Maria relationship is: why did the attempt to elope fail? To begin with, although Maria's request for help reached Vladimir rather late, it is still unclear why he could not manage to kidnap her before the wedding, given his prowess at extraordinary escapades. But even if we accept that there is good reason for his tardiness, it is still obscure why she will not go with him. After all, she had not pronounced a marriage vow; what had happened was that "when the priest turned to her with the customary questions, she shuddered and froze with fear, but she still hesitated, still did not give up hope. However, the priest, not waiting for her reply, pronounced the irrevocable words" (8: 220). Why would these words be "irrevocable" if they were pronounced without her consent and if they were not followed by a consummation of the marriage? And why does she say to Dubrovskii: "It's too late. I am already married. I am the wife of Prince Vereiskii" (8: 221)? V. G. Belinskii suggests that to be kidnaped by a robber from the altar "seemed very 'romantic' to her and therefore very enticing. But Dubrovskii came too late, which pleased her deep down; now she stepped into the role of a faithful wife, that is, the role of another 'heroine.'"[35] By contrast, Wacław Lednicki finds her decision highly moral and compares it with Tatiana's rejection of Onegin, commenting that both heroines—as well as Maria of "The Blizzard," who faithfully waited for Burmin to turn up—demonstrate Pushkin's deep respect for the sacrament of matrimony.[36]

It is true that Maria, like Tatiana and a number of Pushkin's other women, has been brought up in isolation in the country with no other companion but her imagination, fired by works of romantic literature; and it is also true that her words echo Tatiana's famous line: "I have been given to another in marriage" (6: 188). But the two heroines have nothing in common beyond these superficial similarities. Tatiana of Chapter Eight suspects—rightly or wrongly—that her main attraction for Onegin is her brilliant position in high society; she had already become disillusioned with him as she had pored over his marginalia in the library of his abandoned house; although she had not married for passion, she had come to like and respect her husband and she had no wish to hurt his feelings. Her decision, a complex one for she still loves Onegin, grows out of her spontaneous emotions, rather than out of legalistic or moralistic considerations. Maria Troekurova, on the other hand, is not married except in a very narrowly legalistic sense; she has no reason to like or respect Vereiskii, who had coldly refused to heed her entreaties only a couple of days before; and Dubrovskii gives her no motive for doubting his integrity. Her decision to play the role of the faithful wife derives more from literary tradition than from psychology or ethics.

The tradition with which Pushkin's reader immediately identifies the Vladimir-Maria relationship is that of "The Blizzard," but "The Squire's Daughter" is also relevant. The plot there, as we have seen, was the same as we find in *The Bride of Lammermoor*: a conventional love affair between children of hostile families. Pushkin did not take the trouble to look for another scheme for *Dubrovskii*. The idea of dressing up a squire's daughter as a country wench came from *St. Ronan's Well*; in *Dubrovskii*, too, the action turns around a disguise—this time that of a robber as a tutor. Most important, however, is the notion that forms the plot of "The Blizzard": that marriage, once the ceremony has been performed, is indissoluble. It is enunciated by Francis Tyrrel of *St. Ronan's Well* as follows: "Were Clara Mowbray as free from her pretended marriage as law could pronounce her, still with me—*me*, at least, of all men in the world—the obstacle must ever remain, that the nuptial benediction has been pronounced over her and the man whom I must for once call *brother*."[37] Walter Scott must have considered a marriage *de jure* binding even if *de facto* unconsummated—a very effective literary device, for he made the denouement of *The Bride of Lammermoor* turn around it too.[38] In that novel, Lucy Ashton, tricked by her mother into believing that Edgar Ravenswood is engaged to another woman, has just signed the marriage contract with Bucklaw when Edgar, at last informed of what is happening, arrives and forces his way into the castle; he is ready to snatch his fiancée away by force, but when he learns that she has signed the contract (with the actual wedding still four days away), he only upbraids her for her inconstancy and renounces her forever. A notable difference between Scott's two novels and *Dubrovskii* is that

Pushkin makes his heroine, rather than his hero, insist on a rigid adherence to the letter of the law—a difference that possibly tells us something about both the position of woman in nineteenth-century Russian literature and the position of man in nineteenth-century English literature. It is also quite possible that Pushkin transferred the moralizing attitude from male to female simply under the influence of Rousseau's *Julie, ou La nouvelle Héloïse*. Indeed the latter left its traces on *Dubrovskii* not only in the way the heroine embraces virtue, but also in several telling little details.[39]

All these examples of borrowing reveal the enormous gap between Pushkin's highly original study of Russian social conditions—as reflected in his depiction of the revolt—and the conventional romance he appended to it. The gap between the two themes—united in a forced marriage like Maria and Vereiskii—becomes even more obvious if we take a closer look at the novel's style.

4

The legal document that provided the initial inspiration for the novel is a monstrous piece of writing, not only clumsily worded but grammatically incorrect at times. One critic believes that Pushkin would probably have corrected and abbreviated it if he had decided to prepare the manuscript for publication;[40] another, evidently unaware of the history of the manuscript, has commented on the document as a parody of nineteenth-century Russian bureaucratic jargon.[41] In fact, however, the language is no more obscure than that of most official documents of Pushkin's time: legal writers tended to be so maladroit that on occasion their documents had to be returned as incomprehensible.[42]

This large natural rock of an actual document sits squarely in the middle of Chapter Two of *Dubrovskii*, leaving little room for anything else in that chapter; indeed the whole of Volume One had to be landscaped around it. Since it was the cause, with the revolt as its effect, it was imperative that both it and the action surrounding it should be presented objectively: no valid revelations about social processes could be made otherwise. The material itself demanded the kind of omniscient mode of narration that we have seen in *The Blackamoor of Peter the Great.* Although in *Dubrovskii*, as in *Poltava*, there is a villain, his vices are not exaggerated, nor does the responsibility for the subsequent revolt rest with him alone. In order to make this clear, the narrator emphasizes the similarity between Troekurov and his eventual victim, Andrei Dubrovskii: "Of the same age, born in the same social class, and educated the same way, they were to some extent similar in character and disposition" (8: 162). Troekurov is, of course, ungracious in allowing his servant to insult Dubrovskii, but we must not forget that it was the jealous Dubrovskii who had initiated the unpleasant exchange, and that it is his intransigent arrogance that stands in the way of reconciliation. Pushkin seems to be putting the blame on a political system that allowed one of the two men born equal to acquire enormous fortune and power, causing the other to flaunt his pride in irritation. It was also the system, from the Tsar down, that allowed the wealthiest of the province to have uncontrolled power over corrupt courts: if there had been an upright judge, made secure in his position by the central government, Troekurov could not have indulged in his capricious act, provoked more by temporary anger than lasting malice. Thus Dubrovskii and the legal officials, as well as the whole political regime, are just as much at fault as Troekurov, and the latter even receives a measure of our sympathy when his attempt to make up with his former friend leads to such catastrophic results.

All this is told by a "witness of many years," emotionally above the events he relates, yet not as impersonal as the narrator of *The Blackamoor* was. He does not hesitate to judge as he describes Troekurov's "lordly" and "idle" ways and his "riotous amusements," the "vices of an uncultivated man," with a "rather limited mind" (8: 161). But the epithets conveying the value judgments are applied without irony or any other emotional coloring: they are simply statements about the hero as any educated person would see him. Details designed to moderate our dislike of Troekurov are introduced just as calmly. We are told, for instance, that Troekurov's peasants "were devoted to him . . . proud of their master's wealth and reputation," that "he was not avaricious by nature," and that in undertaking the litigation against his neighbor, "satisfied vengeance and the love of power had smothered his more noble sentiments up to a point, but at long last these latter triumphed" (8: 161, 176, 177). The changes in the manuscript indicate that Pushkin was aiming at a calm, balanced view of the character. For example, he hesitated in his choice of words about the attitude of Troekurov's serfs to their master (8: 161, 755); and he crossed out a phrase, "rare was the girl among the house servants who escaped the fifty-year-old satyr's amorous advances" (8: 755), which might have sounded too jarringly censorious for its stylistic context. (The eventual description of the landowner's harem is much more matter-of-fact.)

From the height of his omniscience, the narrator sees the faults of Troekurov's opponent in just as fitting proportions. He tells us bluntly that at the sight of Troekurov's kennels, Dubrovskii "could not help feeling a certain envy" (8: 163). He calls a note Dubrovskii sends to his neighbor "extremely boorish" (8: 164); and he evaluates the hero's letters to the court just as the occasions warrant, that is, the first one as a "rather rude reply," and the second as "quite a businesslike communication" (8: 166, 167). Later he applies the epithet "poor" to Dubrovskii on two occasions (8: 172, 178), implying not so much a personal emotional involvement of his own as the natural attitude anyone would assume toward a man in Dubrovskii's predicament. Similarly, the nurse Egorovna's letter to Vladimir is described as "these rather incoherent lines," though the narrator does not hide his sympathy for the "goodhearted old woman" (8: 172, 173). Value judgments are attached not only to people, but also to facts, situations, and events. The legal document, for example, is introduced with the words: "We will cite that ruling in full, assuming that it will be gratifying to every reader to be apprised of one of the means whereby we in Holy Russia can lose property to which we have an indisputable right" (8: 167).

This last sentence is perhaps the farthest the narrator goes in revealing his attitudes in those parts of *Dubrovskii* not concerned with the romantic plot. In its sarcasm and jocularity it reminds us of the tone of some of the Belkin tales, yet there is a fundamental difference between the one and the other. In Belkin's stories the tone of narration usually reveals more about the narrator's silliness than about his subject: Pushkin's primary aim is to draw attention to his own ironic attitude. In the first six chapters of *Dubrovskii*, by contrast, the emphasis is all on the subject, and when the narrator steps in front of us, announcing his opinions, he does so in order to enliven our impressions of his subject rather than to draw attention to his own personality.

He seems to have the same purpose in mind when he puts the epigraph "On the table once laden with victuals now stands a coffin" at the head of Chapter Four. This quotation—from G. R. Derzhavin's poem "On the Death of Prince Meshcherskii" (1779)—resembles the epigraph to "The Undertaker" in the sense that it is by the same poet and also refers to a coffin. In the earlier story, however, the coffin had both a literal meaning as merchandise and a figurative meaning as a symbol of death. Whoever chose that epigraph—whether it was Belkin, or his narrator, or even the Publisher—did not seem to be aware of the coffin's dual significance and thought of it simply because the undertaker traded in coffins and therefore an epigraph about coffins seemed to be appropriate. Thus Pushkin's hidden purpose with that epigraph was either to laugh at the naïveté of his literary alter egos or at least to play with the possible implications of coffins. There is nothing quite so involved in this case. The epigraph foretells death, and a man dies: the function of the epigraph—far from being an elaborate joke at the expense of the narrator—is simply to add a lyrical touch, enhancing the reader's impression of the subject. All this is done in as straightforward and guileless a manner as the introduction of the narrator's value judgments. This narrator, in general, resembles the one of *A Novel at a Caucasian Spa* (as far as can be judged from so brief a fragment): he is as objective as the narrator of *The Blackamoor*, but he is not as withdrawn or colorless.

When the narrator reported on Troekurov's feeling of satisfaction at his vengeance, he was in effect entering the hero's mind. He does this on many other occasions. He tells us that Troekurov was proud of his kennels, that "Dubrovskii's sudden fit of insanity [after the court announced its decision] made a powerful impression on him and poisoned his triumph," that "he had pangs of conscience," and that "his victory brought no joy to his heart" (8: 171, 176). The narrator sees into Andrei Dubrovskii's mind just as clearly, not only reporting on his envy, but also perceiving the horses he took from Troekurov's serfs as "three enemy horses" and the serfs themselves as "prisoners of war" (8: 165). The point of view shifts from one person to another rapidly, while the narrator is informed about the feelings and thoughts of each.

The passage most characteristic of this multifocused omniscience is the scene of Andrei Dubrovskii's death: first "he recognized Kirila Petrovich" (his own perception); then "his face assumed an expression of terrible confusion" (perceived by his son who sat by him); after the elder Dubrovskii's stroke, a servant comes in to announce Troekurov's arrival, in response to which Vladimir "threw a terrifying glance at him" (terrifying, presumably, to the servant); having received Vladimir's command to order Troekurov off the premises, "the servant gladly rushed from the room to fulfill his master's command" (the point of view remaining with the servant); next Egorovna, after an exchange with Vladimir, went out and "heard the servant deliver his young master's reply" (the point of view passing to her for a paragraph); and finally "the servants rushed into their old master's room," wept over his corpse, washed and dressed it, and "laid it out on the same table at which they had served their master for so many years" (a scene perceived entirely from the servants' point of view, though the only one identified among them is Egorovna; 8: 177–78).

The fast shifts in point of view are matched by equally fast transitions from narration to representation, and vice versa. Chapter One begins with a summary of the two neighbors' past and friendship; there follows the vivid scene of their quarrel, interspersed with dialogue; there is another scene next morning as Troekurov receives Dubrovskii's rude letter refusing to mend relations and leaves for the hunt; the hunt and the events of the following days are given as a rapid connective synopsis;

Dubrovskii's capture of his neighbor's serfs is presented as a scene, though not in much detail; another synopsis provides information about Troekurov's reaction; and his conversation with Shabashkin is another vivid scene. The last page of the chapter rapidly summarizes the ensuing litigation, with the point of view shifting from Dubrovskii to Shabashkin, then back and forth between Dubrovskii and Troekurov until their final recognition of each other on the way to town; it covers the events of at least a month. As M. O. Lopatto notes, in all of Pushkin's prose works "the greatest number of transitions from vivid representation to abstract narration occurs in the uncorrected manuscript of *Dubrovskii*."[43]

If we compare Pushkin's technique with the methods of other great masters of prose, it seems even more striking. To take only one example, Turgenev in *Fathers and Sons* (1861)— also an objective study of social processes—gives a summary description of the Kirsanov family, framed by Nikolai's brief conversations with his servant, in Chapter One; Chapters Two through Six are all scenes that allow us to get acquainted with the characters at first hand; and only in Chapter Seven do we hear another reminiscent summary of Pavel's life, given by Arkadii. Thus Turgenev accomplishes the introduction of the characters and the exposition of the main themes mostly in scenes, with rare transitions to narration. Whether his is a better technique than Pushkin's in *Dubrovskii* is hard to say: as we have seen, Vladimir's presence is always a disturbing influence, but if we confine our attention to those passages detailing the neighbors' quarrel and litigation, and the peasants' participation in the revolt, Pushkin's choice of presentation seems to be very effective.

Dubrovskii is close to *The Blackamoor* in its omniscient mode of narration, in its fast-shifting point of view, and in its frequent oscillations between scene and summary, but as we have seen, its narrator is much more colorful and forthcoming. The greatest difference between the two unfinished works, however—one that represents an enormous step forward for Pushkin the prose writer—is the much more liberal use and considerably improved mastery of dialogue, at least in those parts of *Dubrovskii* not concerned with Vladimir's romance.

It is no accident that linguists tend to single out *Dubrovskii* as one of the earliest exemplars of modern literary Russian amalgamating many varieties of written and colloquial language.[44] Introducing the vernacular into the language of imaginative literature was one of Pushkin's greatest achievements in prose fiction. But he did not achieve it without relying at least to some extent on tradition: those dialogues in *Dubrovskii* not concerned with the love plot are closest in style to Fonvizin's comedies, to Radishchev's *A Journey from Petersburg to Moscow*, and to the satirical works of such other late-eighteenth and early-nineteenth century writers as I. I. Dmitriev and I. A. Krylov. For instance, in giving Troekurov the phrase *sobachii syn* ("son of a bitch," 8: 188), Pushkin must have had *The Young Hopeful* in mind, for he had said in another place: "If *The Young Hopeful*, this singular monument of a popular satire that enthralled Catherine and her brilliant Court, were to appear in our time, our journals would crack jokes over F. Vizin's habits of spelling and would note with horror that Prostakova calls Palashka a *slut* and a *daughter of a bitch*" (11: 155; Pushkin's italics). The older Dubrovskii's phrase "Your kennels are marvelous; I doubt whether your servants live as well as your dogs" (8: 163)—which is central to the novel's plot—echoes Pravdin's words addressed to Skotinin: "I have heard that you treat your pigs incomparably better than your servants" (Act 5, Scene 4).[45]

One of the paradoxical traits of *The Young Hopeful* is that the negative characters, above all the archvillain Prostakova, tend to speak good Russian, whereas the heroes flounder in the rhetoric of the eighteenth-century Enlightenment. Similarly, in *Dubrovskii* the dialogues of Vladimir and Maria are abstract and colorless, whereas the language of the fathers and servants—mercifully outside the sphere of romance—is fresh and racy. There is one great difference between Fonvizin and Pushkin, however: Fonvizin apparently sees the unpolished language of his negative characters as an attribute of their vulgarity, whereas Pushkin relishes every idiom not only for its usefulness in fixing the characters in their social milieu, but also for its sheer beauty. Looking for expressive idiom to add to his characters' speech, he frequently turns to the metaphoric language of proverbs and folk literature. For instance, Troekurov's expression *gol kak sokol* (literally, "naked as a falcon," meaning "poor as a churchmouse"; 8: 162) can be found in the book *A Complete Collection of Russian Proverbs and Sayings, Arranged in Alphabetical Order* (1822), of which Pushkin had a copy;[46] and the phrase *kakov pop, takov i prikhod* (literally, "like priest, like parish," close in meaning to "birds of a feather flock together"; 8: 217), also spoken by Troekurov, is a well-known proverb. Andrei Dubrovskii fares no worse when it comes to expressive language. We hear him speak much less, but what he says Pushkin weighs with as much care as he accords Troekurov. One added feature of his speech, which we do not find in Troekurov's, is the Biblical phraseology provoked by his indignation at court. Calling the courthouse *bozhiia tserkov'* ("church of God," 8: 171), he betrays the fact that he can no longer discern where he is and whether the solemn phrases that crowd into his mind are appropriate to the occasion or not. His comparison of the court officials to dogs reveals that the grievances in his original quarrel with his neighbor (over dogs, the property of Troekurov, just like the members of the court) are welling up from the bottom of his soul—a masterly touch on Pushkin's part, reminiscent of his use of symbolic undercurrents of meaning in "The Stationmaster."

Lopatto, in his stimulating, though not always convincing, study of the form of Pushkin's fiction, shows that the relative weight of dialogues within the text is highest in *Dubrovskii* among all of Pushkin's prose works.[47] Significant as this observation may be in itself, its meaning is somewhat obscured by the fact that the dialogues involving Vladimir and Maria are entirely different in quality from the others. As we have seen, those parts of the novel having to do with the love plot— dialogues and narrative alike—are sketched in carelessly, with heavy use of literary models. Imitative as they are, they do not merit stylistic analysis side by side with the other passages; and if they are statistically included in such an analysis, they reduce the validity of any generalization. An analysis that combines figures for the fertile topsoil of the first six chapters with figures for the hardpan of Vladimir's romance can only yield averages with limited meaning.

It will be more fruitful, I think, if we apply Lopatto's statistical method, not to compare *Dubrovskii* as a whole with other prose works of Pushkin, but to contrast passages of different quality within the novel. If, for instance, a character uses lots of abstract nouns in a conversation that is not a discussion of ideas (e.g., in a love confession), this may indicate a bookish style, not "overheard" by the author in real life, but read in other works of literature.

To test this idea out, let us take a look at three examples of speech patterns: Vladimir's in Chapter Fifteen, where he and Maria agree to elope if she cannot soften her father's heart (8: 211–12); Anton the coachman's in Chapter Three, where he fills Vladimir in on the quarrel as they drive home from the station (8: 174); and Troekurov's in Chapter Nine, where he hosts a dinner party whose main topic of conversation is the robber Dubrovskii (8: 191–96).

Speaker	Total no. of nouns	Number of abstract nouns	Percent of abstract nouns
Vladimir	57	41	71.93%
Troekurov	80	19	23.75
Anton	38	9	23.68

As this tabulation shows, Vladimir's speech is heavily laced with abstract nouns (e.g. "promise," *obeshchanie*; "timidity," *boiazlivost'*; "revulsion," *otvrashchenie*; as against such concrete nouns as "old man," *starik*; "ring," *kol'tso*; and "oak," *dub*). By contrast, Anton, much as he is given to philosophical generalizations, uses relatively few abstract nouns; and the same goes for Troekurov. In fact, the ratio of abstract to concrete nouns in their speech is almost the reverse of the ratio in Vladimir's.

More than likely, making Vladimir's language abstract was a conscious act on Pushkin's part: abstraction could be regarded as Vladimir's characterization. But to have chosen this method of characterization—to have made his hero's language a pastiche of abstract models—is a measure of Pushkin's lack of interest in the character.

Moving on to the narrator's style, we might ask the question: by what means does he convey his characters' emotions? If he can fully convey them through an objective description of the characters' movements, thoughts, and words, he is master of his material and does not frequently need to supplement his meaning by the addition of modifiers with an affective coloring. Let us examine, for instance, the description of Andrei Dubrovskii's capture of his neighbor's serfs:

One day Dubrovskii was driving about his small estate. Approaching a copse of birches, he heard the sound of an ax and, a minute later, the crash of a falling tree. He rushed into the copse and came upon some peasants from Pokrovskoe, who were calmly stealing his timber. Seeing him, they tried to run away, but he and his coachman caught two of them and brought them back to his house in bonds. Three enemy horses were also among the spoils of the victor. Dubrovskii was *exceedingly* angry: never before had Troekurov's men, brigands as everyone knew, dared to play their pranks within the boundaries of his property, since they were aware of his friendly relations with their master. Dubrovskii realized that they were now taking advantage of the breach of friendship that had recently occurred, and he decided, against all military conventions, to teach his prisoners of war a lesson with the same switches that they themselves had cut in his copse, and to set the horses to work, adding them to his own livestock. (8: 165; italics mine)

In this paragraph, relating an emotion-charged incident, the narrator uses only the one modifier "exceedingly" (*otmenno*) to put extra emphasis on the character's feelings. As we see in Table 1, this word represents less than 1 percent of the words in the Russian original. There are, of course, other modifiers in the passage, but these reflect either objective circumstances or

TABLE 1   *Narrator's Use of Modifiers for Affective Purposes*

Chapter and pages in *PSS*[a]	Subject	Total number of words[b]	Affective modifiers	
			Number	As percent of total
1 (8: 165)	A. Dubrovskii's capture of serfs	126	1	0.79%
1 (8: 161–67)	Summary of events through court summons	1,686	22	1.31
16 (8: 213–14)	Masha's attempt to sway her father	475	18	3.79
5 (8: 178–82)	Funeral through beginning of riot	779	31	3.97
15 (8: 211–12)	Elopement plans of Vladimir and Masha	135	14	10.37

[a]The analysis covers full chapters except in the case of the capture of the serfs.
[b]The total number of words is exclusive of all dialogue, and in the case of Chapter 1, of Dubrovskii's letter.

the character's attitudes, and thus they are not directly attributable to the narrator. For instance, the adjective "small" (*maloe*), modifying the noun "estate" (*imenie*), simply conveys the extent of Dubrovskii's land; the adverb "calmly" (*spokoino*), modifying the participle "stealing" (*voruiushchikh*), is a narrated thought of the character's, since it expresses his annoyance over the peasants' self-assured impertinence; and the adjective "enemy" (*nepriiatel'skie*), modifying the noun "horses" (*loshadi*), reflects Dubrovskii's perception of the situation as a warlike encounter. In the whole of Chapter One (excluding dialogues and Dubrovskii's letter, which do not represent the narrator's own words), only slightly more than 1 percent of the words can be described as the narrator's own modifiers (or component parts of his modifier phrases) with affective meaning.[48]

Let us now quote, for comparison, the narrative paragraphs and the narrator's interpolations in the dialogues in Chapter Fifteen (italics mine):

The moon was shining. It was a still July night. The wind rose now and then, and a *light* rustle ran over the entire garden.

Like a *light* shadow, the young beauty drew near the appointed meeting place. Nobody was yet in sight. Suddenly Dubrovskii, coming out from behind the arbor, appeared in front of her.

. . . he said to her in a *soft, sad* voice.

. . . answered Masha.

. . .

Dubrovskii trembled. A *crimson* flush spread across his *pale* face, which, in the next moment, became even paler than before. He remained silent *for a long time, with his head bent.*

. . .

Here Dubrovskii covered his face with his hands and seemed to be gasping for air. Masha wept...

. . . he said with a *bitter* sigh.

He *gently* put his arm around her *slender* waist and *gently* drew her to his heart. She leaned her head *trustingly* on the young robber's shoulder. Both were silent.

Time flew.

. . . said Masha at last.

Dubrovskii seemed to be waking from a trance. He took her hand and slipped a ring on her finger.

. . . he said.

Dubrovskii kissed her hand and disappeared among the trees. (8: 211–12)

The difficulty with selecting modifiers that reflect the narrator's emotional attitudes is that one is forced to make some arbitrary choices.[49] But though certain expressions may be included by some critics and excluded by others, the general drift of the style can nevertheless be measured with a certain degree of accuracy. Some may believe, for example, that the adjective "light" (*legkii*) applied to "rustle" (*shorokh*) is an integral element in the description of the objective setting. I hold that it is not, because it betrays the author's intention to create a romantic mood and because it could be deleted with no harm either to the overall image or to the grammatical structure. Applied to the noun "shadow" (*ten'*), the same adjective invokes an analogy between nature and heroine, and reveals the narrator's intention to present her as an ethereal creature; therefore it too is the narrator's modifier. Further, the adjectives "crimson" (*bagrovym*) and "pale" (*blednoe*) are attributes of Vladimir's passion the narrator wishes to draw to our attention; the word "slender" (*stroinyi*) emphasizes the heroine's youth and beauty; and the expressions "for a long time" (*dolgo*) and "with his head bent" (*potupia golovu*) are descriptive details added by the narrator in order to enhance the emotional effect of the basic facts that have been communicated. Finally, words like "soft" (*tikhim*), "sad" (*pechal'nym*), "bitter" (*gor'ko*), "gently" (*tikho*), and "trustingly" (*doverchivo*) are without any doubt modifiers of an affective nature.

If we accept all these modifiers as belonging to our group, then more than 10 percent of the narrator's own words in Chapter Fifteen are modifiers with an affective meaning. This figure is almost eight times as high as the figure for Chapter One. Between these two extremes stand Chapter Five and Chapter Sixteen.[50] One is tempted to conclude that the smallest number of such modifiers occurs in chapters in which neither Vladimir nor Maria appears; an intermediate number is observable in those chapters where one of the two lovers is present; and the highest number occurs as they both step on the stage.

We have seen in our preceding discussions that Pushkin's syntax tended to be quite complex in fragments of psychological studies such as "The Guests Were Arriving at the Dacha"

TABLE 2   *Narrator's Use of Sentence Types*

Type of sentence	Chapter 1		Chapter 12	
	Number	Percent	Number	Percent
Virtual, elliptical	—	—	1	1.46%
Basic	10	10.76%	17	25.00
Expanded simple	16	17.20	16	23.53
Compound	19	20.43	16	23.53
Complex	16	17.20	9	13.24
Compound-complex	32	34.14	9	13.24
TOTAL	93	100.00%	68	100.00%

and "In the Corner of a Small Square," but was much simpler in the majority of the Belkin tales. Let us examine the question of syntactic complexity in relation to two chapters in *Dubrovskii*: Chapter One, which obviously reflects Pushkin's first design and basic idea, and Chapter Twelve, which relates the two lovers' first rendezvous, Vladimir's disclosure of his identity, and a discussion between the police chief and Kirila Petrovich, and is thus almost wholly devoted to the romantic plot. Again we count only the narrator's own words, leaving aside both dialogues and letters (in which syntactic features may be used for the heroes' characterization). The results are shown in Table 2.

The one elliptical sentence in Chapter Twelve is "But by whom and how?" (*No kem i kak?*; 8: 207). Basic sentences—consisting of no more than a noun phrase and a verb phrase such as "answered the servant" (*otvechal sluga*; 8: 206)—are most frequently used by the narrator when he identifies speakers in a many-sided conversation; the presence of such a conversation in Chapter Twelve accounts, at least partially, for the preponderance of basic sentences in that chapter. With the expanded simple variety are counted those sentences whose basic structure is enriched by complements and modifiers of different kinds, such as "In the meanwhile she kept looking at the clock every minute" (*mezhdu tem ona pominutno pogliadyvala na chasy*; 8: 204).

Compound sentences include both conjunctive and disjunctive compounds, linked either by parataxis or by modified parataxis; since they very often amount to no more than a compilation of simple sentences, they are stylistically very close to the latter. In deciding whether to count a sentence as a compound, I took into account the function of its individual segments. In some cases complete statements can be found in each of two or more segments of a sentence, regardless of whether they share a subject or a predicate. For example, "Andrei Gavrilovich usually shook his head and answered" (*A. G. kachal golovoiu i otvechal obyknovenno*; 8: 162) is no more than an expanded simple sentence, and is counted as such; but "He suffered from the effects of gluttony once or twice a week, and was drunk every evening" (*On raza dva v nedeliu stradal ot obzhorstva i kazhdyi vecher byval navesele*; 8: 161) is counted as a compound.

The complex group includes, first of all, those sentences that contain subordinate clauses; but it also includes those that incorporate other embedded structures functionally close to subordinate clauses. Among the latter we find gerundive and participial phrases, such as "participating in his noisy, sometimes even riotous, amusements" (*razdeliaia shumnye, a inogda i buinye ego uveseleniia*; 8: 161) and "Kirila Petrovich, having never in his life condescended to visit anyone else" (*K. P., otrodu ne udostoivavshii nikogo svoim poseshcheniem*; 8: 162), both of which could be rendered as relative clauses beginning with "who." Also included in the complex category as functionally close to subordinate clauses are noun phrase complements, verb phrase complements, clauses reduced by nominalization, and other embedded segments extensive enough to form recognizable units within the whole. For example, "Troekurov, haughty in his relations with people of the highest rank, treated Dubrovskii with respect . . ." (*T., nadmennyi v snosheniiakh s liud'mi samogo vysshego zvaniia, uvazhal D. . . .* ; 8: 162) contains a phrase that could easily have been rendered as a relative clause; and the verb phrase complement in "the kennelmen and grooms were given orders to be ready by five o'clock in the morning" (*byl otdan prikaz psariam i stremiannym byt' gotovymi k piati chasam utra*; 8: 163) is a reduced version of a possible clause introduced by "to the effect that they be ready." Finally, sentences were counted as compound-complex if they contained at least two main sentences as well as subordinate structures, or at least two conjoined subordinate clauses within a main sentence.

Let me say once again that even if some critics might disagree with one or another of my categorizations, a few disputed items would make only a marginal difference. Accordingly, it seems legitimate to conclude from the data in the table (even if we allow for the purely technical nature of some of the basic sentences) that Chapter One is syntactically much more complex than Chapter Twelve. This is even more evident if we combine the percentages for the first four types of sentences (since they all represent simple style): we find that they account for less than half the sentences in Chapter One, compared with almost three-quarters in Chapter Twelve.

Still, one complex sentence may be very different in length and complexity from another, and for that reason it may give us a more accurate comparison of the two chapters' syntactic features if we count the incidence of embedded segments without regard to the number of sentences. For instance, there is only one such segment in the following compound-complex sentence (my italics here and below): "She was beginning to understand her own heart, and confessed to herself with involuntary vexation *that she was by no means indifferent to the young Frenchman's good qualities*" (8: 203). But there are four in this one: "Everybody envied the accord *reigning between the haughty Troekurov and his poor neighbor*, and everybody marveled at the latter's boldness *when he unceremoniously announced his opinions at Kirila Petrovich's table, not caring whether they contradicted those of his host*" (8: 162). Using this procedure we find that in Chapter One there are 91 instances of embedding in a total of 1,686 words, or one segment for roughly every 18 words; the figures in Chapter Twelve (25 instances of embedding to a total of 708 words) work out to roughly one for every 28 words.

Syntactic complexity implies complexity of thought: though involved structure does not necessarily make for good style, a writer who has complex subject matter on his hands is likely not to limit himself to basic sentences. The quarrel of two representative Russian noblemen, which leads to significant social unrest, is a complicated matter that needs exploring in every connection; and therefore it is not surprising that Push-kin chose to present it to us in complex language. A robber's shedding of his contrived incognito, accompanied by a conventional love confession, on the other hand, involves neither social nor psychological study; and thus there is no need for complex grammar to reflect many-sided connections. The example of *Dubrovskii* demonstrates, once more, that Pushkin is not always at his best when he is at his simplest.[51]

The chapters we have so far discussed were at opposite ends, or close to the opposite ends, of the novel's stylistic spectrum. It is impossible, however, to divide all the chapters neatly into two groups, distinguishing between those that deal with social matters and those that are signed over to romance, because Vladimir makes his appearance, introducing an alien streak into the texture, as early as Chapter Three. His presence, as we have seen, alters the nature of the revolt, but otherwise his influence in Chapters Three through Six is muted: the tone of these chapters is still set by Troekurov and the peasants who rise against him. Only beginning with Chapter Seven does Vladimir move more and more into the center of the novel's stylistic structure.

As his importance grows, Troekurov's diminishes. In the first two chapters Troekurov is undoubtedly the most significant personage; after Chapter Four (his visit to the Dubrov-skiis' house) the effect of his actions is still felt, but we see more of his hirelings than we see of him; beginning with Chapter Seven he becomes a passive spectator of Vladimir's escapades, though he is still portrayed in his social position as the wealthiest landowner of the district, treating the whole neighborhood to a holiday dinner; and finally, after Chapter Eleven, he is so upstaged by Vladimir that the only role remaining for him is the one assigned to him within the romantic plot, that is, the role of a tyrannical father. In playing this stereotyped role, he loses much of the color of his personality, becoming almost as bloodless as Prince Vereiskii. Between these extreme stages of the first chapters and the last, however, there is an intermediate one—Chapter Eight and particularly Chapter Nine—which brings a third style into the novel, distinct both from the epic presentation of the social conflict and from the conventional presentation of the love plot.

Commenting on a writer's use of small detail for character-ization, A. Z. Lezhnev mentions that Pushkin, unlike Balzac, avoids detailing his characters' physical surroundings at the outset, and tends to provide particulars as the plot develops. In *Dubrovskii*, he points out, the characteristics of a rich land-owner's life are sketched in with only a few words at the begin-ning, and further details—such as the pushing of guests into an empty room with a hungry bear—follow later, not as descrip-tive elements, but as actions performed by the characters.[52] It is true that Desforges' encounter with the bear moves the action forward—the courage he displays in that affair fires Maria's imagination—but the action being moved is a love plot that has very little to do with the ways of Russian landowners. As far as Troekurov as a social agent is concerned, that incident is merely a nasty anecdote—of a kind that Pushkin did not in-dulge in at the beginning of the novel, when he was in a hurry to unfold a serious drama. It seems to me, rather, that the inci-dent with the bear evidences, not Pushkin's conscious decision to delay providing characteristic details, but a change of pace in the narration.

A story by one of Troekurov's dinner guests, Anna Savishna, about her encounter with a man who claimed to be Dubrovskii is another case in point. It enters the novel as a direct result of a change in the narrator's attitude to the narrative. In the first six chapters, the narrator acted as an omniscient agent whose main concern was to convey to the reader the meaning of a number of momentous events in as straightforward a manner as possible. His value judgments, which he did not shun, were either openly sarcastic or serious—but never ironic. What he knew he told the reader in so many words. By contrast, as Chapter Seven opens he loses his omniscience, telling us only that "news of the fire spread throughout the neighborhood," that "everybody talked about it" (8: 185), and that some said this, and others that. Anna Savishna's story, in Chapter Nine, is in effect an example of what people of the neighborhood were saying, with no way for the reader to know just what ex-actly had happened. Troekurov remarks after she finishes her story that the thirty-five-year-old man she had met could not have been Dubrovskii, for he was only in his twenty-third year; and we also read the following in Chapter Eleven:

About a month had passed between the time he [Dubrovskii] had taken up the calling of tutor and the memorable holiday feast, yet no one suspected that the modest young Frenchman was in fact the dreaded robber whose name alone was enough to strike terror in the hearts of all the landowners of the neighborhood. All through that month Dubrovskii had not left Pokrovskoe, yet rumors about his robberies did not stop circulating, thanks perhaps to the inventive imagination of local people, or perhaps because his band had continued its exploits even in the absence of its chief. (8: 202)

Instead of giving out reliable information as he did in earlier chapters, the narrator is now teasing the reader, adopting a manner close to that of *The Tales of Belkin*. His coyness has led at least one critic to conclude that Anna Savishna's story is another inconsistency that Pushkin left in inadvertently,[53] though it is more likely to have been planted in the novel as a deliberate joke. However that may be, it is certainly significant that whereas the anecdote about Vladimir's encounter with the bear was at least connected with the love plot, Anna Savishna's story is connected with absolutely nothing—especially if we conclude, as we have to, that the man she met was not Dubrovskii. Why is her story introduced into the novel at all?

The answer seems to be that the narrator—no longer the stern chronicler of momentous events—loves a good yarn over the dinner table. Anna Savishna's story, providing an insight into her way of thinking and speaking and into her relationship with her son and her servants, is an excellent depiction of provincial mores. Similarly, the scene in Chapter Eleven where the stationmaster's wife curses the Frenchman for his whistling depicts the mood of a post station amusingly but contributes nothing to plot development: after all, the Frenchman did not have to be a whistler in order to meet Dubrovskii. Nor does it matter, from the point of view of the action, whether the coachman who dropped the Frenchman off at the town gate "proceeded to a house of entertainment he knew" (8: 202). Continuing the love plot in the absence of serious social interest, the narrator seems to feel he must at least introduce characteristic details about the social milieu, these details also serving as comic relief from the unblessed love affair. Comic anecdotes would have been out of place earlier, when serious social conflicts were coming to a head; but when the anticipated denouement is a conventional one, requiring no great concentration or effort, the narrator has all the leisure on his hands to sit back and enjoy a good joke. This shifting of the author's interest from story line to descriptive detail is a characteristic of the School of Naturalism.

At least one critic has mentioned that some elements of *Dubrovskii*—particularly the character of Spitsyn—"anticipate" the Gogol manner.[54] Indeed Anna Savishna's story about Dubrovskii anticipates the postmaster's tale of Captain Kopeikin in the later *Dead Souls* (1841): both are about robbers, both prove to be totally irrelevant to the respective plot lines, and both dissolve into thin air. Also, we know from *History of the Village of Goriukhino* that Pushkin had anticipated, and not required the example of, Gogol in developing the style that was to be adopted by the School of Naturalism. Yet in the case of *Dubrovskii* it is more correct to speak about Gogol's direct influence on Pushkin than about Pushkin's anticipation of Gogol, for at least one Gogol story, "Ivan Fedorovich Shponka and His Aunt," left remarkable traces on the description of the dinner party at Troekurov's house.

"Shponka" was published in the second volume of *Evenings on a Farm Near Dikanka* at the beginning of 1832 and was, without any doubt, read by Pushkin soon after its publication, if not before. Of all the stories in the two volumes of *Evenings*, it is the most important one because it comes closest in manner to the works of the mature Gogol. It is built on the principle of emphasizing the insignificant detail for humorous effect.

Beginning with the narrator's own "printed cotton trousers and checkered yellow coat,"[55] the clothes of almost every character in "Shponka" are described in minute detail, and one wonders if this was not what inspired Pushkin to add to his manuscript (8: 794) that the ladies at Troekurov's party were "dressed according to yesterday's fashion, in expensive but worn garments" (8: 191). The greatest emphasis is put on eating, both in Gogol's story, in which the hero's biography commences with a traumatic experience involving a pancake, and in Pushkin's chapter devoted to the dinner at Troekurov's house. Both stress other bodily functions as well: Shponka's neighbor Storchenko, for instance, snores enormously; Troekurov's guest Spitsyn coughs and clears his throat before speaking. The greatest similarity is, perhaps, between these two characters: Storchenko has a "two-storied chin,"[56] and Spitsyn is blessed with a "triple chin" (8: 192); one has hidden his uncle's letter, which would have made Shponka heir to a certain part of his property, and the other testifies falsely in order to dispossess the Dubrovskiis.

But in other instances it is Troekurov who takes after Storchenko: both have their gates locked, for instance, so that no guest can escape their hospitality; both reign over their tables in an overbearing manner; and both retire early, which cheers up their guests. Even Shponka's characterization is reflected in one or two of Pushkin's details. For instance, Shponka kisses the ladies' hands at Storchenko's house "like a well-brought-up cavalier"[57]—a term Pushkin may have consciously or unconsciously had in mind when he corrected the word "men" (8: 801) to "cavaliers" (8: 197) to describe the males at the party. Another noteworthy detail of Shponka's behavior is that he helps himself to gravy liberally when he is embarrassed at Storchenko's table, not unlike Storchenko's other guest, Ivan Ivanovich, who comforts himself with turkey when his host calls him a liar. This detail must have appealed to Pushkin greatly because he employed it twice: both Spitsyn, who is ridiculed for living like a pig in a sty, and the police superintendent, who is ridiculed for his meaningless description of the robber chieftain, swallow their host's insults with greasy mouthfuls of fishpie, roast goose, and cabbage.

And finally even Shponka's aunt, so masculine that she should be wearing "a hussar's mustachios and long riding boots,"[58] exerted an influence over the prominent female figure at Troekurov's table, for Anna Savishna, who had originally had just a "plaintive voice" (8: 796), acquired an unfeminine "booming voice" (*tolstyi golos*, 8: 193) in the course of Pushkin's work on the manuscript. All these and many other details aim at humor, creating an atmosphere of jollity that obliterates whatever social criticism might be implied in the satirical descriptions. The focus of *Dubrovskii* has shifted from a dangerous social conflict to a convivial round of buffoonery.

This third, humorous, style of *Dubrovskii*, effective though it is, is nevertheless the result of the tension between the other two styles. Pushkin's transition from a concern with rebellion to romance and humor was somewhat similar to the course he had taken in abandoning his early prose fragments in favor of *The Tales of Belkin*. In that case, the compromise with literary convention had borne some lasting fruit, notably "The Shot" and "The Stationmaster." *Dubrovskii* too might have been better integrated if Pushkin had continued and revised it, but as several historians of literature have pointed out, early in 1833 he became so engrossed in historical material relating to the Pugachev Rebellion that he lost interest in the novel that had been engendered by a mere handful of facts.[59] Even in its unfinished form, however, the novel contains some dialogues and narrative passages that represent a step forward not only from the earlier fragments, but also from *The Tales of Belkin*. Moreover, for Pushkin the encouraging experience with the work on the first few chapters was proof enough that prose writing need not be just another stage for histrionics; and the inspiration derived from one real-life fact pointed toward works to be based, not on a few, but on a whole archive-full of documents.

v. "The Queen of Spades"

I

Pushkin's experiments with an omniscient mode of narration had still not produced a wholly satisfactory novel in *Dubrovskii*, but they came to full fruition a year later in a short story. A triumph of detached narration, "The Queen of Spades" stands at the peak of Pushkin's achievement as a prose writer: it has been called a chef d'oeuvre by Tolstoi and "the height of artistic perfection" by Dostoevskii.[1] Indeed, Dostoevskii borrowed from it heavily: its central character, Hermann, served as a model for both Aleksei Ivanovich of *The Gambler* (1866) and Raskolnikov of *Crime and Punishment* (1866); and the hero of *The Adolescent* (1875), Arkadii Dolgorukii, characterized him as "a colossal personality, an extraordinary type born entirely of St. Petersburg; a type of the Petersburg period."[2] André Gide, recognizing the story's significance in Pushkin's search for an artistic mode at once detached and poetic, has written that "this short masterpiece provides an excellent example of Pushkin's admirable poetic qualities, as well as of his aptitude for self-effacement."[3]

From circumstantial evidence it seems clear that "The Queen of Spades" was written in Boldino in the fall of 1833. Pushkin had requested a leave of absence from his government post in July of that year to gather material for a projected historical novel set in the period of the Pugachev Rebellion. (This was to be *The Captain's Daughter*.) Having received the Emperor's permission in August, he left for Orenburg, Kazan, and Simbirsk—the chief arena of the rebellion—and found a great deal that was to prove valuable both for his future novel and for his monograph, *A History of Pugachev*. Boldino was on his way as he returned from these regions, and he stopped there, early in October, with the intention of writing his novel (15: 81, 83). However, he found himself working only on his monograph (15: 85), with no inspiration for any other kind of writing until the last week of the month (15: 88). At the end of that week he was at last able to report to his wife that he had written "heaps" (15: 89). Evidently, he was unable to cope with his novel, and temporarily suspended work on it to turn to other projects, including *The Bronze Horseman* and "The Queen of Spades."

His friend P. V. Nashchokin recollected that Pushkin had read "The Queen of Spades" to him;[4] the occasion must have been Pushkin's brief visit to Moscow on his way back from Boldino to St. Petersburg in the middle of November.[5] Further, a St. Petersburg acquaintance, V. D. Komovskii, told A. M. Iazykov on December 10, 1833, that Pushkin had "written a prose tale: either 'The Bronze Horseman' or 'The Blank Shot'; I don't remember exactly. One of these is the prose tale, the other one is in verse."[6] The prose tale could only have been "The Queen of Spades," presumably under an earlier title.

The story was published in the third number of Volume Two of *Library for Reading* (March 1834) and was subsequently included, with slight alterations, in *Tales Published by Alexander Pushkin*, which came out in St. Petersburg later the same year. At least one critic—the editor of *Library for Reading*, O. I. Senkovskii—appreciated the story for its style (see 15: 109–11), but what made it so popular with the general public was its striking plot, not its stylistic achievement.

In Chapter One we see a number of young officers conversing after a card game at the house of a certain Narumov early in the morning. One of them, Tomskii, remarks that he wonders why his grandmother never plays, considering that she is in possession of the secret of a row of three winning cards at faro. Prodded by his comrades, Tomskii relates that his grandmother, a Countess, lived in Paris sixty years before, lost a great deal at faro one night, and turned to the adventurer Saint-Germain for help. Saint-Germain did not give her any money, but named three cards that would win if played consecutively. That night she did indeed win back all her previous losses, but afterwards she did not use her secret cards again. Nor did she reveal them to anyone except for one young man called Chaplitskii, who used them as successfully as she had.

Among Narumov's guests is Hermann, an engineering officer of German descent, who loves to watch other people play cards, though he himself never plays. Tomskii's anecdote has a profound effect on Hermann, and he wonders if he could get the secret out of the Countess. Standing in front of her house one day, he notices a pretty young woman at a window—this is the old lady's companion, Lizaveta. Hermann stares at her regularly from the street and eventually slips her a note as she leaves the house. A correspondence starts between them; he confesses his love for her, and she hopes he will deliver her from her onerous position in the tyrannical Countess's house. She writes to him that one night she and the Countess will be out at a ball, and tells him how he can get into the house in their absence. He follows her instructions, but instead of going up to her room, he stays in a study next to the Countess's bedroom, and when the old lady is left by herself after her return from the ball, he questions her about the cards. She says the anecdote was only a joke, but he does not believe her, presses her for an answer, and eventually pulls a gun on her. She dies of fright. He goes up to Lizaveta's room and tells her what happened; she is horrified and disappointed, but lets him out of the house by way of a secret staircase.

During the Countess's funeral service Hermann steps up to her coffin, and it seems to him that she casts a mocking glance at him, screwing up one of her eyes. That night her ghost visits him and tells him that he will win if he bets on the trey, the seven, and the ace on three consecutive nights. He follows her instructions at the house of the famous gambler Chekalinskii and wins on the trey and the seven; but on the third night, when he thinks he has placed his bet on the ace, he finds that a losing card, the queen of spades, is in his hand, and it seems to him that the queen screws up her eye and grins at him. He has lost everything he had and goes out of his mind.

Soon after the publication of the story, on April 7, 1834, Pushkin made the following entry in his diary: "My 'Queen of Spades' is in great vogue. Gamblers are betting on the trey, the seven, and the ace" (12: 324). The popularity of the tale persuaded the playwright A. A. Shakhovskoi to adapt it for the stage in 1836 under the title *Chrysomania*—the first in a series of stage adaptations that culminated in Tchaikovsky's opera (first performed in 1890).

No manuscript of the final version has survived, but a few handwritten fragments of early drafts indicate the first stirrings of the theme in Pushkin's mind and its connection with his other works. On the same sheet of paper on which he wrote one of the outlines for *A Novel at a Caucasian Spa* (1831), Pushkin jotted down some calculations of wins and losses in a game of faro, possibly intending to show the novel's projected hero, Iakubovich, at the gambling table, though he may have been planning to use the theme of faro in some other work. (Let us designate this Fragment 1 for easier reference.)[7]

Pushkin had toyed with the idea of depicting gambling in fiction on previous occasions: his early fragment "Nadenka" showed a group of young men finishing a game of cards late at night; an even smaller fragment, torn off at the margin, bore the words "cards; sold"; and the incident that unfurled Silvio's drama was a quarrel over cards. We also see the theme occurring in his poetry several times. For instance, in *Onegin* there are two references to cardplaying, which he originally intended to treat in much greater detail. One of these is the comparison, in Stanza 37, Chapter Eight, of Onegin's visions to cards falling to the left and to the right in faro; the early draft shows the metaphor expanded into a series of images, culminating in the sentence "He has lost all the stakes of life" (6: 519).[8] The other reference is in Stanza 17, Chapter Two, to "the insidious deuce" (6: 39), which is the final distillation of several draft versions depicting the poet playing faro in his youth. One of these versions contains the phrase "The fateful word *attendez* / Is not on my tongue any more" (6: 282), a word that is the subject of the epigraph to Chapter Six of "The Queen of Spades."[9] Further, the epigraph to Chapter One is an 1828 lyrical fragment (3: 115) that Pushkin wrote, as his friend Anna Kern recollected, with a piece of chalk on the sleeve of his coat during a card game.[10] Finally, the 1827 poem "The Procuress Sat Sadly at the Table," with its treatment of cards as tools of fortune-telling, anticipates the epigraph to the whole story: "The queen of spades signifies secret ill-will."[11]

At about the time Pushkin jotted down Fragment 1—that is, about the time he was working on *A Novel at a Caucasian Spa*—he wrote the following French sentence in one of his copybooks (Fragment 2):

> il y avait dans ses sentiments un abandon
> et dans ses opinions une license qui
> me
> frappoirent, quelque accoutumé que
> je fusse aux libertins de toutes les
> écoles—[12]

("There was a wantonness in his feelings and an unruliness in his opinions that shocked me, accustomed though I was to libertines of all schools.") It is quite possible that this sentence was supposed to characterize Iakubovich and was to be used as an epigraph to the projected novel, but it has also been suggested that in writing it down, Pushkin might have had in mind a future hero like Hermann, and that the sentence might be an early version of the epigraph for Chapter Four of "The Queen of Spades," which ultimately read, "Homme sans moeurs et sans religion!"[13]

If the original sentence was intended to characterize Hermann, it would further confirm what is apparent from other details: that Hermann descends from a line of evil characters clearly distinguishable both in Pushkin's fiction and in his poetry. As we have seen, the outline of "A Devil in Love" called for a diabolical person to corrupt a young man and to drive a young woman insane. A similar devil is incarnated in the person of Varfolomei in "The Lonely Cottage on Vasilev Island."[14] Iakubovich of *Caucasian Spa* is clearly another predecessor of Hermann's. But the most obvious connection—not only in evil intentions but also in a monomaniacal bent—is between Hermann and Silvio: we read at the beginning of "The Shot" that, in the young officers' opinion, Silvio's conscience must be burdened by the death of "some hapless victim of his terrifying skill" (8: 66); just as in Tomskii's opinion Hermann has "at least three crimes on his conscience" (8: 244).[15] The evil side of Hermann's character is also emphasized by a reference to

Mephistopheles (8: 244), who had appeared both in Pushkin's "Scenes from Faust" (1825) and in his "Fragments of a Faust Project" (1825). Significantly, one of these "Fragments" has a young man losing to Death in a game of cards, and in another an ace takes a queen (2: 381, 382).[16] Like Mephistopheles, Napoleon is used symbolically to delineate Hermann's character (8: 244, 245). Although Pushkin had not always condemned Napoleon unequivocally, he did accuse him of "despising mankind" and of regarding "millions of biped creatures" as only a "means" to an end (2: 214, 6: 37).[17]

Since Pushkin makes such an explicit connection between Hermann on the one hand and the malevolent Mephistophelean, Napoleonic, Byronic types on the other, B. M. Eikhenbaum holds that "The Queen of Spades" is basically a parody of a hackneyed literary type.[18] If the story was indeed to be called "The Blank Shot," this also would point to a close tie with the parodical "The Shot." But even if it is true that Pushkin had at one time contemplated that title, he subsequently discarded it, which seems to indicate that he preferred not to evoke an overt association with the earlier story.[19] Moreover, the text of "The Queen of Spades" amply demonstrates that the view of Hermann-as-Mephistopheles is more Tomskii's and Lizaveta's than the narrator's own. When the narrator mentions, for example, that "thanks to the latest novels, her [Lizaveta's] imagination was both daunted and enchanted by this type—actually quite hackneyed by now" (8: 244), the implication is that it is only Lizaveta who sees a Mephistopheles in Hermann, and that this is not an intrinsic feature of Hermann himself. In "The Shot" Pushkin's main concern was to debunk a myth; in "The Queen of Spades" he is creating a myth of death, destruction, and madness, focusing on a descendant of Silvio, who has shed his ancestor's comic aspect.

Whereas Pushkin's early calculations of a faro game and his French sentence about an immoral character (what we have called Fragments 1 and 2) have only a tenuous, remotely possible connection with "The Queen of Spades," there are four fragments (three pages) in one of his copybooks that are undoubtedly early versions of the story. The first one of these (Fragment 3) contains the short poem that was to be retained as the epigraph to Chapter One, and gives a brief description of the dissipated life of a group of young men in St. Petersburg. The sentence "We . . . paid visits to Sofia Astafevna only in order to make the poor old lady mad with our choosiness" (8: 834) provides a further link with "The Procuress Sat Sadly at the Table," in which men pick over a madame's whole collection with no real intention of choosing anyone. But the most important feature of this fragment (3) is that it is written in the first person. Perhaps the partial failure of *Dubrovskii* made Pushkin cautious, tempting him to revert to well-worn disguises like those of Belkin. However that might be, he soon realized that his new subject called for an omniscient point of view: if the narrator was a participant—a member of the young officers' circle—he could not give an inside view of Hermann's delusions.[20]

The second fragment that is obviously an early segment of "The Queen of Spades" (4) introduces a young woman of German background by the name of Charlotte. She lives with her impoverished widowed mother in an apartment across a courtyard from Hermann; she and Hermann fall in love so deeply as "only Germans are capable of in our day and age" (8: 835); but one morning Hermann does not come to greet her as usual. Here the plot line is interrupted, with only a few more sentences telling us that Hermann had inherited a small capital from his father but firmly resolved not to touch even the interest it earned. A young man's love for a widow's daughter links the fragment with *The Little House in Kolomna*, *The Bronze Horseman*, and, most significantly, "The Lonely Cottage on Vasilev Island." Why Hermann does not greet his sweetheart on that particular morning is not indicated, but if the situation is analogous to that in "The Lonely Cottage," then we can surmise that Charlotte was to have a glamorous rival, as Vera of "The Lonely Cottage" has in the person of the Countess I. This would have been something of a conventional arrangement of characters, already exploited in novels like Balzac's *La Peau de chagrin* (1831), in which the domesticated Pauline loses Raphaël—at least temporarily—to the glamorous Foedora. No longer dealing in parody, Pushkin evidently decided not to settle on a stock situation, replacing Charlotte with the *demoiselle de compagnie* Lizaveta and making the Countess so old as to be beyond even the audacious Hermann's amatory reach.

Having dismissed Charlotte, Pushkin proceeded to borrow some features from Liza of the unfinished *A Novel in Letters*—most notably the attributes of an inferior social position. Further underscoring the two heroines' similarity, he converted a passage from a draft version of the novel into the epigraph for Chapter Two of the short story.[21] The passage, in its original form, read as follows: "A short while ago somebody mentioned an epigram that D. [Davydov] had told a nubile coquette when she had tried to make fun of his democratic penchant for ladies' maids: *que voulez-vous madame, elles sont plus fraîches*" (8: 570). In the original manuscript the letter D. acknowledged Denis Davydov's authorship of the phrase, but that acknowledgment was not carried over into the epigraph, and therefore it came as something of a surprise to Davydov when he read "The Queen of Spades" in print. "What a diabolic memory you have," he wrote to Pushkin on April 4, 1834. "Heaven knows when, I told you fleetingly about my rejoinder to M. A. Naryshkina with regard to *les suivantes qui sont plus fraîches*, and you placed this, word for word, as an epigraph for one of the sections of The Queen of Spades. Just imagine my astonishment, or rather delight, when I realized that I had remained in your memory, in the memory of Pushkin, who was at one time my comrade in bottles and has always been my favorite poet, the one closest to my heart" (15: 123).

In working on "The Queen of Spades" Pushkin was fulfilling some of the aspirations inherent in his earlier unfinished works. In addition to the *Novel in Letters* passage, he salvaged the epigraph to Chapter Two of "In the Corner of a Small Square." That epigraph—"Vous écrivez vos lettres de 4 pages plus vite que je ne puis les lire" (8: 145), which referred to a lady's sincere letters to her lover—was now placed (in a slightly changed form) in front of Chapter Three of "The Queen of Spades," there referring to letters from a man whose declarations of sexual passion are fueled by greed.[22]

On the same page with Fragment 4, describing Hermann's involvement with Charlotte, Pushkin jotted down, and subsequently crossed out, two new sets of calculations for a faro game (8: 836, note 4):[23]

40	60
80	120
160	240
280	420

These figures (Fragment 5) show that he evidently hesitated whether to make Hermann's original stake 40,000 or 60,000 rubles. The higher sum would have made the wager even more breathtaking, but for some reason Pushkin decided to discard the idea, eventually settling on 47,000. Whether the initial figure was to be 40 or 60, the sequences indicate that from the start Hermann was to double his money on the first win; to stake all of that on the second card, which was also to win; and to let everything ride again on the third.

The last of the surviving fragments of this early version of "The Queen of Spades" (6) gives no more than a glimpse of Chekalinskii asking for Hermann's name (8: 836). In addition to these fragments (3–6 in our count), which all obviously precede the writing of the final text, scholars have discovered still another, later calculation for a faro game in Pushkin's hand (Fragment 7; 8: 836).

2

Deeply rooted in almost all periods of Pushkin's creative career, "The Queen of Spades" reflects many real facts and people of his life and times. To begin with, it is well known that Pushkin—like Tomskii's father and three uncles—was a "desperate gambler" most of his life. Once in his youth, running out of cash, he staked and lost a batch of lyrical poems as security for 1,000 rubles, and had difficulty recovering them later (8: 115). On December 1, 1826, he wrote his friend P. A. Viazemskii from Pskov to report that instead of working on Chapter Seven of *Onegin* he was losing Chapter Four at *stoss* (the German name for faro). The period when his passion for gambling gripped him most destructively was the late 1820's, after he had returned to Moscow and Petersburg from exile.[24] He was a frequent guest, for instance, at the house of the notorious V. S. Ogon-Doganovskii, who had turned his Moscow residence into a virtual casino; this man was to serve as the prototype for Chekalinskii in "The Queen of Spades." Pushkin's debt of 25,000 rubles, to which he refers in his letter of May–June 1830 to Ogon-Doganovskii, was no doubt incurred in the course of a card game.[25]

After his marriage, as he declared in a letter of January 15, 1832, to M. O. Sudienko, Pushkin supposedly had given up "both cards and dice" (15: 4), but some of his contemporaries were to attest that he continued gambling, on occasion, even during his married years.[26] Of the rich lore of his escapades over the card table, the most interesting episode—in its anticipation of Hermann's preference for gambling over love—is this one, as told by Viazemskii: "Pushkin, during his sojourn in the south of Russia, once traveled several hundred versts to attend a ball, where he hoped to meet the current object of his passion. Having arrived in the town before the beginning of the ball, he sat down to play faro; and he kept at it all night, until broad daylight, scattering to the winds his ready cash, the ball, his love, and all."[27]

Faro, the simplest of games as it was played in Pushkin's time, is the game of the superstitious, for it requires no skill and gives free rein to chance. As is well known, Pushkin believed in some occult powers at least half-seriously. His Kishinev diary (12: 303) and a later letter (13: 257) indicate that during his stay in southern Russia he was a member of a masonic lodge—evidence that he must have been well versed in the meaning of magic numbers. Indeed, he may well have named his gamblers Chaplitskii and Chekalinskii after two well-known members of a Petersburg lodge, E. I. Chaplich and P. P. Chekalevskii.[28]

On one famous occasion, superstition actually saved Pushkin from exile, or even execution. This was when he planned to make an illegal trip to St. Petersburg in December 1825. As several contemporaries recorded, the only reason he returned to Mikhailovskoe was that two hares and a priest crossed his path, which he took as bad omens; if he had persevered in his original intention, he would have arrived in the capital, without permission, just on the eve of the Decembrist uprising and would no doubt have been arrested along with its participants.[29]

Pushkin's fear of evil omens is also reflected in the letters he wrote to his wife during the weeks just preceding his work on "The Queen of Spades": on September 14, 1833, he reported that he had seen a hare as he was leaving Simbirsk and later had to return there because he had run into difficulties in obtaining a driver for the next stage of his journey; and on October 2 he told her that he had approached Boldino with forebodings because he had met some priests on the way. His belief in fortune-telling and his great interest in parapsychological phenomena such as "magnetism" (in the sense of telepathy) quite surprised a university professor and his wife with whom he visited in Kazan during this same trip to the eastern part of European Russia.[30] All this was to be reflected in "The Queen of Spades," not only in Hermann's belief in magic cards, but also in the narrator's references to "Mesmer's magnetism" and to the "hidden galvanism" that seemed to be rocking the old Countess (8: 240).[31]

The game of faro, or farobank, originated in Italy, but became fashionable and acquired its name in the Court of Louis XIV. It was still in vogue during the decades preceding the French Revolution—the time when *la Vénus moscovite* (as the old Countess is described) made her glittering debut in Paris. It was called *pharaon* (8: 228) because one of the honor cards bore the face of an Egyptian pharaoh. It was also often called by its German name, *stoss* (which, as we have seen, Pushkin himself used in his letter to Viazemskii). Among twentieth-century games the closest to the game of Pushkin's day is stuss. (Other banking games, such as blackjack and pontoon, are also related to it.) Although the rules of the game Pushkin is describing are markedly different from those of today's faro, I use that name in order to stay close to Pushkin's terminology.

An 1826 publication defined the rules of the game as follows (a gambler giving instructions to his partner): "Draw a card at random, put it on the table, and place on it as much money as you wish. I will deal from another deck, placing the cards alternately in two stacks; when a card equal in rank to yours falls to my side, I take your money; when such a card falls to your side, you receive from me the same amount of money you have placed on your card."[32] In more formal games "my side" and "your side" were replaced by left and right, a banker (and dealer) winning when a card of the selected rank fell to his right, and the punter (or player) winning when the card fell to the banker's left. The punter drew a card from his own deck either at random or by deliberate choice. Playing with friends he might place it in front of him face up, but this was not a wise practice among strangers, because in revealing his card the punter might help the banker cheat. A cardsharp holding the bank could use a deck of marked cards and on noting a loser on top of the stack, could imperceptibly draw two cards, showing the face of the second.[33] In formal games, the punter guarded against this possibility by placing his card face down on the table, and announced his win or loss when the banker dealt out an identical card (identical only in rank; suits were not differentiated). This is precisely what we see in "The Queen of Spades": when Chekalinskii deals a trey to his left, he does not know that the card is a loser for him and a winner for Hermann until Hermann announces his win, "showing his card" (8: 251).

Cheating was considerably more difficult for the punter: the only thing he could do was to use a deck treated with a sticky powder that would help him deface—and thereby alter the rank—of a card if he saw it was a loser. One of Tomskii's friends suggests that the Countess must have cheated with the aid of just such "powdered cards" (poroshkovye karty; 8: 229).[34]

If no cheating was involved, faro provided an equal chance to dealer and punter.[35] A cautious tactic in the game—which one of Narumov's guests, Surin, claims he has always followed—was called mirandole (igraiu mirandolem; 8: 227). It consisted of small bets, with gains withdrawn rather than left on the table.[36] As Chekalinskii cautions Hermann, it was not usual to place a large bet on the very first card in a deal, or as it was called, betting on a simple, or single (sempelem; 8: 250). Chekalinskii's question after Hermann's first win—"Do you wish to receive your winnings now?" (8: 251)—implies that the banker expects him to continue play, betting on his gain as well as on his original stake. The unusual practice of betting a large sum on only one card on each of three consecutive nights attracts a crowd of onlookers. When they comment at the end, despite Hermann's final loss, on his "splendid punting" (8: 252), they evidently mean that there was an elegance to his cool reserve (only one card at a time) and to his seemingly casual way of scattering such a large sum to the winds.

Chaplitskii's attempt to recoup his 300,000 rubles, as related by Tomskii, also began in an unusual way in that he too placed an enormous sum—50,000 rubles—on his first card; but he went on with the game at one sitting rather than coming back the next night to place an even larger sum on a *simple*. For Chaplitskii, as for the Countess at Versailles, the second card drawn by the dealer—that is, the first card falling to his left, for dealing started on the right—turned out to be a winner; this fast resolution of the bet was called winning *sonica* (*vyigrat' sonica*; 8: 229, 230). Chaplitskii continued his game by bending down a corner of the next card he chose, which meant that he wished to let all his money ride as his new bet, thereby doubling the original sum. This was called *paroli* (8: 230). Bending the corner of a card as a way of signaling the doubling of a bet was a bit tricky, for a player might "absentmindedly" bend his card unintentionally or when he was not entitled to; this was the cause of Silvio's quarrel with the young officer in "The Shot," and it was something Chekalinskii was carefully watching for ("straightened out the odd corner"; 8: 250).

To return to Chaplitskii, after winning on his second card, he bet all his money again, indicating this intention by bending his card in the middle, as if to make a bridge out of it. This redoubling procedure was called *paroli-paix* (8: 230).[37] Once he won on this third and last bet, too, he had 400,000 rubles in hand, that is, "he won back what he had lost and even went away a winner" (8: 230).

In all the cases we have seen so far, the punter chose a new card after each win. But a doubling and a second doubling of the stake on the original card was also possible. This was called *routé*—a practice that Narumov describes as tempting at the beginning of the story.[38]

If a player bets on a ruble, wins, lets the sum ride, and wins again, he ends up with a gain of three rubles in addition to his original one (i.e., 1 + 3; hence this play is called *trois et le va*). If he stakes all this once more and wins, his total gain will be eight rubles (i.e., 1 + 7; *sept et le va*). B. V. Tomashevskii has observed that these betting terms inspire Hermann to say, while he is still struggling against his obsession with cards, that "calculation, moderation, and industry: these are my three reliable cards. They will treble my capital, increase it sevenfold" (8: 235), and that later, when he succumbs to his obsession, the same betting terms guide him in his choice of the trey and the seven as the first two magic cards.[39] At the end of the story, if Hermann had won on the third night as well as on the first two, he would have had his "sevenfold increase" (i.e., his original stake plus seven times as much again). The sequences that Pushkin jotted down as he was planning the story— 40–80–160–280 and 60–120–240–420—clearly indicate that he had this procedure in mind for his protagonist.

In his great duel with Chekalinskii Hermann is the only punter, but this is only because no one else wishes to interfere. Normally several people would punt against the banker— indeed, on Hermann's arrival the first night we see that "there were more than thirty cards on the table" (8: 250). In between actions each player was allowed to change his bet; if he wished to do so he would call out *attendez!* ("wait!"). This exclamation, especially if pronounced with excited emphasis, could sound like a rather rude command, offensive to the banker if he was a man of mature years or high rank. Viazemskii records in his *Old Notebook* that a certain Count Gudovich, having attained the rank of colonel, stopped taking the role of banker in faro, explaining that "it is undignified to subject yourself to the demands of some greenhorn of a sublieutenant who, punting against you, almost peremptorily yells out: *attendez!*"[40] This anecdote (as well as the draft of an *Onegin* stanza that we have seen) may have inspired Pushkin's epigraph to Chapter Six of "The Queen of Spades," which reads:[41]

"Attendez!"

"How dare you say *attendez* to me?"

"Your Excellency, I said *attendez, sir!"*

Given the simple rules of faro—amounting to hardly more than the toss of a coin—whose only complications involved the various sequences of betting, how did Hermann lose? Some critics, who did not read the description of the gambling scene carefully, mistakenly assumed that the Countess's ghost had named two cards correctly but cheated Hermann on the third one.[42] In fact, however, the card that was named, the ace, does come up on the banker's left, meaning that Hermann would win if he had the correct card. He simply has the wrong card, a queen, which had fallen on the banker's right. Hermann intended to choose the ace; he even exclaims, "the ace has won!" (8: 251); but when he turns the card face up, Chekalinskii points out to him that it is the queen of spades. Apparently, he "pulled the wrong card" (*obdernut'sia;* 8: 251) without noticing it, and was so sure of having an ace that he did not check the card, even after he turned it face up, until his attention was drawn to the mistake.

From the point of view of mathematical probability, three cards chosen in advance are highly unlikely to produce three winners in a row. Consequently, some scholars have concluded that "The Queen of Spades" is a fantastic tale.[43] Others have tried to explain away the miraculous elements, saying either that three prechosen cards turning up as winners, though unlikely, is still theoretically possible;[44] or that there never was a secret of three cards, only the secret of the Countess's affairs first with Saint-Germain and later with Chaplitskii;[45] or that Hermann pulled the wrong card because the cards in the fresh pack were still sticky with printer's ink;[46] or, finally, that the queen and the ace, for psychological reasons, might have looked alike to Hermann.[47]

Another question usually perceived as central to the interpretation of the story is whether the Countess's ghost *really* visited Hermann (i.e., was objectively seen by the narrator) or whether Hermann merely had a hallucination. In my opinion, to ask this question is as irrelevant as asking whether Gregor Samsa could *really* have turned into a huge cockroach. If we were to inquire into the *real* circumstances of Hermann's acquisition of the secret of the three cards and into his eventual loss over the card table, we might as well undertake a study of the biological feasibility of the metamorphosis of Kafka's hero. The meaning of imaginative literature is conveyed through its system of symbols, and its significance does not depend on their immediate correspondence to scientifically verifiable reality.

Three magic cards in a winning sequence were not Pushkin's own invention. Nashchokin's reminiscences, as recorded by Bartenev, contain the following passage:

Pushkin himself read "The Queen of Spades" to Nashchokin, and told him that the central plot element was not an invention. The old Countess was created in the image of Natalia Petrovna Golitsyna, mother of the governor-general of Moscow, Dmitrii Vladimirovich Golitsyn. She had actually lived in Paris in just the manner Pushkin described. Her grandson [S. G.] Golitsyn told Pushkin that he had once lost at cards and gone to his grandmother to ask for money. She did not give him money, but told him about three cards that Saint-Germain had designated for her in Paris. "Try them," said grandmother. The grandson bet on the cards and regained his loss. The other elements of the plot are all invented.[48]

Such anecdotes about three winning cards must have been common currency, for a similar one is recorded in connection with one of Catherine II's courtiers, P. B. Passek.[49]

Pushkin's diary confirms that he modeled the old Countess on Princess Golitsyna. In the same entry where he records that people began betting on the trey, the seven, and the ace after the story was published, we find this sentence: "A likeness between the old Countess and Princess Natalia Petrovna has been noted at Court, but no displeasure seems to be indicated" (12: 324). The title Princess appears three times in Chapter One in the first two printed versions of the story—those in *Library for Reading* and *Tales Published by Alexander Pushkin* (8: 837)—errors that Pushkin must have made in the manuscript because he had Princess Golitsyna in mind.

Born in 1741, Golitsyna was ninety-two—older even than her fictional counterpart—when Pushkin wrote his story. Just like the Countess, she had married a man who was her inferior in character and intellect, but unlike the Countess, she had never been attractive. It was one of her daughters, Ekaterina Vladimirovna, who had been renowned for her exceptionally beautiful though always cross-looking face, for which she had earned the nickname *la Vénus en courroux*—a nickname that Pushkin was to transform into *la Vénus moscovite*. Since his maternal grandmother's estate was close to that of the Golitsyns, Pushkin had known Natalia Petrovna since childhood. She was present, like an indispensable ornament, at every Court function in the early 1830's.[50] Moreover, she was held in such high esteem at the Court that a deck of large-format playing cards was especially ordered for her so she could play despite her failing eyesight.[51] Thus contemporaries not only recognized many of her features in Pushkin's description of the Countess, but also associated her name with a special deck of cards.

For all this, she was not the only aristocratic old lady Pushkin took for a model. Bartenev's record of Nashchokin's recollections, quoted above, ends with the following: "Nashchokin made the remark to Pushkin that the Countess was not really like Golitsyna; that she bore a much stronger resemblance to another old lady, Natalia Kirillovna Zagriazhskaia."[52] The influence of Zagriazhskaia (a relative of Pushkin's wife) is confirmed by Viazemskii, who relates that Pushkin loved to listen to her conversation, admiring the individuality behind her imperious ways and trying to capture the flavor of a past century in her words. Pushkin subsequently jotted down several anecdotes he heard from her. She, unlike Golitsyna, had been renowned for her beauty. One detail that the fictional Countess certainly inherited from her was her habit, in old age, of fearing every breeze and of fussing at her servants for not handing her her coat fast enough; when she went on walks, a lackey had to follow after, carrying a whole wardrobe so she could put on more garments as she passed from sun to shade.[53]

Another supposedly real-life element that made its way into "The Queen of Spades" is the following adventure of Pushkin's, as recorded by Bartenev:

During the reign of the present Emperor, there was in St. Petersburg a lady, a friend of the Empress, who occupied a place of high esteem both at the Court and in the best society. Her husband was considerably older than she, but, despite this fact, no taint of gossip blemished the years of her youth; she was beyond reproach even in the eyes of a society that loved slander and intrigue. Pushkin told Nashchokin about his relationship with her apropos of a conversation about will-power. Necessity, Pushkin argued, enables one to refrain from fainting or from a breakdown; these can be postponed till a later time. That illustrious, impeccable lady succumbed at last to the poet's persuasive powers and made an assignation with him at her house. In the evening Pushkin succeeded in entering her magnificent palace; according to their agreement he was to lie under a sofa in the living room and await her return home. He lay there for a long time, losing patience, but he could not abandon the enterprise, for it was dangerous to retrace his steps. At last, having lain in wait for a long time, he heard a carriage drive up. The house began to stir. Two lackeys brought in candelabra and lit up the living room. The mistress of the house came in, accom-panied by some lady-in-waiting: they were returning either from the theater or from the Imperial Palace. After a few minutes of conversa-tion, the lady-in-waiting left in the same carriage. The mistress re-mained alone. "Etes vous là?"—and Pushkin stood before her. They went to her bedroom. They locked the door; the thick, luxurious drapes were drawn. The ecstasies of sensuality gripped them. They gamboled and frolicked. There was a splendid bearskin rug in front of the open fireplace. They took all their clothes off, sprinkled on them-selves all the perfume they could find in the room, and lay on the rug... Time was flying fast amidst the pleasures. At last Pushkin acci-dentally went up to the window, pulled the curtain aside, and noticed to his horror that the sun had already risen, it was broad daylight. What could be done? He threw his clothes on as best he could in his hurry to get out of the house. His mortified hostess led him to the glass double door to the outside, but the servants had already got up. At the door they met an Italian butler. This meeting had such an effect on the hostess that she felt ill; she was on the point of fainting, but Pushkin, squeezing her hand hard, begged her to postpone her swoon till another time and to get him out of the house in his, as well as in her own, interest. The woman pulled herself together. In their critical situation they decided to ask for the help of a third party. The mistress called in her chambermaid, an affected old Frenchwoman, who had got dressed quite some time beforehand, and who was skillful in such situations. They asked her to get him out of the house. She accepted the assignment. She led Pushkin downstairs straight through the hus-band's rooms. The latter was still asleep. The noise of footsteps woke him up. His bed was behind screens. He asked from behind them: "Who is there?" "It's me," answered Pushkin's adroit companion, and led him on through to the entrance hall from which he could exit at no risk: even if somebody had met him there, his appearance there could not have aroused any suspicions. The next day Pushkin offered the Italian butler 1,000 rubles in gold in order to buy his silence; though the man did not want to take the money, Pushkin forced it on him. Thus the affair remained a secret, but during the next four months the illustrious lady could not recall it without feeling ill.[54]

Although Nashchokin mentioned no names originally, the name of Countess Daria Fedorovna Ficquelmont, granddaughter of the famous military leader Mikhail Kutuzov and wife of the Austrian ambassador to Russia, was later entered on the margin of Bartenev's manuscript, and she has generally been considered the heroine of Nashchokin's story.[55]

In addition to using these disguised historical personalities for his major figures, Pushkin used quite a few other personages by name in unimportant contexts. Semen Gavrilovich Zorich, for instance, the person to whom Chaplitskii had lost 300,000 rubles, was Catherine II's favorite in 1777–78;[56] and Count Saint-Germain (d. 1784) was a famous adventurer. Likewise, the Madame Lebrun, Leroy, Montgolfier, and Mesmer mentioned in the description of the Countess's room were all real people.[57]

3

A closeness to life, both personal and historical, distinguishes "The Queen of Spades" from *The Tales of Belkin*, some of which were products of a purely literary inspiration. This does not mean that the later story is wholly unconnected with other works of literature—over the years in fact many of its affinities have been demonstrated by scholars—but these affinities reveal little about the essence of its own design.

Let us briefly survey the literary allusions and inclusions in the story, beginning with the most ancient. The words of the young bishop about the Countess, in his funeral oration— "waiting for the midnight bridegroom, vigilant in godly meditation" (8: 246)—refers to the parable of the Wise and Foolish Virgins in Matthew 25: 1–13. The phrase "How the bread of others savors of salt" (8: 233) with reference to Lizaveta is from Canto 17 of Dante's *Paradiso*. The linking of Hermann with Mephistopheles is ironic not only because it romanticizes the hero, but also because in offering to take the old Countess's sins on his own soul in exchange for her secret, he tries to enter into a contract in which he would act the part of Faust.[58] Another literary classic Pushkin may be alluding to is A.-F. Prévost's *Manon Lescaut* (1731), whose hero, Des Grieux, says: "Je resolus . . . de me priver plutôt de mille choses nécessaires que de la [Manon] borner même pour le superflu"—a sentence just opposite in meaning to Hermann's favorite dictum, that his circumstances do not allow him "to sacrifice the necessary in the hope of gaining the superfluous" (8: 227, 235).[59]

Thematically, of course, "The Queen of Spades" is most intimately connected with works centered on gambling. Pushkin's library contained several handbooks and references on games,[60] but more important are those fictional, dramatic, or biographical works that relate gambling adventures. Pushkin himself refers in the story to the eighteenth-century adventurer Casanova, whose *Mémoires* were being published posthumously in Pushkin's time (12 volumes, 1826–38); it has been suggested that one of the personages in the *Mémoires*, the polite Count Canano, influenced Pushkin in drawing the character of Chekalinskii (though his original model, as we have seen, was Ogon-Doganovskii).[61] A younger contemporary of Casanova's, Count Alessandro di Cagliostro (Giuseppe Balsamo), whose *Compendio della Vita e della Gesta* was published in 1791, described a correct prediction of some winning lottery numbers, which may have served as a source either for Golitsyna's anecdote or directly for "The Queen of Spades."[62] Even closer to Pushkin's story is Karl Gottlieb Samuel Heun's novella "Der Hollandische Jude" (1825), published under the pseudonym Heinrich Clauren: its central character discovers a foolproof mathematical method of winning in banking games, and we see him betting on the trey and the seven.[63] The suggestion, on the other hand, that the soul of a person who died recently can predict winning numbers is made in Victor Hugo's novel *Le Dernier Jour d'un condamné* (1829).[64]

The epigraph to Chapter Five of "The Queen of Spades," attributed by Pushkin to Emanuel Swedenborg (Svedberg), has not been found in the Swedish mystic's works and is assumed to be Pushkin's own playful invention in the spirit of anecdotes circulating about the adventures of the clairvoyant theologian.

According to one anecdote, Swedenborg's wicked old aunt, with whom he had had some litigations, appeared to him three days after her death.[65] Swedenborg also appears as a character in a historical novel by Karl Franz van der Velde called *Arwed Gyllenstierna* (1816). In this work, with which Pushkin was undoubtedly familiar, a king in a card game symbolically represents Charles XII, in much the same way as the queen of spades stands for the old Countess in Pushkin's story.[66]

The title "The Queen of Spades" probably originates from the Swedish romantic writer Clas Johan Livijn's short novel *Spader Dame, en Berättelse i Bref, Funne pá Danviken*, published under the pseudonym Hiarta in 1824 and translated into German by Friedrich Heinrich Karl, Baron de La Motte-Fouqué, under the title *Pique-Dame: Berichte aus dem Irrenhause in Briefen* (1826). In several parts of this novel cards of various ranks and suits assume symbolic significance, and in one place a queen of spades is seen blushing. The most dramatic scene is a card game: the young hero, Schenander, having learned that the wicked Major Leyonbrak has ruined his former sweetheart Marie, tries to take revenge on the major by betting against him on the queen of spades—a symbol of Marie. Schenander wins nine times, but the tenth time he bets on the queen he loses all his money and subsequently goes mad.[67]

A passion for gambling and madness are also connected in Victor Ducange's drama *Trente Ans ou la vie d'un joueur* (1827), which had a successful Petersburg run in the early 1830's.[68] In E. T. A. Hoffmann's novel *Die Elixiere des Teufels* (1815–16), on the other hand, Medardus has the delusion that a queen of hearts has taken on the features of his sweetheart, Aurelie. A shorter work by Hoffmann, "Spielerglück" (1820), may also have inspired some of the details of "The Queen of Spades," such as the downfall of the hero because of a queen.[69]

The description of Hermann's imagination as "unbridled" (*neobuzdannoe;* 8: 238) echoes "The Baleful Consequences of Unbridled Imagination" by the Russian Hoffmannist A. Pogorelskii. In another story by Pogorelskii discussed earlier, "The Poppy-Seed-Cake Woman of the Lafertovo Quarter," it seems to Ivanovna that the dead Woman, lying in her coffin, is opening her mouth and trying to catch Ivanovna by the nose. Such scenes were much in vogue in the 1830's. In "The Corpse's

Joke," a story written about the same time as "The Queen of Spades," V. F. Odoevskii's heroine similarly imagines that her jilted lover, now dead, raises his head and sneers at her as she rides by his hearse on a Petersburg street.

A group of contemporary literary works is alluded to in "The Queen of Spades" in the conversation between the old Countess and her grandson (8: 232):

> "Paul!" called the Countess from behind the screen. "Send me a new novel, will you, but please not the kind they write nowadays."
> "What do you mean, grand'maman?"
> "I mean a novel in which the hero does not strangle either his mother or his father, and which describes no drowned bodies. I am terribly scared of drowned bodies."
> "There are no such novels these days."

No one work has been established in scholarly literature as the exact target of the Countess's comment, but since she did not read Russian novels (as the subsequent conversation reveals), she must have been alluding to a late romantic European trend, known in France as the *Ecole frénétique*.

A number of comments in Pushkin's correspondence and notebooks indicate which contemporary authors he might have had in mind in this context. His critical fragment about Alfred de Musset, for example, describes the young author's first collection of poems and dramatic scenes, *Contes d'Espagne et d'Italie* (1829), as devoted exclusively to "mortal sins, murders, and prurience" (11: 175). In connection with plans to launch a periodical, he wrote to M. P. Pogodin in September 1831:

> One thing that eggs me on is that I am itching to expose and lay in ruins the repulsive churlishness of contemporary French literature. To say aloud once and for all that Lamartine is more boring than Young without having the latter's profundity; that Béranger is not a poet; that V. Hugo lacks vitality, i.e., truth; that A. Vigny's novels are worse than Zagoskin's; that their journals are boorish; and that their critical reviews are no better than those published in our *Telescopes* and *-graphs*. I am convinced that the nineteenth century, in comparison with the eighteenth, is in a mire (I mean in France). Their prose can just barely redeem the execrable stuff they call poetry. (15: 29)

Scattered through Pushkin's correspondence, we find derogatory comments on Jules Janin's *Barnave* (1831; 14: 244), on

Hugo's *Le Dernier Jour d'un condamné* (11: 94, 14: 81), on Eugène Sue's *Plick et Plock* (1831; 14: 166), and on Balzac's works (15: 38). In thinking about the review article he mentioned to Pogodin, he jotted down a list of names and titles (12: 204):

> Barnave, Confession, Femme guillotinée.
> Eugène Sue.
> de Vigny. Hugo.
> Balzac. Scènes de la vie privée, Peau de chagrin,
>   Contes bruns, drolatiques. Musset. Table de nuit.

It is not surprising that this list includes Balzac, for at this time, in the early 1830's, all Pushkin had to judge Balzac by was his early works, which only remotely foreshadowed his future great novels. For instance, the 1831 "L'Auberge Rouge"— which contains the phrase "He was called Hermann, like almost all characters in German literature," and which probably inspired Pushkin in naming his hero[70]—is a tale of murder, treachery, and inner torments worthy of the Frenetic School. *La Peau de chagrin* is closer to the mature Balzac, but even it could inspire Pushkin to no more than a few details for "The Queen of Spades." Raphaël's desperate last-ditch gambling before he attempts suicide, for example, might have inspired Hermann's duel with Chekalinskii; and the conditions under which Raphaël accepts the shagreen—that it will fulfill all his wishes but will shrink after each wish and ultimately kill him—has at least a remote resemblance to Hermann's offer to trade his conscience for the secret of the cards. It has also been suggested that that tour de force of voyeurism, Raphaël's hiding behind the curtain in Foedora's bedroom, might have anticipated Hermann's surreptitious visit to the Countess's house[71]—though, as we have seen, Pushkin scarcely needed a literary model for that scene. Tomskii's suggestion that Hermann might have seen Lizaveta in her room while she was asleep is more likely to be a hint at Raphaël's adventure. But the fact that Pushkin eliminated from his early plans the kind of love triangle on which Balzac's novel is built indicates a deliberate movement away from the French author. What is most interesting in *La Peau de chagrin* from our point of view is that it has a cultural frame of reference very similar to that of "The Queen of Spades": in it, too, some bizarre phenomena are described as *galvanisme moral;* the old shopkeeper is compared to Mephistopheles; Raphaël is overawed by the old man's presence, as if he were standing before Napoleon; the myth of the shagreen is described as one worthy of Swedenborg; and hackneyed Byronic characters are mocked as *petits lords Byrons.*[72] It is as though both works were holding up mirrors to the same trends in contemporary culture.

Closest of all to "The Queen of Spades" is a novel to which we shall have to return in connection with the story's symbolic structure: Stendhal's *Le Rouge et le noir.* As we have seen, Pushkin read it soon after its publication in French: in one letter he wrote that he was "enchanted" by it; in another he commented that it was "a good novel despite some false rhetoric and some remarks made in poor taste" (14: 166, 172). One detail of the novel, the batch of fanciful love letters that Julien Sorel copies mechanically for Madame de Fervaques, may well have inspired Pushkin in presenting Hermann's correspondence with Lizaveta. A more important similarity between Julien and Hermann is that both combine a calculating attitude with a passionate nature.[73]

Le Rouge et le noir aside, not one of the literary works mentioned above has more than a tenuous partial connection with "The Queen of Spades." Whereas in some of the Belkin tales the literary model parodied was a determining factor not only for the detail, but also for the overall design, here Pushkin used details of literary models only as so many tiny building blocks, whose individual shape could not influence the eventual configuration. Magic numbers, hallucinations, portentous cards, and cards transfigured into personalities may have been used by a wide variety of authors from Cagliostro to Hoffmann, but the original literary milieux of these components were alien to Pushkin's intentions, and he used them only as materials for an entirely new structure.

4

V. V. Vinogradov has shown, in an interesting analysis, the many faces of Pushkin's narrator in "The Queen of Spades."[74] In several scenes—such as Tomskii's presentation of his anecdote, the conversation in the Countess's boudoir, and Hermann's tête-à-tête with Lizaveta in her bedroom—the narrator acts simply as a stage director. Elsewhere—where we read, for instance, that "indeed it was already getting light" (8: 230)—he seems to be a participant, rather than just a director acting from behind the scenes.[75] At other times he presents events from the points of view of various characters. In the middle of Chapter Two, for instance, the point of view is Lizaveta's; then we switch to that of Hermann. As in some previous works by Pushkin, these shifts are at times extremely fast. For example, in the bedroom scene (8: 241), the sentence "Suddenly an inexpressible change came over her lifeless face" implies an outside viewer who does not know about Hermann's presence in the Countess's house and therefore does not understand what is frightening her. This represents a shift, because the point of view up to that time had been Hermann's. The next phrase, "Her lips stopped mumbling, and her eyes lit up" seems to be Hermann's perception. But the concluding phrase of the same sentence, "a strange man stood before her," clearly reflects her point of view.

Such rapid shifts make our heads turn fast, so to speak, moving in the direction that the camera moves, but there is nothing incongruous about them. But some other ploys of the narrator are strange indeed. In Chapter One, for instance, he seems to yield the floor to Tomskii, but soon begins to unveil details— the Countess "peeling off her beauty spots and untying her hooped petticoat" (8: 228) and Saint-Germain becoming "thoughtful" (8: 229)—that imply the presence of an omniscient narrator. A reversal in the narrator's role is that, omniscient though he may be, he is as much in the dark about Saint-Germain's secret as Tomskii is.[76] Elsewhere the narrator's detached tone warms to a sympathetic discussion of the plight of the *demoiselle de compagnie*; then he inserts a jarringly sarcastic remark about Hermann's first love letter having been taken from a German novel; still later he chattily comments on the banality of Hermann's literary type—all this in contrast to his otherwise detached manner. These fast shifts result in a strange mixture of the characters' delusions with the narrator's objective insights, and in a multiple perspective that can accommodate fantasy within reality, past within the present, and lyricism within an ironic framework.

Prose fiction, writes Iurii Lotman, developed historically against the background of poetry. Although at first sight prose appears to be closer to ordinary nonartistic language, it is in fact twice removed from it; its simplicity is secondary. "In order for the simple to be perceived as simple and not primitive," Lotman argues, "it must be *simplified*, that is, the artist must consciously *avoid the use* of certain elements of structure, and the viewer or listener must be able to project the text against a background in which these 'devices' would have been used."[77] As Lotman sees it, prose fiction is in a way a negation of poetry; it equals "the text plus the minus-devices of poetic speech."[78]

In turning to prose, as we have seen, Pushkin did indeed negate poetry. In *Onegin* he summarily dismissed the prose of Rousseau, Richardson, and others as mere "poetry." When he tried to show, however, what "prose" actually was, he came so close to nonartistic, discursive language—in *The Blackamoor of Peter the Great*, for instance—that its poetic background could no longer be discerned. To Viazemskii it seemed "as if Pushkin [the prose writer] had been very much on his guard; imposing sobriety on himself, he strove to dispel all suspicion that he might have imbibed poetry. The prose writer locked himself inside the walls of his prose, so that the poet could not even take a peek at him."[79] Although these words referred to the nonfictional *History of Pugachev*, they seem to be equally applicable to some of Pushkin's early fictional efforts. Locking the poet completely out, he was trying to create a prose that represented, not just "poetry-minus," but "poetry-minus-minus." In *The Tales of Belkin* he circumvented the problem by adopting imaginary narrators whose speech was unmistakably marked as fictional; but as we have seen, that mode of narration imposed severe limitations on the complexity of ideas to be conveyed. To create the prose style, and at the same time the artistic style, of an omniscient narrator remained a task still to be accomplished. Pushkin accomplished it in "The Queen of Spades" largely by moving back toward previously abandoned poetic devices.

The greater presence of poetry in "The Queen of Spades" is revealed, above all, by a system of symbols more elaborate than in any previous prose work by Pushkin (though "The Stationmaster" already showed a fairly high level of complexity in this respect). Central to the story's symbolic structure is the setting of the action in the archetypal phases of winter and night. These two phases of nature's cycles, which reinforce each other in mood and significance, are emphasized as early as the second sentence of the story: "The long winter night passed imperceptibly" (8: 227). The theme of winter is fully developed in the scene preceding Hermann's surreptitious visit to the Countess's house: "The weather was terrible: the wind howled; wet snow fell in large flakes; the lights shone dimly; the streets were deserted. Only occasionally did a cabdriver shamble by with his scrawny nag, on the lookout for a late passenger. Hermann stood wearing only a jacket, yet feeling neither wind nor snow" (8: 239). As if to reinforce the mood created by this description, several other hints at winter are scattered through the story: the epigraph to Chapter One twice underlines that cardplaying is a pastime for inclement days; the Countess, at least at one capricious moment, refuses to go on a ride because she thinks a cold wind is blowing; and her heavy fur coat contrasts with Lizaveta's light cloak against the background of the fatal stormy night.

A long winter night is the time when the myth of the magic cards is born, and when the hero, deeply stirred by Tomskii's story though outwardly still denying its significance, embarks on his quest. His encounter with the old lady is also at night; so is the visit of her ghost; and the plot unfolds with Hermann's three-night battle over the card table. Morning, inevitably, brings frustration: after the night when the myth was born, Hermann finds himself wandering on the streets in confusion, not knowing how to, or even whether to, act; his nocturnal mission is defeated as he leaves the Countess's house at dawn, for she has carried the secret of the three cards with her to her grave; and the Conclusion, with its matter-of-fact style, brings the story to an end in sober daylight.

In ritual and in folklore, as Northrop Frye has observed, winter and night are associated with the defeat of the hero, with dissolution, floods, and chaos, with the ogre and the witch as subordinate characters, and with the archetype of satire.[80] Pushkin's usage conforms with these traditional meanings. As the story unfolds, winter and night become metaphors for madness—the ultimate in the triumph of chaos.

It might be objected that such a use of symbolic details was common in romantic literature and represented no innovation. Hoffmann's stories, for example, abounded in symbolic images. Romantic prose, however, belonged simply to "poetry" in Pushkin's estimation: what he was attempting was not a capitulation before an ornamental manner of writing, but a judicious introduction of some poetic elements into an otherwise austere, detached mode.

One device that undeniably sets the author of "The Queen of Spades" apart is the planting of structural elements below the surface. The flowers Karamzin's Poor Liza carries are obvious symbols of her youthful innocent love, and the storm that breaks out after her seduction not only is symbolic, but represents a culminating point in the story's external structure. The details Pushkin uses are often not so obvious. For example, a series of compositional elements—Hermann's aimless wanderings, his insensitivity to cold, his chanting of the magic formula "trey, seven, ace," and the like—prepares us for the denouement by its obvious cumulation, but below this exterior structure some other elements are hidden that reinforce our expectations. At the beginning of Chapter Three, for instance, when Lizaveta is so agitated over Hermann's first letter that she cannot give coherent answers to the Countess during their ride through the city, the old lady rebukes her, saying: "What's the matter with you, child? Are you in a trance or something? Don't you hear me or understand what I'm saying?... Thank God, I don't slur my words and I'm not yet a dotard!" (8: 237). Hermann is not present in this scene, nor is the reference to mental decay made apropos of him, and therefore there is no direct connection between the Countess's remark and the story's denouement; but the idea of losing one's mental powers lingers in the reader's memory, and he will eventually see a connection with explicit details of the plot.

In the description of the winter night quoted above there is a reference to the dimly shining streetlights. Obvious attributes of night, they here become associated with winter as well. We also read that Lizaveta often "went to weep in her own poor room, furnished with a papered screen, a chest of drawers, a small mirror, a painted bedstead, and a tallow candle faintly burning in its brass holder" (8: 234), which creates a further association between faint lights, night, and sadness. Before entering the Countess's house, Hermann stares at his watch in the light of a streetlamp, waiting for the right moment; in the anteroom he sees a servant sleeping in an old armchair under a lamp; that lamp casts a feeble light on the reception hall and the drawing room; a gold sanctuary lamp burns in front of the icon-case in the Countess's bedroom; after she is undressed her maids remove the candles, leaving her seated in the dark except for the sanctuary lamp; and later we see Lizaveta snuffing out the candle in her room as the day breaks. These dim lights are appropriate for the hero's ominous movements. Their meaning becomes fully revealed in the monastery scene, where we see the late Countess's servants standing around her coffin with candles in their hands.[81] Readers familiar with the parable of the Wise and Foolish Virgins—as most of Pushkin's readers must have been—may make a further connection between lamps and death as the young bishop says that "the angel of death found her waiting for the midnight bridegroom, vigilant in godly meditation" (8: 246), for the Biblical virgins, waiting for the bridegroom with lamp in hand, stand as representatives of mankind awaiting the Kingdom of Heaven. In this context, the servant sleeping under the lamp in the Countess's anteroom is seen as a foolish man for not guarding his mistress, and she herself, having the candles sent out of her room, appears to be as unmindful of her destiny as the foolish virgins who forgot to bring oil for their lamps. By the time, finally, when Hermann lights a candle to jot down details of the specter's visit (which took place in moonlight), the ominous nature of all dim lights has come to the surface of the story's symbolic structure.

The bishop's description of the Countess as "vigilant in godly meditation" ironically contrasts with the narrator's (or Hermann's) impression, as she sat in her armchair, that "her dim eyes were completely empty of thought" (8: 240).[82] That she is unprepared to face her destiny—to heed the Lord's voice—is also implied in the words "she did not seem to hear" and "Hermann assumed she was deaf" (8: 241)—words that ironically echo her own scolding of Lizaveta: "Don't you hear me?" Further, when the narrator tells us that at balls the guests would all go up to the Countess "bowing low, as if performing an established rite" (8: 233), we may not think of burial rites, but we come to understand the implied religious significance later, as we see the "numerous guests filing by in order to take their last bow before her who had so long participated in their frivolous amusements" (8: 246). Developing the technique of "The Stationmaster" further, Pushkin carefully plants many details to be followed up later in the text.

The theme of death is linked with that of dark forces of destruction. The linkage between them is evident already in the epigraph to the story: "The queen of spades signifies secret ill-will." A playing card, in the first instance, evokes the image of gambling, with its associated meanings of loss and self-destruction, leading to the idea, common in romantic literature, that life is a great gamble.[83] But cards are used in fortune-telling as well, and the soothsayer who can pry fortune's secrets open can also have a share in manipulating supernatural forces.

The chief occult elements in "The Queen of Spades" are, of course, the magic cards and the Countess's ghost, both essential to plot development. They are accompanied by a series of subsidiary elements, some more obvious in meaning than others. The Count Saint-Germain, for instance, is mysterious enough with his magic cards, but Pushkin heightens the mystery by telling us that the Count pretended to be "the inventor of the elixir of life and of the philosopher's stone" (8: 228). When Tomskii has concluded the first half of his story, Narumov asks him why he did not attempt to acquire his grandmother's cabalistic prowess, to which Tomskii replies: "The devil I haven't!" (8: 229). This, of course, is merely a colloquial usage; nevertheless the idea of the Devil, which ties in with so many surrounding details, lingers on in the reader's memory. Mesmer's magnetism, when it is first mentioned in connection with a list of things, people, and ideas characteristic of the eighteenth century, seems innocent enough, but coupled with the reference to the "hidden galvanism" (8: 240) that seemed to be rocking the Countess in her chair it becomes an indication of arcane powers. The statement that Hermann became "petrified" (*okamanel*; 8: 240) after the Countess's arrival home could be just another colloquial usage if it were not placed in the midst of a multitude of references to sorcery; as it is, it implies entrancement. The Countess herself is "petrified" (8: 245) later, when Hermann, seeking the secret door, comes back to her room and sees her dead in her chair. All these details, now half-hidden, now very close to the surface, become conspicuous when Hermann's exclamation "You old witch!" (8: 242) makes the theme of sorcery explicit.

Hermann himself is, of course, as much involved with the secret of the cards and therefore with occult powers as the Countess. Our perception of him, as we have noted before, is often from the viewpoint of Lizaveta, rather than the narrator, which lends something of a comic flavor to the supernatural in his characterization. The young woman's inordinate fright at the sight of the hero is emphasized at every step: when she first sees him "he was standing there motionless with his eyes fixed on her window" (8: 234), which suggests the posture of a hypnotizer; two hours later, inadvertently glancing out the window, she sees him still there; after dinner she comes back to look for him "with a certain feeling of apprehension"; two days later she feels "frightened, though she did not know why" when she spots him at the entrance to the house, "his face hidden in his beaver collar" and "his dark eyes sparkling from under his cap" (8: 234); she develops the faculty of being able to "sense his approach" (8: 235) as if there were telepathy between them; when she sees him at her carriage door, he hands her a letter "before she had time to recover from her fright"; Hermann's boldness "terrified her" (8: 237), and she is just as "frightened" (8: 238) by the rashness of his second letter; the romantic image she has formed of him "both daunted and enchanted" her; when he comes to her room she speaks to him "in an alarmed whisper" and listens to his story "with horror" (8: 244)—all this in reaction to the advances of a rather insignificant, emotionally unbalanced young man on his way to the lunatic asylum. Lest anybody should misunderstand the comic nature of the situation, the narrator steps directly before us and makes his remark about the banality of Hermann's literary type—"actually quite hackneyed by now" (8: 244).

Satire, a concomitant of night, winter, and sorcery, was not a mode of writing congenial to Pushkin. Gentle irony, as many critics have observed, was more consistent with his poetic temperament. But the theme and mood of "The Queen of Spades" inexorably drew him, if not to downright satirical portrayals, at least to heavy doses of irony. None of the story's three main characters is worthy of admiration, and therefore their fate cannot excite a sense of tragedy; Pushkin sought an effect somewhere between the fearsome and the comic. The comic element is fastened primarily on the character of Lizaveta—perhaps because, unlike the Countess and Hermann, she has a happy ending to her story.

Although the narrator bursts into a pathetic tirade about the plight of the poor *demoiselle de compagnie* in the middle of Chapter Two, he soon descends to a level of realism, explaining that "she was proud; she felt her position keenly, and looked around impatiently waiting for a deliverer" (8: 234). Viewed from this perspective, her fear of Hermann is not a maiden's trepidation before a romantic character, but simply the fear that he will not, after all, turn out to be her "deliverer." Granting him an assignation, she risks her reputation in the hope of acquiring a husband; her "gamble," as one critic has put it, is no purer in motivation than Hermann's.[84] The stiff insincerity of her first note to Hermann conveys how she is weighing the pros and cons of an uncertain situation. The scene in which she receives another letter from him via a bold little milliner's maid and angrily tears it up, claiming that it was not intended for her, is the funniest passage in the story. When she realizes that her expectations of Hermann have been frustrated, she resorts to the conventional moralistic phraseology she used in returning his unopened letter, bemoaning the fact that she has become an unwitting accomplice in the murder of her "benefactress" (8: 245)—hardly the appropriate term for the cantankerous old harridan whose benefactions she has been trying to flee.

Lest all this should still not suffice for a realistic appraisal of Lizaveta's character, the narrator relates in the Conclusion that she "has married a very pleasant young man; he holds a position somewhere in the civil service and has a handsome fortune of his own: he is the son of the old Countess's former steward. Lizaveta Ivanovna is bringing up the daughter of a poor relation" (8: 252). Among the many ironies of the Conclusion—such as the remark that Tomskii is engaged to Princess Polina, one of the debutantes to whom the earlier description "brazen and coldhearted" (8: 234) might very well have referred[85]—the greatest is the implication that the handsome fortune Lizaveta's husband possesses derives from the late Countess's property, for we were told early on that her numerous domestics—including presumably her steward—were "robbing the moribund old woman left, right, and center" (8: 234). Although Lizaveta is not aware of it, the Countess has thus truly become her benefactress, which is a role Lizaveta is now herself taking on by bringing up the daughter of a poor relation. Pushkin's introduction of this poor relation at the end of the story may well have been what inspired M. E. Saltykov-Shchedrin to conclude his *Golovlevs* (1880) with the appearance of "Sis" Nadezhda Galkina, who has been keeping a close eye on Golovlevo in anticipation of inheriting it, and who, in all likelihood, is going to uphold the family's tradition of greed and destructiveness.

Though Hermann's fiendishness appears ridiculously exaggerated when seen with the eyes of Lizaveta, and though the narrator himself seems to be laying it on thick at times, it nevertheless contributes to the story's aura of black magic and doom. The "mysterious force" (8: 236) that draws Hermann to the Countess's house, his Mephistophelean soul, his willingness to barter his conscience for the secret of the three cards, the three crimes Tomskii suspects he has committed in the past, and his Napoleonic profile—which, incidentally, denotes not only Hermann's cold-hearted disregard of other people, but also his impending downfall, since that other foreigner, Napoleon, essentially met his downfall in Russia—all conform with the series of images that accompanied the portrayal of the Countess herself. Lizaveta's exclamation "You are a monster!"

(8: 245) clearly parallels Hermann's calling the Countess a witch. In this tale of night and winter, the ogre and the sorceress are not subordinate characters, but take the roles of central hero and heroine.

Narumov's reference to the Countess's "cabalistic power" (*kabalistika;* 8: 229) hints that numbers play a particularly important role in the occult design of the story. As we have seen, the trey and the seven—central to the plot—derived from the terms *trois et le va* and *sept et le va,* and they were already on Hermann's mind when he said to himself: "Calculation, moderation, and industry: these are my three reliable cards; they will treble my capital and increase it sevenfold." Aleksandr Slonimskii, who was the first critic to establish a connection between these words and the numbers Hermann was to receive from the apparition, wrote up the three numbers as a dactylic line with a masculine ending:

$$\underline{}' \,\smile\; \smile/\underline{}' \,\smile\; \smile/\underline{}'$$
troika, se-mërka i tuz

with the variation

$$\underline{}' \,\smile\; \smile/\underline{}' \,\smile\; // \;\underline{}'$$
troika, se-mërka, (pause) tuz

Pointing out that both three and seven have traditionally been regarded as magical numbers, Slonimskii suggests that the line not only constitutes poetry or incantation by itself, but also affects the surrounding prose text, parts of which can be arranged in trinary rhythmic patterns.[86] Even if we reject—as some critics have done[87]—the idea of prosodic patterns surrounding the words of the incantation, the incantation itself, repeated in the text four times, together with the discordant variant in the Conclusion "trey, seven, queen" (8: 252), undoubtedly enhances the poetic impression that the story's elaborate system of symbols has already created.

Since the publication of Slonimskii's essay, several critics have commented on the significance of the numbers three and seven in Pushkin's text.[88] It needs no detailed documentation that three and seven play enormously important parts in both the Old and the New Testament; it will be enough to refer only to the Holy Trinity and to the seven days of creation. These numbers are also prominent in folklore: let us mention only that in the fall of 1833—that is, at the time Pushkin was work-ing on "The Queen of Spades"—he wrote "The Tale of the Fisherman and the Fish," whose hero, having fished for thirty-three years, goes out one morning and catches a golden fish on the third cast of his net; and that "The Tale of the Dead Princess and the Seven Knights"—Pushkin's version of "Snow White and the Seven Dwarfs"—was also written at this time. Furthermore, those two numbers frequently occurred in ma-sonic rites with which, as we have noted, Pushkin was famil-iar: for example, a masonic ceremony began with the master mason's threefold questioning of his fellow masons; introduc-ing a prospective new member to the lodge, the sponsor had to knock on the door three times, to which the master answered with three blows of his hammer on the table; and at one point during the ceremony the time had to be given as a quarter to seven.[89]

The text of "The Queen of Spades" is studded with threes and sevens. The magic cards number three; Chaplitskii loses 300,000 rubles; three chambermaids attend to the Countess in her boudoir, and three maids rush in later when she rings; she dresses according to the fashions of the 1770's; she is informed that the Princess Daria Petrovna died seven years before; she is eighty-seven years old; Hermann thinks she might die within a week, which is to say, seven days; three old maidservants un-dress her after the ball; the epigraph to Chapter Four is taken from a letter dated May 7 (which perhaps not coincidentally was an unlucky day according to contemporary books on the interpretations of dreams);[90] "less than three weeks" (8: 243) pass between the time Lizaveta first catches sight of Hermann and the night of their tryst; there may be three crimes on Her-mann's conscience; three ladies walk up to Lizaveta and Tom-skii during the ball; the funeral takes place "three days after the fatal night" (8: 246); Hermann's vision occurs at a quarter to three (which is roughly the time of the Countess's death three nights before);[91] there are more than thirty cards on the table when Hermann joins Chekalinskii's group; Hermann's first stake is 47,000 rubles (changed, as we have seen, from 40,000 for obvious reasons); and the number of Hermann's ward at the lunatic asylum is seventeen. Ingenious calculations—which hardly seem necessary—can discover even more threes and sevens hidden in the text.

The pervasive role of the number two in the story has been argued by S. G. Bocharov. He writes that the two responses to the anecdote about the magic cards ("Mere chance!" says one of the guests, followed by Hermann's "A fairy tale!"; 8: 229) introduce a binary structure into the story that is sustained throughout. Its chief manifestations are the dyads of reality and fantasy, love and greed, life sixty years before and in the present.[92] These dyads are most clearly gathered into a focus at the moment when Hermann stands in the Countess's bedroom, choosing between two doors. Lizaveta wrote in her letter that "in her bedroom, behind the screen, you will see two small doors: the one on the right leads to a study, which the Countess never enters; the one on the left opens into a corridor, where you will find a narrow winding staircase: this leads to my room" (8: 239). With the obvious intention of emphasizing this setting, the narrator describes it again as Hermann is actually standing at the doors: "On the right there was the door leading to the study; on the left, another one leading to the corridor. Hermann opened the latter and saw the narrow winding staircase that led to the poor ward's room... But he drew back and went into the dark study" (8: 240). When the women arrive home, Hermann watches through a crack in the study door as Lizaveta goes through the other door, and he hears her steps on the winding staircase—sights and sounds that evoke "something akin to a pang of conscience" in his heart (8: 240). Even without this last remark, it would be clear that the two doors represent a choice for Hermann between love and greed, between beauty and ugliness, between Venus and Mammon— and also, as it turns out, a choice between sanity and madness. It has been suggested that the theme of two doors opening to the left and to the right is recaptured in the gambling scene, when we see cards falling to the left and to the right.[93] Hermann, obsessed with gambling, must choose the door on his right because the winning card falls to the punter's right.

Twos appear unobtrusively elsewhere in the story—as do a wide assortment of other numbers, whose possible cabalistic significance has been discussed by critics.[94] Pushkin, as a former Freemason, may well have been aware of numerological implications. What is most important, however, is not the meaning of a particular number, but the fact that "The Queen of Spades" is as full of numbers as any scientific treatise. It is as though exact measurements were enormously important both to the narrator and to the characters. When Hermann says that the Countess might die within a week or even in a couple of days, he draws attention to the great weight every minute carries in her crepuscular existence. Indeed the majority of the numbers we see in the story designate time: we are told exactly how many days, hours, sometimes even minutes, pass between one event and another; card games and balls do not end just toward the morning, but at exactly stated hours; the Countess's age, though not at first, is eventually specified as eighty-seven; and her friend did not die just some years ago, but exactly seven years before.

Numbers—signposts measuring our finite spatial and chronological movements, reminding us of the closeness of the end—are natural accessories in a tale of night and winter. It is no accident that Hermann, standing under the dim streetlight, fixes his gaze on his watch, impatiently waiting for what he believes will be his moment of fulfillment (what in fact turns out to be his moment of doom). Looking over the objects in the Countess's drawing room, he notices a clock made by the famous Leroy (the work of a long-deceased craftsman measuring the present), and as he waits in the study he hears not just that one clock, but a multitude of clocks, striking at first twelve, then one, then two. And finally, in Chapter Five, the narrator tells us—once more making a watch the harbinger of the witching hour—that Hermann looked at his watch just before the ghost made its appearance.

The hero's passion, appropriately for a tale of destruction, is greed. Its most eloquent formulation is his dream following his first look at the Countess's house: "It was late when he returned to his humble lodging; he could not go to sleep for a long time, and when he finally dropped off, he dreamed of cards, a green table, heaps of bank notes, and piles of gold coins. He played one card after another, bent the corners resolutely, and kept winning, raking in the gold and stuffing the bank notes in his pockets" (8: 236). The next time we see gold as we accompany Hermann on his quest for riches is at night in the Countess's bedroom, where a gold sanctuary lamp burns in front of the icon-case. Since the Countess is a wealthy woman, we assume the lamp to be of pure gold—pure in both material substance and spiritual function. Its implied meaning of timelessness is contrasted with the "worn" gilt coating (8: 239) of the arm-chairs and sofas in the same room. The gold of Hermann's dream reappears at the beginning of Chapter Six, too, when he says, seeing a young girl, "How shapely! Just like a trey of hearts" (8: 249), since the Russian word for hearts is *chervon-nyi* (red), the same word from which *chervonets*, gold coin, is derived.[95]

The image of the trey of ("gold") hearts as a shapely young woman, subsequently linked with a "luxuriant flower" (8: 249) in Hermann's dreams, sums up the connections of several themes that have been in the making throughout the preced-ing chapters. The series decay-old age-greed-egoism-wealth is linked clearly enough, but when it is joined with that of youth-beauty-love, the connections become complicated.

One complication is that the Countess, who performs her chief role in the story as an old woman, is introduced to us in her youth. Her youthful beauty, in line with her later role as a witch, has a sinister side to it. A sensational *Vénus moscovite*, she nearly drives Richelieu to suicide with her cruelty. Her husband, whom she has made into a lackey, fears her "like fire" (8: 228); when he refuses to pay her gambling debt, she slaps him on the face and goes to bed by herself "as an indication of her displeasure" (8: 228). Her sexual attractiveness, which she clearly used to manipulate men for her selfish purposes, is not described directly at first; it is conveyed to us partly by men's reactions to her (a case in point is Saint-Germain's readiness to help her) and partly through references to the external trap-pings of her toilette. She is seen, for example, peeling off her beauty spots and untying her hooped petticoat as she orders her husband to pay her debt.

The idea of an outer shell lacking appropriate inner content is recapitulated in Chapter Two, when we are told that the Countess no longer had "the slightest pretensions to beauty, which had long since faded from her face, but she adhered to all the habits of her youth, strictly following the fashions of the 1770's, spending just as much time on, and paying just as much attention to, her toilette as she had sixty years before" (8: 231). If in Chapter One we perceived a contrast between external beauty and inner cruelty, in the following chapters we are struck by the inappropriateness of the frills and flounces that adorn her aging body. The paraphernalia of her femininity—first seen as beauty spots and hooped petticoat—are now represented by the jar of rouge one of her maids holds, by the hairpins that sit in a box in Chapter Two and come showering off her in Chapter Three, by the mirror—the symbol of a young woman's vanity—in front of which she is seated in both chapters, and by her "tall bonnet with flame-colored ribbons" (8: 231). The epithet flame-colored (ognennogo tsveta), giving an ominously provocative quality to the headgear of an octogenarian, reminds us that her husband used to fear her like fire (kak ognia). And her other bonnet, the one her maids unfasten after her return from the ball, is "bedecked with roses" (8: 240), which reminds us of her portrait, in which she is shown as "a beautiful young woman with an aquiline nose, with her hair combed back over her temples, and with a rose in her powdered locks" (8: 240). This throwback to her youthful days keeps the idea of her sexuality alive; it is, of course, also reinforced by Hermann's wild notion that he might possibly become her lover.

The witchlike union of old age and provocative sexuality—summed up in the oxymoron "misshapen ornament" (8: 233)—culminates in the bedroom scene where, for the first time, the trappings and riggings come off, "the loathsome mysteries of her dress" (8: 240) are revealed, and her actual body, her gray, close-cropped hair, swollen feet, flabby lips, and dim eyes empty of thought, are shown. Her "yellow dress, embroidered with silver" (8: 240), connects a color symbolic of spring and youth with a precious metal that, like gold, represents wealth. When the maids take it off of her, her face assumes the dress's yellow color, with an ironically reversed meaning. Her frivolous attires are contrasted with her simple night clothes and eventually with the white satin robe in which she is buried.

The bishop's reference to the midnight bridegroom, finally, establishes a Biblical union between the wedding feast and the coming of the Kingdom of Heaven, between love and death, between sex and destruction.

Another thing that complicates the connection between the greed-destruction and love-sex themes is the ambiguity of Hermann's own attitudes. As he listened to Tomskii's anecdote, he must have formed an idea of the Countess's sexual nature. The veiled suggestion that she might have acquired the secret of the cards by granting her favors to Saint-Germain and might have passed it on to Chaplitskii in exchange, at that later stage in her life, for *his* favors could be on Hermann's mind as he contemplates becoming her lover. In that scheme sexual love would be the means for the attainment of the secret, that is, eventually of riches. When Hermann finds himself in front of the Countess's house, however, he notices young beauties slipping out of elegant carriages and revealing shapely legs—which presents a different image of sex, not a means to wealth but the prize wealth can bestow. The sight of those elegant ladies seems to be an added stimulus for him to pursue the secret of the cards. The Countess's house, which is both a depository of wealth and the sanctuary where the secret of the magic cards is hidden, is visited by these beautiful creatures: to attain them you have to be rich enough to be admitted along with them as an equal. Thus Hermann connects sexual fulfillment with riches, anticipating Gogol's Akakii Akakievich, who will feel so exhilarated in an expensive new coat that he will giggle at a risqué picture in a shop window.

The narrator deliberately, almost teasingly, plays on these two meanings of sex when he tells us at the end of Chapter Two: "Hermann beheld a fresh young face and dark eyes. That moment sealed his fate" (8: 236). Is this meant to convey to the reader that Hermann, having seen those beautiful dark eyes—the same color as his own—has fallen in love, and Lizaveta will be the prize awaiting him at the end of his financial struggles? Or does it imply that, having found a means to get into the Countess's house, he will never be able to free himself of his obsession with the magic cards, so that his fate is sealed in that sense? At first, as we see him lingering about the house and finally handing a letter to Lizaveta, we may think he is really in love, but soon the narrator informs us that the letter was translated from a German novel. Still another reversal comes when we learn that his subsequent letters "were no longer translations from German," but were "inspired by passion" (8: 238). That passion, however, turns out not to be amatory after all when we are told, in the scene in Lizaveta's room, that "neither the poor girl's tears nor the wondrous charm of her sorrow could move his icy soul" (8: 245). With this, one would think, Hermann's affair with Lizaveta has come to an end, but in fact her image is conjured up again when the apparition tells Hermann: "I will forgive you my death under the condition that you marry my ward, Lizaveta Ivanovna" (8: 247). This could mean to Hermann either that sexual fulfillment will come, after all, when he has won on the three cards; or that he is duty-bound to repay Lizaveta for her help in obtaining the secret; or, finally, that he must atone for his deed by marrying a woman he does not love.

The ambiguities, it seems, are deliberate. Pushkin's treatment of the Hermann-Lizaveta relationship is his highest achievement in the art of implying meaning by association. Lizaveta's presence is not essential to the plot: after all, Hermann could contrive some means to get into the old woman's bedroom even without the ward's help. But without her presence Hermann's pursuit of the magic cards would be simply madness or greed; in either case a drab affair. Although we cannot unequivocally say he really loves Lizaveta, the mere juxtaposition of potential love and actual greed gives greed rank; it lends, simply by association, an air of nobility to Hermann's actions.

Still another complicating factor in the combination of the greed-destruction and love-sex themes is the character of Lizaveta. The first reference to her sexuality is made when the Countess, though unaware of Hermann's existence, accuses her of trying to captivate someone by donning fancy clothes for their ride. This theme is taken up again when the narrator tells us that she is impatiently looking for a deliverer. She, like Hermann, is counting on love to improve her status. In that sense there is no contrast between her and the other two main characters; but other details suggest that she is set in a contraposition to both. She is, for example, obviously one of the *plus fraîches* of the epigraph to Chapter Two, vastly different from their aging mistresses; and indeed the chapter ends with the image of her "fresh young face" (8: 236). Though egotistical herself, she is seen as a victim of self-seeking attitudes when the narrator reports: "The young men, calculating in their whimsical vanity, did not honor Lizaveta Ivanovna with their attention, though she was a hundred times more appealing than the brazen and coldhearted debutantes on whom they danced attendance" (8: 234). There follows a series of intertwined contrasts and parallels between her and the other two main characters. Her mirror and the screen by her bed are mentioned, reminding us of the same objects in the Countess's rooms. As she and the old lady leave for the ball, the latter epitomizes both old age and wealth since she is carried and is wrapped in a sable fur. By contrast, her young ward flits out dressed "in a light cloak, her head adorned with fresh flowers" (8: 239). No other image could represent a greater challenge to the winter night, to the wind and the snow, to senility, and to the "cold egoism" (8: 233) that failed to provide a winter coat for her. Yet soon afterwards the Countess's portrait as a young woman, with a rose adorning her hair, comes within our view, and it seems that Lizaveta, though a contrast to the old lady, is a parallel to the young Countess.

Parallels sometimes curve off to become contrasts. When the two women come home from the ball, we see the Countess being undressed by three chambermaids; and later we are informed that on her arrival home, Lizaveta "hastened to dismiss the sleepy maid who begrudgingly offered her services; she said she would undress by herself" (8: 243). The situations—maids offering help in undressing—are parallel. But contrasts soon follow. Hermann could be in Lizaveta's room, undressing the lovely young woman, but driven by a thirst that love cannot assuage, he prefers the crone's dubious magic to the girl's affections, and he becomes a witness to the "loathsome mysteries" of the Countess's dress. The rose-bedecked bonnet comes off the old lady's head, but Lizaveta remains dressed—symbolically untouched—and the fresh flowers are still in her hair when Hermann eventually comes up to her room. She herself articulates her understanding of Hermann's behavior in terms of a contrast between love and greed, telling herself: "All that was not love! Money was what his soul was craving!" (8: 245). But the contrasts are soon smoothed out: the image of Hermann pressing Lizaveta's "cold, unresponsive hand" (8: 245) is reiterated when the old housekeeper kisses her former mistress's "cold hand" at the funeral (8: 247); and the Conclusion—relating that Lizaveta's charms have captivated the right man, that she has acquired some of the riches of her benefactress, and that she has a young ward of her own—endows her with attitudes unmistakably parallel to those of Hermann and the Countess.

5

With all these intricate symbols, densely packed in a texture where every word carries multiple connotations, Pushkin was clearly inching back toward poetry. "The Queen of Spades" is especially close from this point of view to Onegin and The Bronze Horseman. The shared perception of life as a faro game in Onegin and "The Queen of Spades" has already been mentioned. But the two share a number of other symbolic usages as well. Let us just mention the presentation of winter. In Chapter Five of Onegin Tatiana engages in fortune-telling on a winter night, and would try her hand at sorcery too, if she did not find it so frightening. In Chapter Seven winter is called a "sorceress" (6: 151). Among the subsidiary images surrounding winter we find some shared with "The Queen of Spades," such as snow, mirrors, moonlight, and the color silver, all occurring in the fortune-telling scene. Tatiana's dream is also set in a snow-covered wilderness on a misty winter night; the bear that catches her is a kind of an ogre; she, like Hermann, peeks through a crack in a door, trying to divine the arcane activities inside; she hears glasses clicking as if at a "funeral feast" (6: 104); she sees an assembly of monsters, among them a witch and a spider (the same creature that Hermann identifies with the ace in his dreams); when she opens the door the wind blows out the candles; and Onegin, presiding over these monsters, is obviously endowed with magic power. All these images presaging destruction prepare us for Onegin's stabbing of Lenskii—an explicit prediction of the senseless duel that the two men are going to fight in the next chapter.

The Bronze Horseman shares with "The Queen of Spades" the central themes of destruction, death, and madness, introduced by a howling storm on a November night. The subsidiary symbols used are not identical with those in "The Queen of Spades," but their arrangement around the central themes is very similar. Flood as an archetype of the winter phase in the seasonal cycle is preeminent; it is contrasted by frequent images of boats, islands, and small cottages as symbols of frail human existence. "Cruel winter" (5: 136) is referred to; harshness, coldness, and savagery are also represented by granite, by iron designs, by the "needle" (*igla*; 5: 136) of the Admiralty building, by metal helmets, and by fearsome animals, in the form of lions and stallions, and of the Neva River—a beast carrying its prey after the flood.

The prose writer working on "The Queen of Spades" had clearly not shut the poet out; he even took a sip from his poetic goblet. In doing so Pushkin achieved the kind of synthesis of poetry and prose that was to make fiction the leading genre of the nineteenth century both in Russia and in the West. At the forefront of the literary movements of his time, he was exploring the same techniques as his great French contemporary Stendhal—also known for the austerity and detached manner of his prose style. Just as the title "The Queen of Spades" hints at gambling in the first instance, so also does the title *Le Rouge et le noir*. To be sure, we never actually see Julien Sorel placing a bet. But the theme of gambling associated with red and black (of the roulette board) pervades the novel, for every major decision Julien makes is a gamble.[96] He could settle down to a comfortable life of mediocrity as a partner in Fouqué's business, but he chooses (like Hermann staking his modest capital) the harsh life of the seminary in the hope of a brilliant future. As secretary to the Marquis de la Mole he has excellent prospects, but he proceeds to risk them by getting involved with Mathilde. As a protégé of Madame de Fervaques, he could soon rise to the highest ranks in the clergy, but he pitches this coveted goal against the demands of his pride and passion. Like Pushkin, Stendhal often implies by association: for instance, Madame de Rênal calls love a foolish lottery (Chapter Eight); Julien stops by a café that is also a billiard room on his arrival in Besançon (Chapter Twenty-four); and he is seated at a card table during the conspiring aristocrats' secret night meeting (Chapter Fifty-two).

The colors of the novel's title also allude to blood and mourning and to a number of associated meanings. The holy water in the Verrières church looks like blood as the sun shines on it through red drapes (Chapter Five).[97] Red assumes the prognostic significance of murder and execution; but at the same time it also signifies liveliness, colorfulness, adventure, and revolt against mediocrity—against everything that the black cassock of the priest signified under the reign of Charles X. Black acquires its most prophetic meaning when we see Mathilde wearing it on the anniversary of the execution of Boniface de la Mole (Chapter Forty).

An element common to Pushkin's story and Stendhal's novel is the heavily symbolic meaning attached to time. As Julien contemplates seizing Madame de Rênal's hand when he is sitting in the dark with her and Madame Derville outside the Rênals' château at Vergy, the clock strikes a quarter to ten. He resolves to execute his scheme at exactly ten; and when the clock strikes, "each stroke of its fatal chiming echoed in his breast, making it quiver as if by a physical shock."[98] Similarly, in Chapter Fifteen he is awakened to action—invading Madame de Rênal's bedroom for the first time—by the clock striking two in the morning. The comparison Stendhal introduces at this point—"that noise aroused him as the crowing of the cock had aroused Saint Peter"[99]—reminds one of Pushkin's ironic allusion to the parable of the Wise and Foolish Virgins.

Although Julien shares some traits with Hermann, he is quite different from the Russian: he is basically a positive character whose actions can be seen in a tragic light. For that reason, the symbols that stand for him are also quite different; but even so the technique of portrayal—surrounding the hero with images that will add depth to his character by association—remains the same for both writers. Julien's chief symbol is unrestrained growth. It is stated in Chapter Two—before Julien himself is introduced—that a promenade in Verrières, called Cours de la Fidélité, is lined by beautiful plane trees. But their growth is kept in check by the mayor, Monsieur de Rênal, who has them severely pruned back twice a year in order to make their foliage dense. "I like shade," he argues, "and I have my trees cut to provide shade. I can't imagine what else a tree is made for, especially when, unlike a useful walnut tree, *it does not bring any revenue.*" [100] For Monsieur de Rênal beauty without practical use or profit is unjustifiable. As we read on, we soon realize that Julien is, in the eyes of his family, what a merely decorative tree is for Monsieur de Rênal: he is small, frail, handsome, sensitive, and intelligent; and—unlike his more robust brothers—he is no use to his father at his sawmill and is therefore frequently beaten. The theme of beauty versus usefulness is taken up again in Chapter Eight when Monsieur de Rênal complains that the magnificent walnut trees on the grounds of his château at Vergy—even walnut trees that bring *some* profit—take up space where he could otherwise grow wheat. It is precisely under these trees that Julien walks with Madame de Rênal and the children, beginning their romance—a romance that will develop under an immense lime tree, a few feet from the house, where they spend warm summer evenings. Throughout the novel trees stand for freedom and happiness.

Free-growing trees represent height, and in that sense they are connected with another leitmotif of the novel: that of climbing. After an altercation with Monsieur de Rênal—whose mode of life is symbolically represented by restrictive walls [101]—Julien climbs to a mountaintop to contemplate his situation in Chapter Ten; *debout sur un roc immense* [102] is a typical posture for him, giving him a sense of freedom and power. The related image of climbing ladders—which we see Julien do once going up to Madame de Rênal's window and twice to Mathilde's—has social as well as sexual connotations, because both women are Julien's social superiors.

6

Pushkin and Stendhal are much alike, then, in borrowing from poetry to enrich the potentialities of realistic prose. With his new technique Pushkin had at last removed the second minus from what had seemed to be poetry-minus-minus in *The Blackamoor*, and had arrived at the happy formula of poetry-minus. But in one respect—in the extreme density of its symbolic texture—"The Queen of Spades" is perhaps not removed far enough from poetry. In *Le Rouge et le noir*, Stendhal fashioned a similarly intricate system of symbols—but this is spread over some seven hundred pages. Pushkin's story runs to only twenty-five pages, and so every word weighs as heavily, every phrase is laden with as much associative meaning, as in poetry. In this sense A. V. Chicherin is right in suggesting that "The Queen of Spades" is so condensed that it has the potentials of expansion into a novel.[103] Yet highly condensed as it is, "The Queen of Spades" accomplishes what is accomplished in *Le Rouge et le noir* and what can be accomplished only to a lesser degree in a poetic work: it gives a detailed psychological portrait of the central hero, both through direct characterization and through images that have only indirect connections with him. An elaborate symbolic structure combined with the straightforward explicitness of prose is the best medium for psychological portraiture.

The key to Hermann's behavior is his filial attitude to the Countess.[104] Imploring her to give him the secret of the cards, he says: "For whom are you saving your secret? For your grandsons? They are rich as it is, and they don't even know the value of money" (8: 241). Like a jealous sibling, Hermann would like to push all rivals out of the Countess's heart. Waxing more and more rhetorical in his entreaties, he tries to stir feeling in her aging heart by evoking the image of a newborn babe. When, at the funeral, a relative remarks that Hermann was the Countess's natural son, this is only a joke; but it reinforces the effect of other veiled suggestions in the same direction, all the more so because it was obviously provoked by Hermann's filial-seeming behavior: his lying prostrate on the cold floor for several minutes and his crashing on his back against the ground as if overcome by grief. In the context of such allusions—not necessarily filtered through Hermann's mind, but often communicated by the narrator directly to the reader—one is led to conclude that the Countess's desire to read "a novel in which the hero does not strangle either his mother or his father" (8: 232) is a forewarning about a scene in which a self-appointed son will cause the death of a mother figure.

The Oedipal element in the relationship is obvious from Hermann's thought of becoming the old lady's lover and, indirectly, from the bishop's reference to the "midnight bridegroom." Additional signs pointing in the same direction are the Countess's provocative sexuality even in old age; the flashbacks to her youth emphasizing her attractiveness; and the parallels between her and Lizaveta, confounding the distinction between mother and other females. The most interesting aspect of the Oedipal relationship, however, is Hermann's desire to divine mother's "secret."

It has been remarked that Hermann's nature is revealed at the very beginning, when he watches other people play, trying to learn their secrets, while he himself remains aloof—acting the part of a voyeur.[105] Secretiveness, though this time with no reference to Hermann, is implied in the repeated mentioning of screens: the Countess retires behind one in her boudoir after her conversation with her grandson, and another one is listed among the furnishings of Lizaveta's room. Characteristically, Hermann goes behind a third screen—the one in the Countess's bedroom—on his way to her study. His subsequent spying on the Countess as she undresses and his passionate begging for her secret have religious connotations as well as sexual ones. Attempting to learn the secret of life is the universal filial sin of mankind, for which Adam and Eve were expelled from the Garden of Eden. Revealing a secret is also a central element in the masonic initiation ceremony, based on the legend of Hyram-Abif, the chief architect of Solomon's temple, who was murdered by his workmen because he would not give them a password.[106]

Windows, through which Hermann looks at Lizaveta and the ghost looks at Hermann, represent a related image. Even more important are doors, which are emphasized not only in the centrally placed bedroom scene, where Hermann has to choose between two, but also on other occasions. Earlier, for example,

Hermann watches the doors of the Countess's carriage and the gates of her house close. Later he has to find both the entrance to and the exit from the secret staircase. The ghost's visit is also punctuated by the opening and closing of doors. A door opening can reveal a secret and admit a novice; passing through a gate is a rite of passage. No wonder Hermann dreams of the card seven as a Gothic gate, though he also thinks of it in relation to time, whose passage brings death—another connection between sex and destruction in the story.

There is also a set of images that links Hermann with several older men and these older men with one another. The primary father figure in relation to Hermann is Saint-Germain, who possessed, and passed on to the Countess, the secret Hermann seeks. His name derives from the same root as Hermann's own; and each is described as "a very remarkable man" (*chelovek ochen' zamechatel'nyi*; 8: 228, 243).[107] Another man who acquired, though had not originally possessed, the secret, and whom Hermann therefore wishes to imitate, is Chaplitskii. Eventually all older, wealthy, well-fed males are united in Hermann's mind: "Every portly man reminded him of an ace" (8: 249). Just as in English the word ace has the secondary meaning of a person who excels at something, so the Russian term *tuz* has an added meaning: a person who carries some weight, a "big shot." It has also been remarked that the word *tuz* is close phonetically to *puzo* (paunch), whose derivative, *puzastyi*, denotes the corpulent men associated with aces.[108] The closer Hermann gets to his decisive final gamble, the greater the number of aces that seem to confront him: on the first night we see him "reaching over from behind a corpulent gentleman who was punting at the table" (8: 250), and on the third night "the generals and privy councillors abandoned their whist in order to watch such an extraordinary game" (8: 251). The supreme ace is Chekalinskii himself, who shares a "highly respectable appearance" with Saint-Germain (8: 228, 250), and who "had at one time made millions" just as easily as Chaplitskii had "squandered millions" (8: 229, 249). It is he whom Hermann, imagining he has secured the Countess's help, tries to defeat in a contest that "was like a duel" (8: 251).

But even though Chekalinskii assumes Hermann's own pallor for a short while, both Chekalinskii and the all-powerful mother figure remain beyond the reach of this Mephistopheles who has rebelled against parental order. Telling Hermann that the anecdote was "only a joke" (8: 241), the Countess refuses to take him seriously (which is why he grows so angry); she still mocks his boyish quest when she casts "a mocking glance at him, screwing up one of her eyes" (8: 247) from her coffin; the father and mother figures are obviously in collusion against him, for Chekalinskii imitates the Countess both in smiling and in screwing up his eyes (*prishchurivaias'*; 8: 250); and she laughs at him again, grinning and screwing up her eyes, when he has pulled the wrong card. Chekalinskii not only has a constant smile, even when his hands are shaking, but is also emphatically polite, even "affable" (*laskovo*; twice on 8: 251), as if he were dealing with a child.

The ace, however, is also ominously associated in one of Hermann's dreams with a spider—a threatening, blood-sucking creature.[109] Further, the epigraph to Chapter Six—showing an impudent young man being put in his place by a figure of authority—predicts that Hermann, too, will be frightened of Chekalinskii and all the other aces-turned-spiders who watch his game, and that he will bring on his own defeat. As the game gets under way, Hermann's trey wins against a nine, which recalls the funeral, for the time of that event—"nine o'clock in the morning" (8: 246)—is the only other use of the number in the story. On the second night Hermann's seven wins against a knave, or jack (*valet*, 8: 251), which is even more ominous because the jack is junior to the queen, king, and ace in a deck. When, finally, Hermann repeats "Trey, seven, ace! Trey, seven, queen!" in rapid succession at the madhouse (8: 252), he reveals that he cannot distinguish between the mother and the father who have both conspired against him.

But this confrontation with figures on whom he projected the images of his father and mother still does not explain Hermann in full. An important fact, which has been curiously neglected by critics, is that Hermann is squandering his patrimony. At first we are led to believe that the 47,000 rubles his father left him are sacred to him: he "did not touch even the interest earned by these funds" (8: 235). It is obviously a bourgeois paternal superego we hear vowing that "calculation, moderation, and industry are my three reliable cards" (8: 235); and when Hermann argues before the Countess that "he who cannot guard his patrimony will die in poverty" (8: 241), he is obviously reciting a paternal maxim deeply inculcated in him. Yet his attitude to his inheritance is an ambivalent one. He has not come to terms with it; if he had, he would not have such a cramped awe before it but would try to use it sensibly. He might even lose some of it at cards without having an overwhelming feeling of guilt. As it is, however, his patrimony represents a terrifying test of his prowess and masculinity. If he managed to increase it sevenfold with mother's help (fully winning her love), he would gain his "independence" (8: 235) not only from financial worries, but also from the demands his late father has put on him. If he cannot do it, he might as well destroy it all at once, along with himself.

Hermann's chief burden, then, is the guilt he feels toward his father, who left him the capital. Since he knows he cannot live up to his father's expectations, he is driven to self-punishment: that is the "mysterious force" (*nevedomaia sila*; 8: 236) that draws him to the Countess's house. The same *nevedomaia sila*, we may note, operates in the *Water-Nymph*—in that case explicitly as the hero's pangs of conscience, which draw him to the banks of the Dnieper, where his former sweetheart committed suicide (7: 212). Further, the remark that Hermann "felt no pang of conscience over the old woman's death" (8: 245) implies that he is so preoccupied with a deeper sense of guilt— possibly with the suspected "three crimes on his conscience" (8: 244)—that his latest outward actions could hardly leave a ripple on it. This element in Hermann's characterization may well have been what influenced Dostoevskii in making Raskolnikov unrepentant for his murder of the pawnbroker: Raskolnikov, too, was preoccupied with a deeper sense of guilt, and his outward crime was more a symptom than a cause. Pushkin is so aware of operating with subconscious forces in "The Queen of Spades" that he comes close to formulating a theory of the subconscious: two fixed ideas, his narrator remarks, cannot occupy the same place in one's mind (8: 249).[110] In order to accomplish his gambling mission, Hermann had to suppress his guilt feelings both about his patrimony and about his role in the Countess's death; but these subconscious feelings were what really drove him to Chekalinskii's house.

Freud's statement in his Dostoevskii essay about gambling as self-punishment seems to hold true for Hermann as well: his gambling is a self-destructive act.[111] Its attraction is more magnetic than the charms of Lizaveta or, for that matter, any other woman. "Have you never been tempted?" Narumov asks Surin. "Have you never risked *routé*?" (8: 227). "Young men thronged to his [Chekalinskii's] house, forgetting the balls for the sake of cards and preferring the seductions of faro to the enticements of gallantry," says the narrator (8: 249). Dostoevskii, who developed this aspect of Pushkin's theme in *The Gambler*, demonstrated just this kind of opposition between love and gambling, endowing the latter with the greater attraction. In comparison with Hermann's deeper motive of self-destruction, the psychological drama that he projects on people around him is only a self-delusion: he may pretend he is going to treble his capital and increase it sevenfold; he may think he will marry Lizaveta once he has beaten the evil powers that stand between him and fulfillment in love; he may even populate his chimerical world with imaginary mothers and fathers, and blame them for conspiring against him; but in fact all he wants, deep down, is to blow those 47,000 rubles to the winds and thereby destroy himself.

With its flashes into the deepest recesses of the hero's emotional life "The Queen of Spades" is close, once more, to *Le Rouge et le noir*. From a labyrinth of psychological motives presented by Stendhal, let us mention only that at the end of the novel, the mere arrival of Julien's father in his cell makes Julien think that "he comes at the moment of my death to deal me the final blow,"[112] and, to round out his ambivalent feelings, at the same time he views Madame de Rênal—the person he attempted to murder—"as if she were his mother."[113]

What matters in the psychological portraits drawn by Pushkin and Stendhal is not whether they presented medically accurate cases (they may have made mistakes in that respect), but that they added a new dimension to fiction writing, making it far richer in hidden layers of meaning than any previous fictional work. Their ultimate achievement is a poetic vision, not some new, scientifically verifiable psychological discovery (which, if it occurs, is only an incidental by-product of a work of art).

Pushkin's poetic vision, open to symbolical and psychological complexities, discerns the transitory nature of life and the unity of opposites reconciled by the passage of time. The most striking image perceived by such vision in "The Queen of Spades" is the scene of Hermann's descent by the secret staircase as he leaves the Countess's house. As he descends, he imagines that some "lucky young man," "dressed in an embroidered coat, with his hair combed *à l'oiseau royal,* pressing his three-cornered hat to his heart" (8: 245), might have stolen up this same staircase many years ago to visit the Countess.

Staircases are as important in "The Queen of Spades" as ladders and mountain peaks in *Le Rouge et le noir.* "Walk straight up the staircase," Lizaveta writes to Hermann (8: 239), and on the same page he is shown doing just that, with emphasis on how he first stepped up to the porch and then ran up the stairs to the anteroom. These steps—wide, well-lit, straight—are steps leading to wealth: they are symbolic of Hermann's ambition. The "narrow winding staircase" leading to Lizaveta's room has sexual symbolism, but Hermann climbs it only after the old woman's death, at a time already of anticlimax. His descent by the third staircase—doubly suggestive of sex with its secrecy as well as its narrow, winding course—signals his double defeat, for not only had he not availed himself of an opportunity for an amorous exploit, he had failed to gain even the object of his avaricious quest.

It is at this point that Hermann crosses the path of the lucky champion of love, whose heart, however, has long since turned to dust. Happiness in love may stand as a reproach to Hermann, but the man who experienced that happiness is long dead; neither his amatory luck nor Hermann's frantic chase after phantoms on a winter night will leave a lasting trace. The meeting of the two is an encounter of *oubli* with *regret* (8: 244); and the detached narrator stands over them, contemplating their transient complexities as a "witness of many years."

VI. 'The Captain's Daughter'

Pushkin's interest in the Pugachev Rebellion of 1773–74 can be traced back at least as far as November 1824, when he asked his brother to send him a book on the rebel leader (13: 119). At the beginning of the 1830's, as we have seen in connection with *A History of the Village of Goriukhino* and *Dubrovskii*, questions of riot and revolution were very much on his mind. Moreover, he was probably aware of the fact that peasants on his own family's estate at Boldino had participated in the Pugachev Rebellion.[1]

The first outlines of what was to become *The Captain's Daughter* were inspired by a gift Pushkin received from Nicholas I in February 1832: the *Complete Collection of the Laws of the Russian Empire* (1830), the first series of which covered Russian laws, statutes, and decrees up to November 1825. Volume Twenty of this series contains the various sentences given to the participants in the Pugachev Rebellion. Among those sentenced to exile was a young nobleman, Mikhail Shvanvich, who had been taken prisoner by Pugachev and had subsequently served the rebel cause.[2] Pushkin's first two outlines— one beginning with the words "A fist fight" (8: 930) and the other with "A peasant revolt" (8: 929), both jotted down probably in late summer 1832—show that this traitor to the government was to be the hero of the projected novel.[3] Even his name was retained for the fictional character. In the fall of 1832, however, Pushkin's interest was diverted by the story of another nobleman siding with rioting peasants, who was to become the hero of *Dubrovskii*. Not until after he had run into difficulties with Volume Two of *Dubrovskii* did Pushkin turn once more to the idea of a novel about Pugachev's era. On January 31, 1833, he jotted down a new outline, beginning with the words "Shvanvich is banished to a garrison for unruly conduct" (8: 929).

All three outlines with Shvanvich as the hero show that at this early stage Pushkin was chiefly interested in a character who had betrayed his Empress and his social class. It is indicated that Shvanvich's initial decision to join Pugachev's side would have been connected with his friendship with a robber who had guided him to an inn—which foreshadows the novel's eventual plot. The motivating force of the novel's action, according to these early outlines, was the conflict between Shvanvich's loyalty to his family and friends on the one hand, and his new allegiance to the rebel cause on the other. He would fight on Pugachev's side without any qualms until the rebellion had spread to the region of Nizhnii Novgorod, where his own family's estate was situated; but as soon as his father's peasants began rioting, he would rush to his father's aid, and he would also rescue the daughter of a neighbor, Maria, from the rebels' clutches. This last detail demonstrates that the rescue by the hero of a maiden in distress was part of Pushkin's design from the very beginning. According to both the second and the third outline, the novel would have ended with the elder Shvanvich going to St. Petersburg after the suppression of the rebellion to implore the Empress to pardon his son.

As mentioned earlier, Pushkin had been taken back into government service in 1831 as a historian, working primarily on Peter I. But he took advantage of his access to archival materials to research the times of Catherine II as well. In order to obtain more material on the Pugachev Rebellion for his projected novel, on February 9, 1833, he asked the Minister of War, A. I. Chernyshev, to put at his disposal various documents relating to the famous military leader Prince Aleksandr Suvorov (1730–1800), who had participated, albeit only in the final stages, in the suppression of the rebellion. Suvorov, as Pushkin's subsequent research shows, interested him little, but he could not very well be refused access to archival materials on the famous generalissimo; and while creating the impression that he was working on Suvorov, he could lay his hands on some materials relating to Pugachev. During the following few months he did indeed gain access to a large number of relevant documents from both the Petersburg and the Moscow archives of the Ministry of War, and from other government sources. What he probably had in mind at this stage was to derive further inspiration for characters and situations from the documents, and to gather enough material for a fairly elaborate historical introduction to the novel.

The next two extant outlines, both beginning with the name Basharin (8: 928–29) and dating probably from March 1833, reflect Pushkin's new research.[4] Among the archival materials relating to the taking of Fort Ilinskaia by Pugachev, Pushkin came across the story of Captain Basharin, who had been spared by Pugachev at the request of his soldiers and had served on Pugachev's side for a while, but eventually rejoined the government forces (9: 36, 699). The chief difference between the earlier Shvanvich and the Basharin of the new outlines is that Basharin is not an outright traitor, but a man involuntarily and temporarily caught up in the rebel cause. Pushkin cast aside the historical circumstances under which Basharin's life had been spared, however, and reverted to his earlier idea of a friendly relationship between the hero and a future rebel. A segment of one of the new outlines reads: "On his way, during a blizzard, Basharin saves the life of a Bashkir (le mutilé). The Bashkir saves Basharin's life after the taking of the fort. —Pugachev spares him, saying to the Bashkir: 'You will answer for him with your head.' —The Bashkir is killed" (8: 929). It was presumably after the Bashkir's death that Basharin, no longer bound to Pugachev's side by personal gratitude, could rejoin the government forces. But before doing so, he was to participate (according to another fragmentary part of the outline) in the taking of a fort and would ask Pugachev to give him an officer's daughter as a reward. (Judging by Basharin's generally decent behavior, one can assume that he wanted to save the girl from the other rebels.) Before rejoining the government side, he was also to save the life of his father, who would "not recognize him" (8: 928)— or would pretend not to, ashamed of seeing his son among Pugachev's men. Subsequently Basharin was to excel in fighting against the rebels, and after the crushing of the rebellion, was to take his father to see the captive Pugachev—possibly in order to ask the rebel leader to assure his father that he had not voluntarily betrayed his officer's oath. The role that the father's moral judgment of his son was to play had clearly gained greater importance in comparison with the earlier outlines.

Although Pushkin continued to jot down outlines, he was still far from writing his novel. As he delved deeper into the archival materials, he was more and more drawn to writing a scholarly historical, rather than fictional, account of Pugachev's time. "How many different books one can derive from here!" he exclaimed about his archival work in a letter of March 5, 1833, to M. P. Pogodin. "How many creative ideas can develop!" (15: 53). Soon after, in the second half of April, he set aside his plans for the novel, and in the next five weeks he wrote the first draft of *A History of Pugachev*.

During the summer and fall of that year he was torn between the two projects. On July 22, 1833, he wrote to A. Kh. Benkendorf, his chief contact at Nicholas's Court, seeking permission to work in the archives of Orenburg and Kazan *guberniias*, without mentioning any fictional work in that connection. In Benkendorf's absence, A. N. Mordvinov, head of the Third Department at the time, answered Pushkin, asking why he wished to work in those archives. Pushkin's reply read, in part, as follows:

I have devoted the last two years to historical research alone, without writing a single line of purely literary composition. It is necessary for me to spend about two months in complete solitude in order to take a rest from my more important pursuits and to complete a book that I began a long time ago, which will earn some much needed money. I myself feel embarrassed to be spending my time on such a trifle, but what other choice do I have? It alone can earn for me independence and the means to live with my family in St. Petersburg, where my efforts, thanks to His Majesty, have a more important and useful purpose. . . .

Perhaps His Majesty will wish to know what book exactly it is that I would like to complete in the country: it is a novel that takes place mostly in Orenburg and Kazan, which is the reason I would like to visit those two *guberniias*. (15: 70)

One might suspect that Pushkin referred to his novel solely because he was afraid he might not receive permission to study the sensitive subject of the Pugachev Rebellion; but in fact only a few days after he had written his letter to Mordvinov, he did draft an introduction to the novel, which clearly indicates that he had not lost interest in it.

In this introduction (which was not to be included in the eventual text) the narrator offers his memoirs to his grandson for the young man's moral edification. The grandson, says the narrator, has caused much worry to his parents with his various escapades, and in this respect he is much more like his grandfather than his father (who had been a reliable and dutiful son); but taking after his grandfather "is not such a great misfortune after all. You will see that although the ardency of my passions has led me astray many times, and although I found myself in very difficult situations on several occasions, I came through in the end, living, thanks to God, to a ripe old age, and earning the respect of my family and friends. I predict the same for you, my dear Petrusha, if you will only cherish in your heart two wonderful qualities that I have noticed in you: goodness and honor" (8: 927). This narrator's youthful passions, leading him astray, cannot be equated with the later Grinev's passions, for at this time Pushkin did not yet have the novel's final plot in mind; but it is significant that, already at this early stage, Pushkin had decided to use the voice of a naïve narrator, a successor of Belkin's, for the telling of his tale.

As his letter of September 19 to his wife indicates, Pushkin was still planning a fictional work even after he had obtained permission to travel and had gone to Orenburg. On his way back from that region, as we saw in connection with "The Queen of Spades," he stopped in Boldino in order to do some writing in solitude; but as soon as he arrived there, the inspiration for the novel seems to have disappeared. On October 8, a week after his arrival, he reported to his wife that he had been working exclusively on his historical study of the Pugachev Rebellion; and he mentioned for the first time that he might ask for permission to publish it, and that the project might bring in some money. On October 11 he instructed his wife to ask his friend P. A. Pletnev to copy out for him all the decrees relating to Pugachev in the *Complete Collection of the Laws of the Russian Empire.* On October 21 he wrote to her: "I've been having a headache and a nagging feeling of depression all this time; it's a little better now. I've begun much, but haven't been in the mood for anything: heaven only knows what's happening to me" (15: 88). By the time he joyously reported to her, on October 30, that he had written "heaps" (15: 89), the idea of the novel had clearly been put aside. The major works he brought back to Petersburg with him were "The Queen of Spades," *The Bronze Horseman*, and the scholarly *History of Pugachev*. His letter of December 6, 1833, to Benkendorf, in which he asked for permission to publish the *History*, contained the following explanation: "At one time I had planned to write a historical novel dealing with Pugachev's times, but having found a great deal of material, I abandoned my original project and wrote *A History of the Pugachev Rebellion*" (15: 98).

Historical scholarship—facts and figures and documented accounts without the fiction writer's histrionic tricks—attracted Pushkin at this time much more than the writing of novels did. Later, after the publication of *A History of Pugachev*, he described to I. I. Dmitriev how he had felt working on it:

I wrote it for myself, not imagining that I would be able to publish it. My only concern was to arrive at a clear account of rather tangled events. Readers love anecdotes, local color, etc., but I relegated all that to the notes. As for those wise men who are upset because I have presented Pugachev as Emelka Pugachev, and not as Byron's Lara, I am happy to refer them to Mr. Polevoi, who will no doubt be willing to undertake, for the appropriate price, to idealize this personage according to the latest fashion." (15: 21)

In the light of this statement, Pushkin's earlier remark to Mordvinov, depreciating the writing of novels as a trifle, to which one resorted solely for the sake of money, acquires greater credibility. Pushkin, naturally, had to write to Mordvinov in language a bureaucrat would comprehend; but the evidence shows that he was not merely adapting his tone to his addressee: he himself preferred a straightforward historical account to a fictional one. Pushkin's scholarly monograph on Pugachev related to his fictional project in somewhat the same way as the first half of *Dubrovskii* had related to the second: in both cases the question arose whether to write with or without "fashions." *Dubrovskii* had been abandoned because the romantic plot had not interested Pushkin; in the case of the later project he decided, at least for the time being, to do without a romantic plot. With a surprising gesture of leniency and generosity, Nicholas I not only permitted Pushkin to publish *A History of Pugachev*, but granted him a government loan to cover the cost of publication. He did require a few changes—he insisted, for example, that a villain like Pugachev could not have his own history, and that the monograph should therefore be called *A History of the Pugachev Rebellion* (15: 121)—but on the whole he interfered little. Pushkin proceeded to prepare the work for the printer. Writing all the notes and arranging all the documents required more than half a year. *A History of the Pugachev Rebellion* (whose title was to be restored to *A History of Pugachev* in later editions) finally appeared in print in December 1834. It consisted of two volumes, the first one representing the narrative part, and the second containing a number of source materials. Pushkin compiled an additional set of notes, intended for the Tsar alone, which he submitted to Nicholas along with the two volumes on publication. These notes (first published in the latter half of the nineteenth century)[5] are included in modern editions as an essential addendum to the *History*.

By far the most reliable of the printed foreign sources Pushkin was able to make use of for his *History* was a French translation of an anonymous German essay, "Zuverlässige Nachrichten von dem Aufrührer Jemelian Pugatschew, und der von demselben angestifteten Empörung," first published in 1784.[6] In Russian little had been printed that related directly to Pugachev, but there were some biographies and autobiographies of military leaders who had participated in the crushing of the rebellion, such as A. I. Bibikov, I. I. Mikhelson, and A. V. Suvorov. A. I. Levshin's survey of the Ural Cossacks, published in 1823, proved helpful particularly in sketching in the background to the rebellion. Books on the geography of the region and on the various nationalities living there were also available.[7]

Some of Pushkin's most important sources, however, were unpublished manuscripts that he was able to borrow in the course of his research. Perhaps the most significant among these was the Academician P. I. Rychkov's eyewitness account of the siege of Orenburg, which Pushkin printed in full in the second volume of his *History* (9: 206–355). The archivist and historian D. N. Bantysh-Kamenskii, who was at this time preparing his multivolume *Dictionary of Noteworthy People of the Russian Land* (1836), put at Pushkin's disposal some twenty short biographies of various people connected with the events of 1773–74, including Pugachev. Finally, to mention just one more of the many sources, the poet I. I. Dmitriev's then-unpublished memoirs, which Pushkin borrowed in June 1833, contained an eyewitness account of Pugachev's execution. (This was to be printed partially in the text of the *History* and fully in the notes; 9: 79–80, 147–48.)[8]

Added to all these sources, of course, were the numerous documents that Pushkin either borrowed from various Petersburg or Moscow archives or perused in Orenburg.[9] One difficulty was that he could not obtain permission to open the sealed case against Pugachev himself until after the publication of his *History*.[10] Last but not least among his sources were oral accounts of Pugachev's times from eyewitnesses or their descendants: the fabulist I. A. Krylov, for example, told him what he had learned from his father, Andrei Krylov, who had been among the defenders of the fortress at Iaitskii Gorodok (9: 492); and Pushkin was able to find quite a few survivors of the rebellion in the Orenburg region during his visit there in September 1833. Indeed some of the liveliest details for many scenes of the *History*—the siege of Kazan; the taking of Tatishchev; the fate of Kharlova, the young widow Pugachev took for his concubine; the betrayal of Pugachev by his comrades—derived from interviews Pushkin had conducted with old Cossacks in the Kazan and Orenburg regions.[11]

Although Pushkin's research was extensive, there were limitations to the resources available to him. It has been noted, for example, that he was able to find less information on the last phase of the rebellion—when the uprising, initiated by disgruntled Cossacks and spreading to oppressed national and religious minorities, had turned into a general social revolution, involving vast masses of Russian seignorial peasantry.[12] Moreover, he perhaps concentrated too much of his attention on purely military maneuvers for the simple reason that, as he himself said (15: 42), it had required so much effort to disentangle the various commanders' confusing and contradictory reports. He might be accused of partiality for some commanders, such as Bibikov and Mikhelson, and undue severity toward others. Be that as it may, *A History of Pugachev* is nevertheless an outstanding historical work, not only by the standards of Pushkin's own time, but also by those of modern scholarship. It is founded strictly on evidence, whether written or oral. Fifty years after its publication, when N. Dubrovin compiled his three-volume work on *Pugachev and His Companions* (1884), he had much more extensive resources to explore and a more mature scholarly tradition to build on; yet his findings only confirmed and further elaborated Pushkin's view of the rebellion.[13]

It is all the more surprising, then, that Pushkin's work earned so little respect among pre-revolutionary Russian historians. V. O. Kliuchevskii, writing in 1880, thought that Pushkin was at his best as a historian when he was not trying to be one.[14] Another critic, N. Firsov, accused him of seeing history as a result of isolated acts by outstanding leaders;[15] but as several scholars have pointed out since, just the opposite is true: in fact Pushkin shows that Pugachev's choices were severely limited by the Cossacks he led; that the rebellion was engendered by social conditions and repressive governmental policies; and that Pugachev's military successes were largely due to the almost unanimous support he received from the masses wherever he went.[16] This was the conclusion Pushkin drew in his special notes for Nicholas: "All the common people were on the side of Pugachev. The clergy sympathized with him—not only the priests and monks, but even the archimandrites and archbishops. Only the nobility was openly on the government's side. Pugachev and his companions had tried at first to win over the nobles, too, but their own interests conflicted too strongly with those of the nobles" (9: 375). And: "If we analyze the measures taken by Pugachev and his companions, we must admit that the rebels chose the most reliable and effective means of achieving their goals. The government's actions, by contrast, were weak, slow, and ill-advised" (9: 375–76). These were brave words spoken directly to a Tsar. They testify to Pushkin's full realization that the upheavals of 1773–74 had been caused by social and political conditions, and that if such upheavals were to be avoided in the future—as he fervently hoped they would be—those conditions would have to be changed.

In *A History of Pugachev* Pushkin fully succeeded in expressing the ideas that he had attempted to formulate in the unfinished *History of the Village of Goriukhino* and *Dubrovskii*. At the same time he achieved a new triumph as a prose stylist. The chief stylistic characteristic of *A History of Pugachev* is that Pushkin not only quotes word for word from his sources, but allows the language of witnesses and documents to inform that of the narrator, with emphasis on carefully selected vivid expressions. Pushkin's technique of selecting the vivid and expressive is shown at its clearest in an unpublished compilation by the Soviet scholar R. V. Ovchinnikov, in which the original documents are typed side by side with the notes Pushkin took from them and with the *History*'s text.[17] This extremely interesting compilation reveals that Pushkin usually cast aside archaisms that were obscure, clumsy, or lacking in expressive power, while picking out, often underlining, those that could serve to lend the text a historical flavor.

Another Soviet scholar, G. Blok, has even argued, analyzing Pushkin's use of source materials, that Pushkin's passages dealing with particular events expanded or contracted, not according to the extent of purely factual sources he had available, but according to how much vividly expressive material he had found.[18] This method, if indeed it was as pervasive as Blok claims, represented an intrusion of the fiction writer into the realm of the historian. What is more important from our point of view, however, is that in his *History* Pushkin the prose stylist had achieved his ideal of objectivity: although the narrator's tone is consistent enough to bring coherence to the diverse sources, his personality as narrator is so inconspicuous that his function is reduced simply to conveying "thoughts and thoughts," as befits "stern prose."

By this time, however—and this is one of the striking features of the mature Pushkin—"stern prose" did not necessarily mean the antithesis of poetry. One of Pushkin's sources in studying the Pugachev Rebellion was folklore, and he allowed elements of folk poetry to enter the text along with the other details that bore the imprint of the period. We read, for example, in Chapter Five:

The spring thaw set in, clearing the rivers of ice; the corpses of those killed at Tatishchev floated downstream, past the forts. Wives and mothers stood on the riverbanks, trying to identify their husbands or sons among the corpses. An old Cossack woman wandered along the Iaik by Nizhne-Ozernaia every day, drawing the floating corpses to the bank with a crooked stick and saying, "Is that you, my child? Is it you, my Stepushka? Are these your black curls, washed by the waves?" And when she saw an unfamiliar face she gently pushed the corpse away. (9: 51)

The grieving mother's words had clearly been taken from folk poetry: Pushkin's notes indicate that he had heard them from an old Cossack woman called Buntova in the village of Berda (9: 497). Since Buntova identified the grieving mother as a certain Razina (which Pushkin acknowledged in a footnote; 9: 112), Nicholas I recognized in the passage a reference to Stenka Razin, the leader of a Cossack rebellion a century earlier, and forbade Pushkin to include the passage, calling it irrelevant to Pugachev (9: 471)—in truth probably not wishing to see a continuity in popular uprisings so plainly demonstrated.[19]

The voice of popular tradition echoes occasionally in the characterization of Pugachev too, contrasting with the epithet "villain" applied to him elsewhere. For example, the following passage, stylistically incongruous with the preceding description of the horrors Pugachev had unleashed on Kazan, clearly reflects a view of Pugachev as folk hero: "Thus had the poor convict celebrated his return to Kazan, whence he had escaped only a year before! The prison where he had been waiting for a sentence of lashes and forced labor had now been burned down by him, and the prisoners, his comrades of yore, had been released" (9: 66). The narrator's tone gathers lyrical force especially toward the end of the book, as he describes Pugachev's betrayal by his Cossacks, his journey to Moscow as a captive, and his execution. The source of lyricism, however, is not always folk tradition; we also sense a poetic quality, for instance, in the description of Bibikov's last days. In that case the poetic quality derives from the tone of Bibikov's own letters. Whenever a lyrical potential inheres in the objective material itself, the narrator allows it to develop, while he himself remains above it all, contemplating history from an epic height.

2

Although *A History of Pugachev* represented a great achievement, Pushkin evidently did not feel it had exhausted the topic, for after its publication he once more took up the idea of treating the same period in a fictional work. Sometime in late 1834 or early 1835 he jotted down another outline for the novel. This fragmentary outline, beginning with the words "Valuev arrives at the fort" (8: 930), is quite close to the plot of the eventual *Captain's Daughter*, except that it does not refer to a duel. Its hero, Valuev, was to be wounded during a successful defense of the fort, nursed back to life at the commandant's house, and captured only when the rebels had taken the fort in a second assault. This means that Valuev—unlike the eventual Grinev— would have actually shed his blood fighting for his Empress.

This outline did not immediately lead to the writing of the novel. Work on the project had evidently not progressed very far by the fall of 1835, when Pushkin retired to Mikhailovskoe to write in solitude for a while; and even from there he kept reporting to his wife that inspiration (presumably for the novel, though he did not state this explicitly) was not coming (see 16: 47, 48, 50). One letter indicated that he had done some work (16: 53); but shortly before his return to Petersburg he complained to Pletnev: "I've never had such a fruitless autumn in my life" (16: 56). However, financial pressures were mounting; *A History of Pugachev* was not selling well and had generally little success with the public (see his diary entry dating back to February 1835; 12: 337); and Pushkin's long-standing ambition to write a historical novel was still unfulfilled. He finally began writing the first draft of the novel in late 1835, and continued working on it through the spring and early summer of 1836. The first draft was followed by a clean copy later that summer and in the early fall. This final copy is extant and serves as the basis of the definitive text.

In the novel, as it eventually emerged, Pushkin pretends

to be giving a firsthand account of the rebellion by an eye-witness—a young man named Petr Grinev who, after receiving a meager education at his father's country house, is sent to serve as a cadet in a remote fort, Belogorsk, close to Orenburg. On his way there he first loses one hundred rubles to an older officer, Ivan Zurin, at billiards in Simbirsk, then is caught in a blizzard. Fortunately, he meets a stranger, who guides him to a wayside inn; the next morning he gives the man his hareskin coat as a token of his gratitude.

At the fort he finds life dull but pleasant. He grows fond of his commandant, Captain Mironov, and his family, eventually falling in love with the captain's daughter, Masha. Another young officer serving in the fort—banished there from St. Petersburg for a duel—is Aleksei Shvabrin, who was at one time also attracted to Masha and even proposed to her, but was rejected. Grinev writes a love poem to Masha and reads it to Shvabrin; the latter makes some impertinent comments; and the two decide to fight a duel. At first they are prevented from executing their plan by the commandant's wife, Vasilisa Egorovna; but eventually they fight, and Grinev is wounded because of the distracting arrival of his old servant, Savelich. Grinev is taken to the captain's house and is nursed back to life; when he recovers he proposes to Masha. She accepts on the condition that his parents consent to the marriage.

His father not only refuses to consent to the marriage, but even threatens to have his son transferred to another post. In the meanwhile, however, the Pugachev Rebellion breaks out; Belogorsk is occupied; the captain, his inseparable comrade Ivan Ignatich, and Vasilisa Egorovna are all killed; and Grinev is only saved because Pugachev turns out to be the man he gave his hareskin coat to on the way to Belogorsk. Pugachev wants Grinev to join the rebels, but he refuses; the rebel leader lets him go. He sets out for Orenburg, leaving behind Masha, who escaped rape and murder by hiding in the local priest's house, pretending to be a niece of the priest's wife.

In Orenburg Grinev advocates offensive action against the rebels, but since both the governor and his council prefer to wait for help safe behind the city's walls, his only opportunities to fight are afforded by sorties. During one of these he meets Belogorsk's former Cossack sergeant, Maksimych (now a rebel), who has brought him a letter from Masha. In it she tells him that Shvabrin, who went over to Pugachev's side and was appointed commandant of Belogorsk, is trying to force her to marry him. Grinev leaves Orenburg without permission, accompanied by Savelich, to rescue her. They try to skirt the village of Berda, where Pugachev has his headquarters, but thanks to old Savelich's slowness, they are caught by rebel sentries. Brought before Pugachev and his associates, Grinev declares that he was going to rescue an orphan mistreated by Shvabrin. The rebel chief's associates do not believe Grinev's story and want to execute him, but Pugachev once again decides to spare him; indeed accompanies him on his journey to Belogorsk. They find Masha in a pitiful state, imprisoned by Shvabrin; Pugachev liberates her, whereupon Shvabrin reveals that she is the captain's daughter; but even this information does not swerve Pugachev from his merciful intentions. He pardons Shvabrin and lets the young couple go.

They safely drive through Pugachev country, claiming to be a close associate of his, until government troops arrest them for their claim. It so happens that the commander of these troops is Zurin, to whom Grinev lost at billiards some time before; Zurin allows Masha to proceed to Grinev's parents with Savelich and lets Grinev stay with his regiment. When the rebellion is finally put down, Grinev prepares to go home, but Zurin suddenly receives an order to arrest his young comrade and have him transported to Kazan, to appear before the commission investigating the rebellion. The accusation, leveled against him, as it turns out, by Shvabrin, is that he joined Pugachev's side. He could justify himself but does not wish to bring Masha's name into the business. He is sentenced to penal servitude in Siberia.

In the meanwhile the old Grinevs have grown fond of the orphaned Masha and are looking forward to her marriage with their son when he returns. The news of his arrest and trial shatters them; the old Grinev believes that his son was really a traitor. Masha, however, guesses what happened before the Investigating Commission; she goes to Petersburg, accidentally meets Catherine II in the park of Tsarskoe Selo, and secures a royal pardon for her fiancé.

The first draft of the novel contained an additional chapter, which Pushkin took out of the manuscript and preserved under the title "Omitted Chapter" (8: 906).[20] This chapter, detailing the hero's visit to his father's estate in the grips of riot, originally followed the sentence "Zurin received orders to cross the Volga" in the final text (8: 364), and would have taken the action up to the point of the hero's arrest. Its last three paragraphs, beginning with the words "I will not go into the details of our campaign" (8: 383), are very close to the description of the last phase of the rebellion near the end of Chapter Thirteen (8: 364). There has been some speculation in scholarly literature about Pushkin's reasons for omitting this chapter:[21] he probably did so because it turned out to be incompatible with the general idea of the novel as it took shape. For example, in this chapter the young hero, called Bulanin, tries to rescue his parents and Masha from rebel captivity, and is reconciled with his father. If these details had been left in, the father could not have accepted the Investigating Commission's judgment of his son's guilt, which would have made the novel quite different; for the elder Grinev's loss of faith in his son is an essential feature of the final text. Also, Bulanin of the omitted chapter mortally wounds the village notary, Andriushka, whereas in the published text we never see Grinev do any harm to anyone: all we come across are general references to his participation in sorties and campaigns.

Pushkin also made several corrections in the final copy of the manuscript. One of the most significant had to do with refining the relationship between Grinev and Pugachev: at first Pushkin had Grinev going directly to Pugachev to ask for his help in Chapter Eleven; but in the corrected text he is caught by Pugachev's men and hits on the idea of asking for the rebel leader's help only when he is brought before him. If the original version had been left uncorrected, Grinev's friendship with Pugachev would have gone beyond what the young officer's oath of allegiance to the Empress allowed.[22]

Another significant change, which could shed light on how Pushkin's ideas were developing, concerns the date of the elder Grinev's retirement. Originally, Pushkin entered the year 1762 (8: 858), which might have simply referred to Peter III's February 1762 edict exempting the nobility from obligatory state service.

But if we consider the elder Grinev's association with Count Burkhard Christoph Münnich, one-time President of the War College (mentioned in the same paragraph), then we may well take that date as an indication that the elder Grinev, like Münnich, had adhered to his oath of allegiance to Peter III during the palace revolution of June 1762, in which Catherine II ousted her husband from the throne. This detail would then have lent greater poignancy to the young (Peter!) Grinev's friendly relations with Pugachev, who claimed to be Peter III. (The Tsar had actually been killed shortly after the palace coup, but rumors circulated that he was in hiding, and several impostors appeared on the scene, claiming to be Peter.) An extant fragment containing Pushkin's calculation of the younger Grinev's age (8: 928) shows that the reason Pushkin changed the date 1762 to the less specific 17— in the final version (8: 279) was that if the father had not married until after he retired in 1762, the young Petr could not have been eighteen in 1773, the year of the Pugachev Rebellion.

In the latter half of September 1836, Pushkin asked the censor P. A. Korsakov, who was an old friend, to read the novel. This request implied that Pushkin did not intend to publish the novel under his name (otherwise he would have had to submit it to Nicholas I through Benkendorf), and that he meant to publish it separately, rather than in *The Contemporary*, the journal he had launched earlier that year (for he would then have sent it to the censor for the journal, A. L. Krylov). Korsakov agreed, and Pushkin submitted the first half of the manuscript to him. The copying of the second half was completed by October 19, and the manuscript was submitted to Korsakov on the 24th of that month. Korsakov was somewhat perplexed by Pushkin's intention to publish the work anonymously and asked a number of questions; but eventually he approved the text with a few minor deletions (such as a scene in which Mironov's ragtag soldiers did not know left from right, even though they crossed themselves before attempting about-faces—8: 299, 921—and a remark about the government troops taking away from the peasants whatever had been left behind by Pugachev's hordes—8: 364, 925). On November 1 Pushkin read some of his novel at a gathering at Viazemskii's house.[23] Finally, after Pushkin decided to run the novel in his new journal after all, *The Captain's Daughter* was published, without the author's name, on December 22, in Volume Four of *The Contemporary* for 1836.[24]

The research Pushkin had done for *A History of Pugachev* is behind every line of *The Captain's Daughter*. It has been suggested that the fictional Belogorsk is modeled on Fort Tatishchev, where the rebels brutally murdered all the officers, and where the commander's wife was "hacked to pieces" (9: 19).[25] In drawing the character of Captain Mironov, Pushkin probably had the commandants of several forts in mind, but he was particularly inspired by the stories Krylov had told him about his father. The commandant of Fort Nizhne-Ozernaia, whose execution is reported with no mention of his name in Chapter Six of the novel, was Major Kharlov, whose attractive widow was to become Pugachev's concubine and was eventually to be murdered by his associates. (Masha refers to her in her letter to Grinev in Chapter Ten of the novel.)

Some documentary details that appear in the novel cannot be found in the narrative part of the *History*, either because, being unessential to a historical account of the events, they were relegated to the source materials, or because Pushkin came across them after the publication of the *History*. The name Grinev, for example, originates from Second Lieutenant A. M. Grinev, mentioned in a government report dated January 10, 1775, as one of the officers at first suspected of treason but later acquitted (9: 191).[26] Pugachev's companion Beloborodov is given a more expressive characterization in the novel than in the *History*, because Pushkin received more information about him after the text of the *History* had been sent to the printers.[27] A list of stolen goods Savelich hands to Pugachev, obviously too trifling an affair to be included in the *History*, was derived from a petition a certain Court Councillor Butkevich had submitted to the government in the hope of being compensated for the losses he had suffered during the rebellion.[28] (Pushkin, however, used the document as a humorous touch: he makes a servant, rather than a nobleman, submit the list, and not to government authorities, but to the rebel leader himself.) Finally, a reading of Pushkin's notes reveals that some of the colorful details, characterizations, or turns of phrase that he had copied from documents found their way directly into the novel, bypassing the *History*. To give just one example, a report by the governor of Kazan, Jacob von Brandt, dated November 26, 1773, describes how he instructed commandants of forts to "defend themselves to the last drop of their blood" and "to try to stop [Pugachev's] further advance, to repulse him completely... and to attempt to crush and entirely destroy him."[29] These phrases reappear, in slightly altered form, in the general's letter to Captain Mironov and in Grinev's words about defending the fort in Chapter Six of the novel (8: 314, 319).

It is even more interesting to observe how Pushkin turned the factual accounts of the *History* into vivid representations in the novel. In the *History* we are given the facts about the meeting of the council in Orenburg in preparation for Pugachev's siege, about sorties out of the city, about Pugachev's headquarters at Berda, about his companions and revelries, and about his feeling that he was under the control of his Cossacks; in the novel we witness the debates at the council meeting and see an individual participating in a sortie; we are present at a quarrel between two of Pugachev's chief associates and hear Pugachev himself voice his complaint about his hands being tied. The novel's vivid details are often fictional—once the camera "zooms in" on a scene, no amount of documentary evidence can provide all the components of description—but we sense that at least the depictions of the surroundings, if not necessarily the characterizations, are rooted in fact.

Nevertheless, Pushkin did not rely exclusively on documentary sources for the novel, but drew on some literary sources as well. He may have been familiar, for example, with N. I. Strakhov's story "Gratitude" (1810), about a nobleman who had been kind to his neighbor's servant on several occasions, and had subsequently been spared by Pugachev and allowed to go free at the servant's request.[30] And perhaps the most important single source for the plot was a story entitled "My Grandmother's Tale," published in the 1832 issue of the *Neva Almanac* under the initials A.K., which related a young noblewoman's escape from the clutches of Pugachev's companion Khlopusha.[31]

3

Considering that *The Captain's Daughter* was the child of such long labor and difficult birth, how did it turn out? In judging the novel's aesthetic qualities, one must ask, above all, whether Pushkin succeeded, for all this effort, in creating an artistic unity from the diverse elements he had borrowed from history.

The Captain's Daughter, even though its action is set in the midst of a bloody revolt, contains surprisingly little violence. Grinev has a prophetic nightmare during the blizzard that foreshadows a massacre, but only in a remote way; and though he is wounded quite seriously in his duel with Shvabrin, his wound turns out to be a blessing, for he awakes to find himself in the tender care of Masha. The first physical marks of cruelty appearing in the novel are the mutilated features of the Bashkir whom Mironov's men capture prior to the siege of the fort; similar tokens of savage governmental repression are brought to our attention at the beginning of Chapter Ten, when Grinev sees a group of mutilated convicts on his way to Orenburg, and in Chapter Eleven, when he is struck by Khlopusha's disfigured face. But all these faces had been deformed a long time before, and they appear only as witnesses to a cruel past, far removed from the time of the action, just as Mironov's participation in the Turkish and Prussian campaigns seems to be a legend of bygone days.[32] In the present, as soon as the mutilated Bashkir opens his mouth to show a short stump in place of his tongue, his torture is stopped; moreover, Grinev the narrator hastens to soften the impact of the scene by reflecting on the progress that has been made since those ruthless days. Unmitigated violence, vividly described for us, appears only in Chapter Seven when the Cossack deserters hurl the loyalist Kalmyk Iulai's severed head over the palisade. That event serves as a prelude to the most violent scene in the novel: the execution of the elderly Captain Mironov, of his comrade-in-arms Ivan Ignatich, and of his wife, Vasilisa Egorovna. Finally, the theme of beheading recurs at the very end of the novel, where we are told that Pugachev nodded to Grinev before his head was cut off; but that scene, once more, is remote; it belongs to history; and it is narrated rather than vividly described. The execution of the Mironovs takes place exactly halfway through the novel, and indeed it occupies a central place in it. But as an unalloyed scene of violence it stands strangely isolated in the context of the narrative, which—unlike *A History of Pugachev* with its naturalistic display of betrayal, debauchery, and cruelty—generally oscillates between the mildly comic and the mildly sentimental. It seems that the main question for the critic in judging the novel is whether the tragic note of the execution is brought into harmony with the novel's generally comic tone.

Most elements of the plot are so obviously conventional or melodramatic as to suggest parody. Grinev's gift to the stranger who guides him to safety, for example, is a traditional opening for a plot, which has been compared to Iurii's saving of Kirsha at the beginning of M. N. Zagoskin's *Iurii Miloslavskii*,[33] and to the folktale motif of a strong beast being helped by a weaker creature, to whom it will later do a good turn.[34] Other chance meetings of import are Grinev's with Zurin in Chapter Thirteen and, above all, Maria's with Catherine II in the park at Tsarskoe Selo in Chapter Fourteen. The latter encounter, resulting in a tongue-in-cheek denouement for the novel, has often been compared to Jeanie Dean's meeting with Queen Caroline in Chapter Thirty-seven of Scott's *The Heart of Midlothian* (1830).[35] Pushkin may well have been alluding to Scott; what is more important, however, is that he deliberately chose a cliché of wide currency in popular literature,[36] as if wishing to put the reader on notice that the tale he was telling was something of a joke. Other conventional elements in the plot are the choice between love and duty with which Grinev is confronted, as in a classical tragedy;[37] the presence of the melodramatic villain Shvabrin;[38] and Grinev's refusal to reveal his secret (his desertion from Orenburg in order to save Masha)—a device for slowing plot development.[39] Perhaps the most contrived situation in the story is Grinev's capture by Pugachev's men outside Berda: since in the final version Grinev is not deliberately seeking the rebel leader, there is no reason why he could not have gone toward Belogorsk along a different route, avoiding the lion's den.[40] The resulting implausibility is not likely to have been simply a careless mistake on Pushkin's part as he reworked the chapter, for it fits well into his overall design.

What renders the conventional elements comic is the naïve tone of Grinev—a literary descendant not only of Ivan Petrovich Belkin, but also of the various artless personae Pushkin had used in his polemical exchanges in journals.[41] Pushkin presents the tale as if it had indeed been sent to him by the heirs of a survivor of the rebellion; as if it were indeed a genuine document, an eyewitness account, precious to Pushkin the historian. In order to make Grinev authentic he surrounds him with quotations from, and allusions to, eighteenth-century literature. The epigraph to Chapter One is from Ia. B. Kniazhnin's comedy *The Braggart* (Act 3, Scene 6); to Chapter Four, from Kniazhnin's comedy *Eccentrics* (Act 4, Scene 12); to Chapter Nine, from M. M. Kheraskov's lyrical poem "Separation"; and to Chapter Ten, from Kheraskov's epic poem *Rossiade* (Canto 11). The epigraphs to Chapters Eleven and Thirteen are both thought to be Pushkin's own compositions in imitation of the eighteenth-century authors to whom they are attributed: the fabulist A. P. Sumarokov and Kniazhnin.[42]

Some of these epigraphs, in addition to providing an eighteenth-century atmosphere, create a humorous context for the action. Let us quote the one taken from *The Braggart* as an example:

> "In no time he'll be a captain in the Guards."
> "No need for that; I had the ranks in mind."
> "Handsomely said: they'll put him through the grind.
> . . .
> "And who's his father?"

The first line is spoken by the character Verkholet in reference to his rival in love, Zamir. Pretending to be a rich, influential Count, Verkholet claims he could make Zamir a captain of the Guards if only Zamir was not so rude and inconsiderate. The person answering is Cheston, the wise old man of the comedy; what he implies is that serving in the active army would be better for a young man's character. Verkholet, who does not know that Cheston is Zamir's father, misunderstands Cheston's words and imagines that the old man is siding with him against Zamir. This dialogue at cross-purposes adds a comic touch to the elder Grinev's resolve to send his son to Orenburg instead of Petersburg.

The other quotation from Kniazhnin puts a comic complexion on Chapter Four, since it is drawn from a scene in which two servants fight a ludicrous duel—hardly the kind the young Grinev envisaged for himself. But the most obviously humorous references are to D. I. Fonvizin's *The Young Hopeful*, which, as we have seen, Pushkin had used for ironic purposes many times before. The subjects that the young Petr's tutor Beaupré is supposed to be teaching him—"French, German, and all the sciences" (8: 280)—echo a quotation from Fonvizin's comedy (Act 1, Scene 6), where Prostakova boasts that a foreign tutor, Adam Vralman, is teaching her adolescent son "French and all the sciences." Pushkin's Beaupré was a barber back in France; Fonvizin's Vralman turns out, at the end of the comedy, to have been a coachman in his native Germany. This and other allusions to *The Young Hopeful*, hidden in the text, indicate the similarity of the Grinevs to the Prostakovs. And when we see yet another quotation from the comedy at the head of Chapter Three—"Old-fashioned people, my dear sir"—we suspect that the characters introduced in this chapter will also be ludicrous.[43]

Pushkin obviously intended that the narrator's vision should be limited. If the conventional situations and the melodramatic image of the villain Shvabrin are functions of Grinev's personality as narrator, so is the two-dimensional character of Masha. Sensible, modest, virtuous, angelic, she is not allowed any human failings. In the manuscript version of Chapter Six Grinev reports that she was jealous of Kharlova, when, during a stay at the Mironovs', the pretty wife of the commandant of Fort Nizhne-Ozernaia had carried on a long conversation with Grinev (8: 878); but Pushkin decided to launder even that touch of color out of her personality.

The only expansion of the point of view in the novel is Grinev's own double perspective. Like the narrator of "The Shot," he tells his tale from a distance of many years, with the result that events are seen now through the eyes of his young, impetuous self, now through those of his old, mellowed self. The humor arising from this double perspective is that the transitions from a callow to a more mature perception are at times too fast. In Chapter One we see Petr as a totally uneducated young oaf, yet in Chapter Four, only a few months later chronologically, he is already writing poetry that is to win the praise (albeit dubious) of Sumarokov. Similarly, his only military training has been to watch the inept Mironov struggle with his veterans, yet when he converses with the director of the Orenburg customhouse in Chapter Ten, he presumes to judge that the man was "not well versed in the military arts" (8: 339), and when the city council decides to take defensive action, he describes its members as "untrained and inexperienced people" (8: 340). Where had he himself acquired so much knowledge of the military arts and so much experience? Some critics have seen these abrupt transitions as a structural flaw,[44] but it is more likely that Pushkin planted them deliberately for the sake of humor. The presence of Grinev the narrator suffuses the whole work with gentle irony.

In addition to the humorous devices so far mentioned, there is one in the novel that has received relatively little attention in critical literature: the device of frustrating the reader's expectations. The title of Chapter One suggests that the young hero will become an officer of the Guards, which in his eyes would be "the ultimate in the wellbeing of men" (8: 281). After his father's perverse decision to send him into the regular army instead, he feels that all his "brilliant hopes were dashed" (8: 282). But his new destination also raises certain expectations, though of a different kind, both in his and in his reader's mind: we now think he will "learn to sweat, to get used to the smell of gunpowder, [and to be] a soldier, not an idler" (8: 282). What in fact happens is that Zurin, claiming to be instructing him in the ways of the service, gets him drunk, hustles him out of a hundred rubles at billiards, and takes him to Arinushka's. Zurin's repeated insistence that all this is essential for the service reminds one of the brothers Ostap and Andrii Bulba's liquid initiation into the life of the Cossack *sech*; and the whole scene, with Zurin's previous opponent, the billiard marker, forced to crawl on all fours under the table on each loss, has a Gogolesque flavor.

Having presented himself to the governor, Andrei Karlovich,

in Orenburg, the young Grinev realizes that he is being sent to "a godforsaken fort on the edge of the Kirgiz-Kaisak steppes" (8: 293). He is disappointed, but he imagines that his new surroundings will be impressive at least in their rugged severity: "I tried to picture to myself Captain Mironov, my future commanding officer, and the image that came to mind was that of a stern, short-tempered old man, ignorant of everything except the service, and ready to put me under arrest on bread and water for the merest trifle"; and "I looked in every direction, expecting to see fearsome bastions, towers, and a rampart" (8: 294). Instead, he arrives at "a small village bounded by a palisade" (8: 294) and commanded, not by a stern captain, but by the redoubtable and querulous Vasilisa Egorovna (strongly reminiscent of Vasilisa Kashporovna in Gogol's "Ivan Fedorovich Shponka and His Aunt"). She quarters Grinev at the house of Semen Kuzov in order to punish the man for having allowed his horse to get into her vegetable garden. The chief duty of Ivan Ignatich as an officer, it seems, is to hold a hank of yarn on his outstretched hands for Vasilisa Egorovna to wind. The day's main event in the fort is that "in the bathhouse Corporal Prokhorov got into a scuffle with Ustinia Negulina over a tubful of hot water" (8: 296), reminding us of such Gogolian women as Agafia Fedoseevna, who bit off the assessor's ear, or Gapka, whom Ivan Ivanovich threatened to let loose on the mayor in the tale of the two Ivans. (In the manuscript version Corporal Prokhorov gets into a fight with another man, the Cossack Petr Negulin, but Pushkin crossed "Petr" out and entered "Ustinia," obviously to heighten the comic effect; 8: 869.) To continue the list of absurdities, the fort's only cannon has not been fired for the last two years because its boom would frighten the captain's daughter; and the garrison soldiers cannot tell left from right, even though, in order to avoid mistakes, they usually cross themselves before making about-faces. The most farcical detail, however, twisting the style of the narrative beyond all pretense of realism into a gnarl of grotesque hyperbole, is the scene in which the captain, clad in dressing gown and nightcap, drills his doddering veterans, while Vasilisa Egorovna insists that the drill should be halted because dinner is ready and the cabbage soup is getting cold, and because her husband does not know the first thing about drills anyway (8: 297).[45] Grinev, who had hoped to become a dashing officer of the Guards in St. Petersburg, is justly "overcome by dejection" and bemoans: "This was the place where I was condemned to spend my youth" (8: 296).

The one person who could bring a sense of adventure to this uninspiring village is the romantic villain Shvabrin, and indeed it is his quarrel with Grinev that follows next to raise expectations. He challenges Grinev with the ominous words, "You are not going to get away with that"; and Grinev, after responding to his adversary in kind, comments to the reader: "At that moment I could have torn him to pieces" (8: 301). But Ivan Ignatich, the only other officer in the fort and therefore the only person Grinev can ask to be his second, is busy with needle in hand, stringing up mushrooms for Vasilisa Egorovna when Grinev comes to him. The good old man refuses to participate in the duel and suggests: "If he swore at you, you curse him back; if he hit you in the mug, you bash him on the ear; and once more, and again; and then go your separate ways" (8: 302). In Belogorsk all romantic notions are soon translated into the prose of domestic reality. The young men's first attempt at dueling is thwarted by a handful of veterans, who were commandeered to arrest them, not by the captain, but by his wife; she berates the duelers as if they were naughty boys, tells the maid to lock their swords away in the storeroom, and describes dueling simply as murder (an early example of *ostranenie*—the device of looking at a familiar phenomenon with fresh eyes). Even the outcome of the eventual duel, though serious enough, is brought about by the comic Savelich, dashing to protect Grinev, whom he still regards as a little boy entrusted to his care.

Expectations are inflated to ludicrous proportions as Grinev awaits the rebels' expected attack on the fort.[46] "It is our duty to defend the fort to the last breath" (8: 319), he declares (these words, similar to the phrase we have cited from von Brandt's report, were originally to be spoken by Captain Mironov, but Pushkin signed them over to Grinev in the manuscript; 8: 877); on the eve of the assault, in an "agitated state of mind," he awaits danger "impatiently, with a feeling of noble ambition" (8: 321); and he waxes even more solemn the next morning, when Masha tries to smile at him before the siege begins: "I involuntarily grasped the hilt of my sword, remembering that I had received it from her hands the evening before, as if for the defense of my beloved. My heart glowed. I imagined myself her knight-protector. I longed to prove that I was worthy of her trust, and waited impatiently for the decisive moment" (8: 322).

These chivalrous attitudes, however, are incongruous with the way the rest of the characters prepare to defend the fort. When Mironov receives the general's letter alerting him to Pugachev's approach, he has to trick his wife to get her out of the house in order to be able to hold a council with his officers without her; he has to lock up Palashka the maid in the storeroom to prevent her from eavesdropping on the council; and when he is said to be "prepared for the assault" (8: 315), this means that he is ready to take a barrage of questions from his wife. The ensuing description centers on how Vasilisa Egorovna wheedles the military secret out of the guileless Ivan Ignatich, and on how her husband, Ivan Kuzmich, fails to trick her for a second time. The tone of these descriptions befits, not preparations for a serious battle, but some farcical carryings-on—like Ivan Ivanovich's scheme to saw the posts of Ivan Nikiforovich's goose pen.

Nevertheless, Grinev has vowed to defend the fort to the last breath, and we await his heroic actions. He does in fact dash out of the fort with Ivan Kuzmich and Ivan Ignatich, but the frightened garrison does not follow: "At that moment the rebels charged and burst into the fort. The drum fell silent; the garrison threw down their weapons; I was hurled to the ground, but I got up and entered the fort with the rebels. The commandant, wounded in the head, stood in the midst of a group of villains, who were demanding the keys from him. I was on the point of rushing to his aid, but some hefty Cossacks seized me and bound me with their belts" (8: 324). "I was on the point" is a phrase well chosen to describe Grinev's action: he had been on the point of becoming a dashing officer of the Guards, of serving in a fort of austere magnificence, of teaching a villain a lesson in a duel, and of shedding his blood in defense of his beloved, but somehow, each time, something interfered.

Leaving aside the scene of Mironov's execution for the moment, let us follow the same pattern of frustrated expectations in further chapters of the novel. In Orenburg, Grinev awaits the meeting of the council "impatiently" (8: 339), just as he awaited battle earlier; and in front of the council he makes a strong case for offensive action, assuring his audience that Pugachev could not stand up to a professional army; what he gets in reply from the director of the customhouse, who speaks after him, is the sobering and prosaic suggestion that the town should take neither offensive nor defensive measures, but should simply take "bribing measures," that is, offer an award for Pugachev's head. We are told that Grinev often participated in sorties against the besiegers of Orenburg, but the only time we see him in one he is "about" to strike down a Cossack with his Turkish saber when the man, taking his hat off, reveals himself as Maksimych, the sergeant at Grinev's old post, greets him cordially, and hands him a letter from Masha (8: 341).[47] Her letter could be expected to encourage Grinev to fight her parents' murderers, but in fact it reproaches him for not taking enough care of himself during sorties; with its reproach it stands in the same relationship to Grinev's "heroism" as his mother's entreaties to take care of his health stood in relation to his father's command to guard his honor in Chapter One. Further, Grinev's earnest pleading of Masha's fate before the commandant of Orenburg, General Andrei Karlovich, and his request to lead a troop to liberate the fort before she is forced to marry Shvabrin elicits the unromantic suggestion that "it is better for her to be Shvabrin's wife for the time being, since he can protect her under the present circumstances; and after we've shot him, God will provide other suitors for her" (8: 343); on the outskirts of Berda Grinev once again swings his saber at a sentry, but the man is saved by his thick hat; Grinev tries to gallop away, but has to come back because of his bungling servant; and he is threatened with execution once more, only to be spared once more.

Every unfulfilled expectation, it would seem, amounts to a lesson in realism. All fanciful notions are dashed against the prosaic facts of ordinary life. Scenes like Grinev's encounter with the Cossack Maksimych even suggest that the simple af-

fairs of individuals should take precedence over political alle-
giances and large issues of history. Indeed *The Captain's Daughter*, like some of Walter Scott's novels, has been interpreted as a
quest for simple humanitarian values amid conflicting fanati-
cisms.[48] This interpretation would be entirely convincing if
history were presented in an unfalteringly comic vein throughout the novel; if chivalric sallies inevitably ended up in a joke
while nobody got hurt—or at least death and cruelty were only
accessories to a stage setting, to be eluded by every character
the reader intimately knew. But the reader cannot ignore the
scene of the Mironovs' execution.

At first sight Grinev's behavior during the executions seems
to fall into the same ironic pattern of unfulfilled expectations.
He is captured with loud threats of retribution for not obeying
the rebels' "Sovereign"; he is led into Pugachev's presence to be
tried along with Ivan Kuzmich and Ivan Ignatich; both are
hanged for their defiance of the pretender, and now it is Grinev's
turn. "I was looking at Pugachev boldly," we read, "ready to repeat the answer my noble comrades had given him" (8: 325). He
is not asked any questions, however, because Shvabrin has de-
nounced him, and Pugachev does not even want to bother with
him; he is being led to the gallows. He is "on the point" of becoming a martyr. But then Savelich throws himself at Pugachev's feet, begging for his young master's life; Pugachev recognizes them both and pardons Grinev. Once more, a personal
gesture—gratitude for a hareskin coat—prevails over historical
forces; human sympathy triumphs over fanaticism. What about
Ivan Kuzmich and Ivan Ignatich, however?

They hang on the gallows, and continue hanging while the
rebel leader, their murderer, tries to make friends with Grinev.
Their corpses are brought into focus on several occasions (mostly
added to the manuscript later; see 8: 883, 885): we see them in
the daylight when some Bashkirs pull the boots off their feet,
and at dusk, looming dark and terrible as Grinev goes to see
Pugachev; the moon lights them up when Grinev goes back to
his lodging that evening; they hang over the next morning's
gathering; and Grinev takes a last look at them as he leaves for
Orenburg. Even more terrifying is the body of Vasilisa Egorovna, who has been slashed by a saber for lamenting her hus-

band's death and left lying stripped naked near the porch until the next day, when someone throws a piece of matting over her body.

Yet despite these horrifying scenes, the narrator does not abandon his tone of light banter. The two old officers have already been hanged, and Grinev is about to lose his life, when we read: "I was dragged under the gallows. 'Don't be scared, don't be scared!' repeated my executioners, wishing, in all truth perhaps, to give me courage" (8: 325). The Cossack who conveys Pugachev's demand that Grinev attend him describes the "Sovereign" in the following terms: "Well, Your Honor, everything shows that he's a person of distinction: at dinner he was pleased to eat two roast suckling-pigs, and he had his steam bath so hot that even Taras Kurochkin couldn't bear it: he had to hand the besom to Fomka Bikbaev and could just barely revive himself with cold water" (8: 329). The manner, once more, is Gogol's, down to the trick of casually mentioning two hitherto unheard-of characters with the assumption that the reader knows all about their habits. No less Gogolesque is the remark with which Andrei Karlovich receives the news of Vasilisa Egorovna's murder: "She was a good-hearted lady, and what an expert at pickling mushrooms!" (8: 338). From among other similar details let us mention only the list of stolen goods Savelich presents to Pugachev in the shadow of the gallows: the act of presenting it is so improbable, and the list itself so funny, that the scene creates a farcical atmosphere.

Some critics hold that the scene of execution is perceived relatively lightly because Grinev the narrator is an eighteenth-century man, used to cruelty, and because there is an element of justice in popular retribution against officers of governmental troops.[49] The chief question from the point of view of our investigation is not, however, whether the narrator should condemn the cruelty under his eyes or not, but whether his description of it blends in with the stylistic context of the narrative.[50]

Marina Tsvetaeva has suggested that we can accept the executions in their context as we accept violence in a fairy tale: Pugachev is not an ordinary human being in our perception, but an incarnation of the evil of popular imagination, the wolf or robber of folklore.[51] The novel does indeed incorporate even more elements of folklore than *A History of Pugachev* did. Epigraphs for several chapters and the songs cited within the text are all traceable to popular songs.[52] Masha was described by one of Pushkin's own contemporaries as a heroine out of a *bylina*—a traditional heroic poem.[53] Pugachev has not only been likened to a fairy-tale beast or a robber, but his hyperbolic, larger-than-life image is reminiscent of the presentation of folk heroes; even his physical appearance—in a red caftan, riding a white horse, with saber drawn—is evocative of the cheap popular prints known as *lubki*.[54] Finally, Catherine II comes to the rescue of the hero and heroine every bit as a fairy godmother would.[55] One might add that the scene of execution is modeled on the trinary structure of the folktale: Ivan Kuzmich and Ivan Ignatich perish in the clutches of the dragon, but the third "knight," Grinev, escapes.

Yet despite the undoubted presence of these elements, a fairy-tale atmosphere does not explain the problem under discussion. Tsvetaeva would be right if Pugachev were an exclusively evil figure and if the violence were committed against some remote personages with whom the reader had had no opportunity to identify; in that case "we" as readers would acknowledge the existence of evil in the abstract but would not be hurt by it ourselves; we would emerge victorious from a fight against it. But in fact the Mironovs were "us," endearing despite their laughable characteristics; and we cannot see their demise without pain. Moreover, Pugachev is far from being all evil: he is, in Tsvetaeva's own description, the most enchanting character in the novel.

Pugachev's charm brings us to another, related question, that of the romantic element in his presentation. It is perfectly plausible that he would, as the real-life Pugachev did, spare a loyalist out of gratitude for a personal favor. It is still believable that he might summon the loyalist officer to an interview in the hope of gaining his allegiance. But it is beyond credibility that he would let the officer rejoin the opposite side; that he would send presents after him; that he would receive him with kindness a second time despite the suspicious circumstances of the officer's arrival in his camp; and that he would leave camp, army, siege, and all, in order to rescue the officer's sweetheart, at once forgiving him for a fraud, offering himself as "father by proxy" for his wedding, and making him privy to his innermost thoughts. It is precisely these unrealistic details that make Pugachev attractive, for he emerges as the eagle of the Kalmyk tale he tells, as a lonely giant likely to be betrayed by his cohorts, a misunderstood hero seeking the friendship of a kindred spirit.[56] His greatness is that he is condemned from the beginning, and he knows it. His violent acts, it would seem, are redeemed by his acceptance of his own death in the concluding paragraph of the novel. But are they? Such a Pugachevian perspective is in jarring contrast to the lovingly mocking, intimately indulgent attitude that the narrator has shown toward Pugachev's victims. Prior to the scene of the execution the only kind of romanticism we encountered was Grinev's highfalutin chivalry—put on display only in order to be debunked. The debunking was accomplished partly by frustrating expectations and partly by submerging fanciful notions in the quagmire of Russian provincial banality. But now, after the execution, notably with the evocative song Pugachev and his associates sing at the end of the evening, an entirely new, serious romantic strain enters the novel's stylistic structure, and we are asked to accept the executions under the spell of its fairy-tale atmosphere. The different stylistic strands that converge on the central scene of the executions are clearly incongruous.

Incongruity is the hallmark of the grotesque, and indeed we have seen that some elements, especially in the description of the Mironovs, do bring the style close to the grotesque; but on the whole it is unlikely that Pushkin was aiming here at the kind of grotesque effect that he had achieved, for example, in "The Undertaker."[57] Nor is *The Captain's Daughter* in the style of the *Ecole frénétique*: and therefore it cannot treat the gory as gleefully as it is treated, for example, in Victor Hugo's *Notre Dame de Paris* (1831). Is the structure of *The Captain's Daughter* flawed, then, by a certain stylistic incongruity?[58] Perhaps a partial solution to the problem may be found in the Grinev-Pugachev relationship.

It has been argued persuasively that in addition to the elder Grinev, both Mironov and Pugachev assume something of a fatherly role in relation to the young Petr, and that the hero's progress through the novel is a process of gaining independence from parental tutelage.[59] Andrei Grinev is a cross-grained father, bent on curbing his son's freedom, threatening to thrash him for his duel as if he were a little boy, and thwarting his plans of marriage. When his son is convicted of treason, he accepts the verdict and will have nothing further to do with "a publicly dishonored traitor" (8: 370)—a marked difference in attitude from that of Shvanvich's father in the earlier outlines, who would have gone to Petersburg to beg mercy for his son. What is particularly remarkable about the old Grinev's belief in his son's guilt is that it persists even though he has heard from Masha and Savelich a full account of why Petr went over to the rebel side. One is reminded of Taras Bulba's condemnation of Andrii for his desertion of military duties in pursuit of love.[60]

Young Petr, on his part, does everything contrary to his father's wishes. Behaving like "a young whelp who had broken loose for the first time" (8: 283) in Simbirsk, he fails the first moral test upon leaving home (as if deliberately rejecting the maxim, "Cherish your honor from a tender age"—8: 277, 282— with which his father had sent him off); and insisting on continuing the journey despite the threat of a blizzard, he fails the first test of wisdom to which he is exposed. He throws himself into the duel hotheadedly, clearly against his elders' wishes, as though it were some kind of rite of passage into manhood. Clearly regarding Savelich as a deputy of his father's, he thinks to himself as they argue over his gambling debt, "If at this decisive moment I did not gain the upper hand over the obstinate old man, it would be difficult to free myself from his tutelage later on," and at the conclusion of that scene he states his intentions quite explicitly: "I wanted to shake myself loose and prove that I was no longer a child" (8: 285). When the old German general Andrei Karlovich asks Petr what his father means by the phrase *"derzhat' v ezhovykh rukavitsakh"* ("to hold in a mailed fist"; literally, "to hold in hedgehog-hide gloves"), he translates it—reasserting his previous quest for independence— as "to treat kindly, not too severely, to allow as much freedom as possible" (8: 292). Two reproachful statements by Savelich—

"You're beginning to play your pranks early" (8: 284), pronounced after the Simbirsk episode, and "Why the great haste? It'd be something else if you were hurrying to your wedding" (8: 287), when the travelers are caught in the blizzard—both express an effort to hold Grinev back from his headlong rush into independence, and both foreshadow his confrontation with his father over his plan of marrying early. Captain Mironov, too, plays a restraining role in relation to the young man, both when he censures him for his duel and when he advises him to give up writing verse—that is, indulging in amorous sentiments.

One could go a step further and argue that Petr seeks liberation not just from paternal authority, but from parental authority in general. If he were more dutifully bound to his mother he would not risk his life in a duel—an act that causes her to fall sick with fright and worry. Moreover, he fights the duel in defiance not so much of Captain Mironov as of Vasilisa Egorovna, who is the weightiest authority figure in Belogorsk.

Pugachev is also something of a parental figure,[61] but his relationship with Petr is nevertheless quite different from that of the elder Grinevs, Savelich, and the Mironovs. He appears in Grinev's life at a moment when the young man needs guidance both in escaping from the blizzard and in a new psychological orientation. Petr's search for new guidance was already apparent from his readiness to succumb to the older officer Zurin's seductive ploys; but Zurin of course did not prove worthy of respect or sympathy; those feelings were to be reserved for the much more gallant Pugachev. Rapport between Grinev and the rebels' future leader is established almost as soon as they meet for the first time. It is characteristic, for instance, that although Pugachev is strong and authoritative, he does in the blizzard just what the inexperienced and lost young man had recommended: to forge ahead despite the dangers. Another reason why Grinev feels kinship for his guide is that Pugachev had pawned his coat at an inn—having obviously behaved just as Grinev had in Simbirsk. Here is a different paternal figure to follow; and it is no accident that just as Pugachev is leading Grinev's wagon to safety, Petr has a dream in which his feared father ("My first thought was an apprehension that my father might be angry with me"; 8: 289) is replaced by Pugachev. This new father, though he heaps corpse on corpse with his axe, gently invites Petr to receive his blessing.

Further, a contest between Pugachev and Mironov as authority figures takes place in Chapter Seven, not only in a physical but also in a psychological sense: Pugachev, the charismatic leader, is able to rally his men again after they have been scattered by cannon fire; but Mironov, despite his momentary advantage, is unable to make the garrison troops follow his charge. The contrast between Pugachev's violence to others and his kindness to the young Grinev is emphasized anew when Grinev visits him after the execution of the Mironovs, observing that "his features, regular and rather pleasant, had nothing ferocious about them" (8: 330). When, eventually, Pugachev makes Grinev laugh with him toward the end of that scene, we have the impression that the young man has in some way been seduced into betraying the dead Mironovs, who had been his substitute parents. The leader of the rebels has become Grinev's guide in rebelling against parental authority. Pugachev's liberating influence on the young hero and the latter's gratitude for it are emphasized several times: the rebellion is described as giving Grinev's soul "a powerful and salutary shock" (8: 312); he says the happiness of his whole life depends on Pugachev; and he becomes so attached to the rebel leader that he declares: "God is my witness, I'd be glad to repay you with my life for what you've done for me" (8: 356).

Most important of all, Grinev could never have married his Masha if the rebellion had not occurred and Masha's parents had not been killed, because his father would have had him moved to a different location and would have continued opposing his marital plans. What Grinev outwardly abhors—the execution of his prospective in-laws—turns out to be the greatest benefaction to him.[62] From a psychological point of view, the novel could be described as the story of a young man's violent rebellion against parental restraints, but with this peculiar feature: that he does not stain his hands with blood. It is Pugachev who commits the murder for him by proxy and suffers the punishment for it by proxy. Since Pugachev has murdered the Mironovs, Grinev does not have to raise his hand against his own parents.

Admittedly, this interpretation does not solve the problem of the disunity of the various modes of presentation in the novel. Whichever way we interpret *The Captain's Daughter*, the execution scene retains a jarring quality. But if we take the novel's psychological dimension into consideration, we can appreciate that the disunity we sense is a reflection in the artistic form of Pushkin's probings into new, complex, even disconcerting, contents.

VII. Last Prose Works

I

Pushkin's interest in scholarly historical writing was by no means confined to *A History of Pugachev*. Indeed the Pugachev Rebellion represented only a side interest compared with the subject that had attracted him for a long time and became the central concern of his last years—the epoch and personality of Peter the Great.

As we have seen, Pushkin had begun collecting material about Peter's life and times as early as the mid-1820's. The subject subsequently inspired two poetic masterpieces—*Poltava* and *The Bronze Horseman*—but two attempts at treating it in fiction—*The Blackamoor of Peter the Great* and a projected "Story About a Strelets" (1833–34)—were abandoned. The deeper Pushkin delved into published sources and archival materials (from the early 1830's on), the more he was drawn to writing a historical monograph, which he hoped would be his chef d'oeuvre—a lasting contribution to scholarship, arising like a "bronze monument" (15: 154). One of the reasons that he could not tear himself away from St. Petersburg was that if he had retired from the Tsar's service he would have lost access to the archives (see 15: 165, 171; 16: 37). By 1837 he had compiled a large volume of notes and preliminary sketches.

After Pushkin's death V. A. Zhukovskii looked at these materials and sought Nicholas I's permission to hand them over to censors with a view to possible publication. The censors, after crossing some passages out, eventually gave the manuscript back to Pushkin's widow, but she was unable to find a publisher. Two segments of the material were later published by P. V. Annenkov.[1] The bulk of the manuscript, however, remained in the possession of Pushkin's heirs, some parts to be lost, others to be accidentally recovered in 1917. Only after Ilia Feinberg's careful study of the extant parts in the 1950's did it become clear that the manuscript consisted, not just of notes Pushkin took in the course of his historical research, but also of whole passages in which he had already consolidated his source materials and summarized his own opinions.[2] It appears that he was only a year or two away from completing the work.

Despite gaps in the chronological presentation of events and despite the sketchiness of many parts, *A History of Peter I* shows qualities corresponding to Pushkin's ideal of an objective historical narrative. Documented facts, critical comments on the reliability of source materials, and sound conclusions follow each other in the tightly woven text. Wherever subjective judgments appear—"He must have been drunk" (10: 198); "He was a strange monarch" (10: 241); "a tyrannical law" (10: 245)—it is clear that Pushkin was just making parenthetical notes for himself, rather than formulating the final text. In such historical narrative there was no need for the narrator to assume any role other than that of a detached chronicler. Factual details invoke the full horror of the epoch. People are starved in captivity; they are tortured; their tongues are cut out and their fingers chopped off; we see them beheaded or broken on the wheel. After Peter has subdued their rebellion, Streltsy line the road all the way from the village of Alekseevskoe to Moscow, begging for mercy, with their heads voluntarily placed on executioners' blocks (10: 25). The chief spectacle in a triumphant march after a military victory is a captured traitor, pulled along in a cart equipped with gallows and hung around with knouts (10: 29). It is observed that Peter's son Aleksei, during his interrogations, at first wrote his statements in a firm hand, and then, after being whipped, in an unsteady hand (10: 246).

Other descriptions bring the color of the period alive in less brutal ways. A "theological debate" precedes a riot by the Streltsy (10: 12); a dwarf steps out of an enormous pie at a feast marking the baptism of the Tsarevich Petr Petrovich (10: 217); "one hundred adult soldiers" are sent as a present to the Prussian

King (10: 218); and every citizen is required to go to confession at least once a year, under penalty of a fine equaling twice his annual income (10: 221). When the material itself is so rich, the presentation can be matter-of-fact without becoming dry. What interests Pushkin most is Peter's character. The Emperor comes alive, first of all, in his colorful speech, of which Pushkin records as much as he can. Braving a stormy sea, Peter reassures his fellow sailors with the words: "Have you ever heard of a Tsar drowning?" (10: 39). Faced with a risky situation, he writes: "But if you fear misfortune, you will never find fortune" (10: 111). He calls boats imported from England his "foster children" compared to those built in his own shipyard (10: 197); he disparages a Swedish Prince's statesmanship because the Prince "carries his behind on very thin legs" (10: 204); and when the Tsaritsa Marfa Matveevna (Fedor Alekseevich's widow) dies, he strictly forbids people "to bewail her now or at any time in the future" (10: 219; Pushkin's italics).

Peter's most attractive features, as they emerge in Pushkin's presentation, are his tremendous energy, his quick mind, and his ability to divide himself among a great variety of pursuits. He sends his orders to the Russian army from a "carpenter's shed" while working as an apprentice in a Dutch shipyard (10: 37). Soon after issuing his Table of Ranks, he works in a Kaluga mine and takes eighteen three-kopeck pieces as wages (10: 257). While on military campaigns, he collects rare plants, gives orders to capture rare animals for a zoo, and confers with scholars; and—at once a seeker of enlightenment and a predator—he has an occupied Finnish city's whole municipal library packed up and sent to Russia (10: 199). His attention to small details, however, often turns into pettiness: he issues, for instance, orders against the use, under penalty of exile, of nails and braces in shoemaking because the metal would spoil the leather (10: 216); he forbids people, on pain of severe punishment, to throw themselves on their knees before him on the muddy streets of his new city under construction (10: 69); and he requires "all the citizens to take part in excursions on the Neva on Sundays and holidays" (10: 244; Pushkin's italics).

The most horrifying aspect of Peter's personality, which Pushkin records in ample detail, is his cruelty. It is demonstrated, above all, in the torture and trial of his son Aleksei. In this context, however, while avoiding none of the horror and grossness of Peter's behavior, Pushkin also captures some finer psychological details: it is on the very day of Aleksei's death that Peter launches a new ship, rewards the *son* of one of his associates for his services, and ends up in a drunken orgy. When his other son, Petr Petrovich, in whom he had sought solace, dies of an illness the following year, Pushkin concludes that "this death finally broke Peter's iron soul" (10: 255). In Peter Pushkin found a character of enormous complexity, as full of psychological peculiarities and contradictions as any character invented by a novelist, and as great in his passions, ambitions, and achievements as any hero of epic poetry.

In addition to an incisive character study, *A History of Peter I* offers a view of the changeability and insecurity of human existence. No sooner has Peter concluded an uneasy truce with the Turks in the south than the Swedes attack him in the north; no sooner has he defeated the Swedes than a shift in West European alliances changes the international situation to Russia's disadvantage; while Peter engages in diplomacy and study abroad, there are riots and conspiracies at home; and his family cannot be trusted any more than his lieutenants, what with his own son becoming the symbol of popular resistance to his reforms and his wife being unfaithful to him just when he most needs her support. The central theme of *A History of Peter I* is the transience of man's historical existence.

A History of Peter I represents the farthest point Pushkin reached in the direction of objectivity, away from poetic gestures and histrionics. Not content with his achievements as a poet, dramatist, and fiction writer, he strove, especially in his last years, to be a leader of Russian intellectual life in general. For this reason a great deal of his output during the last years was discursive prose—journalism, literary criticism, and political and philosophical commentary as well as historical scholarship. Among his nonfiction prose writings of the last period, apart from *A History of Peter I*, "A Journey to Arzrum" stands out as one of the best.

The final text of this work, based partly on the notes he took during his journey to the south in 1829 and partly on ethno-

graphic information he subsequently gathered, was written in
1835.³ At first glance it appears to be very close to the journalistic pieces of his last years, especially to the anecdotes he published under the heading *Table Talk*: it is chatty, digressive,
now lyrical, now flippant; it ranges over personal reminiscences,
political questions, and problems of literary creation; it mixes
ethnography with subjective impressions. On closer examination, however, this seemingly lightweight travelogue proves to
be quite intricately structured. Iu. N. Tynianov has observed
that the image the "Journey's" narrator projects about himself
is doubly ironic: he is not Pushkin, but an average Russian nobleman pronouncing judgments appropriate to his social background (about the Circassians, for instance); and he is a civilian
observing military action, puzzled and uncomprehending, anticipating the role of Pierre Bezukhov on the field of Borodino.⁴
A war that from a distance might seem heroic breaks into prosaic details in his description. In general, "A Journey to Arzrum"
can be read as a profaning of romantic themes: scholars have
remarked that some of Pushkin's lyrical poems about the Caucasus are here given in prose,⁵ and that the narrator's references
to Pushkin's earlier verse tales, such as *A Prisoner of the Caucasus*, amount to something of a parody.⁶ However, at the same
time as his poems are recast in prose, his prose style acquires
greater flexibility and moves closer to poetry.⁷ Finally, as still
another scholar has pointed out, the travelogue is so structured
that the dynamism of the journey and the static nature of the
descriptions create a paradox.⁸

   Close to "A Journey to Arzrum" in genre is the short story
"Kirdzhali" (1834).⁹ The name of its hero, from which it takes
its title, is derived from the Balkan Turkish word *kircali*, meaning marauder or irregular soldier. Some early scholars assumed
that this hero, designated by a common noun rather than by a
proper name, was an invention of Pushkin's, but subsequent research has shown that there was indeed in Moldavia a robber
chief called Kirdzhali, who joined Alexander Ypsilanti's uprising with his band in 1821, escaped to Russia after the Hetairists' defeat near Skuliany, was arrested by the Russian authorities in 1823, and was handed over to the Turks. He escaped

from prison that year, but was recaptured and hanged in 1824.[10] Pushkin, who took some notes about the leading Hetairists while living in Kishinev (12: 190–91), obviously heard about Kirdzhali's extradition to Turkey at the time it happened. The name first occurs in Pushkin's works in an 1823 lyrical fragment known as "A Civil Servant and a Poet"; and some lines he jotted down in 1828 were intended for a verse tale entitled *Kirdzhali*. The civil servant who tells the narrator of the short story about Kirdzhali's arrest and subsequent fate was modeled on a person Pushkin had met in Kishinev.[11] But for all that "Kirdzhali" is based on historical facts and on an eyewitness account, its version of how the hero escaped from prison after his extradition is wholly fictitious: as Pushkin has it, Kirdzhali befriends his guards while awaiting his execution, promises to reveal a secret treasure to them, and fights free when they agree to take him to the site of the supposed treasure. It is most likely that Pushkin took this element of the plot from a Moldavian ballad.[12] Pushkin's failure to mention Kirdzhali's subsequent execution—though he obviously knew about it—also relates the story to a type of ballad in which the hero's triumph was an obligatory ending.[13]

Part fiction, part historical fact, part anecdote, part legend, "Kirdzhali" has perplexed critics who wished to assign it to a definite genre.[14] In manner it is close to "A Journey to Arzrum" and *Table Talk*: it is narrated in a light, anecdotal style as if told in a company of friends after dinner; it contains digressions, unnecessary from the point of view of plot development (e.g., about the Moldavian wagon called a *căruță*; 8: 257); it relates with gusto such details as a Russian major named Khorchevskii chasing the Turks away with a wag of his finger; and it makes light of gory scenes such as the fat Hetairist Kantagoni thrusting a Turk's spear further into his own stomach in order to be able to reach his enemy with his saber. This light manner seems to be incongruous with the legendary air of the story. It is, however, possible to discern an underlying structure that integrates the disparate elements: it has been argued that by giving credit to a legend at the end of the story, the narrator subverts the credibility of all the foregoing historical information, turning the story into an ironic anecdote, epitomized by the question mark on which it ends ("Isn't Kirdzhali something?"; 8: 260).[15] Pushkin's last years saw the genesis of several other fictional plans and fragments. Two of these—the plans for "A Story About a Strelets" and the fragment "I Have Often Thought About This Horrifying Family Scene" (ca. 1833)—are belated attempts to treat the Peter-Hannibal theme in fiction. The brief outline "Crispin Arrives in the Guberniia" (1833–34) hints at a comic situation of mistaken identities, a twist that Gogol was to adopt, at Pushkin's suggestion, for the plot of his comedy *The Government Inspector* (1836). The fragment "In 179.. I Was Returning" (1835) sets the scene for a romance between an officer and a young noblewoman, but gives very little indication of further developments.

There is more substance to *A Russian Pelham* (1834–35), of which two brief chapters and four outlines have remained.[16] The name of the hero (and the title, bestowed posthumously) obviously derives from Edward Bulwer Lytton's *Pelham, or Adventures of a Gentleman* (1828), which Pushkin had in his library both in the English original and in a French translation. Chapter One of Pushkin's text gives the family background of the hero, but gives it so sketchily that one wonders if even this fragment, appearing as a chapter, was not intended only as an outline to be fleshed out later. Sketchy as the chapter is, it still contains enough information for the reader to see that Pushkin planned to develop a complicated character, who grows up in a broken family, constantly battling against the woman his father lives with and against the son she has brought into the household. Chapter Two is even sketchier, giving only basic information about the central character's sojourn at a German university and his preparations for returning home.

The outlines give some hint of what was to happen later. The connection with Bulwer Lytton's novel—with whose rambling style Pushkin could obviously not have sympathized—is that Pushkin's hero, too, would have been exposed to a variety of experiences in a variety of social situations, ranging over foreign lands, Petersburg, and Russian country estates. The outlines indicate that the Russian Pelham (Pelymov in some variants; 8: 975) would have gone through a number of stormy love affairs, would have been friendly with a scapegrace called Fedor Orlov, would have got into trouble with the authorities because of Orlov, would have retired—like Onegin—to the country for a while, and would have associated with a number of future Decembrists. (The action of the projected novel, judging by the real-life names mentioned and the real-life events hinted at, was to take place in the late 1810's—the period Pushkin spent in St. Petersburg before his exile.) It is not clear whether the historical personalities appearing in the outline would have retained their true identity or would have been renamed for the novel,[17] but it is certain that Pushkin intended to portray psychologically complex characters within a panorama of Russian life.

Pushkin's last unfinished fictional piece is known by the name of its heroine, Maria Schoning (1836). It begins with a correspondence between Anna Harlin, a former servant in the Schoning household, and Maria, whose father has just died, leaving her with nothing but a backlog of taxes owed to the city of Nuremberg. The letters, three in all, are followed by a scene, related in the third person, of the auction at which Maria loses everything she and her father had had. This much of Pushkin's Russian text is accompanied in the manuscript by a précis in French of the supposedly real-life story of Maria Schoning, taken from a French collection of criminal case histories.[18] We learn from the précis that Maria, driven to utter penury and insulted by the police, who took her for a prostitute, contemplated suicide but was saved by her former maid Anna. She went to live with Anna, who was married to a disabled veteran and had two children. For a while the arrangement worked out, the two women supporting Harlin and the children, but later tragedy struck: job opportunities dried up, Anna fell sick, Harlin died, and the children were on the verge of starvation. Maria decided to put both Anna and herself out of the way, thereby qualifying the children for admission to an orphanage. To this end she made a false confession to the police, saying that she had delivered a baby with Anna's help, and that they had then murdered and buried it. Anna, when she understood Maria's purpose, confirmed the story; both were sentenced to death;

Maria tried to rescind her false confession just before their execution, but it was too late: Anna was beheaded and Maria died of fright before she got to the executioner's block. What element in this odd melodrama aroused Pushkin's interest? Maria's second letter in Pushkin's text already gives a hint that he was chiefly interested in her distraught emotional state: at her father's funeral and memorial service she feels now faint, now restored to full strength, now lightheaded, now inclined to laugh. Most likely, Pushkin intended to explore her mind further, trying to show what drove her to seek death in such a strange way: after all, the children were not hers and *her* death was not required for getting them into an orphanage; and even if she thought she had to die, she did not have to choose such a humiliating means of suicide. Pushkin must have sensed the potential of an inner urge for self-destruction and self-humiliation in her character, which would have related her to Hermann and Volskaia.

2

Although chronologically not the last, by far the most important fictional fragment of Pushkin's final years was *Egyptian Nights*. Like "The Queen of Spades," this unfinished work is linked with several themes that Pushkin treated in different genres over a decade. One of its central themes, that of Cleopatra, was originally anticipated in the historical elegy bearing her-name, written in the fall of 1824. Writing "Aurelius-Victor" (3: 678) on the manuscript of the first draft of this poem, Pushkin indicated that he was using a late Roman historical source— a compilation called *Liber de Viris Illustribus Urbis Romae*, attributed to Sextus Aurelius Victor.[19] The last short chapter of this work (Chap. 86) is devoted to Cleopatra and contains the following sentence: "She was so lustful that she often prostituted herself and so beautiful that many men paid with their lives for a night with her."[20] Although this sentence is ambiguous ("paying with their lives" could mean that men sacrificed themselves in duel or battle in exchange for Cleopatra's love, or that they risked their lives stealing into her chamber at night, or anything else), Pushkin read it as an unequivocal indication that Cleopatra had her lovers' heads chopped off, by a pre-arranged bargain, after an amorous night.

Having made a fair copy of the first draft of the poem, Pushkin laid it aside for the time being.[21] He returned to the project again four years later, in the fall of 1828, establishing iambic tetrameter as the uniform meter throughout the poem (the first version had contained some hexameters) and introducing several changes that helped define his idea more clearly. The most important of these changes is the elimination of Cleopatra's second pronouncement of her challenge. In the first version we hear her admirers "praise her in chorus" and "crowd around her throne," calling her their "idol" (3: 679), all of which makes her suspect their sincerity; her challenge seems to be a desire to elicit true devotion; the men's response to her challenge is a stunned silence; she has to repeat it; and when three volunteers finally step forward we have the feeling that they are doing their duty to their despotic Queen at least as much as they are following the dictates of their own hearts. But in the 1828 version Cleopatra's challenge makes her guests' "hearts quiver with passion" (3: 130) even as it strikes them with horror; their confused murmurs do not last long; and she does not need to repeat her offer because the three volunteers step forward while she is still contemptuously surveying the crowd's first reaction. In this second version she is the life and soul of the feast, to all appearances perfectly happy with her guests; and she grows pensive momentarily only in order to devise the most extravagant sexual game she can think of to crown her happiness with perfect bliss. And the men rise to meet her destructive flame with their own self-destructive pride or sexual passion. This mutually satisfying meeting of flame and air is, perhaps, what makes Cleopatra of the second version also more compassionate: in the first version she just "feasted her eyes" (*liubovalas'*; 3: 685) on the third, very young volunteer; now she is either casting a "sad glance" (*grustnyi vzor*; 3: 131) at him, as one variant has it, or looks at him with "tender feeling" (*s umileniem*; 3: 692), as the variant preferred in more recent editions reads.[22]

Like its 1824 predecessor, the 1828 version was put aside for possible future use. One opportunity for using the poem presented itself to Pushkin in connection with "A Tale of Roman Life" (also known by its beginning, "Caesar was traveling"), which he started to work on in 1833 and turned to again in 1835. Of this attempt at a historical novella there remain, first of all, three fragments of prose text. We see the writer Titus Petronius receiving news that he has fallen out of favor with Nero. He decides to end his own life rather than await his fate at the hand of Caesar.[23] The subject, these fragments hint, was to be Petronius's attempt to die a noble death. The manuscript indicates that Pushkin intended to insert into the prose text translations of two odes, one by Anacreon, dealing with old age and death, the other by Horace, recounting, possibly with deliberate exaggeration, how the poet had taken to his heels on the battlefield—a topic also related to the question of courage or cowardice in the face of death.[24] Incorporating these verses into the prose, Pushkin was attempting to combine two genres that he had at one time regarded as irreconcilable. The work that was to emerge would probably have been close to Menippean satire—the genre to which Petronius's own *Satyricon* belonged.[25]

In addition to these three fragments we have an outline on this project in Pushkin's own hand. It calls for a scene in which Petronius is lying in a warm bath, now opening his vein to let the blood flow, now bandaging it up to prolong his life a little more, while several close friends entertain him with anecdotes and pleasant conversation. The first story intended to cheer the last moments of the dying Petronius was to be "about Cleopatra" (8: 936). Exactly what Pushkin meant by this phrase and the following one, "our discussions of the matter," is not clear. If indeed the poem about Cleopatra's challenge was to be recited, then the mode of death her three prospective lovers had chosen would have been the subject of the discussion.[26] But it is also possible that Pushkin was simply referring to Cleopatra's own suicide, in which case "A Tale of Roman Life" would have little connection with the earlier poems relating Cleopatra's amorous exploits. What makes a connection with the earlier poems more likely is that Cleopatra's suicide—her preference for death over heartbreak and humiliation—would have been a matter plainly understandable to Petronius and his friends and would have called for little discussion. The question of whether one should sacrifice one's life for a night of fulfillment seems much more likely as a topic for debate.

However that may be, "A Tale of Roman Life" did not get beyond the first fragments and outline, and later, probably in 1835, Pushkin thought of incorporating the Cleopatra poem in another prose work, known by its first sentence, "We Were Spending the Evening at Princess D.'s Dacha." The extant manuscripts of this work consist of several fragments, some in draft, some in clean copy. The first of these describes a social gathering where, in the course of conversation, an anecdote about Madame de Staël is told—supposedly she once asked Napoleon whom he considered the most outstanding woman in the world, to which he answered, "The one who has borne the most children" (8: 420). A young man called Aleksei Ivanovich says he considers Cleopatra the most remarkable woman who has ever lived, and in proof he recites the story of Cleopatra's challenge, partly in prose, partly in verse (supposedly written by his poet friend N.). After the recitation the guests discuss whether a Cleopatra could exist under the conditions of modern life; and in the concluding fragment Aleksei Ivanovich asks a young woman, Volskaia, if she thinks that any Russian woman in the 1830's would be willing to enter into the kind of contract Cleopatra concluded with her prospective lovers. She answers in the affirmative, though not necessarily in relation to herself, and Aleksei Ivanovich abruptly leaves, presumably to think the matter over.

The setting of "We Were Spending the Evening at Princess D.'s Dacha" immediately calls to mind the earlier fragment "The Guests Were Arriving at the Dacha." The fact that Pushkin here again called his heroine Volskaia also seems to indicate that he was attempting to rework a previously abandoned theme. Furthermore, it is revealing that Nina Voronskaia of Chapter Eight of *Onegin*, modeled on the same prototype as Volskaia, is called "the Cleopatra of the Neva" (6: 172).[27] Pushkin was evidently planning to resume his psychological study of complex people of his own time, creating a Cleopatra in a modern Petersburg setting.

This change in geographical and chronological setting had

several consequences for Pushkin's treatment of the Cleopatra theme. To begin with, Napoleon's stodgy view of women, which one of the guests, Sorokhtin, ironically characterizes as the straightforward opinion of a genius, provides a trivial framework for Cleopatra's story. The other guests come forward with their candidates for the title of the most admirable woman in the world, mentioning the names of Madame de Staël herself, the Maid of Orleans, Queen Elizabeth I, the Marquise de Maintenon, and Madame Roland, until at last Aleksei Ivanovich suggests Cleopatra. The Cleopatra of the 1828 poem was unique and poetic in the grandeur of her extravagant desires; the Cleopatra of this fragment is brought into the conversation apropos of trivia and is compared to other women of varying claims to fame. What was originally intended to produce one great flash of indivisible impression has now become the object of analysis.

As Valerii Briusov has emphasized, one of the original Cleopatra's appealing features was her unabashed avowal of her inclinations.[28] She flung her challenge at the whole assembly, with a "bright look" (s vidom iasnym; 3: 130) and surveyed her guests' reaction with a "contemptuous glance" (3: 131). The three men who accepted her challenge also stepped out, in front of everyone, with "bold gait" and with "a bright look in their eyes" (iasny ochi; 3: 131). Aleksei Ivanovich, by contrast, is embarrassed to tell his anecdote, and Volskaia, who is supposed to become a Cleopatra of the Neva in the course of the action, coyly pleads with him not to tell it, "primly casting down her fiery eyes" (8: 421). Their hostess assumes Aleksei Ivanovich's anecdote will be slightly off-color, but assures him it will be all right to tell it, for they have all just seen Dumas Père's melodrama Antony (1832), and a copy of Balzac's La Physiologie du mariage (1829) is lying right there on the mantelpiece. Instead of a striking poetic fantasy, we are now dealing with a salacious anecdote, exposed to the light of nineteenth-century views of sex.

The "Cleopatra" Aleksei Ivanovich proceeds to recite is also changed by this new context. Its prose fragments are highly stylized, reflecting the literary taste either of Aleksei Ivanovich himself or of his poet friend. They represent perhaps the most poetic prose Pushkin ever wrote: one critic has justly commented that they might have been written by Gogol.[29] An introduction to Cleopatra's feast, much more elaborate than what we have seen in the earlier poems, describes the sultry Alexandrian night that fuels the Queen's passion. Because of the exotic details of this scene,[30] the subject appears much further removed from nineteenth-century Petersburg than it did in the earlier poems. With its three hundred youths, three hundred maidens, and three hundred black eunuchs serving the guests, the introduction brings a fairy land of fantasy to Princess D.'s dacha. Perhaps the theme that follows will be more presentable to the guests in this garb.

The verses that eventually develop the theme bring another change. In the earlier variants Cleopatra was accepted as she was, without explanation; now her motives are analyzed. Aleksei Ivanovich's friend introduces his poem by asking what makes her so restless and dissatisfied when she has at her disposal all the power, wealth, admiration, and sensual pleasure she could possibly want? (A draft version even describes a male harem in which "bashfully passionate" youths await her orders; 8: 995). The answer he devises is that "Her oversated senses sicken, / With barrenness of feeling stricken" (8: 423). Her satiety suggests that she is a creature of the late and declining Roman Empire, a victim of decaying morals confined to a definite period. The remote Queen of a fairy tale is paradoxically subjected to historical analysis.

Just as Aleksei Ivanovich had expected, his listeners take his anecdote as an indecent one. One suggests that it should be communicated to the "shameless" George Sand (8: 423), who could adapt it to contemporary mores. Another guest objects that the anecdote belongs exclusively to the ancient world, which leads to the chief question of whether a Cleopatra could exist in modern times. Although it is not always indicated in the ensuing conversation who is speaking, the context shows that the statements supporting an affirmative answer to this question all belong to Aleksei Ivanovich. "Couldn't you find one among today's women," he argues, "who would want to test in deed the truth of what men repeat to her every minute— that her love is dearer to them than their lives?" (8: 424). But this does not satisfy his interlocutors, who want to know about practical details. A latter-day Cleopatra, one of them objects, would not have the Egyptian Queen's power to enforce the contract when the time came: "You cannot draw up such agreements on legal paper and have them notarized in civil court" (8: 424).

Aleksei Ivanovich's answer, that a man could give his word of honor to commit suicide, is also ridiculed: somebody suggests that the man could change his mind and leave for foreign lands the next morning, making a fool of his lady. None of Aleksei Ivanovich's arguments—that life is not such a treasure after all, that mere existence without fulfillment is worthless—sound convincing against the skeptical, quite possibly trivial and unimaginative, but nonetheless common-sense counterarguments of his interlocutors. Why would a woman want to kill a man if she loved him? How could he love her if he thought she was a heartless creature, coveting his life? The discussion amounts to the exposing of poetic notions of passion to a flatfooted analysis in prose. Finally, pressed into a corner, Aleksei has to admit that he does not have mutual affections in mind: "As for requited love... that I do not demand: why should it be anyone's business if I am in love?" (8: 424). This admission implies that both parties to Cleopatra's contract would be driven by their inner compulsions, with very little regard for each other, and if they happened to find mutual fulfillment, it would be more or less coincidental. Such a notion takes the discussion beyond romantic clichés of "love" into the realm of self-absorbed neurotic patterns of behavior. Perhaps this is why one of Aleksei Ivanovich's interlocutors insists on changing the subject at this point.

The last prose fragment of the story underscores once more the enormous difference between the Egyptian Queen's Court and the Petersburg salon. Instead of making his offer publicly, Aleksei Ivanovich leans over Volskaia, as if examining her needlework, and whispers. At first she does not answer; he has to repeat his question. But the most telling ironic reversal is that in this situation it is the prospective victim who offers the contract to his coy destroyer.[31]

Anna Akhmatova has suggested that the final exchange between Volskaia and Aleksei Ivanovich provides a striking dramatic ending to the story and therefore we should regard "We

Were Spending the Evening" as a completed work. What other details could we wish for, argues Akhmatova: surely not a description of the delights of the lovers' night or of the "lucky man's" subsequent suicide?[32] One must object, however, that a melodramatic suicidal outcome of Aleksei Ivanovich's involvement with Volskaia is by no means assured. Pushkin did not plant hints at possible other denouements in the text for nothing. Since we have been told that a man might just not keep his word, making a fool of his lady—which would be a farcical ending—we need to know for sure whether Aleksei Ivanovich will or will not turn out to be such a man. Since we have also been told that a woman who loved her man would want to spare him (such a possible outcome with regard to the Queen's youngest victim was inherent even in the 1828 "Cleopatra"), we want to find out whether Volskaia will or will not be such a woman. If she decided to release him from his word of honor, there could simply be a comic resolution to the affair. Thus we have at least three possible denouements to the narrative,[33] and since the text gives no reliable indication of which one it will be, we cannot regard the story as completed. One could even claim that the discussion preceding Aleksei Ivanovich's offer to Volskaia not only leaves the outcome of his involvement with her open, but positively prognosticates a development that he does not expect. One critic has aptly remarked that the Cleopatra anecdote was probably meant to serve this narrative in the same way as the anecdote about the three winning cards serves the plot of "The Queen of Spades": it was to provide the impulse for the action but eventually lead the hero astray.[34]

It is accepted that Pushkin had in all likelihood abandoned his plans for "We Were Spending the Evening" before he turned to *Egyptian Nights* in the fall of 1835.[35] The novel would therefore represent still another attempt to use the Cleopatra theme. It consists of three short chapters in prose and two poems, which though not actually attached to the prose parts, have traditionally been incorporated in the work because of their obvious thematic relevance.

The hero of the unfinished novel is a young aristocrat named Charskii, who is also a poet. An Italian improvisatore, visiting in St. Petersburg, comes to ask him, as a fellow artist, to help him set up a performance. Charskii at first thinks that the man is an itinerant musician and finds it offensive to be described as his fellow artist, but when he learns that his visitor is an improvisatore, he promises to help. That evening he persuades a Princess to let the Italian give his performance in her reception room; and the next morning he comes to the improvisatore's poor hotel room to communicate the good news. As a token of his gratitude, the Italian offers to improvise for him on the spot. Charskii suggests the theme mentioned earlier: *"A poet chooses the subjects of his songs himself: the crowd has no right to command his inspiration"* (8: 268; Pushkin's italics); and the Italian improvises a poem of astonishing beauty.

The evening of the performance arrives: the Italian asks his audience to suggest topics, writing them on slips of paper, which are subsequently placed in an urn. It is hard for the improvisatore to find someone to draw a topic from the urn, but eventually a young woman of majestic beauty volunteers. The topic drawn is "Cleopatra and her lovers." Which of her many lovers did the person who named the topic have in mind, the Italian asks. No one knows who suggested the topic, but for some reason everybody turns to a plain, bashful girl, who made a suggestion at the urging of her mother. The girl does not respond. Charskii eventually breaks the embarrassing silence by acknowledging the topic as his own and explaining Cleopatra's contract with her lovers. There follows the Italian's improvisation on the Cleopatra theme, after which the narrative breaks off.

The beginning of Chapter One—a description of Charskii's position in society as a poet—is a new version of an earlier unfinished piece of writing, which we have discussed under the title "A Fragment."[36] The chief difference between the character described in the 1830 "Fragment" and Charskii is that Charskii, being rich, does not depend on royalties for his livelihood. It appears that Pushkin introduced this change in order to be able to contrast a rich, independent Russian poet with the poor Italian improvisatore. It is also notable that unlike the character of "A Fragment," Charskii is not said to be descended from an ancient family that has fallen on hard times by the nineteenth century. A draft of *Egyptian Nights* shows that at first

Pushkin even toyed with the idea of placing Charskii at the opposite end of the social scale, stating that "his uncle, a tax-farmer in Saratov, had left him a handsome estate" (8: 839). If Pushkin had left this variant unchanged, Charskii would have emerged as one of those upstarts whom Pushkin had mockingly called aristocrats in several earlier pieces. Such a social background, however, would have detracted from the clear-cut contrast between Charskii and the Italian. The occupation Pushkin eventually gave to the uncle—"vice-governor at a prosperous time" (8: 263)—still derogates the source of Charskii's wealth, but at least it does not set him apart from the general run of the nobility.

Several possible prototypes for the Italian improvisatore have been mentioned in scholarly literature. The poet whose improvisations seem to have inspired Pushkin most was Adam Mickiewicz. In April 1828, in fact, Pushkin's apartment was the scene of one of the Polish poet's brilliant performances.[37] According to an eyewitness, Pushkin cried out after one of Mickiewicz's improvisations: "Quel génie, quel feu sacré, que suis-je après de lui!"[38] However, some of the actual details of the Italian's performance in *Egyptian Nights* appear to have been taken from another source: from the improvisations of a young German by the name of Maximilian Langenschwarz, who performed in St. Petersburg in April and October of 1832.[39] It is possible that Pushkin also heard about Tommaso Sgricci, the best-known improvisatore of the time in Western Europe, who had at one time improvised on the theme of "Cleopatra's Death" and who was notorious, just like Pushkin's character, for his greed.[40] Further, the scene of the improvisatore's arrival at Charskii's just when the young man is engrossed in his writing may have been inspired by a visit that a certain Alexandre Vattemare, an itinerant actor, mimic, and ventriloquist, had paid to Pushkin at an inopportune time for the purpose of soliciting his patronage.[41] Finally, the romantics' penchant for describing improvisations, resulting in works like Madame de Staël's *Corinne* (1807), Samuel Taylor Coleridge's *Improvisatore* (1827), and V. F. Odoevskii's "Improvisatore" (1833), must have had its share of influence on Pushkin.[42]

The Italian's first improvisation in *Egyptian Nights* originates in Stanzas Twelve and Thirteen of the unfinished verse tale *Ezerskii* (1832–33). These stanzas, forestalling criticism of the poet's choice of his hero and defending the poet's freedom of inspiration, were partially reworked by Pushkin in 1835, and another six lines, beginning with the words "Such is the poet: like the North" (8: 854–55), were added. These materials were so clearly intended for *Egyptian Nights* that few scholars argue with the decision of Pushkin's posthumous editors, Zhukovskii and Pletnev, to include them in the text.[43] But Pushkin had obviously not finished his revision of the verses, which do not fully live up to the narrator's description of them as "fiery stanzas" (8: 268).[44] Since Pushkin undertook to stylize his "Cleopatra" for "We Were Spending the Evening," it stands to reason that he would have similarly wanted to adapt the stanzas from *Ezerskii* to the conditions of *Egyptian Nights*.[45]

For the Italian's second improvisation editors have traditionally adopted the 1828 version of "Cleopatra." The question could be raised whether the 1835 fragments of the poem, reworked for "We Were Spending the Evening," would serve the purposes of *Egyptian Nights* better. These fragments, however, do not add up to a full coherent version (we do not see the prospective lovers stepping forward); and both their position in Pushkin's notebook and their stylistic characteristics indicate that they were meant for "We Were Spending the Evening."[46] But even if these particular fragments were not fit for *Egyptian Nights*, we must assume that Pushkin, had he completed his project, would have revised his 1828 poem for the novel. Both improvisations included in the standard editions must be regarded as simply the closest available approximations to what Pushkin probably intended.

Dostoevskii claimed in an article in 1861 that *Egyptian Nights* was a completed work.[47] He was no doubt right in the sense that the existing narrative fully develops and brings to conclusion certain themes. Yet some parts of the text seem to call for continuation. Why would Pushkin imply a parallel between the "majestic young beauty" (8: 273), drawing a theme from the urn with a self-assured, unruffled dignity, and Cleopatra, if he did not intend to create a Cleopatra of the Neva? These textual hints and the shared Cleopatra theme have persuaded some scholars that "We Were Spending the Evening" could be transformed into a continuation of *Egyptian Nights* if one took Aleksei Ivanovich's recitation out and assumed that the gathering at the dacha took place after the Italian's performance.[48] This assumption, however, takes too much liberty with the available texts: Pushkin had probably abandoned "We Were Spending the Evening" before he made a new attempt to use the Cleopatra theme in *Egyptian Nights*. It is likely that *Egyptian Nights* represents a fragment of a novel in which the mores of contemporary society would have been depicted, but since we do not know how Pushkin would have continued the novel, we must confine our analysis to the material we have.

These virtually plotless chapters represent a tightly structured and self-contained exposition of the nature of the poet's work. The two problems treated in this connection are the poet's relationship to society and the moral value of his creative efforts. The Italian improvisatore's relationship to society is relatively simple: he is poor; he needs to market his skill as a craftsman; he greedily seizes whatever rewards he can get.[49] The irony of his situation is, however, that his most marketable commodity is not so much his genuine art as the exotic air surrounding his personality. To be sure, he has to be able to hold forth glibly once he is up on the platform; but his sheer fluency, his striking appearance, his outward show of creative effort, and above all his foreignness count more than the quality of his poetry. Charskii understands this from the very beginning, telling the Italian: "I hope that you will have success: our society here has never yet heard an improvisatore. People's curiosity will be aroused; it is true that Italian is not in use among us, and therefore you will not be understood, but that doesn't matter: the main thing is that you should be in vogue" (8: 267).[50] One critic has commented that the literal failure of the improvisatore's audience to understand Italian is symbolic of the public's general failure to comprehend the poet.[51]

Although Charskii understands the Italian's need to appeal at a superficial level, he himself would never hunt for popularity in a similar way. For this reason he is unpleasantly struck by the improvisatore's theatrical attire just before the performance. He thinks at that moment that a poet should not look like an "itinerant mountebank" (*zaezzhii figliar*; 8: 271). But when he actually sees the improvisatore's showy figure on the platform he comes around to the Italian's view of what the public needs. (That view, in fact, is in line with what Charskii himself had said earlier about arousing curiosity.)

It appears, then, that playing cheap tricks in order to gain popularity is a concession an indigent poet must make. Given freedom from financial pressures, the poet should be able to ignore the wider public and create only for a small select group. The Italian says to Charskii before his first improvisation: "Where could I find a better audience? You are a poet, you will understand me better than any of them, and your quiet encouragement will be dearer to me than a whole storm of applause" (8: 268). And in the next chapter, when the Italian hears the theme "Cleopatra e i suoi amanti," he does not understand it, his imagination is not fired by it, until Charskii, another poet, explains it to him. Poetry, it is implied, is practiced by poets, for poets.

If this is so, Charskii should be the happiest of poets, for he, in contrast to the Italian, is not obliged to sell the products of his inspiration. The "genuine friends" (8: 264), to whom he confesses that he knows true happiness only in his moments of poetic inspiration, comprise, presumably, his small select audience. (By "fellow men of letters"—8: 264—whose company he shuns, he obviously means vulgar types of the literary marketplace, and not genuine poets.) Yet—and this is one of the reasons Pushkin needs him in addition to the improvisatore—he frets about his relationship to society much more than the Italian does. If public reaction to his works bothers him, he could refuse to publish them and could simply read them to his select friends. But he does publish them, and therefore his complaints about the public's reaction to them are somewhat disingenuous. He is compelled by an inner urge to create, and he needs a public, however imperfect its understanding may be. The Italian may have needed a poet as an intermediary, but his theme had originally been suggested by a member of the audience, and the product that finally emerged was an artistic experience of sorts for everybody present. Pushkin's most telling comment on the interaction between author and public is that the poet depicted in the Italian's first improvisation is walking along ostensibly oblivious to everything and everybody; but in fact "someone detains him from behind" (8: 269).

The "someone" represents another kind of demand society makes on poets. A poet, he insists, should not wander around aimlessly, stooping to unworthy subjects; he should soar to heaven, for "A genuine poet ought to deem / Of his inspired anthems worthy / None but an elevated theme" (8: 269). In an outline connected with this passage in *Ezerskii*, Pushkin had jotted down: "Why unworthy heroes? What can you do? I have seen Ypsilanti, Paskevich, and Ermolov" (5: 410). This revealed that in defending his choice of an ordinary man for a hero, Pushkin was answering those critics who had reproached him for not writing odes to the glory of Russian arms after his journey to Arzrum, and particularly for not singing the praises of the commander of the Caucasian army, I. F. Paskevich.[52] The Italian's improvisation is an eloquent assertion of the poet's right not to be swayed by such public demands. The underlying irony is that this assertion itself is a response to a public demand—Charskii, in this case, representing the public.

It has been argued that the topic of the first improvisation ("A poet chooses the subjects of his songs himself: the crowd has no right to command his inspiration"), though suggested by Charskii, must have been close to the improvisatore's own heart since it was central to the nature of his art.[53] But the question arises: what would the Italian have done if an "elevated" topic, such as the singing of an army's glory, had been suggested to him? The obvious answer is that he would have created an equally impassioned improvisation on that subject. Pushkin could not have forgotten that he had glorified Ermolov's subjugation of the Caucasus in his Epilogue to *A Prisoner of the Caucasus*, and that the Polish uprising of 1830 had prompted him to write such nationalistic poems as "To the Slanderers of Russia" (1831), "A Borodino Anniversary" (1831), and "He Lived Among Us" (1834)—the last one censuring Mickiewicz for *his* nationalism. We are, once more, confronted with the chameleon poet's "negative capability," with his role playing, with his total absorption in his subject. Pushkin's nationalistic poems were products of momentary inspiration; in other moods, other moments, his inspiration took him in entirely different directions. Having to respond with equally beautiful poetry to contradictory demands was, then, not just the improvisatore's professional predicament, but the plight of the poet in general. It is revealing that the Italian's words about the "close tie between one's own inspiration and another's external will" had originally read in a draft as "the close tie between inspiration and external nature" (8: 270, 849). Pushkin's original thought, evidently, was that nature itself provided the contradictory stimuli that the poet could not help responding to. The improvisatore's audience setting unexpected themes for him is analogous to life at large inspiring the poet in capricious ways.

The essential closeness of the Italian improvisatore and the poet Charskii becomes clear as the story unfolds. Despite their contrasting features—poverty and wealth, ostentation and reticence, a romantic view of inspiration as "the divine presence" (8: 274)[54] and a skeptical description of it as "nonsense" (drian'; 8: 264)—the Italian is right when he insists to Charskii: "You are a poet just as I am" (8: 268). The most vivid manifestation of their oneness is the way they create the second improvisation together. There is a deliberate ambiguity about who suggested the Cleopatra theme in the first place: only the plain young woman's blushing and tears betray that she must have made the suggestion; but even if she is sufficiently implicated by her tears, we do not know—as the Italian does not know—exactly what she had in mind. She might have meant Caesar and Antony as Cleopatra's lovers. But Charskii, acting as if he were the improvisatore, accepts the ambiguous topic, puts his own interpretation on it, and passes it on to the Italian in an act of collective creation.[55]

The attribute of the improvisatore—and by extension of the poet—that makes him at once a great artist and a morally inconsistent human being is his capacity for making his own whatever he comes in contact with, that is, a heightened sensitivity. This was the attribute Pushkin's prophet acquired in the 1826 lyric by that title: once the seraph had touched his eyes and ears, he could equally perceive a tremor in the empyrean, the angels' flight, the reptiles' movement underwater, and the sprouting of the vine in the valley. It is interesting to note that Kipriano, the hero of Odoevskii's "Improvisatore," becomes a great artist when a magician endows him with the capacity "to know everything, to see everything, to understand everything."[56] This endowment is so awesome, however, that Kipriano cannot survive it.

It is their shared capacity to adapt to their poetic material that makes Charskii and the Italian identify with Cleopatra. In the first improvisation the poet defends his right to a lowly subject; in the second one he demonstrates that such a subject can indeed be transformed into poetry. The poet's acceptance of perverted sexuality instead of an elevated theme for his subject is like the wind's stubborn habit of stirring up dust in the ravine instead of inflating the sail that eagerly awaits it; like the eagle's whim of sitting on a decrepit stump instead of alighting on a lofty tower; like Desdemona's caprice in loving an old Moor instead of a young Italian. The poet can choose a subject unworthy in the eyes of the virtuous philosopher, because the poet "lives in gusto, be it foul or fair, mean or elevated." All he needs is that some quality in the subject—the grandeur of Cleopatra's unabashed passion—should capture his imagination.

Pushkin does not give an answer to the problem he explores in *Egyptian Nights*. While exploring it, he indulges in the very assumption of roles—equally identifying with Charskii, the Italian, and Cleopatra—that is the target of his exploration. Moreover, not only does he indulge in an assumption of roles—associated with the changing colors of the chameleon poet—but he resorts to poetic techniques to a greater degree than ever before in prose.

We find some of the same techniques employed here that we saw in "The Queen of Spades": for example, the contrasting descriptions of Charskii's study on the one hand and the Italian's hotel room on the other characterize the heroes through allusive details. Other such details expand the Desdemona-poet-Cleopatra similarity into a series of parallels: both the poet of the first improvisation and Cleopatra cast their eyes *down*, after moments of exaltation, in search of new desires or inspiration; both Cleopatra with her challenge and the Italian with his request for themes bewilder their audiences; and urns—symbolic of fate—are used both for allotting Cleopatra's nights to her lovers and for choosing a theme for the improvisatore. But in *Egyptian Nights* Pushkin goes even further than he went in "The Queen of Spades": here, as in some of the other fragments of the last years, he introduces verses into the body of prose. Moreover, his prose style has by now become so versatile that it can be adapted to the norms of romantic prose when the context so requires, as in the description of inspiration seizing the Italian.[57]

Pushkin had originally thought that prose writing would eliminate the many different masks poetry seemed to require. He did indeed pursue till the end of his life the kind of stern objective prose that produced *A History of Pugachev* and drew him to *A History of Peter I.* But that was scholarly prose; when he tried his hand at fiction he soon discovered that it could not be all thought and thought without decorative frills. Of the two fictional works that Pushkin held close to nonfiction—*The Blackamoor of Peter the Great* and "Kirdzhali"—the first remained unfinished and the second was too bare and blank to be among his best. The colorful *Tales of Belkin* amounted to a resumption of playacting on the part of the author. Although conventional in mode, they engendered a productive trend that eventually gave rise to *The Captain's Daughter.* But the use of simplehearted narrators severely limited Pushkin's scope in exploring ideas and characters, and therefore he groped for modes of presentation capable of conveying greater complexities. Creating the omniscient narrator of *Dubrovskii* was a step in the right direction, but full success with the omniscient mode came only when Pushkin endowed his detached narrator with some of the techniques of poetry in "The Queen of Spades."

What called for a greater presence of poetry were exigencies of characterization. Pushkin learned—anticipating even post-Freudian writers—that allusions, symbols, juxtapositions, were more versatile than analysis in elucidating character. An analytical conclusion may be correct in defining a particular psychological phenomenon, but a poetic text evokes much more varied echoes in humanity's subconscious archetypal store of experience. Therefore poetic techniques were most important to Pushkin when he tried to create, in many promising but tantalizingly incomplete pieces, the Russian psychological novel.

Descriptions full of symbols and allusions would have been unthinkable at the time when Pushkin was casting the prose of Rousseau, de Staël, and Richardson aside as "poetry." At that time he had certain theoretical expectations of prose as an antithesis to poetry. But prose, like Dunia the Prodigal Daughter, refused to follow the prescribed course. A continuing tension between two trends—one toward a sparse, austere style, the other toward poetic techniques—was what produced the rich variety of Pushkin's prose fiction.

Notes

Notes

Complete authors' names, titles, and publication data for the works cited by bracketed number are given in the Bibliography, pp. 341–70.

Chapter One

1. [P. A.] Viazemskii, "O *Kavkazskom plennike*, Soch. A. Push-kina," *Syn otechestva*, 82, No. 49 (1822): 115–26; Letter of Sept. 27, 1822, to A. I. Turgenev, in Saitov [482], 2: 274.

2. Tomashevskii [85], pp. 406–7.

3. Ernest J. Simmons, *Pushkin* (New York: Vintage, 1964), p. 92.

4. Victor Erlich, *The Double Image: Concepts of the Poet in Slavic Literatures* (Baltimore: Johns Hopkins Univ. Press, 1964), pp. 22f.

5. Lionel Trilling discusses the novel from this point of view. See his "Jane Austen and *Mansfield Park*" in Boris Ford, ed., *From Blake to Byron* (Harmondsworth, Eng.: Penguin, 1957), pp. 119–29.

6. Jane Austen, *Mansfield Park* (London: Zodiac, 1967), pp. 252–53.

7. Austen's name does not appear in the indexes to the Academy edition of Pushkin; nor are any of her novels listed in the catalogue of Pushkin's library. See Modzalevskii [479]; and B. L. Modzalevskii, "Biblioteka Pushkina: Novye materialy," *Literaturnoe nasledstvo*, 16–18 (1934): 985–1025.

8. See, for example, Tatiana A. Wolff, "Shakespeare's Influence on Pushkin's Dramatic Work," *Shakespeare Survey*, 1952, pp. 93–106. A full survey of scholarly works dealing with the subject is given by M. P. Alekseev, "Pushkin i Shekspir," *Pushkin: Sravnitel'no-isto-richeskie issledovaniia* (Leningrad: Nauka, 1972), pp. 240–80.

9. By "Shakespeare's hypocrite" Pushkin means Angelo of *Measure for Measure*.

10. August Wilhelm von Schlegel, *Über dramatische Kunst und Litteratur: Vorlesungen*, 2d ed. (Heidelberg: Mohr & Winter, 1817), 3: 55.

11. *Ibid.*, pp. 70–71.

12. *Ibid.*, p. 226.

13. George H. Mead, *Movements of Thought in the Nineteenth Century* (Chicago: University of Chicago Press, 1936), pp. 63, 75.

14. Letter of Oct. 27, 1818, to Richard Woodhouse, in *The Letters of John Keats*, ed. M. B. Forman, 4th ed. (London: Oxford Univ. Press, 1952), pp. 226–27.

15. Letter of Dec. 18, 1817, to George and Thomas Keats, *ibid.*, p. 71.

16. Letter of Nov. 22, 1817, to Benjamin Bailey, *ibid.*, p. 66.

17. *Ibid.*, p. 67.

18. See A. Bestuzhev, "Vzgliad na staruiu i novuiu slovesnost' v Rossii," *Poliarnaia zvezda* (1823; reprint Moscow: Akademiia Nauk SSSR, 1960), p. 26; and O. Somov, "Obzor rossiiskoi slovesnosti za 1828 god," *Severnye tsvety*, 1829, pp. 82–83.

19. V. F. Pereverzev, *U istokov russkogo real'nogo romana* (Moscow: GIKhL, 1937), p. 48.

20. Bestuzhev, "Vzgliad na staruiu" (as cited in note 18, above).

21. Eikhenbaum [108], pp. 60–62.

22. Sidiakov [138], pp. 20–24. For a more detailed comparison of Pushkin's early prose with that of Batiushkov, see Sidiakov [140], pp. 10–16.

23. Gaevskii [226].

24. Tomashevskii [85], p. 33.

25. Tomashevskii [85], p. 36, suggests that the name Fatam derives from the Latin word *fatum*. It is more likely, however, that it is connected with Fatima, daughter of Muhammad, whose name was spelled by Denis Diderot and Jean Le Rond d'Alembert as "Fathima ou Fathama" in *Encyclopédie, ou Dictionnaire raisonné des sciences, des arts et des métiers* (Paris: Briasson, 1751–65), 6: 429. Pushkin must have simply left off the feminine ending of her name. The novel's Eastern, rather than Roman, setting seems also to point in the direction of an Arabic or Persian name.

26. Gaevskii [226], p. 158; Annenkov [13], p. 22.

27. For details about this quatrain, see Alekseev [225], pp. 11–12.

28. Liprandi [165].

29. See Tsiavlovskii & Tsiavlovskaia [168].

30. *Duka* published by A. Hîjdău in *Vestnik Evropy*, 23–24 (1830): 181–207; and *Dabizha* published by B. Hîjdău in *Syn otechestva*, 1 (1838): 230–39.

31. According to historical sources, Dafna was Dabija's wife, not his daughter, and the burning of the palace had occurred before Dabija's reign began. For full details about the legends and about the historically verifiable facts, see Bogach [162], pp. 137–80; and Dvoichenko-Markova [164].

32. Source of the title identified by Oksman [469].

33. For details of Pushkin's work on the project, see Tsiavlovskaia [470].

34. The occasion has been described by Anna Kern, who was present; see her *Vospominaniia* (Leningrad: Academia, 1929), p. 253.

35. "Uedinennyi domik na Vasil'evskom," published under the

pseudonym "Tit Kosmokratov" in *Severnye tsvety*, 1829, pp. 147–217. Poorly received by critics at the time, the story was forgotten until 1912, when Titov's letter of Aug. 29, 1879, to A. V. Golovin, revealing the background of the story, was published in A. I. Del'vig, *Moi vospominaniia* (Moscow: Izd. Moskovskogo Publichnogo i Rumiantsevskogo Muzeev, 1912), 1: 157–58. The story was soon published as "Uedinennyi domik na Vasil'evskom: Rasskaz A. S. Pushkina, zapisannyi V. P. Titovym" in the newspaper *Den'*, 81–83 (Dec. 22–24, 1912): 22–24; and subsequently in other periodicals and in separate editions. A number of scholars commented on it at this time; see Bibliography, pp. 368–69.

36. For a comparison of Titov's story with Pushkin's original outline of "Vliublennyi bes," see Pisnaia [464].

37. See V. P. Titov, "Monastyr' sv. Brigitty," *Severnye tsvety*, 1831, pp. 156–76. A comparison of Titov's two stories can be found in Stepanov [467], pp. 129–30.

38. *Severnye tsvety*, 1829, p. 174. The statue of the Commander is mentioned with reference to Molière's *Dom Juan* (1665), Act 4, Scene 12. I do not think Botnikova is right in trying to trace Pushkin's sentence to a passage in E. T. A. Hoffmann's story "Der Magnetiseur" (1814; in Vol. 2 of *Fantasiestücke in Callots Manier*). In Hoffmann there is only the sudden appearance of the character Alban, with no reference to the statue of the Commander; see Botnikova [25], p. 93. In other respects the parallels Botnikova shows between "Dar Magnetiseur" and "Uedinennyi domik" are convincing.

39. For a further discussion of Hoffmannesque elements in the story, see Passage [65], pp. 116–30; and Ingham [44], pp. 124–29.

40. See Akhmatova [457], pp. 196–202.

41. Vinogradov is reported to have pointed out that the style veers further away from Pushkin's toward the end of the story; see Akhmatova [457], p. 198. Vinogradov's lecture on the subject, delivered on Dec. 18, 1962, at the State Pushkin Museum in Moscow, has not been published. Kodjak [461] makes an interesting argument in favor of a strong presence of Pushkin's speech pattern in the story.

42. Akhmatova [457], p. 201. The story has generally not been recognized as genuinely Pushkin's. In the 10-volume Academy edition it is included only as an appendix; see [6]; 9: 507–40.

43. Liprandi [165], p. 1410.   44. Feinberg [32], pp. 245–80.

45. *Ibid.*, pp. 281–93.   46. Frumkina [33], p. 66.

47. N. L. Stepanov, "Pis'ma Pushkina kak literaturnyi zhanr," in Stepanov, *Poety i prozaiki* (Moscow: Khudozhestvennaia literatura, 1966), p. 95.

48. See Vinokur [146].

49. Frumkina [33], pp. 66–68.

50. Introduction to *The Letters of Pushkin*, tr. J. Thomas Shaw (Bloomington: Indiana Univ. Press, 1963), 1: 42.

51. V. F. Khodasevich, *O Pushkine* (Berlin: Petropolis Verlag, 1937),

pp. 136–40. On the broad range of poetic devices Pushkin employed in his letters, see also L. Grossman, "Kul'tura pisem v epokhu Pushkina," in Grossman, *Stat'i o Pushkine* (Moscow: Federatsiia, 1930), p. 243.

52. V. V. Sipovskii, "A. S. Pushkin po ego pis'mam," in *Pamiati L. N. Maikova: Sbornik* (St. Petersburg: Tip. Imp. Akademii Nauk, 1902), pp. 458, 466. For further details and for a bibliography on the subject, see William Mills Todd, III, *The Familiar Letter as a Literary Genre in the Age of Pushkin*, Studies of the Russian Institute, Columbia University (Princeton, N.J.: Princeton Univ. Press, 1976), especially pp. 104–7, 141–48, 211–13.

53. See, for example, Stepanov [145], p. 26.

54. Feinberg [32], p. 282.

55. See Sorokin [78], p. 463. See also Sidiakov [139].

56. Sidiakov [139], pp. 130–31.

57. Eikhenbaum's expression: [31], p. 167.

58. Lezhnev [119], pp. 11–17.

Chapter Two

1. *Severnye tsvety*, 1829, pp. 111–24; and *Literaturnaia gazeta*, 1830, No. 13: 99–100.

2. *Sovremennik*, 6 (1837): 97–145. For full details about the dates and circumstances of Pushkin's work on the novel, see Lapkina [157].

3. Feinberg [32], pp. 265–67.

4. See *Rukoiu Pushkina* [10], pp. 34–49; and Pushkin [5], 12: 434–37. For further details about Abram Hannibal, see M. Vegner, *Predki Pushkina* (Moscow: Sovetskii pisatel', 1937), pp. 11–151; Veresaev [485], 1: 25–31; and V. Nabokov, "Pushkin and Gannibal: A Footnote," *Encounter*, 19, No. 1 (1962): 11–26.

5. On the Osipovs' library, see M. Semevskii, "Progulka v Trigorskoe," *S-Peterburgskie vedomosti*, No. 139 (May 24, 1866).

6. "O chastnoi zhizni Imperatora Petra I," "Ob uveseleniiakh russkogo dvora pri Petre I," "O pervykh balakh v Rossii," "O chastnoi zhizni russkikh pri Petre I," in A. O. Kornilovich, *Sochineniia i pis'ma* (Moscow: Akademiia Nauk SSSR, 1957), pp. 149–203 (originally published in *Russkaia starina* in 1824).

7. Pointed out by Feinberg [32], pp. 306–7.

8. Suggested by Arminjon [14], p. 70.

9. For details on Pushkin's use of, and distortion of, historical materials, see Levkovich [54], pp. 181–88; and Iakubovich [114].

10. It is interesting that both of these sentences betraying the author's presence can be traced to literary sources. The first one, as Akhmatova [150], p. 110, points out, was inspired by Adolphe's humble devotion to Ellénore in Chaps. 2 and 3 of Constant's novel. The second one, as Tomashevskii [84], p. 416, mentions, is a paraphrase of a sentence from Charles Nodier's *Le Peintre de Saltzbourg* (1803):

"C'est une chose admirable et pleine de charme que de suivre un grand génie dans son course" (entry for Oct. 9: [480], p. 78).

11. From the Preface to *Tales of a Traveller* (1824); see Irving [478], 2: 12. In addition to Austen's novels, Johann Wolfgang Goethe's *Die Wahlverwandtschaften* (1809) is an early example of a detached, third-person narrative, but there is no evidence that Pushkin had read this particular work.

12. On Pushkin's familiarity with Walpole's works, see Vatsuro [91].

13. On Irving's and Hoffmann's popularity in Russia, see Proffer [67]; Passage [65]; and Ingham [44].

14. Scott [483], 1: 3. Alexander the Corrector was a name assumed by Alexander Cruden (1701–70), best known for his *Complete Concordance to the Holy Scriptures* (1737). Among other works, he published *The Adventures of Alexander the Corrector* (in 3 parts, 1754–55).

15. "C'est un de mes principes, qu'il ne faut pas s'ecrire. L'artiste doit être dans son oeuvre comme Dieu dans la creation, invisible et tout-puissant; qu'on le sente partout, mais qu'on ne le voie pas." See Flaubert's letter of March 18, 1857, to Mlle. Leroyer de Chantepie in Gustave Flaubert, *Oeuvres complètes* (Paris: L. Conrad, 1910–27), Correspondance, Série 4 (1854–61), p. 164. For a discussion of the author's disappearance into the background in the 19th-century novel, see Richard Stang, *The Theory of the Novel in England, 1850–1870* (New York: Columbia Univ. Press, 1959), pp. 91–110.

16. This does not seem quite so natural to V. I. Lavretskaia, who writes ([52], p. 81): "The first time his [Ibrahim's] portrait is seen through the eyes of the frivolous, corrupt Countess. . . . The second time we perceive his features with the eyes of Natasha, a simple, unspoilt, pure Russian girl: it is understandable that she was frightened by the Negro's unusual appearance, which had appealed to the satiated Countess."

17. Emphasized by Blagoi [22], p. 260.

18. Dymshits [476], p. 325.

19. Pointed out by Akhmatova [150], pp. 103, 110.

20. Modzalevskii [479], p. 210. Pushkin was much more complimentary about Constant's language in his brief article announcing Viazemskii's forthcoming translation of *Adolphe* in 1830: "It will be interesting to see how Prince Viazemskii's experienced and lively pen has overcome the difficulties of metaphysical language—of a language that is always graceful, that is of high society, and that is often inspired"; [5], 11: 87. Although the epithets Pushkin chose are complimentary, they do not reflect his own aspirations as a prose stylist.

21. F. V. Bulgarin, "Vtoroe pis'mo iz Karlova na Kamennyi ostrov," *Severnaia pchela*, 1830, No. 94: cols. 1–8.

22. Bulgarin's lampoon is referred to by Oksman in his notes to *Arap Petra Velikogo* [4], 4: 713. Oksman also states that in the spring of 1828 Pushkin's attention was drawn away from prose by the idea of *Poltava*, and that he must have thought M. N. Zagoskin's work *Iurii*

Miloslavskii (1829)—which had been published by the time Pushkin might have returned to his project in prose—solved the problem of creating a Russian historical novel. Pushkin's works of subsequent years, however, argue otherwise: it is clear that he was not about to cede the field to another historical novelist. Shklovskii [136], pp. 29–35, holds that Pushkin's "Plany povesti o strel'tse" represented a broader design for the theme of *Arap*, and that he abandoned the novel because this new design would have necessitated rewriting chapters already published. The "Plany" Shklovskii cites (dated 1833–34) seem to me to have only a tenuous connection with *Arap*; but even if they are connected with it, it is still not clear why Pushkin let his project lie for five or six years and then decided to redesign it.

23. See Lapkina [157], p. 308; Lavretskaia [52], p. 86; and Blagoi [22], p. 273. See also Petrov [128], pp. 76–77.

24. See Khodasevich [156], pp. 168–69.

25. Pushkin's biographer N. L. Brodskii attributes Pushkin's difficulties to a problem in developing the plot: Pushkin, he conjectures, must have come to the conclusion that if he used the same situation twice—an unfaithful wife delivering a baby of an embarrassing color—he might not be able to maintain interest. See Brodskii, *A. S. Pushkin: Biografiia* (Moscow: GIKhL, 1937), p. 573. Brodskii's conjecture is hardly convincing: Pushkin's intention, quite clearly, was not simply to repeat the situation, but to reverse it ironically—a clever device indeed. Blagoi [22], p. 273, believes that the didactic purpose of giving Nicholas a lesson proved to be incompatible with the realistic principles of writing that Pushkin was beginning to espouse in the late 1820's. Further, Abramovich [149], p. 67, suggests that Pushkin could probably not reconcile his realistic presentation of history with his romantically colored portrait of Ibrahim. Skvoznikov [76], p. 71, connects Pushkin's difficulties with his inability, at this early stage, to contain the complexities of the plot of a historical novel within the confines of his own stylistic principles of prose. And Petrunina [287], p. 102, argues that Ibrahim, of foreign origin and not psychologically bound up with Russian social groups, was not the right choice for Pushkin if his intention was to depict the social struggles of Peter's time. Closest to my own interpretation is that of Bocharov [24], pp. 115–24, which sees a tension between the narrative point of view and the historical theme in the novel.

26. Dymshits [476], p. 455.

27. See Nadezhdin's review of *Poltava* in *Vestnik Evropy*, 1829, Nos. 8 and 9: 287–302, 17–48.

28. Dymshits [476], p. 455.

29. For an analysis of the language of Rzhevskii and his circle, see Bogorodskii [154], pp. 211–19.

30. Gladkova [112], p. 310, argues that Chap. 3 simply continues the conversation between Minskii and the Spanish tourist begun in Chap. 1.

31. See, for example, Vodovozov [230].
32. Chicherin [102], p. 83.   33. Lezhnev [119], p. 293.
34. Chicherin [103], p. 132.   35. Chicherin [102], pp. 84–85.
36. See N. K. Gudzii, "Istoriia pisaniia i pechataniia *Anny Kareninoi*," in L. N. Tolstoi, *Polnoe sobranie sochinenii* (Moscow: GIKhL, 1928–53), 20: 577–78. See also Gornaia [228]; and E. Maimin, "V spore s uchitelem," *Neva*, 2 (1962): 175–76.
37. See Brodskii, *A. S. Pushkin* (cited in note 25, above), p. 588.
38. See Gladkova [112], p. 313.
39. See the comments of Oksman [4], 4: 762; and of Modzalevskii [2], 2: 304–7. The prototypes for several other characters in the unfinished novel have been identified by Vainshtein & Pavlova [229].
40. From "Alcibiade," one of the *Contes Moraux* (1765). See *Oeuvres complètes de Marmontel*, nouvelle ed. (Paris: Verdière, 1818–19), 3: 19.
41. See Odintsov [124], p. 411.
42. Sidiakov [137], p. 38.
43. Vinogradov [96], p. 523.
44. Iu. N. Tynianov, *Arkhaisty i novatory* (Leningrad: Priboi, 1929), pp. 283–86.
45. For details, see Vol'pert [445]. See also V. Shklovskii's brief discussion of Pushkin's models for the epistolary form in *Za i protiv: Zametki o Dostoevskom* (Moscow: Sovetskii pisatel', 1957), p. 28.
46. Lotman [444] draws attention to the fact that Liza's description of *Clarissa* corresponds to the French translation of the novel, *Lettres angloises, ou Histoire de Miss Clarisse Harlowe* (Paris, 1777), with a Preface by the translator, the Abbé Prévost. The edition was in Pushkin's library.
47. Briusov [100], p. 267. Ivanov-Razumnik [45], p. 83, claims that "the further development of the plot is clear: Vladimir will abandon both [girls] and will return to St. Petersburg in order to resume an Oneginian way of life."

Chapter Three

1. *Vestnik Evropy*, 1820, No. 11: pp. 213–20.
2. *Syn otechestva*, 61, Nos. 15–17 (1820): 120–28, 160–65, 217–18.
3. All these pseudonyms occurred in *Vestnik Evropy* in the early 1820's.
4. *Vestnik Evropy*, 1829, Nos. 8 and 9: 287–302, 17–48; and 1930, No. 7: 183–224.
5. This is the chronology given by Tomashevskii in [6], 6: 759. The dating of the drafts in earlier editions of Pushkin's collected works is confusing and obviously tentative. Some of the argument surrounding the question can be found in Gukasova [398], pp. 77–78.
6. Pointed out by Kodjak [404], p. 86.

7. See, for example, Berkovskii [391], p. 250. Berkovskii's view derives, at least in part, from that of Apollon Grigor'ev, who also saw Belkin as an incarnation of the Russian native principle, satirically contrasted to the alien type of Sil'vio. This idea was discussed by Grigor'ev in several articles; see, for example, [36], pp. 19−28.

8. The enormous distance between Pushkin and Belkin—ignored by so many critics—is emphasized by Ovsianiko-Kulikovskii: [64], pp. 57−59.

9. Vinogradov [96], p. 539, points out the discrepancy between the bookish tone of the Introduction and the irony of the epigraph.

10. Discussed by Jan M. Meijer in van der Eng [415], p. 114.

11. See Iakubovich [400], p. 163; and Simmons [75], pp. 257−58.

12. Introduction to Scott's *Tales of My Landlord*: [483], 5: viii.

13. Sir Walter Scott, *The Waverley Novels* (London: John C. Nimmo, 1898), 8: 456. The sentence is missing from the 1829 edition.

14. *Moskovskii telegraf*, 42, No. 22 (1831): 255.

15. I remain unconvinced by Timmer's argument [237] that these dates may have referred to 1835, rather than 1830.

16. *Sovremennik*, 7 (1837): 197−200.

17. Mal'tsev [56], pp. 95−99, notes the connection between the fragment "Esli zvanie liubitelia otechestvennoi literatury" and the Belkin of *Goriukhino*, but, missing Pushkin's irony, he assumes that both represent mouthpieces for Pushkin's own political and literary opinions. As for the *Latest Handbook of Composition* Belkin refers to, this was not an invention of Pushkin's: Nikolai Gavrilovich Kurganov (d. 1796), a professor of the Naval Academy, had indeed published many editions of a *Pismovnik, soderzhashchii v sebe nauku rossiiskogo iazyka so mnogim prisovokupleniem raznogo uchebnogo i poleznozabavnogo veshchesloviia*, which was still popular in Pushkin's time (first published, under a different title, in 1769; known as *Pismovnik* from the 4th ed., 1790, on). It was a small encyclopedia, containing a Russian grammar, readings, and sundry appendixes providing useful information. V. Sechkarev has conjectured that Pushkin must have had only a superficial acquaintance with the book, for he treated it with more scorn than the actually rather useful volume deserved; see Sechkarev's Preface to *Pismovnik*, 5th ed. (Würzburg: Jal-Reprint, 1978; originally published in 1793).

18. Blagoi [20], p. 159, demonstrates that some of the details of Belkin's education coincide with those of Mitrofan in D. I. Fonvizin's *Nedorosl'*.

19. Cherniaev [27], pp. 571−75, points out that M. E. Saltykov-Shchedrin's *Istoriia odnogo goroda* (1869−70) also was inspired by Pushkin's *Istoriia sela Goriukhina*. For further details, see Gritsai [233].

20. Chicherin [105], p. 10, speaks of a "Gogolesque logic" pervading both *Povesti Belkina* and *Goriukhino*.

21. See, for example, M. Makarov, "Perekol, ili I moia derevnia dol-

zhna prinadlezhat' istorii," *Syn otechestva*, 42 (1817), cited in Alekseev [232], p. 74.

22. Strakhov [79], p. 54, was the first to draw attention to Karamzin's *Istoriia* as a possible target for Pushkin's parody.

23. N. M. Karamzin, *Istoriia gosudarstva Rossiiskogo* (St. Petersburg: Voennaia tip. Glavnogo shtaba Ego Imp. Vel., 1815–24), 1: 3.

24. *Ibid.*, p. 104.   25. *Ibid.*, p. 70.
26. *Ibid.*, p. 69.   27. *Ibid.*, p. 72.
28. *Ibid.*, p. 73.   29. *Ibid.*, p. 112.

30. *Rukoiu Pushkina* [10], pp. 167–79. See also Pushkin [5], 11: 125–27. Polevoi's *Istoriia* as a possible target of Pushkin's parody suggested by Cherniaev [27], pp. 521–31.

31. *Literaturnaia gazeta*, 1, Nos. 4 and 12 (1830): 31–32, 96–98.

32. N. Polevoi, *Istoriia russkogo naroda*, 2d ed. (Moscow: Tip. Avgusta Semena pri Imp. Med.-Khirurgicheskoi Akad., 1830), 1: 5.

33. *Ibid.*, p. xix.

34. *Ibid.*, p. 5.

35. Some passages seem to indicate an affinity between *Goriukhino* and *Don Quixote*. For example, Belkin sits over his copybook chewing on his pen and wondering what to write in much the same manner as Cervantes, in a quandary over his Prologue; inspiration is brought to Belkin by his housekeeper, to Cervantes by a friend.

36. *Vestnik Evropy*, 1823, No. 5: 70.

37. See Feinberg [32], pp. 22–24.

38. Scott [483], 5: iv.

39. Irving [478], 1: 382.

40. *Ibid.*, 2: 11. Gukasova [398], p. 88, draws attention to the fact that Narezhnyi's Prince Chistiakov also spends some time trying his hand at various kinds of literary creation. The scene Gukasova refers to can be found in *Rossiiskii Zhil'blaz* (Moscow: Gos. izd., 1938), 2: 24–29.

41. As fully demonstrated by Alekseev [232], pp. 77–86.

42. *Selected Writings of Washington Irving*, ed. S. Commins (New York: Modern Library, 1945), p. 421. In the 1840 edition the phrase is given as "from the dirt": [478], 1: 48. Another passage close to *Goriukhino* in its pomposity is Nicol Jarvie's identification of his parents in Chap. 31 of Scott's *Rob Roy* (1817): "My mother, Elspeth Macfarlane, was the wife of my father, Deacon Nicol Jarvie—peace be wi' them baith": [483], 4: 415.

43. Sipovskii [236], pp. 50–57, cites as one possible source G. W. Rabener, "Ein Auszug aus der Chronike des Dörfleins Querlequitsch, an der Elbe gelegen" (1742); and Alekseev [232], pp. 75–76, offers two more: an 1828 Moscow pamphlet, *Rukopis' pokoinogo Klementiia Akimovicha Khabarova*; and Paul-Louis Courier de Méré, *Gazette de village* (1823).

44. See P. E. Shchegolev, *Pushkin i muzhiki: Po neizdannym materialam* (Moscow: Federatsiia, 1928), p. 91.

45. All these details are taken from Shchegolev, *ibid.*, pp. 79–93. For a cautionary note about Shchegolev's description of Pushkin's attachment to Ol'ga, see V. Veresaev [Smidovich], "Krepostnoi roman Pushkina" in Veresaev, *V dvukh planakh: Stat'i o Pushkine* (Moscow: Nedra, 1929), pp. 180–202.

46. The documents of the case are reprinted in S. A. Orlov, *Boldinskaia osen': Ocherk* (Gorky: Gor'kovskoe knizhn. izd., 1962), pp. 64–65. Orlov gives a bibliography of both primary and secondary sources for Pushkin's connections with Boldino and Kistenevo (pp. 53–55). For some later findings, see I. Vorob'eva, "Novoe o 'krepostnoi liubvi' Pushkina," *Voprosy literatury*, 16, No. 8 (1972): 250–52.

47. For details, see Walter N. Vickery, "*The Water-Nymph* and *Again I Visited*: Notes on an Old Controversy," *Russian Literature Triquarterly*, 3 (Spring 1972): 195–205.

48. Shchegolev, *Pushkin* (cited in note 44, above), p. 93.

49. Because the spelling Gorokhino was used in the manuscript, the fragment was published as *Istoriia sela Gorokhina* until Vengerov argued in favor of Goriukhino in his 1910 edition; see [1], 4: 226. Goriukhino has been accepted ever since. However, as Gukasova [41], pp. 239–42, argues, one should bear in mind the implications of all variants in a case like this, where the author never prepared a definitive text for publication.

50. Alekseev [232], p. 84, also comes to this conclusion.

51. Belinskii [99], p. 577.

52. Oksman, in [4], 4: 718. On the same page Oksman conjectures that Pushkin moved the last two tales to the front in order to bring the sequence in line with the "inner chronology" of the stories. But Vinogradov [96], pp. 344–45, suggests that thematic considerations must have guided Pushkin's hand in rearranging the sequence: the titles, as published, indicate a transition from adventure to character. Still another theory has been advanced by Kodjak, who argues that the sequence given in the Publisher's footnote is the correct one, for it reflects the original order. The Publisher's reason for changing the original order, the argument goes, was his fear of censorship: the prologue to "Stantsionnyi smotritel'," with its suggestion that mind should yield to mind rather than rank to rank, might have caught the censor's eye if it stood at the front of the volume. The Publisher's footnote about the narrators, Kodjak claims, is Pushkin's shrewd way of telling us that we should read the tales beginning with "Stantsionnyi smotritel'"; see [404], pp. 83–84, and for further details, [403].

53. Connection with the Irving story mentioned by Berkovskii [391], p. 289.

54. Mentioned by Botsianovskii [26], p. 189.

55. Liubovich [405], p. 263, draws attention to this ironic reversal of the theme.

56. Discussed by Vinogradov [96], pp. 455–56.

57. See the entry for Sept. 8 in Nodier [480], pp. 48-49. Connection established by Tomashevskii [84], pp. 416-17.
58. Lednicki [425].
59. See van der Eng [415], p. 16.
60. Scott [483], 17: 315. Connection between the two works pointed out by Iakubovich [401], p. 106.
61. Connection noted by Pushkin's contemporary P. A. Katenin; see "Vospominaniia P. A. Katenina o Pushkine," *Literaturnoe nasledstvo*, 16-18 (1934): 642.
62. "Mol'er! tvoi dar, ni s ch'im na svete nesravnennyi" (1808), identified in Pushkin [6], 6: 764.
63. See Liubovich [405], pp. 266-69; Gippius [396], pp. 22-27; and Vinogradov [96], p. 436.
64. A. P. Novosiltseva, in *Razgovory Pushkina*, comp. S. Gessen and L. Modzalevskii (Moscow: Federatsiia, 1929), p. 154.
65. Akhmatova [190], pp. 162-64, puts an entirely different interpretation on the "happy endings" in these tales: Pushkin, facing his marriage with grave doubts, was trying to persuade fate to bring happy endings.
66. Cherniaev was the first critic to comment on the connection in some detail: [27], pp. 244-45.
67. The two nightmares compared by Gershenzon [258].
68. For some additional comments on the connection between "Baryshnia-krest'ianka" and *Onegin*, see Al'tman [418].
69. Cherniaev [27], p. 263.
70. Vinogradov [96], pp. 548-49, 552, comments on the sentimentality of the style in these two passages.
71. Unbegaun [413], pp. xxii-xxiii, provides possible French models for some of Miss K.I.T.'s phrases.
72. Pushkin [5], 8: 84, 111. The references are to Francesco Petrarch, *Rerum Vulgarum Fragmenta*, No. 132; and to a French edition of J. P. F. Richter's *Pensées de Jean-Paul: Extraites de tous ses ouvrages*, tr. Augustin de Lagrange (Paris: F. Didot, 1829), p. 153.
73. Emphasized by Stepanov [145], pp. 276-77. Bocharov [24], pp. 143-57, too sees Belkin as a device that Pushkin adopted in order to combine a wide range of narrative voices, from the uneducated to his own.
74. Cherniaev [27], p. 286.
75. A. Belkin "Poteriannaia dlia sveta povest'," *Biblioteka dlia chteniia*, 10 (1835): 134-50. Berkovskii [391], pp. 301-2, comments on this parody.
76. Pointed out by Vinogradov [96], p. 551.
77. Pointed out by van der Eng [415], p. 18.
78. Lezhnev [119], pp. 28-35, 177-98.
79. Abakumov [387], pp. 70-73.
80. Bestuzhev-Marlinskii [474], p. 105.

81. Discussed by Iakubovich [401], pp. 111–17.
82. See Passage [65], pp. 41–45; and Ingham [44], pp. 41–47, 133–34.
83. Bestuzhev-Marlinskii [474], p. 252.
84. Pointed out by Vinogradov [96], p. 544.
85. *Ibid.*, p. 565.
86. See Lezhnev [119], p. 112.
87. Pointed out by Vinogradov [96], pp. 464–65. Vinogradov's ideas have been developed further by S. G. Bocharov in his outstanding article "O smysle 'Grobovshchika' (K probleme interpretatsii proizvedeniia)": [423].
88. An excellent discussion of the meaning of Pushkin's reference to Shakespeare and Scott can be found in Clayton [30].
89. Emphasized by Iskoz [402], pp. 191–93.
90. Parallel pointed out by Berkovskii [391], p. 316.
91. Lednicki [117], p. 114.
92. Gogol' [477], 3: 170. Schultz's phrase, "Zhivoi bez sapog oboidetsia, a mertvyi bez groba ne zhivet," is a distorted version of the proverb "Zhivoi bez sapog oboidetsia, a mertvyi bez groba ne oboidetsia" ("The living can do without boots, but the dead can't do without a coffin"). See *Poslovitsy russkogo naroda: Sbornik V. Dalia* (Moscow: GIKhL, 1957), p. 284. The distortion of the Russian proverb, fitting for the German cobbler, was introduced into the text deliberately, which is evident from the original manuscript containing the correct version: [5], 8: 628.
93. Shaw [442], p. 133, emphasizes this feature of the story's structure.
94. See Busch [435], p. 409. Busch mentions further (p. 413) that Chap. 2 is also related by I.L.P. as something that occurred in the distant past: he seems to have an ironic attitude to his former self, whose admiration for the Count was out of all proportions.
95. *The Giaour* (1813), in *The Complete Poetical Works of Byron* (Boston: Houghton Mifflin, 1905), p. 319.
96. E. A. Baratynskii, *Polnoe sobranie stikhotvorenii* (Leningrad: Sovetskii pisatel', 1957), p. 252.
97. *Ibid.*, p. 255.
98. *Ibid.*, pp. 257–58.
99. Baratynskii was evidently not offended by Pushkin's ironic use of his poem: in Pushkin's description he "neighed and pawed the ground" as he heard Pushkin's reading of *Povesti Belkina* in Dec. 1830: [5], 14: 133.
100. Lerner [438], p. 130.
101. Bestuzhev-Marlinskii [474], pp. 240, 244.
102. *Ibid.*, p. 52.
103. Lauren G. Leighton discusses Bestuzhev's "penchant for false heroics and extraordinary passions" in connection with this story. See his *Alexander Bestuzhev-Marlinsky* (Boston: Twayne, 1975), p. 87. On Pushkin's use of "Vecher na bivuake" in "Vystrel," see also Leigh-

ton, "Marlinskij's 'Ispytanie': A Romantic Rejoinder to *Evgenij Onegin*," *Slavic and East European Journal*, 13, No. 2 (1969): 208; and Shaw [442], pp. 125–26.

104. A. A. Bestuzhev-Marlinskii, *Polnoe sobranie sochinenii* (St. Petersburg: Tip. III otdeleniia sobstvennoi E. I. V. Kantseliarii, 1838), 6: 13.

105. Pointed out by Busch [435], p. 414. Kodjak [437], pp. 206–8, draws attention to some further similarities between the two works.

106. Connection between *Hernani* and "The Shot" mentioned in Lerner [438], p. 133. The name Silvio may have been inspired by de Silva; or else it may have come from Jules Janin's novel *L'Ane mort et la femme guillotinée* (1829), which introduces a character named Sylvio in Chap. 19.

107. Petrovskii [439], pp. 176–80.

108. Van der Eng [415], pp. 12–16, 69–82, describes this technique in detail.

109. *The Complete Poetical Works of Byron* (cited in note 95, above), p. 367.

110. Argued interestingly by Kodjak [437], pp. 203–4.

111. Blagoi [19], pp. 228–33.

112. In Kodjak's opinion ([437], pp. 199–200), Chap. 2 is symmetrical only with the latter half of Chap. 1 (Silvio's story). In this connection, I would suggest taking into consideration Petrovskii's idea ([439], pp. 180, 194) that the difference between the chapters can be attributed to two factors: one, that Chap. 2 introduces a subsidiary, rather than the central, character, and two, that the suspense is created in Chap. 1 and therefore Chap. 2, providing the climax, requires a less elaborate structure.

113. See Berkovskii [391], pp. 279–84; Blagoi [19], pp. 236–38; Gukasova [398], p. 22; Kodjak [437], pp. 204, 211; and Makogonenko [55], p. 149.

114. Shaw [442], p. 127, emphasizes the success of Silvio's revenge.

115. *Ibid.*, p. 111.

116. See A. L. Bem, "Dostoevskii—genial'nyi chitatel'." in *O Dostoevskom: Sbornik statei*, ed. A. L. Bem (Prague: V. D. Kolesnikov, 1933), 2: 17.

117. Dostoevskii [475], 5: 149–50. It might also be mentioned that Sil'vio's decision not to kill his adversary must have inspired the future Father Zosima's behavior in "The Russian Monk" section of *The Brothers Karamazov*.

118. Gippius [396], p. 29.

119. Dostoevskii [475], 5: 148.

120. Kodjak [437], pp. 194–95.

121. Slonimskii's phrase (*chto-to v rode nizosti*): [77], p. 511.

122. This detail may have also come from *Hernani*, in which Doña Sol throws herself between Don Carlos and Hernani to prevent a duel

(Act 1, Scene 2); begs Don Carlos on her knees to pardon Hernani (Act 4, Scene 4); and throws herself at de Silva's feet (Act 5, Scene 6). One might add that de Silva is also compared both to *le diable* (Act 5, Scene 1) and to *le tigre* (Act 5, Scene 3), and that on his arrival with the horn he declares, anticipating both Silvio and the Water-Nymph, "C'est mon heure" (Act 5, Scene 5).

123. Liprandi as the main prototype suggested by Grossman [436], pp. 203–32. See also S. Shtraikh, "Znakomets Pushkina—I. P. Liprandi," *Krasnaia nov'*, 1935, No. 2: 212–18. But Lerner [438], pp. 128–29, suggests that Silvio was probably a composite of features taken from both literary and real-life models. In addition to Liprandi, he mentions the notorious duelist F. I. Tolstoi ("The American"; 1782–1846) and Pushkin's one-time friend Aleksandr Raevskii (1795–1868) as possible prototypes; and he refers to the duel between the famous scapegrace A. I. Iakubovich (1792–1845) and the celebrated writer A. S. Griboedov (1795–1829), postponed for a year, as a possible source for the plot of "Vystrel."

124. K. K. Danzas, "Poslednie dni zhizni i konchina Aleksandra Sergeevicha Pushkina," in Dymshits [476], p. 499.

125. The similarity between Silvio and Salieri pointed out by Iskoz in [1], 4: 187. See also Bem [390], p. 99.

126. See A. A. Akhmatova, "*Kamennyi gost'* Pushkina," *Pushkin: Issledovaniia i materialy*, 2 (1958): 191.

127. The most acrimonious criticisms of Pushkin were made by Nadezhdin in his reviews of *Poltava* and Chap. 7 of *Evgenii Onegin* in *Vestnik Evropy*, 1829, Nos. 8 and 9: 287–302, 17–48, and 1830, No. 7: 183–224, respectively; by F. V. Bulgarin in his reviews of the same two works in *Syn otechestva*, 3, Nos. 15 and 16 (1829): 36–52, 102–10, and *Severnaia pchela*, 1830, Nos. 35 and 39: cols. 1–6 (in both), respectively; and by N. Polevoi in his review of Chap. 7 of *Onegin* in *Moskovskii telegraf*, 32, No. 6 (1830): 238–43. For details, see Paul Debreczeny, "The Reception of Pushkin's Poetic Works in the 1820's: A Study of the Critic's Role," *Slavic Review*, 28, No. 3 (1969): 398–99, 406.

128. Odinokov [123], p. 39, draws attention to this incongruity.

129. N. M. Karamzin, *Izbrannye sochineniia* (Leningrad: Khudozhestvennaia literatura, 1964), 1: 607. Blagoi [20], p. 147, draws attention to Pushkin's probably deliberate imitation of the introduction to "Bednaia Liza."

130. Van der Eng [415], p. 31.

131. Published in the almanac *Uraniia*, 1826, pp. 15–39.

132. For Vinogradov's discussion of this epigraph, see [96], pp. 465–68. Vinogradov draws attention to an interesting point: that Pushkin changed the stationmaster's rank from Viazemskii's *gubernskii registrator* to *kollezhskii registrator*.

133. Kodjak [404], p. 81, draws attention to this parallel between "O narodnom obrazovanii" and "Stantsionnyi smotritel'."

134. *Ibid.*
135. V. A. Zhukovskii, *Sobranie sochinenii* (Moscow: GIKhL, 1959–60), 4: 401.
136. Mentioned by Gukasova [398], pp. 49–50.
137. Mentioned by Vinogradov [96], p. 572. It is interesting that Pushkin introduced this feature only in the final version of the text; see [5], 8: 652.
138. Some of this recurrent imagery is analyzed by Blagoi [19], pp. 243–44.
139. Gershenzon was the first critic to analyze the symbolic significance of the pictures; see [35], pp. 123–26.
140. Gershenzon [35], p. 123, points out that such pictures must have been common in the Russian provinces in the first half of the 19th century, for a description similar to Pushkin's can be found in V. A. Sollogub's novel *Tarantas* (1845), Chap. 4, "Stantsiia."
141. Vinogradov [434], p. 24, draws attention to the "profound metaphorical significance" of the wolf and the sheep in the story.
142. The contrasting parallel between the two works has been discussed by several critics. See, for example, Gippius [396], pp. 17–18; Blagoi [20], pp. 147–54; and van der Eng [415], pp. 31–32.
143. See, for example, Gukasova [398], pp. 58–61.
144. See Uzin [414], pp. 16–17; and Savvin [432].
145. I. I. Dmitriev, "Karikatura," in *Polnoe sobranie stikhotvorenii* (Leningrad: Sovetskii pisatel', 1967), p. 277.
146. Van der Eng [415], pp. 33, 53.
147. Viazemskii [486], 8: 443–46.
148. This is Tomashevskii's conjecture; see his Introduction to A. A. Del'vig, *Polnoe sobranie stikhotvorenii* (Leningrad: Sovetskii pisatel', 1959), p. 29.
149. Suggested by Berkovskii [391], p. 323.
150. Uzin [414], p. 16.
151. See Gershenzon [35], p. 126; and Berkovskii [391], p. 336.
152. See V. G. Belinskii, *Polnoe sobranie sochinenii* (Moscow: Akademiia Nauk SSSR, 1953), 7: 498–500; and F. M. Dostoevskii, *Sobranie sochinenii* (Moscow: GIKhL, 1956–58), 10: 449.
153. Vickery [92], p. 97, discusses this question.

Chapter Four

1. *Teleskop*, 4, Nos. 13 and 15 (1831): 135–44, 412–18. For details of the techniques Pushkin employed in these two articles, see J. Thomas Shaw, "The Problem of the *Persona* in Journalism: Puškin's Feofilakt Kosičkin" in *American Contributions to the Fifth International Congress of Slavists*, Sofia, September 1963, Vol. 2: *Literary Contributions* (The Hague: Mouton, 1963), pp. 301–26.
2. Oksman is hardly justified in his claim that *Roslavlev* is a finished work: [4], 4: 731. Filippova [446] also tries to prove, in my opin-

ion unsuccessfully, that Pushkin expressed in his fragment all he wished to express, and therefore *Roslavlev* should be considered completed.

3. Gukovskii [449] draws attention to the fact that an attack on Russian women who married French prisoners of war was published in *Syn otechestva*, 1813, No. 26, and that the story of such a woman, written by F. F. Ivanov in the form of a letter to the editor, appeared in the journal *Amfion*, 1815, No. 1.

4. Tomashevskii [450], pp. 87–89, shows that Pushkin's portrait of the Russian social climate in *Roslavlev* derives, at least partially, from Mme. de Staël's *Dix Années d'exil* (1820).

5. See, for example, Grushkin [448], pp. 325–32; and Petrov [128], pp. 97–100.

6. Discussed by Glukhov [447].

7. M. N. Zagoskin, *Roslavlev, ili Russkie v 1812 godu* (Moscow: N. Stepanov, 1831), 1: 92.

8. The testimony of Pushkin's friend, P. V. Nashchokin, confirms that Pushkin's main interest was in developing Polina's character: "*Roslavlev*, as Pushkin himself said, had been written because Pushkin did not like Polina's character in Zagoskin's novel: she seemed too flat to him, and he wanted to show how he would have characterized her." See Bartenev [473], p. 39.

9. The phrase "Il n'y a de bonheur que dans les voies communes" is from the very end of *René* (1802). See F. R. Chateaubriand, *Atala, René, Le dernier Abencérage*, ed. F. Letessier (Paris: Garnier, 1962), p. 244. Pushkin slightly misquotes it as "Il n'est de bonheur que dans les voies communes": [5], 8: 154.

10. *Moskovskii telegraf*, 42, No. 23 (1831): 254–56. See also reviews in *Severnaia pchela*, 255 (1831): cols. 1–3; *Teleskop*, 6, No. 21 (1831): 117–25; and *Literaturnye pribavleniia k Russkomu invalidu*, 93 (1831).

11. The fragment was first published by Bartenev in *Russkii arkhiv*, 1881, No. 3, pp. 466–68. For details about the plot outlines and the characters' real-life prototypes, see Izmailov [443]; and Oksman's notes, [4], 4: 771–74.

12. For details about the Rimskii-Korsakov family, see M. O. Gershenzon, *Griboedovskaia Moskva*, 2d rev. ed. (Moscow: M. & S. Sabashnikov, 1916), which is based on the family's archives. The kidnaping episode is mentioned on p. 140.

13. It may be argued that Tolstoi interferes with the child's vision, allowing him to see Iakov both from the front and from the back simultaneously; but this does not alter the fact that the scene is reflected in the child's mind.

14. P. A. Viazemskii, *Fon-Vizin* (St. Petersburg: Tip. Dep-ta vneshnei torgovli, 1848), p. 52. Pushkin had read Viazemskii's book in manuscript before October 1832; see [11], p. 4, and for the passage quoted, p. 27.

15. Bartenev [473], p. 27. For further details about Ostrovskii, see Stepunin [186]. It has also been documented that the character of the neighbor who gained the land, Troekurov, as it eventually emerged in Pushkin's novel, was modeled largely on the famous local tyrant of the Tula and Riazan' provinces, L. D. Izmailov (1764–1834); see Engel' [171].

16. Pushkin and Nashchokin probably acquired such a document through the services of a certain D. V. Korotkii, who was employed by the State Board of Trustees (of estates taken under state guardianship); see [4], 4: 734.

17. See Shliapkin [184], citing Case No. 37 in *Dela Pskovskoi provintsial'noi kantseliarii*, ed. I. I. Vasil'ev (Pskov: 1884), p. 57.

18. See A. Eremin, *Pushkin v Nizhegorodskom krae* (Gorky: Gor'-kovskoe oblastnoe gos. izdatel'stvo, 1951), p. 166. A description of this case can be found in *Deistviia Nizhegorodskoi gubernskoi uchenoi arkhivnoi komissii: Sbornik statei, opisei i dokumentov* (Nizhnii Novgorod: I. K. Vladimirskii, 1909), 8: 272. A legend about still another Dubrovskii, also a victim of injustice, is reported to have been widespread in a region not far from Moscow; see M. Prishvin, "Dubrovskii (Issledovanie kraeveda)," *Sovetskoe kraevedenie*, 1935, No. 12: 47–49.

19. Soboleva [185], p. 79, draws attention to the relevance of this detail to *Dubrovskii*. According to A. Iatsimirskii ([1], 4: 278), another real-life incident, the rescue of a cat from a fire at the Bol'shoi Theater in Moscow, served as a model for the scene in which the blacksmith Arkhip saves a cat from the flames of Dubrovskii's house.

20. These are the passages about the respective young heroes' arrival home; compare [5] 8: 128–29 and [5] 8: 175.

21. See Veresaev [485], 2: 142–43.

22. M. Ia. Fon-Fok was the head of the Third Section (political police) from 1826 till his death in 1831; N. I. Grech was co-editor of *Syn otechestva* and *Severnaia pchela* with Bulgarin.

23. P. I. Shalikov was the editor of a ladies' journal called *Damskii zhurnal*.

24. First published, in a form mutilated by censorship, in 1841 in *Sochineniia Aleksandra Pushkina* [8], 10: 101–240. For the subsequent publishing history of the restored text, see [4], 4: 734.

25. Berezin's analysis of the novel's language, for instance, contains no warning to the students that they are dealing with a text not intended by the author to be a textbook example: [169]. Even Soboleva, who presents the relevant facts about Pushkin's work on the novel, maintains that "*Dubrovskii*, in the shape it came to us, is perceived as an integrated, logically concluded narrative, of great artistic worth": [185], p. 4.

26. This is one of the inconsistencies Lerner has drawn attention to; see [179], pp. 184–85. Soboleva [185], p. 21, also points out that Vladimir could not have spent a month at Troekurov's house by the

feast day of Oct. 1 if his father had died at the end of September. It seems to me that this is not necessarily an inconsistency: though it is not stated clearly, one has to assume from the context that almost a year passes between Andrei's death and Vladimir's arrival at the Troekurovs'.

27. See Soboleva [185], p. 20.

28. Discussed in Kubikov [177], p. 87. See also Sergievskii [69], pp. 52-53.

29. This incongruity noted by Skvoznikov [76], p. 74.

30. A. Iatsimirskii discusses the place of Schiller's drama in the tradition of robber romanticism in [1], 4: 273.

31. It is hard to agree with the suggestion of Izmailov [115], p. 484, that *Hernani* may have been the most decisive influence on Pushkin's novel. In Izmailov's opinion, Pushkin may even have stopped working on the manuscript because he saw he was coming too close to Hugo's original. In fact *Hernani* was only one of many literary sources Pushkin exploited for his novel.

32. For a discussion of Vulpius's novel, its imitations, and its translations, see A. Iatsimirskii in [1], 4: 275.

33. Scott [483], 4: 523.

34. In addition to these obvious sources, Tomashevskii has drawn attention to a lesser known French novel—*Les Mauvais Garçons* by Alphonse Royer and Auguste Barbier (published anonymously in 1830)—that probably served as a model for Pushkin, at least in describing the siege of the robbers' camp by government troops. The hero of this novel, with his dual existence as both lover and robber, continues the tradition of Nodier's *Jean Sbogar*—another possible source for Pushkin. Tomashevskii also mentions George Sand's second novel, *Valentine* (1832), as a work somewhat similar to *Dubrovskii* in theme and familiar to Pushkin; see [187], pp. 947-57; and [84], pp. 410-21. Finally, a Russian novel, D. N. Begichev's *Semeistvo Kholmskikh* (published anonymously in 1832), in which a landowner organizes his peasants into a band of robbers, has been mentioned as another possible source; see Shklovskii [136], p. 83; and Petrunina [181], p. 143.

35. Belinskii [99], p. 578.

36. Lednicki [178], p. 72.

37. Scott [483], 17: 362. I am confining my comments to the published text of *St. Ronan's Well*, leaving out of consideration the possibility, contained in the original manuscript, that Clara's marriage to Bulmer might have actually been consummated. For details of this question, see Francis R. Hart, *Scott's Novels: The Plotting of Historic Survival* (Charlottesville: Univ. of Virginia Press, 1966), p. 280.

38. On *The Bride of Lammermoor* as a possible source for *Dubrovskii*, see Zhirmunskii [98], p. 85.

39. See Rozova [183], pp. 67-69. Other motifs, mostly clichés of love scenes, were borrowed by Pushkin from other French authors.

Tomashevskii [84], pp. 416–18, draws attention, for example, to the motif of the heroine's white dress flittering among the trees of a park, found both in Nodier's *Le Peintre de Saltzbourg* (entry for Sept. 17) and in Sand's *Valentine* (Chap. 14), which Pushkin uses twice: in the scene of Vladimir's homeward journey in Chap. 3 and in the latter's recounting of the growth of his love in Chap. 12. Setschkareff [70], p. 176, also suggests that the scene of Andrei Dubrovskii's death may have been inspired by the scene of Godfrey Bertram's death in Scott's *Guy Mannering* (1815); see also Zborovets [189]. Drawing still another parallel, Bayley [16], p. 341, says that Dubrovskii "is not a Robin Hood figure, or even a Karl Moor, but more like Kleist's Michael Kohlhaas [in the novel by that name, 1810], whose acceptance of the social order is transformed into violent rejection when his eyes are opened by personal experience."

40. See Iakubovich [173], p. 130.

41. See Berezin [169], p. 51.

42. One such case was recorded in Nizhnii Novgorod Province in 1817; see N. I. Dranitsyn, comp., "Opis' del Lukoianovskogo uezdnogo suda 1802, 1811, 1814–1817 gg." in *Deistviia Nizhegorodskoi gubernskoi uchenoi arkhivnoi komissii*, 8: 143–44. One might add that the preposterous petitions Gogol' quotes in the tale of the two Ivans were also based on actual legal documents; see the commentary to the story in Gogol' [477], 2: 756.

43. Lopatto [121], p. 30.

44. See, for example, Orlov [63], p. 114.

45. See Blagoi [20], p. 161.

46. *Polnoe sobranie russkikh poslovits* [481], p. 44.

47. Lopatto [121], p. 35.

48. The 22 modifiers I have counted in Chap. 1 are (the page references are to [5], vol. 8) *barskuiu, shumnye, buinye, neobrazovannogo, izbalovannyi, pylkogo, ogranichennogo* (p. 161); *nadmennyi, nadmennym* (p. 162); *laskovo, goriachii, surovo, gromko* (p. 163); *vskochiv s posteli bosoi* (p. 164); *otmenno, raskhazhivaia tiazhelymi shagami* (p. 165); and *gordo* (p. 167). (Each word, including prepositions, is counted separately, regardless of whether it forms a modifier by itself or is a component of a modifying phrase.)

49. The aspect of Lopatto's method that received most severe criticism after the publication of his essay was his arbitrariness in categorizing words with different stylistic colorings. See Loks [120].

50. The 31 modifiers I have counted in Chap. 5 are (the page references are to [5], vol. 8) *bednogo, pechal'nyi, gromko, pospeshno* (p. 178); *sil'no, dolgo, nepodvizhno, tikhoe, zhivo* (p. 179); *dolgo, s zharom, serdito, zadykhaias', ostroi, s pritvornym khladnokroviem* (p. 180); *derzkim, grozno, uzhasneishie, pospeshno, zvuchnyi, velichestvennyi, tikhon'ko, s unizhennymi poklonami, s prezreniem* (p. 181); and *sukho* (p. 182).

The 18 modifiers I have counted in Chap. 16 are *tikhon'ko, nimalo, napriamik, zhalobnym golosom, bednaia* (p. 213); and *v otchaianii, s izumleniem, dolgo, bednaia, plamenno, dolgo, gluboko, nepodvizhno, temnoe, pechal'nymi* (p. 214). As explained in note 48, each word is counted separately.

51. Predtechenskaia [182], p. 15, correctly observes that "Pushkin does not strain to simplify a sentence just for the sake of brevity. When the accuracy and clarity of expression require complex structures, he does not shun them. This is particularly true of *Dubrovskii*, which differs from all other works of Pushkin by a higher percentage of complex sentences." The one thing that reduces the validity of this statement is that Predtechenskaia, like Lopatto, considers the unfinished text of the novel as a monolithic whole.

52. Lezhnev [119], pp. 183–84.   53. Soboleva [185], p. 21.
54. *Ibid.*, p. 57.   55. Gogol' [477], 1: 284.
56. *Ibid.*, p. 289.   57. *Ibid.*, p. 298.
58. *Ibid.*, pp. 293–94.
59. See Oksman's commentary, [4], 4: 735; Tomashevskii [86], p. 146; and, for a more recent work, N. N. Petrunina "*Istoriia Pugacheva*: Ot zamysla k voploshcheniiu," *Russkaia literatura*, 8, No. 3 (1974): 183.

Chapter Five

1. See A. B. Gol'denveizer, *Vblizi Tolstogo* (Moscow: Kooperativnoe izd. i Golos Tolstogo, 1922), 1: 217; and *Neizdannyi Dostoevskii: Zapisnye knizhki i tetradi 1860–1881 gg.*, *Literaturnoe nasledstvo* (Moscow: Nauka, 1971), 83: 610.

2. Dostoevskii [475], 13: 113.

3. Gide [344], p. 142.

4. Bartenev [473], p. 46.

5. See Oksman's commentary, [4], 4: 739.

6. Veresaev [485], 2: 185. (Originally published in *Istoricheskii vestnik*, 14 [1883]: 538.)

7. *Rukoiu Pushkina* [10], p. 333.

8. Connection between this draft version of *Onegin* and "Pikovaia dama" noted by Vinogradov [383], pp. 102–3.

9. Noted by Oksman, [4], 4: 743.

10. Vatsuro et al. [484], 1: 395. Manuilov [364], p. 94, points out that Pushkin's lyrical fragment is a playful imitation of K. F. Ryleev's poem "Akh, gde te ostrova" (1822 or 1823).

11. Lerner [360], pp. 132–33, draws attention to the connection between the poem and "Pikovaia dama."

12. *Rukoiu Pushkina* [10], p. 215.

13. *Ibid.*, p. 216.

14. Connection between the two stories discussed by Khodasevich [49], pp. 71, 91.

15. Connection noted by Iakubovich [350], p. 57.

16. Connection between these fragments and "Pikovaia dama" emphasized by Kodjak [355], p. 112.

17. Meilakh [57], p. 634, discusses Napoleon's image in Pushkin's poetry in relation to "Pikovaia dama."

18. B. M. Eikhenbaum, *Stat'i o Lermontove* (Moscow: Akademiia Nauk SSSR, 1961), p. 200.

19. Argued by Sidiakov [138], p. 110.

20. Argued by Gershenzon [35], p. 106.

21. Connection first noted by Lerner [360], p. 158.

22. Noted by Manuilov [364], p. 100.

23. Pushkin's calculations are set side by side for convenience. They in fact run seriatim in the manuscript.

24. For a summary of Pushkin's gambling contacts at this time, see Iakubovich [350], pp. 61–62.

25. Manuilov [364], p. 96.

26. See N. M. Iazykov's letter of Dec. 22, 1831, and A. P. Arapova's reminiscences in Veresaev [485], 2: 127, 151.

27. Viazemskii [487], p. 85.

28. Suggested by Weber [385].

29. See the statements about this occasion by N. I. Lorer (quoting Pushkin's brother Lev), M. I. Semevskii, M. P. Pogodin, and P. A. Viazemskii, all in Veresaev [485], 1: 293–95.

30. See A. A. Fuks, "A. S. Pushkin v Kazani," in Vatsuro et al. [484], 2: 219–20. For further details about Pushkin's interest in "magnetism," see A. A. Kononov, "Zapiski," *Bibliograficheskie zapiski*, 2, No. 10 (1859): 305–6. Pushkin's experience with a soothsayer, recounted by Aleksandra Fuks, is also mentioned, along with other details, in Nashchokin's recollections; see Bartenev [473], pp. 40–41.

31. Friedrich Anton Mesmer (1734–1815) was an Austrian physician who attributed induced somnambulism to a power similar to magnetism, which he called "animal magnetism." Luigi Galvani (1737–98) was a professor of anatomy at the University of Bologna who attributed the twitching of a frog's leg when touched with a scalpel to electricity generated by the animal's muscles and nerves. Although the findings of these two men were ultimately to lead to important scientific discoveries, in the early 19th century their names were connected in the public mind with mysterious phenomena. In my opinion, Alekseev [325], pp. 95–101, is wrong in claiming that Pushkin uses the terms *magnetizm* and *galvanizm* in "Pikovaia dama" in a purely scientific sense, in keeping with the education and perceptions of Hermann. For one thing, this contradicts the testimony of Pushkin's contemporaries about his discussion of these subjects. And for another, the word *skrytyi*, used as an attribute of *galvanizm*, points to the presence of some dark forces as perceived by Hermann. What sort of scientifically verifiable electricity could Hermann have assumed to be operating in the Countess's armchair?

32. *Zhizn' igroka, opisannaia im samim, ili Otkrytye khitrosti kar-*

tochnoi igry (Moscow: 1826–27), 2: 199; quoted in Vinogradov [383], p. 76.

33. Described by Chkhaidze [336], p. 457.

34. Vinogradov [383], pp. 85–86, describes this method of cheating.

35. Chkhaidze does not substantiate his claim, in a second article on the subject ([337], pp. 87–88), that the advantage was on the banker's side.

36. Vinogradov [383], pp. 79–80, offers explanations of all the gambling terms used in the story. But gambling terms, as well as the rules of the games, were subject to frequent change, and therefore historians disagree on the definitions. Chernyshev, for instance, defines the term *igrat' mirandolem* differently ([335], p. 404); and Tomashevskii accepts Chernyshev's definition for his notes to the story ([6]: 6: 774). In this particular case I find Vinogradov's definition, also accepted by Chkhaidze, more consistent with the context of the story. For Chkhaidze's definitions, see [336]: 456–57. The term *igrat' mirandolem* presumably originates from the name of the Italian Mirandola family (Mirandole in French spelling).

37. *Paroli-paix* is another term that has been defined differently by different scholars; it seems to me that in this particular case Vinogradov's definition ([383], p. 79) is most consistent with the context of the story. Vladimir Nabokov gives a conflicting definition in his translation of *Eugene Onegin*, rev. ed. (Princeton, N.J.: Princeton Univ. Press, 1975), 2: 260.

38. Vinogradov's definition: [383], p. 79.

39. See Tomashevskii's letter to André Meynieux, published in *Pouchkine, Oeuvres complètes*, ed. A. Meynieux (Paris: André Borne, 1953–58), 3: 500, note 5. Tomashevskii's formula is further discussed by Rosen in [372], p. 271, note 7, and [373].

40. Viazemskii [487], p. 135.

41. Connection between Viazemskii's anecdote and Pushkin's story noted in Pushkin [3], 6: 279.

42. See, for example, Khodasevich [49], p. 90; and Shklovskii [136], p. 65.

43. See chiefly Slonimskii [378], p. 173; and, among more recent studies, Kodjak [355], p. 100.

44. Kashin [353], p. 29; Sidiakov [138], p. 117.

45. De Labriolle [357], pp. 266–69.

46. Chkhaidze [336], p. 459.

47. Rosen [372], pp. 265–67.

48. Bartenev [473], pp. 46–47.

49. M. I. Pyliaev, *Staroe zhit'e: Ocherki i rasskazy* (St. Petersburg: A. S. Suvorin, 1892), pp. 28–29, quoted in Vinogradov [383], pp. 88–89.

50. For details about her, see Lerner [361].

51. See Rabkina [370], p. 215.

52. Bartenev [473], p. 47.

53. See Viazemskii [487], pp. 130–32.

54. Bartenev [473], pp. 36−37.

55. For details, see *ibid.*, Introduction; and M. Tsiavlovskii, "Pushkin i grafinia D. F. Fikel'mon," *Golos minuvshego*, 2 (1922): 108−23.

56. Identified by Oksman, [4], 4: 741.

57. Elisabeth Vigée-Lebrun (1755−1842) was a Parisian portrait painter; Julien Leroy (1686−1759) and his son Pierre (1717−85) were famous French watchmakers; and the brothers Joseph Michel Montgolfier (1740−1810) and Jacques Etienne Montgolfier (1745−99), of Annonay, France, launched the first hot-air balloon in 1783. On Mesmer, see note 31, above. To mention one more possible connection with historical personalities, there has been some speculation that in describing Hermann's Napoleonic features, Pushkin alluded to the Decembrist Pavel Pestel', who was noted for his likeness to the French Emperor. See Oksman's notes, [4], 4: 741−42. Oksman also connects Pestel' with the epigraph to Chap. 4, chiefly because Pushkin's diary entry for Nov. 24, 1833, suggests he considered Pestel' dishonest.

58. Von Gronicka [37], pp. 66−67, comments that if Hermann resembles Faust at all, he is a parody, rather than a serious Russian replica, of Goethe's hero.

59. See Antoine-François Prévost d'Exiles, *Histoire du Chevalier des Grieux et de Manon Lescaut* (Paris: Garnier-Flammarion, 1967), p. 73. Some scholars, however, have suggested other possible sources for Hermann's dictum. Stenbock-Fermor, for one, has found a similar phrase—"Sait on gré du superflu à qui vous prive de nécessaire?"—in Pierre-Augustin Caron de Beaumarchais' *Mariage de Figaro* (1784); see [144], pp. 120−21. Leighton, on the other hand, connects Hermann's dictum with a statement that Antoine C. J. de Noailles, French ambassador to Russia in the 1810's, is said to have made: "Russians are generally concerned with and seek in everything the superfluous without having even the necessary"; see Leighton [358], pp. 468−69, note 33, citing quotation in M. T. Florinsky, *Russia: A History and Interpretation* (New York: Macmillan, 1955), 2: 735.

60. Iakubovich found a slip of paper, marking a chapter about games and gamblers, between pages 284 and 285, Vol. 2, in Pushkin's set of *Miroir historique, politique et critique de l'ancien et du nouveau Paris, et du Département de la Seine* by Louis-Marie Prudhomme (Paris: n.p., 1807); see [349], p. 208.

61. Lerner [360], p. 159. On Casanova's punting against Canano, see Vol. 4, Chap. 19, of A. Machen, trans., *The Memoirs of Casanova*, 6 vols. (New York: Putnam [1959−61]). The French original and Italian editions have different divisions into volumes and chapters.

62. Grossman's claim ([38]; p. 68) that Cagliostro had correctly predicted three numbers has been repeated by several commentators; but more recently Rosen has drawn attention to the fact that Cagliostro's prediction involved five numbers, none of which bore any relation to Pushkin's 3 or 7; see [372], p. 271, note 8.

63. A Russian translation of the novella under the title "Golland-

skii kupets" was published in *Syn otechestva*, 101, No. 9 (1825): 3 – 51; the same issue of the journal contained an article about Finland by Mme. de Staël, with notes by A. A. Mukhanov. Since Pushkin entered into polemics with the latter (see [5], 11: 27 – 29), it has been assumed that he probably read the novella as well. For details, see Vinogradov [383], pp. 87 – 88; and Gribushin [346], pp. 86 – 88. Kashin [353], p. 34, suggests that another possible source for Pushkin's numbers 3 and 7 is the line "Utroit', syn, usemerit'" in F. Glinka's poem "Brachnyi pir Toviia" ("Tobias's Wedding Feast," 1828).

    64. Noted by Vinogradov [383], p. 89.

    65. For details, see Iakubovich [349], pp. 210 – 11; Sharypkin [376], pp. 131 – 36; and C. R. Sigstedt, *The Swedenborg Epic* (New York: Bookman Associates, 1952), p. 256.

    66. See Iakubovich [349], pp. 209 – 12; and Vinogradov [383], pp. 95 – 96. A copy of the novel was kept in the library of Pushkin's neighbors, the Osipovs, at Trigorskoe; see B. L. Modzalevskii, "Poezdka v s. Trigorskoe v 1902 godu," *Pushkin i ego sovremenniki*, 1 (1903): 31. Some chapters of it appeared in Russian translation in *Moskovskii vestnik*, 1828, No. 3: 279 – 301; and Pushkin jotted down its title in one of his notebooks: see *Rukoiu Pushkina* [10], p. 313.

    67. See Nabokov, *Onegin* (cited in note 37, above), 3: 97; Egunov [339]; Clayton [338]; and Sharypkin [376], pp. 129 – 30.

    68. Noted by Iakubovich [349], p. 207.

    69. Hoffmann connections noted in [3], 6: 279; Vinogradov [383], p. 96; Passage [65], p. 138; and Ingham [44], pp. 134 – 39. In Pushkin's library a French translation of Hoffmann's novel *L'Elixir du diable* appears under the false authorship of Carl Spindler; see *Pushkin i ego sovremenniki*, 9 – 10 (1910): 341. According to a contemporary, Pushkin was very much interested in Hoffmann around the time he worked on "Pikovaia dama"; see V. V. Lents, "Prikliucheniia lifliandtsa v Peterburge," in Veresaev [485], 2: 184. (Originally published in *Russkii arkhiv*, 1878, No. 1: 441 – 42.)

    70. Noted in [3], 6: 279.

    71. Lerner [360], p. 142. Lerner also sees a similarity between Hermann and Raphaël, and between the old Countess and the owner of the antique shop. Further, Gregg [345], pp. 280 – 81, finds Balzac's Foedora akin to Pushkin's Countess in her youth, and suggests that Lizaveta may have some connection with the poor *demoiselle de compagnie* who warns Raphaël of the conspiracy against him toward the end of *La Peau de chagrin*.

    72. H. de Balzac, *La Peau de Chagrin* (Paris: Garnier, 1964), pp. 27, 29, 30, 39, 46.

    73. Discussed by, among other critics, Sidiakov [142], pp. 210 – 12. Sidiakov also suggests (p. 207) a certain affinity between "Pikovaia dama" and some stories by Prosper Mérimée, such as "Le Vase étrusque" (1830) and "La Double Méprise" (1833). For other surveys of

Pushkin's attitude to French authors of his time, see Zhirmunskii [98], pp. 90–94; Tomashevskii [84], pp. 161–70; Chicherin [101]; and, for one particular parallel, Sharypkin [375].

74. Vinogradov [383], pp. 105–13.

75. Vinogradov [383], pp. 105–6, points out that several sentences, especially at the beginning of Chap. 1, have no definite subject, with the verbs expressing the action of a general first-person plural. Bocharov [24], p. 191, adds that this almost-first-person mode of narration may derive from the first-person presentation in the original draft ([5], 8: 834).

76. Noted by Bocharov [24], pp. 192–93.

77. Iu. M. Lotman, *Lektsii po struktural'noi poetike. Vvedenie: Teoriia stikha* (Providence, R.I.: Brown Univ. Press, 1968), p. 53.

78. *Ibid.*, p. 52.

79. Viazemskii [486], 2: 375.

80. Northrop Frye, "The Archetypes of Literature" in Frye, *Fables of Identity: Studies in Poetic Mythology* (New York: Harcourt, Brace, 1963), p. 16.

81. Connection made by Bitsilli [330], p. 559. Meanings implied through association in Pushkin's poetry are discussed at length by Bitsilli in *Etiudy o russkoi poezii* (Prague: Legiografie, 1926), pp. 65–224.

82. Noted by Vinogradov [96], p. 594.

83. Vinogradov [383], pp. 100–104, discusses the symbolic meaning of cards. For further comments, see Lotman [362].

84. Shaw [377], p. 124.

85. Noted in *ibid.*, p. 122.

86. Slonimskii [378], pp. 176–77.

87. Slonimskii's analysis was disputed most strongly by Lezhnev: [119], pp. 120–28. Tomashevskii, in a study devoted to prose rhythms using "Pikovaia dama" as a sample text, came to the conclusion that poetic rhythmic patterns are perceived within the texture of prose only if they are specially marked through such means as anaphora or structural parallelism; see [382], p. 317.

88. See Bitsilli [330], p. 558; de Labriolle [357], p. 263; Rosen [372], pp. 255–58; and Leighton [359].

89. See A. N. Pypin, *Russkoe masonstvo: XVIII vek i pervaia chetvert' XIX veka*, ed. G. V. Vernadskii (Petrograd: Ogni, 1916), pp. 47–61; and Weber [385], pp. 439–42.

90. See Vinogradov [96], p. 588.

91. Discussed by Rosen [372], p. 258.

92. Bocharov [24], pp. 186–88.

93. Kodjak [355], pp. 92–93.

94. See Rosen [372], pp. 256–58; and Leighton [358], [359].

95. Noted by Rosen [372], p. 262.

96. Title's two colors first connected with games of chance by Arsène Houssaye, *Histoire de 41ᵉ Fauteuil de l'Académie Française*

(Paris: H. Plon, 1861), p. 335. Jules Marsan objects that if the two colors were referring to roulette they would be in the feminine gender and the title would have to be *La Rouge et la noire*; see his introduction to the novel in Stendhal, *Oeuvres complètes*, ed. Jules Marsan (Geneva: Edito Service, n.d.; reprint of the 1923 ed., Paris: Champion), 1: xlix. For further discussion of the question, see Pierre Martino, "*Le Rouge et le noir*: La Signification du titre," *Le Divan*, Nov. 1923, pp. 575–77. It seems to me that even if the grammatical form of the title precludes an exact reference to roulette, the two colors produce at least an oblique association with gambling.

97. Symbolic significance of this description pointed out by Boris Reizov in "Pourquoi Stendhal a-t-il intitulé son roman *Le Rouge et le noir*?," *Studi Francesi*, 11, No. 32 (1967): 300.

98. Stendhal, *Le Rouge et le noir*, 2 vols. (Paris: Nelson, 1957), 1: 85.

99. *Ibid.*, p. 133.

100. *Ibid.*, p. 15.

101. The symbolic significance of walls in the novel discussed by Martin Turnell, "*Le Rouge et le noir*," in *Stendhal: A Collection of Critical Essays*, ed. Victor Brombert (Englewood Cliffs, N.J.: Prentice-Hall, 1962), pp. 16–17.

102. *Le Rouge et le noir* (cited in note 98, above), 1: 198.

103. Chicherin [103], p. 130.

104. As shown by Schwartz & Schwartz [374], p. 282.

105. *Ibid.*, p. 277.

106. See Pypin, *Russkoe masonstvo* (cited in note 89, above), pp. 71–75; and Weber [385], p. 440.

107. Noted by Kodjak [355], p. 100.

108. Rosen [372], p. 262.

109. Hermann's associations and dreams have been interpreted variously by Shaw [377], p. 120; Schwartz & Schwartz [374], p. 287; Rosen [372], pp. 262–65; and Kodjak [355], p. 97.

110. Pushkin's anticipation of the idea of the subconscious noted by Rosen [372], p. 259.

111. Sigmund Freud, "Dostoevsky and Parricide," in *Dostoevsky: A Collection of Critical Essays*, ed. René Wellek (Englewood Cliffs, N.J.: Prentice-Hall, 1962), p. 109.

112. Stendhal, *Le Rouge et le noir* (cited in note 98, above), 2: 361.

113. *Ibid.*, p. 341.

Chapter Six

1. See Mal'tsev [56], p. 146; and M. D. Kurmacheva, "Uchastie krest'ian Nizhegorodskogo S. Boldina v krest'ianskoi voine 1773–1775 gg," in *Voprosy sotsial'no-ekonomicheskoi istorii i istochnikovedeniia perioda feodalizma v Rossii: Sbornik statei k 70-letiiu A. A. Novosel'skogo* (Moscow: Akademiia Nauk SSSR, 1961), pp. 151–56.

2. *Polnoe sobranie zakonov Rossiskoi imperii*, 1st series, Vol. 20

(St. Petersburg: Tip. II Otdeleniia E. I. V. Kantseliarii, 1830), No. 14.233, pp. 9–10.

3. In the large Academy edition these outlines are given as Nos. 5 and 4.

4. Oksman [284], p. 29, was the first to suggest that the outlines with Shvanvich as the hero preceded the one with Basharin. Petrunina has further refined Oksman's chronology, arguing convincingly that the outline given as No. 5 in the large edition, beginning with the words "Kulachnyi boi," must have been written first; see Petrunina & Fridlender [66], pp. 73–82.

5. *Bibliograficheskie zapiski*, 6 (1859): 179–81; *Poliarnaia zvezda*, 6 (1861): 128–31; *Zaria*, 12 (1870): 418–22.

6. Published in *Magazin für die neue Historie und Geographie*, ed. A. F. Büsching (Halle: J. J. Curts Wittwe, 1784), 18: 1–50. A French translation was published by Jean-Charles-Thibault Laveaux in *Histoire de Pierre III, Empereur de Russie* (Paris: Maison La Briffe, 1799), 2, No. 13: 255–360. For details, see G. Blok, *Pushkin v rabote nad istoricheskimi istochnikami* (Moscow: Akademiia Nauk SSSR, 1949), pp. 90–140.

7. For details see R. V. Ovchinnikov, *Pushkin v rabote nad arkhivnymi dokumentami ('Istoriia Pugacheva')* (Leningrad: Nauka, 1969), pp. 17–19.

8. For further details of the manuscripts available to Pushkin, see *ibid.*, pp. 19–24.

9. For a full account, see *ibid.*, 26–185.

10. Pushkin received the permission in the summer of 1835; see [5], 16: 45. Access to this material and new information from other sources prompted him to plan a second edition of *Istoriia Pugacheva*, but he did not live to carry out this plan.

11. For his notes on information gathered there, see [5], 9: 494–97. A chapter-by-chapter analysis of Pushkin's sources can be found in Anna Chkheidze, *'Istoriia Pugacheva' A. S. Pushkina* (Tbilisi: Izd. SSR Gruzii "Literatura i iskusstvo," 1963), pp. 58–89.

12. *Ibid.*, p. 54.

13. This is Michael Karpovich's conclusion; see his "Pushkin as an Historian" in *Centennial Essays for Pushkin*, ed. S. H. Cross and E. J. Simmons (New York: Russell & Russell, 1937), p. 197.

14. Kliuchevskii [50], p. 147.

15. N. Firsov, "Pushkin kak istorik (Obshchaia kharakteristika)," in [1], 6: 246.

16. See V. Ia. Briusov, "Pushkin pered sudom uchenogo istorika," in Briusov, *Moi Pushkin* (Moscow: Gos. izd., 1929), pp. 173–87; and D. Sokolov, "Neskol'ko zamechanii k kommentariiu prof. N. N. Firsova na *Istoriiu Pugachevskogo bunta*," *Pushkin i ego sovremenniki*, 29–30 (1918): 18–27. Among major Soviet publications that both complete and correct Pushkin's findings, let me mention V. V. Mavrodin et al., eds., *Krest'ianskaia voina v 1773–1775 gg. Vosstanie Puga-*

cheva, 3 vols. (Leningrad: Leningradskii gos. univ., 1961–70); and the collection of documents *Pugachevshchina*, 3 vols. (Moscow: Gos. izd., 1926–31).

17. R. V. Ovchinnikov, Arkhivnye istochniki *Istorii Pugacheva*: Sbornik arkhivnykh dokumentov i tekstov Pushkina, Institut russkoi literatury (Pushkinskii dom), Arkhivnyi fond 244: A. S. Pushkin, op. 31, No. 109.

18. Blok, *Pushkin* (cited in note 6, above), pp. 66–68.

19. For further details see Izmailov [268], p. 296.

20. First published in *Russkii arkhiv*, 3, No. 1 (1880): 218–27.

21. See, in particular, Oksman [283], p. 258; and Gillel'son & Mushina [260], pp. 176–80.

22. For a discussion of this change, see Tomashevskii, "Pervonachal'naia redaktsiia XI glavy *Kapitanskoi dochki*," in [86], pp. 281–90.

23. Saitov [482], 3: 347.

24. Although he included the novel in his journal, Pushkin did not give up the idea of publishing it in book form: in early January 1837 he had made arrangements with a publisher to print it as Vol. 1 of a two-volume edition of his fiction, but the project fell through with his death on Jan. 29, and only one copy of this projected separate edition of the novel survived. For details, see N. Smirnov-Sokol'skii, *Rasskazy o prizhiznennykh izdaniiakh Pushkina* (Moscow: Izd. Vsesoiuznoi knizhnoi palaty, 1962), pp. 402–6.

25. See Gillel'son & Mushina [260], p. 99.

26. Two other historical personages who might have contributed to Pushkin's fictional account of the fate of Grinev were a nobleman, Il'ia Aristov, who had fought on Pugachev's side (see [5], 9: 704–9), and the Protestant pastor mentioned in Chap. 8 of *Istoriia Pugacheva*, whose life Pushkin spared because the pastor had given him alms when he was a prisoner in Kazan (see [5], 9: 68).

27. For details, see Oksman [284], p. 65.

28. *Ibid.*, pp. 94–100.

29. Ovchinnikov, Arkhivnye istochniki (cited in note 17, above), pp. 60–61.

30. For details, see Petrunina & Fridlender [66], pp. 113–14.

31. The tale has been republished in the "Literaturnye pamiatniki" edition of *Kapitanskaia dochka* (Moscow: Nauka, 1964), pp. 123–46. Its author has been identified as A. P. Kriukov; for details, see Brang [250]; and Fokin [257].

32. Skvoznikov [76], p. 78, argues convincingly that the participation of Ivan Kuz'mich and Ivan Ignat'ich in these campaigns is a matter of "a distant past, beyond the framework of the narrative," unlikely to change our perception of these characters as peaceable ones.

33. Petrunina & Fridlender [66], p. 107. The description of the blizzard may have been inspired also by S. T. Aksakov's "Buran" (1834).

34. See V. Shklovskii, *Gamburgskii schet* (Leningrad: Izd. pisatelei v Leningrade, 1928), p. 31.

35. George Saintsbury, who reviewed the English translation of *Kapitanskaia dochka* published in *Russian Romance* (London: King & Co., 1875), was the first critic to point out the connection; see [292]. Among the most important subsequent studies comparing Pushkin's novel, not only with *The Heart of Midlothian*, but also with other Scott novels, above all *Rob Roy*, are M. Gofman "*Kapitanskaia dochka*" in [1], 4: 355–57; Neiman [280]; Iakubovich [265]; Davie [254]; and Greene [113], pp. 213–15.

36. Iakovlev [264] draws attention to a story, published in *Detskoe chtenie dlia serdtsa i razuma* (Moscow: Univ. tip. u N. Novikova, 1786), 7: 110–11, that relates the chance meeting of a poor orphan girl with a gentleman who invites her to the Imperial Palace; he turns out to be the Emperor Joseph II, and generously provides for her. It is also noteworthy that in I. I. Lazhechnikov's *Poslednii novik* (1833) the hero, Vladimir, is saved by a boatful of sailors, whose kind captain, covering the freezing Vladimir with his own coat, turns out to be Peter I (see Part 4, Chap. 3). Pushkin emphasizes the conventionality of the situation also by modeling his description of Catherine II on a well-known portrait (1791) by V. L. Borovikovskii; see Shklovskii [134], p. 68.

37. See Sidiakov [138], p. 192.

38. Shvabrin first called melodramatic by Belinskii [99], p. 577.

39. See Shklovskii [295], p. 22.

40. Pointed out by Tomashevskii [86], p. 289.

41. See Shklovskii [136], pp. 100–101; and Oksman [284], pp. 88–89.

42. For detailed commentary on the epigraphs to the novel, see Shklovskii [136], pp. 96–128; Shklovskii [134], pp. 76–82; and Stenbock-Fermor [144], pp. 113–18.

43. This last quotation is from Act 3, Scene 5, of *Nedorosl'*. The most detailed consideration of Pushkin's allusions to Fonvizin's comedy can be found in Blagoi [20], pp. 159–60.

44. See, among others, Gofman (cited in note 35, above), pp. 366, 370–71; and Tsvetaeva [303], pp. 125–26.

45. Toibin [300], p. 84, notes the grotesque nature of these descriptions.

46. Bayley [16], p. 388, notes the technique of frustrating expectations in this instance.

47. Grinev's gesture of "almost" striking the Cossack Maksimych reminds one of Girei of *Bakhchisaraiskii fontan* (1823), who halted his sword midair, distracted by the memory of his Maria. Pushkin later recalled how his friend A. Raevskii roared with laughter over Girei's melodramatic gesture: [5], 11: 145.

48. This is Lotman's interpretation of the novel; see [273]. For a similar interpretation of some of Scott's novels, see Francis R. Hart, *Scott's Novels: The Plotting of Historic Survival* (Charlottesville: Univ. Press of Virginia, 1966), chaps. on *Waverley*, *The Heart of Midlothian*, and *Peveril*, especially pp. 19, 25, 29, 129, 144.

49. The argument that Grinev, as an 18th-century man, is less

shaken by the sight of cruelty than a later reader would be is presented in Odinokov [123], pp. 56–57. Makogonenko [275], p. 53, draws attention to the difference between the behavior of the simple villagers who witness the executions in *Kapitanskaia dochka* and the horrified reaction of the populace on hearing of the murder of Boris Godunov's children in the tragedy by that name. He attributes this difference to a perception of the Mironovs' execution as a just act. Mal'tsev [56], p. 185, argues that Grinev's relative equanimity in the face of the cruelties committed by the rebels testifies to his deep humanitarian concern for the cause of the simple people.

50. Gusev [43], p. 569, perceiving a polarity in modes of presentation, offers the suggestion, puzzling at least to me, that "the death of the captain and of his wife 'reconciles' the two atmospheres—the serious and the laughable, tragedy and comedy."

51. Tsvetaeva [303], p. 113. A similar view is expressed by Skvoznikov [76], pp. 79–81.

52. The epigraphs for Chaps. 1, 5, 6, and 8 derive from *Novoe i polnoe sobranie rossiiskikh pesen*, ed. M. D. Chulkov (Moscow: Univ. tip. N. Novikova, 1780), as follows: *Chap. 1*, Part 3, No. 68; *Chap. 5*, Part 1, Nos. 176, 135; *Chap 6.*, Part 1, No. 125; *Chap. 8*, Part 2, No. 130. The epigraph for Chap. 12 derives from a nuptial song Pushkin himself had recorded, and the one for Chap. 14 from *Polnoe sobranie russkikh poslovits* [481], p. 141. Grinev's poem about Masha ("Mysl' liubovnu istrebliaia") is a slightly altered version of a song from *Novoe i polnoe sobranie rossiiskikh pesen*, Part 1, No. 34. Shvabrin's song ("Kapitanskaia doch'") derives from *Sobranie narodnykh russkikh pesen*, ed. N. L'vov and I. Prach (St. Petersburg: Tip. Gornogo uchilishcha, 1790), p. 85. Finally, the barge haulers' song Pugachev and his men sing in Chap. 8 ("Ne shumi, mati zelenaia") is also from *Novoe i polnoe sobranie rossiiskikh pesen*, Part 1, p. 147.

53. Viazemskii [486], 2: 377.

54. Toibin [301], pp. 125, 136.

55. Davie [254], p. 8.

56. For a vivid characterization of Pugachev as a romantic hero, see Tsvetaeva [303], pp. 122–39.

57. Zvoznikov [312], p. 125, writes that Pushkin's treatment of Vasilisa Egorovna, shifting from mockery to compassion, is akin to Gogol''s attitude to his characters in "Starosvetskie pomeshchiki" (1835). Zvoznikov's comment is perceptive, but it still leaves open the question of whether Gogol''s technique of combining incongruities is in accord with the overall atmosphere of Pushkin's work.

58. The only critic I am aware of who has stated this outright, claiming that "the horrors described in it [*Kapitanskaia dochka*] do not accord with Grinev's peaceable character and with the calm tone of his memoirs," is Lopatto: [121], p. 14.

59. Anderson [241].

60. Taking an unauthorized leave of absence in order to see to a private affair is, of course, less of an offense than joining Pugachev in order to fight against the Empress; but it is nevertheless an act of insubordination, which no army can tolerate during a war. Therefore I think Makogonenko [275], p. 85, is wrong in claiming that Catherine II restores justice at the end of the novel, rather than simply pardoning Grinev.

61. Anderson [241], p. 482. Although Mikkelson [276], p. 309, too, considers Pugachev a paternal figure in relation to Grinev, he sees him as more of a historical father to "all the outcasts of the Russian Empire" than as a psychological one to Grinev the individual.

62. The ambivalence of Grinev's feelings toward Pugachev is analyzed very interestingly by Besançon [244], pp. 165–70.

Chapter Seven

1. Annenkov [13], pp. 399–404.
2. Feinberg [32], pp. 38–52.
3. A fragment had already appeared in *Literaturnaia gazeta*, 1830, No. 8: 57–59.
4. See Iu. N. Tynianov, "O 'Puteshestvii v Arzrum,'" in his *Pushkin i ego sovremenniki* (Moscow: Nauka, 1969), pp. 200–205.
5. E. Etkind, *Razgovor o stikhakh* (Moscow: Detskaia literatura, 1970), pp. 175–78.
6. Anthony Olcott, "Parody as Realism: The *Journey to Arzrum*," *Russian Literature Triquarterly*, 10 (Fall 1974): 245–59.
7. Sidiakov [138], p. 168.
8. Krystyna Pomorska, "O chlenenii povestvovatel'noi prozy," in *Structure of Texts and Semiotics of Culture*, ed. J. van der Eng and Mojmir Grygar (The Hague: Mouton, 1973), pp. 359–63.
9. First published in *Biblioteka dlia chteniia*, 7, No. 12 (1834).
10. For a full discussion of findings relating to Kirdzhali, see Trubetskoi [320], pp. 309–16; Trubetskoi [321], pp. 333–37; Dvoichenko-Markova [313]; and Oganian [318]. Pushkin's year 1821 for the date of Kirdzhali's deportation is an error; it should be 1823.
11. See Oksman's notes, [4], 4: 743.
12. See Koroban [317]; and Dvoichenko-Markova [313], p. 44.
13. Dvoichenko-Markova [313], p. 45.
14. See, among others, Oksenov [319].
15. Kodjak & Wynne [316], pp. 44–62.
16. There is still another brief outline, beginning with the words "Les deux danseuses," that seems to be related to the Pelham project.
17. For identification of historical personalities appearing in the outlines, see Oksman's notes, [4], 4: 774–77; V. Briusov, "Neokonchennye povesti iz russkoi zhizni," in [1], 4: 269; Kazantsev [453]; and Shesterikov [455].

18. "Infanticide: Procès de Maria Schoning et d'Anna Harlin, Nuremberg, 1797" in Vol. 2 of *Causes célèbres étrangères, publiées en France pour la première fois et traduites de l'italien, de l'allemand etc. par une société de jurisconsultes et de gens de lettres* (Paris: C. L. F. Panckoucke, 1827), pp. 200–213, quoted in Iakubovich [322], pp. 150–53.

19. As Vershnev's comments indicate in "My provodili vecher na dache" ([5], 8: 421), Pushkin knew that there was some doubt about the authorship of *De Viris*. The text of this work has been preserved in several manuscripts, of which two types can be distinguished: (1) manuscripts that contain only *De Viris*, from which, however, the last nine lives, including that of Cleopatra, are missing, and (2) two manuscripts of the 15th century that contain *Origo Gentis Romanae* and *Aurelii Victoris Historiae Abbreviatae* (also known as *Liber de Caesaribus*) in addition to *De Viris*; this version contains the last nine chapters but lacks almost all of the first chapter. The full text, incorporating both manuscript traditions, can be found in Franciscus Pichlmayr's definitive edition, *Sexti Aurelii Victoris Liber de Caesaribus* (Leipzig: B. G. Teubner, 1911). Scholars generally agree that Sextus Aurelius was the author of *Liber de Caesaribus*, but not the author of the other two works contained in the corpus. The identity of the author of *De Viris* has not been established. For further details, see Donald W. Wade, "*Liber de Viris Illustribus Urbis Romae*: A Translation, with Introduction and Notes," Thesis, Univ. of North Carolina, Chapel Hill, 1964, pp. i–v; Chester G. Starr, "Aurelius Victor, Historian of Empire," *American Historical Review*, 61 (1955–56): 574–86; and Martin Schanz, *Geschichte der römischen Literatur*, Müllers Handbuch der klassischen Altertumswissenschaft, 8 (Munich: C. H. Beck'sche Verlagsbuchhandlung, 1959), 4: 1, 65–67, 72, 75.

20. Pichlmayr's edition, p. 74; Wade's translation, p. 74 (both cited in the preceding note). The reliability of *De Viris* as a historical source is doubtful; see Ilse Becher, *Das Bild der Kleopatra in der griechischen und lateinischen Literatur* (Berlin: Akademie-Verlag, 1966), pp. 92–93.

21. For details of the history of the text, both of the Cleopatra poem and of related fragments, see Bondi [192]; and Tomashevskii, "Kleopatra," in [86], pp. 55–65.

22. See Pushkin [6], 6: 389. O'Bell [211], p. 39, discusses the softening of Cleopatra's image in the 1828 version.

23. Pushkin took the historical details about Petronius from Tacitus's *Annales*, Book 16, Chaps. 18–20.

24. The first verse inserted is Pushkin's translation of Anacreon's Ode 56; the second, of Horace's Ode 7, Book 2; and the line on which Pushkin's fragment ends is from Horace's Ode 2, Book 3.

25. See Cherniaev [27], p. 481.

26. Pointed out by Petrunina [214], p. 25.

27. Oksman (in [4], 6: 762) suggests A. F. Zakrevskaia as the proto-

type for both Vol'skaia and Voronskaia. Akhmatova [190], p. 178, on the other hand, suggests that the prototype for Vol'skaia, at least of "My provodili vecher," if not of the earlier fragment, might have been Karolina Soban'skaia (Sobańska), a married woman separated from her husband, with whom Pushkin had something of a romantic involvement early in 1830. See also L. A. Chereiskii, *Pushkin i ego okruzhenie* (Leningrad: Nauka, 1975), p. 385. Another character in "My provodili vecher" is identified by Pushkin himself in a draft version ([5], 8: 990, note 12) as Titov (the man who had written down his oral narrative, "Uedinennyi domik na Vasil'evskom"). For more details, see Bikerman [323]. Still other prototypes for characters appearing in the fragment are suggested by Gillel'son [324], pp. 16–19, on the basis of D. S. Fiquelmont's diary. The edition Gillel'son refers to is Nina Kauchtschischwili, *Il diario di Dar'ja Fedorovna Fiquelmont*, Publicazioni dell'Universiteta Cattolica del Sacro Cuore, Contributi—Serie terza, scienze filologiche e letteratura, 18 (Milan: Societa Editrice Vita e Pensiero, 1968).

28. Briusov [193], p. 109.

29. Petrunina [214], p. 26, note 7.

30. Analyzed by Tomashevskii [86], pp. 59–61. Tomashevskii suggests that for these more elaborate details Pushkin turned to Plutarch's *Vitae Parallelae* (Chap. 26 of the Life of Antony), possibly with the mediation of Shakespeare's *Antony and Cleopatra*.

31. Noted by O'Bell [211], pp. 194–95.

32. Akhmatova [190], pp. 179–80.

33. Noted by O'Bell [211], p. 193.

34. *Ibid.*, p. 194.

35. See Petrunina [214], p. 26, note 8.

36. The description of Charskii reiterates ideas Pushkin had expressed in various forms over a decade. Its most notable antecedents can be found, apart from "Otryvok," in Pushkin's letter of late May–early June, 1825, to Bestuzhev; in his journalistic fragment "Al'manashnik" (1830); in the "Lomonosov" chapter of his "Puteshestvie iz Moskvy v Peterburg"; at the end of his unfinished poem "Osen'" (1833), where he describes the onset of inspiration; and in a number of other poems mentioned in connection with the problem of the poet's relations to society: above all in "Poet," "Poet i tolpa," "Poetu," and "Otvet anonimu." Tomashevskii has also noted that the scene of a little boy treating the poet to a reading of the poet's own distorted verses is probably based on a real-life experience of Pushkin's, recorded by B. M. Fedorov in his diary in May 1827. See Pushkin [6], 6: 777; and Veresaev [485], 1: 366.

37. See Viazemskii's letter of May 2, 1828, to his wife, quoted by M. Borovkova-Maikova in "Mitskevich v pis'makh P. A. Viazemskogo k zhene," *Zven'ia*, 3–4 (1934): 219–20. On Pushkin's attitude to Mickiewicz's improvisations, see Lednicki [205], pp. 25–26, 71–81; and Weintraub [223], pp. 131–37.

38. A. E. Odyniec, *Listy z podrozy* (Warsaw: Gebethner i Wolff, 1875), 1: 54, quoted in Lednicki [205], p. 26.

39. See various items about Langenschwarz in *Severnaia pchela*, 1832, Nos. 115, 117, 140, and 238 (May 21, May 24, June 21, Oct. 8). For discussions of his possible influence on Pushkin, see Stolpianskii [218]; Kazanovich [202]; Lednicki [205], p. 71; and Weintraub [223], pp. 135–36.

40. See Gillel'son [324], p. 16; and *Il diario di D. F. Fiquelmont* (cited in note 27, above), p. 57.

41. See the anecdote told by S. N. Goncharov in P. A. Efremov, "A. S. Pushkin," Chap. 6, *Russkaia starina*, 28 (May 1880): 95–96; and Lednicki [205], p. 71.

42. Weintraub [223], pp. 119–31, discusses these and other possible sources. It has also been suggested that Jules Janin's *Barnave* (1831) exerted an influence on Pushkin's theme; see Lednicki [206], p. 253.

43. See *Sovremennik*, 8 (1837): 5–24; and subsequent editions.

44. Bondi [192], pp. 192–96.

45. Argued by Petrunina [214], p. 44.

46. *Ibid.*, p. 26, note 8.

47. Dostoevskii [195].

48. See, primarily, Gofman [198].

49. Akhmatova [190], p. 177, among others, has observed that the epigraph to Chap. 2—"Ia tsar', ia rab, ia cherv', ia bog," taken from Derzhavin's ode "Bog" (1784)—refers to the two sides of the Italian's nature, inspired and mercenary. One might add that the puerile epigraph to Chap. 1, taken from Georges Mareschal Bièvre's *Almanach des calembours* (1771), serves as a contrast to the lofty art of the improvisatore.

50. The themes suggested to the Italian by the Petersburg public have to do either with superficial sensationalism or with topics of the day. "La famiglia dei Cenci" refers to the murder, in 1598 by his own family, of the wealthy Roman Francesco Cenci, which served as a basis for both Percy Bysshe Shelley's *The Cenci* (1819) and Adolphe Custine's *Beatrix Cenci* (1833). "L'ultimo giorno di Pompeia" was the theme of a painting by K. P. Briullov exhibited in St. Petersburg in 1834. "La primavera veduta da una prigione" bears a relationship to Maroncelli's improvised hymn, which is mentioned in Chap. 87 of Silvio Pellico's *Le Mie Prigioni* (1832). (The text of the hymn itself is given by Pellico's fellow prisoner Maroncelli in an appendix.) "Il trionfo di Tasso" was a topical theme because of N. V. Kukol'nik's play *Torquato Tasso*, performed in St. Petersburg in 1833. The sources of these themes have been identified by Tomashevskii: Pushkin [6], 6: 778. The Cleopatra theme, which draws a guffaw from the men when the Italian questions its implications, is no different until the Italian transforms it into poetry.

51. Matlaw [208], p. 105.

52. Pushkin was still on the road when the military correspondent

of *Severnaia pchela*, I. Radozhitskii, expressed a hope that the poet would derive inspiration from his visit to the Turkish front; see *Severnaia pchela*, 1829, No. 101 (Aug. 22): col. 8. Bulgarin subsequently censured Pushkin for his failure to do so; see his review of Chap. 7 of *Onegin*, *Severnaia pchela*, 1830, No. 35 (March 22): cols. 1–6. For Paskevich's expression of disappointment over Pushkin's silence, see his letter of 1831 to Zhukovskii, quoted by Oksman in [4], 4: 785. Pushkin himself refers to repercussions of this matter in his Preface to "Puteshestvie v Arzrum."

53. Emphasized by Sidiakov [138], p. 144.

54. This phrase, *"priblizhenie boga"* in Russian, may have been influenced by A. Glagolev's description of the awakening of an improvisatore's inspiration as *"priblizhenie Apollona"*; see his "Ital'iantsy (Otryvok iz puteshestviia po Italii)," *Moskovskii vestnik*, 12 (1827): 327. Connection pointed out by V. E. Vatsuro in B. P. Gorodetskii et al., eds., *Pushkin: Itogi i problemy izucheniia* (Moscow: Nauka, 1966), p. 216.

55. Noted by O'Bell [211], pp. 231–32.

56. V. F. Odoevskii, *Russkie nochi* (Munich: W. Fink, 1967), p. 217. (Reprint of the 1913 ed.)

57. Presence of poetic techniques in *Egipetskie nochi* noted by Sidiakov [138], pp. 147–48.

Selected Bibliography

Selected Bibliography

Major Pushkin Editions Cited

[1] *Biblioteka velikikh pisatelei: Pushkin.* Ed. S. A. Vengerov. 6 vols. St. Petersburg: Brokgauz-Efron, 1907–11.
[2] Pushkin, A. S. *Pis'ma.* Ed. B. L. Modzalevskii. 3 vols. Moscow: Gos. izd., 1926–35.
[3] ———. *Polnoe sobranie sochinenii.* Prilozhenie k zhurnalu Krasnaia niva. 6 vols. Moscow: GIKhL, 1930–31.
[4] ———. *Polnoe sobranie sochinenii.* Ed. M. A. Tsiavlovskii. 6 vols. Moscow: Academia, 1936–38.
[5] ———. *Polnoe sobranie sochinenii.* Ed. V. D. Bonch-Bruevici et al. 17 vols. Moscow: Akademiia Nauk SSSR, 1937–59.
[6] ———. *Polnoe sobranie sochinenii.* Ed. B. V. Tomashevskii. 10 vols. Moscow: Nauka, 1962–66.
[7] Shliapkin, I. A., ed. *Iz neizdannykh bumag Pushkina.* St. Petersburg: M. M. Stasiulevich, 1903.
[8] *Sochineniia Aleksandra Pushkina.* Ed. V. A. Zhukovskii et al. 11 vols. St. Petersburg: Tip. zagotovleniia gos. bumag, 1838–41.
[9] *Sochineniia Aleksandra Pushkina.* Ed. P. V. Annenkov. 7 vols. St. Petersburg: P. V. Annenkov, 1855–57.
[10] Tsiavlovskii, M. A., et al., eds. *Rukoiu Pushkina: Nesobrannye i neopublikovannye teksty.* Moscow: Academia, 1935.
[11] Vatsuro, V. E., and M. I. Gillel'son. *Novonaidennyi avtograf Pushkina.* Moscow: Nauka, 1968.

Critical Studies with Some Consideration of Pushkin's Prose Fiction

[12] Akhmatova, A. A. *O Pushkine: Stat'i i zametki.* Leningrad: Sovetskii pisatel', 1977.
[13] Annenkov, P. V., ed. *A. S. Pushkin: Materialy dlia ego biografii i otsenki proizvedenii.* 2d ed. St. Petersburg: Obshchestvennaia pol'za, 1873.
[14] Arminjon, Victor. *Pouchkine et Pierre le Grand.* Paris: Cinq Continents, 1971.

[15] Azadovskii, M. "Pushkin i fol'klor." In Azadovskii, *Literatura i fol'klor*. Leningrad: GIKhL, 1938, pp. 5–64.

[16] Bayley, Jo.n. *Pushkin: A Comparative Commentary*. Cambridge: Cambridge Univ. Press, 1971.

[17] ———. "Pushkin's Secret of Distance," *Oxford Slavonic Papers*, n.s. 1 (1968): 74–84.

[18] Blagoi, D. D. "Dostoevskii i Pushkin." In K. N. Lomunov et al., eds., *Dostoevskii—khudozhnik i myslitel': Sbornik statei*. Moscow: Khudozhestvennaia literatura, 1972, pp. 344–426.

[19] ———. *Masterstvo Pushkina. Vdokhnovennyi trud. Pushkin—master kompozitsii*. Moscow: Sovetskii pisatel', 1955.

[20] ———. "Pushkin i russkaia literatura XVIII veka." In D. D. Blagoi and V. Ia. Kirpotin, eds., *Pushkin rodonachal'nik novoi russkoi literatury: Sbornik nauchno-issledovatel'skikh rabot*. Moscow: Akademiia Nauk SSSR, 1941, pp. 101–66.

[21] ———. *Sotsiologiia tvorchestva Pushkina*. 2d rev. ed. Moscow: Mir, 1931.

[22] ———. *Tvorcheskii put' Pushkina, 1826–1830*. Moscow: Sovetskii pisatel', 1967.

[23] Blagoi, D. D., et al., eds. *Istoriia russkoi literatury*. Vol. 6, Moscow: Academiia Nauk SSSR, 1953, pp. 161–368.

[24] Bocharov, S. G. *Poetika Pushkina: Ocherki*. Moscow: Nauka, 1974.

[25] Botnikova, A. B. *E. T. A. Gofman i russkaia literatura*. Voronezh: Izd. Voronezhskogo univ-ta, 1977.

[26] Botsianovskii, V. F. "K kharakteristike raboty Pushkina nad novym romanom." In A. Poliakov, ed., *Sertum bibliologicum v chest' Prezidenta Russkogo bibliologicheskogo obshchestva A. I. Maleina*. Petrograd: Gosizdat, 1922, pp. 182–93.

[27] Cherniaev, N. I. *Kriticheskie stat'i i zametki o Pushkine*. Kharkov: Iuzhnyi krai, 1900.

[28] Chernyshevskii, N. G. Review of *Sochineniia Aleksandra Pushkina*. In Chernyshevskii, *Polnoe sobranie sochinenii*. Vol. 2. Moscow: GIKhL, 1949, pp. 424–516. Originally published in *Sovremennik*, Nos. 2, 3, 7, 8 (1855).

[29] Chicherin, A. V. *Ocherki po istorii russkogo literaturnogo stilia. Povestvovatel'naia proza i lirika*. Moscow: Khudozhestvennaia literatura, 1977.

[30] Clayton, John D. "Parody and Burlesque in the Work of A. S. Pushkin: A Critical Study," Ph.D. dissertation, University of Illinois, Urbana, 1971.

[31] Eikhenbaum, B. M. "Problemy poetiki Pushkina." In Eikhenbaum, *Skvoz' literaturu*. Leningrad: Academia, 1924, pp. 157–70.

[32] Feinberg, I. *Nezavershennye raboty Pushkina*. 3d, enlarged ed. Moscow: Sovetskii pisatel', 1962.

[33] Frumkina, R. M. *Statisticheskie metody izucheniia leksiki*. Moscow: Nauka, 1964.

[34] Gasiorowska, Xenia. *The Image of Peter the Great in Russian Fiction.* Madison: Univ. of Wisconsin Press, 1979.

[35] Gershenzon, M. O. *Mudrost' Pushkina.* Moscow: Knigoizd. pisatelei v Moskve, 1919.

[36] Grigor'ev, Apollon. "Vzgliad na russkuiu literaturu so smerti Pushkina." In Grigor'ev, *Sobranie sochinenii.* Ed. V. O. Savodnik. Vol. 6. Moscow: I. N. Kushnerev, 1915, pp. 1–81. Originally published in *Russkoe Slovo,* Nos. 2 and 3 (1859).

[37] Gronicka, André von. *The Russian Image of Goethe.* Philadelphia: Univ. of Pennsylvania Press, 1968.

[38] Grossman, Leonid. "Iskusstvo anekdota u Pushkina." In Grossman, *Etiudy o Pushkine.* Moscow: L. D. Frenkel', 1923, pp. 37–75.

[39] Grushkin, A. *K voprosu o klassovoi sushchnosti pushkinskogo tvorchestva.* Leningrad: GIKhL, 1931.

[40] ———. "Obraz narodnogo geroia v tvorchestve Pushkina," *Pushkin: Vremennik Pushkinskoi komissii,* 3 (1937): 424–41.

[41] Gukasova, A. G. *Boldinskii period v tvorchestve A. S. Pushkina.* Moscow: Prosveshchenie, 1973.

[42] Gukovskii, G. A. *Pushkin i problemy realisticheskogo stilia.* Moscow: GIKhL, 1957.

[43] Gusev, V. "Pushkin i nekotorye sovremennye problemy teorii stilia." In S. Mashinskii, ed., *V mire Pushkina: Sbornik statei.* Moscow: Sovetskii pisatel', 1974, pp. 545–72.

[44] Ingham, Norman. *E. T. A. Hoffmann's Reception in Russia.* Würzburg: Jal-Verlag, 1974.

[45] Ivanov-Razumnik, R. *Sochineniia.* Vol. 5: *Pushkin i Belinskii: Stat'i istoriko-literaturnye.* Petrograd: M. M. Stasiulevich, 1916.

[46] Izmailov, N. V. "Pushkin i V. Odoevskii." In N. V. Iakovlev, ed., *Pushkin v mirovoi literature.* Leningrad: Gos. izd., 1926, pp. 289–308.

[47] Jones, L. G. "Syntactic Replication in Russian Prose Fiction." In *American Contributions to the Seventh International Congress of Slavists* (Warsaw, Aug. 21–27, 1973), Vol. 1: *Linguistics and Poetics.* Ed. Ladislav Matejka. The Hague: Mouton, 1973, pp. 157–68.

[48] Kalinine, P. "L'Ecole frénétique française et la prose romantique en Russie (1831–1836)," *Revue des Etudes Slaves,* 49 (1973): 231–41.

[49] Khodasevich, V. F. "Peterburgskie povesti Pushkina." In Khodasevich, *Stat'i o russkoi poezii.* Petrograd: Epokha, 1922, pp. 58–96.

[50] Kliuchevskii, V. O. "Rech', proiznesennaia v torzhestvennom sobranii Moskovskogo Universiteta 6 iiunia 1880 g., v den' otkrytiia pamiatnika Pushkinu." In Kliuchevskii, *Sochineniia.* Vol. 7. Moscow: Izd. sotsial'no-ekonomicheskoi literatury, 1959, pp. 145–52.

[51] Kostka, Edmund. *Glimpses of Germanic-Slavic Relations from Pushkin to Heinrich Mann.* Lewisburg, Pa.: Bucknell Univ. Press, 1975.

[52] Lavretskaia, V. I. *Proizvedeniia A. S. Pushkina na temy russkoi istorii.* Moscow: Uchpedgiz, 1962.

[53] Lednicki, Wacław. *Bits of Table Talk on Pushkin, Mickiewicz, Goethe, Turgenev, and Sienkiewicz.* The Hague: Mouton, 1956.

[54] Levkovich, Ia. L. "Printsipy dokumental'nogo povestvovaniia v istoricheskoi proze pushkinskoi pory," *Pushkin: Issledovaniia i materialy,* 6 (1969): 171–96.

[55] Makogonenko, G. P. *Tvorchestvo A. S. Pushkina v 1830-e gody (1830–1833).* Leningrad: Khudozhestvennaia literatura, 1974.

[56] Mal'tsev, M. *Tema krest'ianskogo vosstaniia v tvorchestve A. S. Pushkina.* Cheboksary: Chuvashskoe gos. izd., 1960.

[57] Meilakh, B. *Pushkin i ego epokha.* Moscow: GIKhL, 1958.

[58] ———, ed. *Russkaia povest' XIX veka: Istoriia i problematika zhanra.* Leningrad: Nauka, 1973.

[59] Mirsky, D. S. *Pushkin.* London: Routledge, 1926.

[60] Modzalevskii, B. *Pushkin.* Leningrad: Priboi, 1929.

[61] Myshkovskaia, L. "O printsipakh pushkinskogo stilia." In Myshkovskaia, *O masterstve pisatelia: Stat'i 1932–1959 gg.* Moscow: Sovetskii pisatel', 1967, pp. 107–36.

[62] Odintsov, V. V. *O iazyke khudozhestvennoi prozy.* Moscow: Nauka, 1973.

[63] Orlov, A. S. "Pushkin—sozdatel' russkogo literaturnogo iazyka." In A. M. Deborin, ed., *Sto let so dnia smerti Pushkina: Trudy pushkinskoi sessii AN SSSR, 1837–1937.* Moscow: Akademiia Nauk SSSR, 1938, pp. 97–115.

[64] Ovsianiko-Kulikovskii, D. N. *Sobranie sochinenii.* Vol. 4: *Pushkin.* St. Petersburg: Obshchestvennaia pol'za i Prometei, 1911.

[65] Passage, Charles E. *The Russian Hoffmannists.* The Hague: Mouton, 1963.

[66] Petrunina, N. N., and G. M. Fridlender. *Nad stranitsami Pushkina.* Leningrad: Nauka, 1974.

[67] Proffer, Carl R. "Washington Irving in Russia: Pushkin, Gogol and Marlinsky," *Comparative Literature,* Vol. 20, No. 4 (1968): 329–42.

[68] Sazonova, S. S. *Pushkin o sovremennoi proze i ee zadachakh.* Riga: Latviiskii gos. univ. im. P. Stuchki, 1976.

[69] Sergievskii, I. V. "Pushkin v poiskakh geroia." In Sergievskii, *Izbrannye raboty: Stat'i o russkoi literature.* Moscow: GIKhL, 1961, pp. 40–59.

[70] Setschkareff (Sechkarev), V. *Alexander Puschkin: Sein Leben und Sein Werk.* Wiesbaden: Otto Harrassowitz, 1963.

[71] Sharypkin, D. M. "Pushkin i 'nravouchitel'nye rasskazy' Marmontelia," *Pushkin: Issledovaniia i materialy,* 8 (1978): 107–36.

[72] Shevyrev, S. Review of *Sochineniia Aleksandra Pushkina, Moskvitianin,* 5, No. 9 (1841): 236–70.

[73] Shtein, S. *Pushkin i Gofman: Sravnitel'noe literaturnoe issledovanie.* Acta et Commentationes Universitatis Tartuensis / Dorpatensis, B: Humaniora, Vol. 13, Tartuskii Univ., 1928.

[74] Sidiakov, L. S. "Proza i poeziia Pushkina: Sootnoshenie i vzai-

modeistvie," Avtoreferat dissertatsii na soiskanie uchenoi stepeni filologicheskikh nauk, Tartuskii gos. univ., 1975.

[75] Simmons, E. J. *English Literature and Culture in Russia (1553–1840)*. Cambridge, Mass.: Harvard Univ. Press, 1935.

[76] Skvoznikov, V. D. "Stil' Pushkina," *Teoriia literatury*, 3 (1965): 60–97.

[77] Slonimskii, A. L. *Masterstvo Pushkina*. 2d rev. ed. Moscow: GIKhL, 1963.

[78] Sorokin, Iu. S. *Razvitie slovarnogo sostava russkogo literaturnogo iazyka: 30-e–90-e gody XIX veka*. Moscow: Nauka, 1965.

[79] Strakhov, N. N. *Zametki o Pushkine i drugikh poetakh*. 3d ed. Kiev: I. P. Matchenko, 1913. Originally published in St. Petersburg in 1888.

[80] Striedter, Jurij. "Poetic Genre and the Sense of History in Pushkin," *New Literary History*, 8, No. 2 (1977): 293–309.

[81] Struve, P. "Walter Scott and Russia," *The Slavonic Review*, 11, No. 32 (1933): 397–410.

[82] Tamarchenko, D. E. *Iz istorii russkogo klassicheskogo romana: Pushkin, Lermontov, Gogol'*. Moscow: Akademiia Nauk SSSR, 1961.

[83] Toibin, I. M. "Voprosy istorizma i khudozhestvennaia sistema Pushkina 1830-kh godov," *Pushkin: Issledovaniia i materialy*, 6 (1969): 35–59.

[84] Tomashevskii, B. V. *Pushkin i Frantsiia*. Leningrad: Sovetskii pisatel', 1960.

[85] ———. *Pushkin: Kniga pervaia (1813–1824)*. Moscow: Akademiia Nauk SSSR, 1956.

[86] ———. *Pushkin: Kniga vtoraia. Materialy k monografii (1824–1837)*. Moscow: Akademiia Nauk SSSR, 1961.

[87] ———. "Voprosy iazyka v tvorchestve Pushkina," *Pushkin: Issledovaniia i materialy*, 1 (1956): 126–84.

[88] Trensky, Paul I. "Peter the Great in Pushkin," *Zapiski russkoi akademicheskoi gruppy v SShA*, 7 (1973): 239–50.

[89] Tynianov, Iu. N. "Pushkin." In Tynianov, *Arkhaisty i novatory*. Leningrad: Priboi, 1929, pp. 330–66.

[90] Vatsuro, V. E. "Pushkin i problemy bytopisaniia v nachale 1830-kh godov," *Pushkin: Issledovaniia i materialy*, 6 (1969): 150–70.

[91] ———. "Uolpol i Pushkin," *Vremennik Pushkinskoi komissii*, 1967–68 (published 1970): 47–57.

[92] Vickery, Walter N. *Alexander Pushkin*. New York: Twayne, 1970.

[93] Vinogradov, I. "Put' Pushkina k realizmu," *Literaturnoe nasledstvo*, 16–18 (1934): 49–90.

[94] Vinogradov, V. V. *Iazyk Pushkina: Pushkin i istoriia russkogo literaturnogo iazyka*. Moscow: Academia, 1935.

[95] ———. *Ocherki po istorii russkogo literaturnogo iazyka XVII–XIX vv*. 2d ed. Moscow: Uchpedgiz, 1938.

[96] ———. *Stil' Pushkina*. Moscow: Ogiz, 1941.

[97] Vorob'ev, P. G. "Poslovitsy i pogovorki v tvorchestve Pushkina." In N. A. Glagolev, ed., *A. S. Pushkin: 1837–1937*. Moscow: Uchpedgiz, 1937, pp. 168–84.

[98] Zhirmunskii, B. M. "Pushkin i zapadnye literatury," *Pushkin: Vremennik Pushkinskoi komissii*, 3 (1937): 66–102.

Critical Studies of Pushkin's Prose Fiction

[99] Belinskii, V. G. "Sochineniia Aleksandra Pushkina: Stat'ia odinnadtsataia i posledniaia." In Belinskii, *Polnoe sobranie sochinenii*. Vol. 7. Moscow: Akademiia Nauk SSSR, 1953, pp. 576–79. Originally published in *Otechestvennye zapiski*, 48, No. 10 (1846).

[100] Briusov, V. Ia. "Neokonchennye povesti iz russkoi zhizni." In [1], listed above, Vol. 4, pp. 264–70.

[101] Chicherin, A. V. "Pushkin, Merime, Stendal' (O stilisticheskikh sootvetstviiakh)," *Pushkin: Issledovaniia i materialy*, 7 (1974): 142–50.

[102] ———. "Pushkinskie zamysli prozaicheskogo romana." In Chicherin, *Vozniknovenie romana-epopei*. Moscow: Sovetskii pisatel', 1958, pp. 66–119.

[103] ———. "Put' Pushkina k prozaicheskomu romanu." In Chicherin, *Idei i stil'*. Moscow: Sovetskii pisatel', 1965, pp. 92–142.

[104] ———. "Ritm i stil' pushkinskoi prozy." In Chicherin, *Ritm obraza: Stilisticheskie problemy*. Moscow: Sovetskii pisatel', 1973, pp. 210–23.

[105] ———. "Spornye voprosy stilia pushkinskoi prozy," *Voprosy russkoi literatury*, 1966, No. 1: 7–13.

[106] Drobysheva, L. Ia. "Rol' inversii v proze Pushkina," *Issledovaniia po russkomu iazyku. Uchenye zapiski Omskogo gos. ped. inst-a im. A. M. Gor'kogo*, Vol. 76, 1973. Omskii gos. ped. inst., 1973, pp. 45–50.

[107] Druzin, V. "Proza Pushkina," *Rezets*, 1929, No. 31: 13, No. 33: 12, No. 35: 13–14.

[108] Eikhenbaum, B. M. "Put' Pushkina k proze." In N. V. Iakovlev, ed., *Pushkinskii sbornik pamiati Professora S. A. Vengerova*. Moscow: Gos. izd., 1923, pp. 59–74.

[109] Eshtein, A. "Proza Pushkina v russkoi kritike," *Literaturnyi sovremennik*, 1936, No. 3: 183–205.

[110] Ferrell, J. O. "The Syntax of the Gerund and Participle in Pushkin's Prose Works." Ann Arbor, Mich.: Univ. Microfilms, 1949.

[111] Fokht, U. "Proza Pushkina v razvitii russkoi literatury." In D. D. Blagoi and V. Ia. Kirpotin, eds., *Pushkin rodonachal'nik novoi russkoi literatury: Sbornik nauchno-issledovatel'skikh rabot*. Moscow: Akademiia Nauk SSSR, 1941, pp. 435–70.

[112] Gladkova, E. "Prozaicheskie nabroski Pushkina iz zhizni 'sveta,'" *Pushkin: Vremennik Pushkinskoi komissii*, 6 (1941): 305–22.

[113] Greene, Militsa. "Pushkin and Sir Walter Scott," *Forum for Modern Language Studies*, 1, No. 3 (1965): 207–15.

[114] Iakubovich, D. "Pushkin v rabote nad prozoi," *Literaturnaia ucheba*, 1930, No. 4: 46–64.

[115] Izmailov, N. V. "Khudozhestvennaia proza." In B. P. Gorodetskii et al., eds., *Pushkin: Itogi i problemy izucheniia*. Moscow: Nauka, 1966, pp. 460–85.

[116] Kozmin, N. "Pushkin-prozaik i frantsuzskoe ostroslovie XVIII veka (Shamfor, Rivarol', Riul'er)," *Izvestiia po russkomu iazyku i slovesnosti AN SSSR*, 1, No. 2 (1928): 536–58.

[117] Lednicki, Wacław. "The Prose of Pushkin," *Slavonic and East European Review*, 28, Nos. 70 (1949): 105–22, and 71 (1950): 377–91.

[118] Lerner, N. O. *Proza Pushkina*. 2d ed. Petrograd: Kniga, 1923.

[119] Lezhnev, A. Z. *Proza Pushkina*. 2d ed. Moscow: Khudozhestvennaia literatura, 1966.

[120] Loks, K. "Problema stilia v khudozhestvennoi proze." In V. Ia. Briusov, ed., *Problemy poetiki*. Moscow: Zemlia i fabrika, 1925, pp. 45–60.

[121] Lopatto, M. D. "Povesti Pushkina: Opyt vvedeniia v teoriiu prozy." In S. A. Vengerov, ed., *Pushkinist: Istoriko-literaturnyi sbornik*. Vol. 3. Petrograd: Tip. A. F. Dresslera, 1918, pp. 1–163.

[122] Mikhailov, A. D. "Pushkin i Stendal'." In K. V. Pigarev et al., eds., *Iskusstvo slova: Sbornik statei k 80-letiiu Chlena-korrespondenta AN SSSR D. D. Blagogo*. Moscow: Nauka, 1973, pp. 125–34.

[123] Odinokov, V. G. "Pushkin i prozaicheskii roman." In Odinokov, *Problemy poetiki i tipologii russkogo romana XIX veka*. Novosibirsk: Nauka, 1971, pp. 35–60.

[124] Odintsov, V. V. "Dialog u Pushkina," *Izvestiia Akademii Nauk SSSR, Seriia literatury i iazyka*, 25, No. 5 (1966): 410–17.

[125] ———. "Printsipy postroeniia pushkinskogo dialoga," *Izvestiia Akademii Nauk SSSR, Seriia literatury i iazyka*, 33, No. 3 (1974): 275–78.

[126] Patrick, George Z. "Pushkin's Prose Writings." In Samuel H. Cross and Ernest J. Simmons, eds., *Centennial Essays for Pushkin*. New York: Russell & Russell, 1937, pp. 119–30.

[127] Pereverzev, V. F. "Pushkin v bor'be s russkim 'plutovskim romanom,'" *Pushkin: Vremennik Pushkinskoi komissii*, 1 (1936): 164–88.

[128] Petrov, S. M. *Istoricheskii roman A. S. Pushkina*. Moscow: Akademiia Nauk SSSR, 1953.

[129] Pospelov, I. "Iz nabliudenii nad iazykom pushkinskoi prozy," *Knizhnye novosti*, 1936, No. 10: 18–24.

[130] Pospelov, N. S. "Iz nabliudenii nad sintaksisom iazyka Pushkina (Bessoiuznye sochetaniia predlozhenii v pushkinskoi proze)," *Materialy i issledovaniia po istorii russkogo literaturnogo iazyka*, Institut iazykoznaniia, 3 (1953): 176–99.

[131] Prokopovich, E. N. "Iz nabliudenii nad sintaksisom vremen v khudozhestvennoi proze A. S. Pushkina," *Russkii iazyk: Sbor-

nik trudov, Moskovskii gos. ped. inst. im. V. I. Lenina, 1975, pp. 252–58.

[132] Salfeld, Hans-Eduard. "Die Erzähltechnik Puschkins unter motivationspsychologischen Geschichtpunkten gesehen," *Die Welt der Slaven*, 18 (1973): 308–16.

[133] Seleznev, Iu. "Proza Pushkina i razvitie russkoi literatury (K poetike siuzheta)." In S. Mashinskii, ed., *V mire Pushkina: Sbornik statei*. Moscow: Sovetskii pisatel', 1974, pp. 413–46.

[134] Shklovskii, V. "A. S. Pushkin." In Shklovskii, *Zametki o proze russkikh klassikov*. 2d ed. Moscow: Sovetskii pisatel', 1955, pp. 18–86.

[135] ———. "Pushkin's Prose." In *Pushkin: A Collection of Articles and Essays*. Moscow: The USSR Society for Cultural Relations with Foreign Countries, 1939, pp. 106–15.

[136] ———. *Zametki o proze Pushkina*. Moscow: Sovetskii pisatel', 1937.

[137] Sidiakov, L. S. "*Evgenii Onegin* i nezavershennaia proza Pushkina 1828–1830 godov (Kharaktery i situatsii)." In E. A. Maimin et al., eds., *Problemy pushkinovedeniia: Sbornik nauchnykh trudov*. Leningrad: Leningradskii gos. ped. inst. im. A. I. Gertsena, 1975, pp. 28–39.

[138] ———. *Khudozhestvennaia proza A. S. Pushkina*. Riga: Latviiskii gos. univ. im. P. Stuchki, 1973.

[139] ———. "Nabliudeniia nad slovoupotrebleniem Pushkina ('Proza' i 'poeziia')," *Pushkin i ego sovremenniki*, Uchenye zapiski Leningradskogo gos. ped. inst.-a im. A. I. Gertsena, 434 (1970): 125–34.

[140] ———. "Nachal'nyi etap formirovaniia pushkinskoi prozy," *Pushkinskii sbornik*, Uchenye zapiski Latviiskogo gos. univ.-a im. P. Stuchki, 106 (1968): 5–23.

[141] ———. "Publitsistika v khudozhestvennoi proze Pushkina (Nezavershennye proizvedeniia rubezha 1830-kh godov i opyt *Evgeniia Onegina*)," *Pushkinskii sbornik*. Uchenye zapiski Leningradskogo gos. ped. inst.-a im. A. I. Gertsena, 1973, pp. 42–58.

[142] ———. "Pushkin i razvitie russkoi povesti v nachale 30-kh godov XIX veka," *Pushkin: Issledovaniia i materialy*, 3 (1960): 193–217.

[143] ———. "Pushkinskaia proza i zadachi ee izucheniia," *Izvestiia Akademii Nauk SSSR, Seriia literatury i iazyka*, 34, No. 5 (1975): 418–25.

[144] Stenbock-Fermor, Elisabeth. "Some Neglected Features of the Epigraphs in *The Captain's Daughter* and Other Stories of Puškin," *International Journal of Slavic Linguistics and Poetics*, 8 (1964): 110–23.

[145] Stepanov, N. L. *Proza Pushkina*. Moscow: Akademiia Nauk SSSR, 1962.

[146] Vinokur, G. B. "Pushkin-prozaik." In Vinokur, *Kul'tura iazyka:*

Ocherki lingvisticheskoi tekhnologii. Moscow: Rabotnik prosveshcheniia, 1925, pp. 179–88.

[147] Voskresenskii, E. *Povesti Pushkina. (Opyt razbora).* Yaroslavl: Tip. Gubernskoi zemskoi upravy, 1888.

[148] Zvoznikov, A. A. "Issledovanie prozy Pushkina v poslednie gody," *Russkaia literatura,* 1975, No. 1: 187–202.

Critical Studies of Individual Prose Works

Arap Petra Velikogo (The Blackamoor of Peter the Great; unfinished)

[149] Abramovich, S. L. "K voprosu o stanovlenii povestvovatel'noi prozy Pushkina (Pochemu ostalsia nezavershennym *Arap Petra Velikogo),*" *Russkaia literatura,* 17, No. 2 (1974): 54–73.

[150] Akhmatova, A. A. "*Adol'f* Benzhamena Konstana v tvorchestve Pushkina," *Pushkin: Vremennik Pushkinskoi komissii,* 1 (1936): 91–114.

[151] Auslender, S. "*Arap Petra Velikogo.*" In [1], listed above, Vol. 4, pp. 104–12.

[152] Belkin, D. I. "*Arap Petra Velikogo* Pushkina i *Persidskie pis'ma* Montesk'e,*" Literaturnye sviazi i traditsii,* Uchenye zapiski Gor'kovskogo gos. univ.-a im. N. I. Lobachevskogo, 160 (1973): 122–30.

[153] ———. "Zametki o pushkinskoi traktovke natsional'nogo i obshchechelovecheskogo v obraze afrikantsa Ibragima Gannibala," *Literaturnye sviazi i traditsii,* No. 3: *Mezhvuzovskii sbornik,* Gor'kovskii gos. univ. im. N. I. Lobachevskogo, 1972, pp. 52–63.

[154] Bogorodskii, B. L. "O iazyke i stile romana A. S. Pushkina *Arap Petra Velikogo,*" *Uchenye zapiski Leningradskogo gos. ped. inst.-a im. A. I. Gertsena,* Kafedra russkogo iazyka, 122 (1956): 201–39.

[155] Iakubovich, D. "*Arap Petra Velikogo,*" *Pushkin: Issledovaniia i materialy,* 9 (1979): 261–93.

[156] Khodasevich, V. F. "Praded i pravnuk." In Khodasevich, *O Pushkine.* Berlin: Petropolis Verlag, 1937, pp. 166–76.

[157] Lapkina, G. A. "K istorii sozdaniia *Arapa Petra Velikogo,*" *Pushkin: Issledovaniia i materialy,* 2 (1958): 293–309.

[158] ———. "Roman A. S. Pushkina *Arap Petra Velikogo.*" Avtoreferat dissertatsii na soiskanie uchenoi stepeni kandidata filologicheskikh nauk, Leningradskii univ., 1952.

[159] Lerner, N. O. "Zametki o Pushkine (Dva epigrafa k *Arapu Petra Velkogo),*" *Pushkin i ego sovremenniki,* 16 (1913): 19–76.

[160] Oksman, Iu. G. "Mnimye stroki Pushkina." In B. L. Modzalevskii et al., eds., *Atenei: Istoriko-literaturnyi vremennik.* Vol. 1–2. Leningrad: Atenei, 1924, pp. 164–66.

[161] Tuzova, L. "Portret v romane A. S. Pushkina *Arap Petra Veli-*

kogo." Trudy Kirgizskogo gos. univ.-a, Filologicheskie nauki, Vol. 21, Seriia "Voprosy poetiki," No. 3 (1975): 11–19.

"Dafna i Dabizha, moldavskoe predanie 1663 goda" ("Dafna and Dabija, a Moldavian Legend of 1663"; lost draft)

[162] Bogach, G. "Dva istoricheskikh moldavskikh predaniia." In Bogach, *Pushkin i moldavskii fol'klor.* 2d rev. ed. Kishinev: Kartia Moldoveniaske, 1967, pp. 131–80.

[163] Dvoichenko-Markoff, E. "Puškin and the Rumanian Historical Legend," *American Slavic and East European Review,* 7 (1948): 144–49.

[164] Dvoichenko-Markova, E. M. "Pushkin i narodnoe tvorchestvo Moldavii i Valakhii." In Dvoichenko-Markova, *Russko-rumynskie literaturnye sviazi v pervoi polovine XIX veka.* Moscow: Nauka, 1966, pp. 54–58.

[165] Liprandi, I. P. "Iz dnevnika i vospominanii," *Russkii arkhiv,* 1866, No. 4: 1410–11.

[166] Tomashevskii, B. V. "Nezavershennye kishinevskie zamysli Pushkina." In M. P. Alekseev, ed., *Pushkin: Issledovaniia i materialy.* Trudy 3-ei vsesoiuznoi pushkinskoi konferentsii. Moscow: Akademiia Nauk SSSR, 1953, pp. 171–212.

[167] Trubetskoi, B. *Pushkin v Moldavii.* Kishinev: Kartia Moldoveniaske, 1976, pp. 145–46.

[168] Tsiavlovskii, M., and T. Tsiavlovskaia. "Dnevnik Dolgorukova," *Zven'ia,* 9 (1951): 5–20.

Dubrovskii (unfinished)

[169] Berezin, B. M. "Rabota nad iazykom povesti A. S. Pushkina *Dubrovskii* v srednei shkole," *Russkii iazyk v shkole,* 1949, No. 3: 45–55.

[170] Eikhenbaum, B. "Pushkin i Lermontov," *Smena,* 1937, No. 2: 20.

[171] Engel', S. "Rasskaz o Troekurove," *Prometei: Istoriko-biograficheskii al'manakh serii "Zhizn' zamechatel'nykh liudei,"* 10 (1974): 106–13.

[172] Gukovskii, G. A. "*Dubrovskii* Pushkina." In E. F. Napravnik, *Dubrovskii.* Leningrad: Gos. ordena Lenina Akademicheskii teatr opery i baleta im. S. M. Kirova, 1948, pp. 5–16.

[173] Iakubovich, D. "*Dubrovskii.*" In A. S. Pushkin, *Dubrovskii.* Ed. D. Iakubovich. Leningrad: Khudozhestvennaia literatura, 1936, pp. 125–46.

[174] ———. "Nezavershennyi roman Pushkina (*Dubrovskii*)." In I. Oksenov, ed., *Pushkin: 1833 god.* Leningrad: Pushkinskoe obshchestvo, 1933, pp. 33–44.

[175] Iatsimirskii, A. "*Dubrovskii.*" In [1], listed above, Vol. 4, pp. 271–86.

[176] Kaletskii, P. "Ot *Dubrovskogo* k *Kapitanskoi dochke*," *Literaturnyi sovremennik*, 1937, No. 1: 148–68.

[177] Kubikov, I. N. "Obshchestvennyi smysl povesti *Dubrovskii*." In N. K. Piksanov, ed., *Pushkin: Sbornik vtoroi*. Moscow: Gos. izd., 1930, pp. 81–109.

[178] Lednicki, Wacław. "Bits of 'Table Talk' on Pushkin. II: *The Nest of Gentlefolk* and 'The Poetry of Marriage and the Hearth,'" *American Slavic and East European Review*, 5 (1946): 72–98. Reprinted in [53], listed above.

[179] Lerner, N. O. "Pushkinologicheskie etiudy. XXI: O *Dubrovskom*," *Zven'ia*, 5 (1935): 182–86.

[180] ———. "Zametki o Pushkine: I. Anna Rodionovna i niania Dubrovskogo," *Pushkin i ego sovremenniki*, 7 (1908): 68–78.

[181] Petrunina, N. N. "Pushkin na puti k romanu v proze: *Dubrovskii*," *Pushkin: Issledovaniia i materialy*, 9 (1979): 141–67.

[182] Predtechenskaia, E. A. "Rabota A. S. Pushkina nad iazykom povesti *Dubrovskii*." Avtoreferat dissertatsii, predstavlennoi na soiskanie uchenoi stepeni kandidata filologicheskikh nauk, Saratovskii gos. univ., 1955.

[183] Rozova, Z. G. "*Dubrovskii* Pushkina i *Novaia Eloiza* Russo," *Voprosy russkoi literatury*, 1971, No. 18: 64–69.

[184] Shliapkin, I. A. "Melochi o Pushkine. III: *Dubrovskii* Pushkina," *Pushkin i ego sovremenniki*, 16 (1913): 105–7.

[185] Soboleva, T. P. *Povest' A. S. Pushkina 'Dubrovskii.'* Moscow: Akademiia Pedagogicheskikh Nauk RSFSR, 1963.

[186] Stepunin, I. "Prototip pushkinskogo Dubrovskogo," *Neman*, 1968, No. 8: 180–84.

[187] Tomashevskii, B. V. "Pushkin i romany frantsuzskikh romantikov (K risunkam Pushkina)," *Literaturnoe nasledstvo*, 16–18 (1934): 947–60.

[188] ———. "Sud'ba Dubrovskogo," *Kniga i revoliutsiia*, 1923, No. 11–12: 9–12.

[189] Zborovets, I. V. "*Dubrovskii* i *Gai Mennering* V. Skotta," *Vremennik Pushkinskoi komissii*, 1974 (published 1977): 131–36.

"Duka, moldavskoe predanie XVII veka" ("Duca, a Moldavian Legend of the 17th Century"; lost draft). *See entries under* "Dafna i Dabizha."

Egipetskie nochi (*Egyptian Nights*; unfinished)

[190] Akhmatova, A. A. "Neizdannye zametki Anny Akhmatovoi o Pushkine" (comp. and ed. E. G. Gershtein), *Voprosy literatury*, 1970, No. 1: 176–87.

[191] Bagdasariants, Ia. "K istorii teksta *Egipetskikh nochei*." In M. P. Alekseev, ed., *Pushkin: Stat'i i materialy*. Vol. 2. Odessa: Odesskii dom uchenykh, 1926, pp. 88–91.

[192] Bondi, S. M. "K istorii sozdaniia *Egipetskikh nochei*." In Bondi, *Novye stranitsy Pushkina: Stikhi, proza, pis'ma*. Moscow: Mir, 1931, pp. 148–205.

[193] Briusov, V. Ia. "*Egipetskie nochi*." In Briusov, *Moi Pushkin*. Ed. N. Ķ. Piksanov. Moscow: Gos. izd., 1929, pp. 107–18.

[194] Čirpak-Rozdina, E. "*Egipetskie nochi* A. S. Pushkina," *Studia Slavica*, 19 (1973): 373–90.

[195] Dostoevskii, F. M. "Otvet *Russkomu vestniku*." In Dostoevskii, *Polnoe sobranie khudozhestvennykh proizvedenii*, Vol. 13. Moscow: Gos. izd., 1930, pp. 198–220. Originally published in *Vremia*, May 1861.

[196] Garibian, D. A. "Nekotorye stilisticheskie nabliudeniia nad tekstom *Egipetskikh nochei* Pushkina i Briusova." In K. V. Aivazian et al., eds., *Briusovskie chteniia 1962 goda*. Erevan: Armianskoe gos. izd., 1963, pp. 232–45.

[197] Ginzburg, L. *O lirike*. Moscow: Sovetskii pisatel', 1964, pp. 202–4.

[198] Gofman, M. L. (Modeste Hofmann) '*Egipetskie nochi*' s polnym tekstom improvizatsii ital'iantsa, s novoi chetvertoi glavoi— Pushkina, i s Prilozheniem (zakliuchitel'naia piataia glava). Paris: S. Lifar, 1935.

[199] Gorlin, M. "*Noce Egipskie* (Kompozycja i geneza)," *Etudes littéraires et historiques*, Institut d'Etudes Slaves de l'Université de Paris, 1957, pp. 139–56.

[200] Gorokhova, R. M. "K tekstu *Egipetskikh nochei*," *Vremennik Pushkinskoi komissii*, 1966 (published 1969): 49–50.

[201] Iakovlev, N. V. "Iz razyskanii o literaturnykh istochnikakh v tvorchestve Pushkina. III: Pushkin i Kol'ridzh." In Iakovlev, ed., *Pushkin v mirovoi literature*. Leningrad: Gos. izd., 1926, pp. 137–45.

[202] Kazanovich, E. "K istochnikam *Egipetskikh nochei*," *Zven'ia*, 3–4 (1934): 187–204.

[203] Kirpotin, V. "Dostoevskii o *Egipetskikh nochakh* Pushkina," *Voprosy literatury*, 1962, No. 11: 112–21.

[204] Komarovich, V. L. "Dostoevskii i *Egipetskie nochi* Pushkina," *Pushkin i ego sovremenniki*, 29–30 (1918): 36–48.

[205] Lednicki, Wacław. "Mickiewicz's Stay in Russia and His Friendship with Pushkin." In Lednicki, ed., *Adam Mickiewicz in World Literature: A Symposium*. Berkeley: Univ. of California Press, 1956, pp. 13–104.

[206] ———. "Pochemu Pushkin ne okonchil *Egipetskie nochi*?," *Novyi zhurnal*, 90 (1968): 244–55.

[207] Malein, A. "Pushkin, Avrelii Viktor i Tatsit." In N. V. Iakovlev, ed., *Pushkin v mirovoi literature*. Leningrad: Gos. izd., 1926, pp. 11–12.

[208] Matlaw, Ralph E. "Poetry and the Poet in Romantic Society as

Reflected in Pushkin's *Egyptian Nights*," *Slavonic and East European Review*, 33, No. 8 (1954): 102–19.

[209] Novitskii, P. I. "*Egipetskie nochi* Pushkina." In A. S. Pushkin, *Egipetskie nochi*. Leningrad: Academia, 1927, pp. 37–81.

[210] Nusinov, I. "*Antonii i Kleopatra* Shekspira i *Egipetskie nochi* Pushkina." In Nusinov, *Pushkin i mirovaia literatura*. Moscow: Sovetskii pisatel', 1941, pp. 285–348.

[211] O'Bell, Leslie C. "The Problematics of Puškin's *Egipetskie noči* in the Creative History of His Work." Ph.D. dissertation, Harvard Univ., 1978.

[212] Odinokov, V. G. "*Egipetskie nochi* A. S. Pushkina v protsesse 'ukrupneniia' zhanra," *Khudozhestvennoe tvorchestvo i literaturnyi protsess*, Izd. Tomskogo Univ.-a, 1 (1976): 26–33.

[213] Ostrovskaia, M. "Nepriurochennyi otryvok *Egipetskikh nochei* Pushkina," *Vestnik literatury*, 1921, No. 9: 7.

[214] Petrunina, N. N. "*Egipetskie nochi* i russkaia povest' 1830-kh godov," *Pushkin: Issledovaniia i materialy*, 8 (1978): 22–50.

[215] Rzhevsky, L. "Strukturnaia tema *Egipetskikh nochei* A. Pushkina." In Andrej Kodjak and Kiril Taranovsky, eds., *Alexander Puškin: A Symposium on the 175th Anniversary of His Birth*. New York: New York Univ. Press, 1976, pp. 126–34.

[216] Shervinskii, S. V. "Iz *Egipetskikh nochei*." In Shervinskii *Ritm i smysl: K izucheniiu poetiki Pushkina*. Moscow: Akademiia Nauk SSSR, 1961, pp. 137–55.

[217] Sidiakov, L. S. "K izucheniiu *Egipetskikh nochei*," *Pushkin: Issledovaniia i materialy*, 4 (1962): 173–82.

[218] Stolpianskii, P. N. "Bibliograficheskie primechaniia k nekotorym proizvedeniiam Pushkina," *Pushkin i ego sovremenniki*, 17–18 (1913): 35–44.

[219] Toibin, I. M. "*Egipetskie nochi* i nekotorye voprosy tvorchestva Pushkina v 1830-kh godakh," *Uchenye zapiski Orlovskogo ped. inst.-a*, 30 (1966): 122–24.

[220] Val'be, B. "*Egipetskie nochi*," *Zvezda*, 1937, No. 3: 143–57.

[221] Vitberg, F.A. "Bibliograficheskaia zametka," *Severnyi vestnik*, 1895, No. 10: 316–17.

[222] Voitolovskii, L. "O Pushkine," *Zvezda*, 1927, No. 5: 141–51.

[223] Weintraub, Wiktor. "The Problem of Improvisation in Romantic Literature," *Comparative Literature*, 16, No. 2 (1964): 119–37.

[224] Zhirmunskii, V. "*Egipetskie nochi* Valeriia Briusova." In Zhirmunskii, *Valerii Briusov i nasledie Pushkina*. Petrograd: El'zevir, 1922, pp. 52–86.

Fatam (lost fragment)

[225] Alekseev, M. P., ed. *Literaturnyi arkhiv: Materialy po istorii literatury i obshchestvennogo dvizheniia*. Vol. 3. Moscow: Akademiia Nauk SSSR, 1951, pp. 11–12.

[226] Gaevskii, V. P. "Pushkin v litsee i litseiskie ego stikhotvoreniia," *Sovremennik*, 97, No. 7 (1863): 155–58.

[227] Glebov, G. S. "Utrachennaia skazka Pushkina," *Pushkin: Vremennik Pushkinskoi komissii*, 4–5 (1939): 485–87.

"Gosti s"ezzhalis' na dachu" ("The Guests Were Arriving at the Dacha"; fragment)

[228] Gornaia, V. "Iz nabliudenii nad stilem romana *Anna Karenina*: O pushkinskikh traditsiiakh v romane." In D. D. Blagoi et al., eds., *Tolstoi-khudozhnik: Sbornik statei*. Moscow: Akademiia Nauk SSSR, 1961, pp. 181–206.

[229] Vainshtein, A. L., and F. P. Pavlova. "K istorii povesti Pushkina 'Gosti s"ezzhalis' na dachu,'" *Vremennik Pushkinskoi komissii*, 1966 (published 1969): 36–43.

[230] Vodovozov, N. V. "Neokonchennaia povest' A. S. Pushkina," *Uchenye zapiski Moskovskogo gos. ped. inst.-a im. V. P. Potemkina*, 94, No. 8 (1959): 71–104.

Istoriia sela Goriukhina (*A History of the Village of Goriukhino*; unfinished)

[231] Akulova, E. A. "Nabliudeniia nad iazykom i stilem *Istoriia sela Goriukhina* A. S. Pushkina," *Uchenye zapiski kafedry russkogo iazyka Leningradskogo gos. ped. inst.-a im. A. I. Gertsena*, 76 (1949): 203–10.

[232] Alekseev, M. P. "K *Istorii sela Goriukhina*." In Alekseev, ed., *Pushkin: Stat'i i materialy*. Vol. 2. Odessa: Odesskii dom uchenykh, 1926, pp. 70–87.

[233] Gritsai, Iu. F. "*Istoriia sela Goriukhina* A. S. Pushkina—literaturnyi prototip *Istorii odnogo goroda* M. E. Saltykova-Shchedrina," *Voprosy russkoi literatury*, 1973, No. 1: 19–26.

[234] Gukasova, A. G. "*Istoriia sela Goriukhina* Pushkina," *Uchenye zapiski Moskovskogo gos. ped. inst.-a im. V. I. Lenina*, 70, No. 4 (1954): 63–110.

[235] Iskoz, A. [Dolinin]. "*Istoriia sela Goriukhina*." In [1], listed above, Vol. 4, pp. 237–46.

[236] Sipovskii, V. V. "K literaturnoi istorii *Istorii sela Goriukhina*," *Pushkin i ego sovremenniki*, 4 (1906): 47–58.

[237] Timmer, Charles B. "The History of a History: A. S. Puškin and *The History of the Village of Gorjuchino*," *Russian Literature*, 1 (1971): 113–31.

[238] Vengerov, S. A. "Goriukhino, a ne Gorokhino." In [1], listed above, Vol. 4, p. 226.

Kapitanskaia dochka (*The Captain's Daughter*)

[239] Akimova, T. M. "Narodnye udalye pesni v tvorchestve A. S. Pushkina," *Iz istorii russkoi i zarubezhnoi literatury*, Mordovskii gos. univ. imeni N. P. Ogareva, 2 (1968): 3–25.

[240] Aleksandrov, V. "Pugachev (Narodnost' i realizm Pushkina)." In Aleksandrov, *Liudi i knigi*. Moscow: Sovetskii pisatel', 1956, pp. 5–40.

[241] Anderson, Roger B. "A Study of Petr Grinev as the Hero of Pushkin's *Kapitanskaia dochka*," *Canadian Slavic Studies*, 5 (1971): 477–86.

[242] Astaf'eva, O. V. "Obraz Pugacheva v povesti Pushkina *Kapitanskaia dochka*," *Uchenye zapiski Taganrogskogo ped. inst.-a*, 1 (1956): 113–30.

[243] Beletskii, A. I. "K istorii sozdaniia *Kapitanskoi dochki*," *Pushkin i ego sovremenniki*, 38–39 (1930): 191–201.

[244] Besançon, Alain. *Le Tsarévitch immolé: La Symbolique de la loi dans la culture russe*. Paris: Plon, 1967, pp. 161–81.

[245] Blagoi, D. D. "*Kapitanskaia dochka*." In Blagoi, *Ot Kantemira do nashikh dnei*. Vol. 2. Moscow: Khudozhestvennaia literatura, 1973, pp. 213–31.

[246] Blinova, E. M. "Ustnoe narodnoe tvorchestvo v proizvedeniiakh Pushkina o Pugacheve i fol'klor iuzhnogo Urala." In A. S. Pushkin, *Kapitanskaia dochka; Istoriia Pugacheva*. Cheliabinsk: Oblastnoe izd., 1937, pp. 312–20.

[247] Blok, G. "Put' v Berdu (Pushkin i Shvanvichi)," *Zvezda*, 1940, No. 10: 208–17, and No. 11: 139–49.

[248] Borovoi, S. "O prototipe odnogo iz geroev *Kapitanskoi dochki*," *Russkaia literatura*, 1966, No. 2: 194–95.

[249] Borovskii, Ia. M. "K tekstu *Kapitanskoi dochki*." In N. A. Meshcherskii et al., eds., *Voprosy teorii i istorii iazyka: Sbornik statei, posviashchennyi pamiati B. A. Larina*. Leningrad: Leningradskii univ., 1969, p. 39.

[250] Brang, Peter. *Puškin und Krjukov: Zur Entstehungsgeschichte der 'Kapitanskaja dočka.'* Berlin: Otto Harrassowitz, 1957.

[251] Cherniaev, N. I. *'Kapitanskaia dochka' Pushkina: Istoriko-kriticheskii etiud*. Moscow: Universitetskaia tip., 1897.

[252] Chernyshev, V. "Zametka k Pushkinu (Proiskhozhdenie pesenki Grineva 'Mysl' liubovnu istrebliaia')," *Pushkin i ego sovremenniki*, 2 (1904): 25–26.

[253] Daichik, A. B. "Printsipy istorizma v povesti A. S. Pushkina *Kapitanskaia dochka*," *Aktual'nye voprosy sovremennoi nauki (Nekotorye voprosy gumanitarnykh nauk)*, Dnepropetrovskii gos. univ. im. 300-letiia vossoedineniia Ukrainy s Rossiei, 2 (1972): 81–88.

[254] Davie, Donald. "*The Captain's Daughter*: Pushkin's Prose and Russian Realism." In Davie, *The Heyday of Sir Walter Scott*. New York: Barnes & Noble, 1961, pp. 7–20.

[255] Emerson, Caryl. "Grinev's Dream: *The Captain's Daughter* and a Father's Blessing," *Slavic Review*, 40, No. 1 (1981): 60–76.

[256] Fokin, N. I. "K istorii sozdaniia *Kapitanskoi dochki* A. S. Push-

kina," *Uchenye zapiski Ural'skogo ped. inst.-a,* 4, No. 3 (1957): 97–124.

[257] ———. "K voprosu ob avtore 'Rasskaza moei babushki' A. K.," *Uchenye zapiski Leningradskogo universiteta,* Vol. 261, Seriia filologicheskikh nauk, No. 49: Russkaia literatura XIX veka (1958): 155–63.

[258] Gershenzon, M. O. "Sny Pushkina." In Gershenzon, *Stat'i o Pushkine.* Moscow: Academia, 1926, pp. 99–101.

[259] Giliarova, E. S. "Iz nabliudenii nad ritmom pushkinskoi prozy," *Naukovi zapiski Kievskogo derzh. univ-a im. T. G. Shevchenka,* Vol. 12, filologicheskii sbornik No. 5 (1953): 103–13.

[260] Gillel'son, M. I., and I. B. Mushina. *Povest' A. S. Pushkina 'Kapitanskaia dochka': Kommentarii.* Leningrad: Prosveshchenie, 1977.

[261] Gofman, M. L. "*Kapitanskaia dochka.*" In [1], listed above, Vol. 4, pp. 353–78.

[262] Gribushin, I. I. "O pesniakh v *Kapitanskoi dochke,*" *Vremennik Pushkinskoi komissii,* 1975 (published 1979): 85–89.

[263] Guliaev, V. G. "K voprosu ob istochnikakh *Kapitanskoi dochki,*" *Pushkin: Vremennik Pushkinskoi komissii,* 4–5 (1939): 198–211.

[264] Iakovlev, N. V. "K literaturnoi istorii *Kapitanskoi dochki,*" *Pushkin: Vremennik Pushkinskoi komissii,* 4–5 (1939): 487–88.

[265] Iakubovich, D. "*Kapitanskaia dochka* i romany Val'ter Skotta," *Pushkin: Vremennik Pushkinskoi komissii,* 4–5 (1939): 165–97.

[266] ———. "Ob epigrafakh k *Kapitanskoi dochke,*" *Uchenye zapiski Leningradskogo ped. inst.-a im. A. I. Gertsena,* 76 (1949): 111–35.

[267] Izmailov, N. V. "*Kapitanskaia dochka.*" In G. M. Fridlender, ed., *Istoriia russkogo romana.* Vol. 1. Moscow: Akademiia Nauk SSSR, 1962, pp. 180–202.

[268] ———. "Orenburgskie materialy Pushkina dlia *Istorii Pugacheva* i *Kapitanskoi dochki.*" In Izmailov, *Ocherki tvorchestva Pushkina.* Leningrad: Nauka, 1975, pp. 270–302.

[269] Kaletskii, P. "Ot *Dubrovskogo* k *Kapitanskoi dochke,*" *Literaturnyi sovremennik,* 1937, No. 1: 148–68.

[270] Kotel'nikova, L. M. "Izuchaia *Kapitanskuiu dochku,*" *Kazan' v istorii russkoi literatury,* Kazanskii gos. ped. inst., 3 (1972): 109–15.

[271] Kuleshov, V. I. *Literaturnye sviazi Rossii i Zapadnoi Evropy v XIX veke.* Moscow: Izd. Moskovskogo univ-a, 1965, pp. 198–205.

[272] Kupreianova, E. N. *'Kapitanskaia dochka' A. S. Pushkina: Materialy dlia chtenii i lektsii.* Leningrad: Pushkinskoe obshchestvo, 1947.

[273] Lotman, Iu. "Ideinaia struktura *Kapitanskoi dochki.*" In M. Efimov et al., eds., *Pushkinskii sbornik.* Pskov: Pskovskii gos. ped. inst. im. S. M. Kirova, 1962, pp. 3–20.

[274] Lukács, Georg. *The Historical Novel*. Tr. Hannah and Stanley Mitchell. London: Merlin Press, 1962, pp. 72–73.
[275] Makogonenko, G. P. *'Kapitanskaia dochka' A. S. Pushkina*. Leningrad: Khudozhestvennaia literatura, 1977.
[276] Mikkelson, Gerald E. "The Mythopoetic Element in Pushkin's Historical Novel *The Captain's Daughter*," *Canadian-American Slavic Studies*, 7 (1973): 296–313.
[277] Mrevlishvili, T. N. "Rechevaia kharakteristika personazhei povesti A. S. Pushkina *Kapitanskaia dochka*." In Mrevlishvili, *O iazyke russkikh pisatelei*. Tbilisi: Izd. Tbilisskogo univ.-a, 1972, pp. 36–49.
[278] Nedosekin, V. I. "Pushkinskie assotsiatsii pri izuchenii arkhivnogo materiala v kurse literaturnogo kraevedeniia (K voprosu o prototipe obraza Grineva iz *Kapitanskoi dochki* A. S. Pushkina)," *Izvestiia Voronezhskogo gos. ped. inst.-a*, 72 (1968): 37–44.
[279] Neiman, B. V. "Couleur locale v *Kapitanskoi dochke* (K voprosu o vliianii Val'ter-Skotta)." In N. K. Piksanov et al., eds., *Pamiati P. N. Sakulina: Sbornik statei*. Moscow: Kooperativnoe izd. pisatelei, Nikitinskie subbotniki, 1931, pp. 147–55.
[280] ———. "*Kapitanskaia dochka* Pushkina i romany Val'ter-Skotta," *Sbornik otdeleniia russkogo iazyka i slovesnosti AN SSSR*, 101, No. 3 (1928): 440–43.
[281] Nezelenov, A. "Kak i pochemu propushchena odna glava iz povesti *Kapitanskaia dochka*," *Novoe vremia*, No. 1744 (1881): 2–3.
[282] Odintsov, V. "Semanticheskie arkhaizmy v *Kapitanskoi dochke* A. S. Pushkina," *Russkii iazyk v natsional'noi shkole*, 1967, No. 6: 16–18.
[283] Oksman, Iu. G. "Primechaniia k tekstu romana *Kapitanskaia dochka*." In A. S. Pushkin, *Kapitanskaia dochka*. Seriia "Literaturnye pamiatniki." Moscow: Nauka, 1964, pp. 245–60.
[284] ———. "Pushkin v rabote nad *Istoriei Pugacheva* i povest'iu *Kapitanskaia dochka*." In Oksman, *Ot 'Kapitanskoi dochki' k 'Zapiskam okhotnika.'* Saratov: Saratovskoe knizhnoe izd., 1959, pp. 5–133.
[285] Orlov, A. S. "Narodnye pesni v *Kapitanskoi dochke* Pushkina," *Khudozhestvennyi fol'klor*, Gos. Akademiia Khudozhestvennykh Nauk, 2–3 (1927): 80–95.
[286] Petrunina, N. N. "K tvorcheskoi istorii *Kapitanskoi dochki*," *Russkaia literatura*, 13, No. 2 (1970): 79–92.
[287] ———. "U istokov *Kapitanskoi dochki*." In [66], listed above, pp. 73–123.
[288] Poliakov, A. "Kartina burana u Pushkina i S. T. Aksakova." In N. V. Iakovlev, ed., *Pushkin v mirovoi literature*. Leningrad: Gos. izd., 1926, pp. 287–88.
[289] Prianishnikov, N. E. "Proza Pushkina (Iz nabliudenii nad poeti-

koi *Kapitanskoi dochki*)." In Prianishnikov, *Zapiski slovesnika*. Orenburg: Orenburgskoe knizhnoe izd., 1963, pp. 5–26.

[290] Prorokova, A. "K analizu stilia pushkinskoi prozy." In K. A. Alaverdov, ed., *Stil' i iazyk A. S. Pushkina: 1837–1937*. Moscow: Uchpedgiz, 1937, pp. 123–29.

[291] Rossel's, V. "Perevod i natsional'noe svoeobrazie podlinnika." In V. Rossel's, ed., *Voprosy khudozhestvennogo perevoda: Sbornik statei*. Moscow: Sovetskii pisatel', 1955, pp. 165–212.

[292] Saintsbury, George. "New Novels," *The Academy*, May 29, 1875, p. 552.

[293] Sarychev, A. P. "Kharakter i obstoiatel'stva v *Kapitanskoi dochke* A. S. Pushkina," *Voprosy russkoi literatury*, Uchenye zapiski Moskovskogo gos. ped. inst.-a im. V. I. Lenina, 405 (1970), 57–88.

[294] Shklovskii, V. *Povesti o proze, razmyshleniia i razbory*. Vol. 2. Moscow: Khudozhestvennaia literatura, 1966, pp. 28–65.

[295] ———. "V zashchitu sotsiologicheskogo metoda," *Novyi Lef*, 1927, No. 3: 20–25.

[296] Skobelev, V. P. "Pugachev i Savel'ich (K probleme narodnogo kharaktera v povesti A. S. Pushkina *Kapitanskaia dochka*)," *Pushkinskii sbornik*, Uchenye zapiski Leningradskogo gos. ped. inst.-a im. A. I. Gertsena, 483 (1972): 43–58.

[297] Stankiewicz, Eugenia. "Statisticheskii analiz leksiki A. S. Pushkina na osnovanii *Evgeniia Onegina* i *Kapitanskoi dochki*." In Bohdan Galster, ed., *O poetyce Aleksandra Puszkina*. Poznan: Uniwersytet im. Adama Mickiewicza, 1975, pp. 101–7.

[298] Strakhov, N. *Kriticheskii razbor 'Voiny i mira.'* St. Petersburg: Tip. Maikova, 1871, p. 210.

[299] Syroegina, G. "Rechevye stili v *Kapitanskoi dochke* A. S. Pushkina." In K. A. Alaverdov, ed., *Stil' i iazyk A. S. Pushkina: 1837–1937*. Moscow: Uchpedgiz, 1937, pp. 130–51.

[300] Toibin, I. M. "Iz nabliudenii nad poetikoi *Kapitanskoi dochki* (*Kapitanskaia dochka* i *Istoriia Pugacheva*)," *Voprosy literatury i metodiki prepodavaniia*, Uchenye zapiski Kurskogo gos. ped. inst.-a, 73 (1970): 71–99.

[301] ———. "O *Kapitanskoi dochke* Pushkina (K probleme natsional'nogo svoeobraziia)," *Voprosy literatury*, Uchenye zapiski Kurskogo gos. ped. inst.-a, 94 (1972): 116–38.

[302] Trubitsyn, N. "Pushkin i russkaia narodnaia poeziia." In [1], listed above, Vol. 4, pp. 63–64.

[303] Tsvetaeva, Marina. "Pushkin i Pugachev." In Tsvetaeva, *Moi Pushkin*. Moscow: Sovetskii pisatel', 1967, pp. 105–60.

[304] Turbin, V. N. "Kharaktery samozvantsev v tvorchestve A. S. Pushkina," *Filologicheskie nauki*, 1968, No. 6: 85–95.

[305] Tuzova, M. F. "Leksicheskii kommentarii k povesti A. S. Pushkina *Kapitanskaia dochka*," *Uchenye zapiski Moskovskogo oblastnogo ped. inst.-a im. N. K. Krupskoi*, Vol. 109, Trudy kafedry russkogo iazyka, No. 7 (1961): 624–29.

[306] Udodov, B. T. "O dvukh geroiiakh veka (Shvabrin i Pechorin)," *Sbornik materialov vtoroi nauchnoi sessii vuzov Tsentral'no-Chernozemnoi zony, Literaturovedenie*, Izd. Voronezhskogo univ.-a, 1967, pp. 3–13.

[307] Vinogradov, A. F. "Tematicheskie modifikatsii v arkhitektonike romana A. S. Pushkina *Kapitanskaia dochka*," *Russkaia literatura XIX veka: Voprosy siuzheta i kompozitsii*, Uchenye zapiski Gor'kovskogo gos. univ.-a im. N. I. Lobachevskogo, 132 (1972): 78–80.

[308] Vinogradov, V. V. "Iz istorii stilei russkogo istoricheskogo romana," *Voprosy literatury*, 1958, No. 12: 134–35.

[309] Vladimirskaia, N. M. "Pugachevskoe vosstanie v khudozhestvennoi proze Pushkina i Lermontova," *Pushkinskii sbornik*, Pskovskii gos. ped. inst. im. S. M. Kirova, 1968, pp. 48–55.

[310] Vol'pert, L. I. "Pol'sko-russkii epizod *Foblasa* i pugachevskaia tema u Pushkina," *Izvestiia Akademii Nauk SSSR, Seriia literatury i iazyka*, 32 (1974): 270–74.

[311] Vorob'ev, V. "Iazyk Pugacheva v povesti Pushkina *Kapitanskaia dochka*," *Russkii iazyk v shkole*, 1953, No. 5: 23–29.

[312] Zvoznikov, A. A. "Osobennosti izobrazheniia russkogo natsional'nogo kharaktera v proze Pushkina (*Kapitanskaia dochka*)," *Russkaia literatura*, 1976, No. 1: 123–31.

"Kirdzhali"

[313] Dvoichenko-Markova, E. M. "Pushkin i narodnoe tvorchestvo Moldavii i Valakhii." In Dvoichenko-Markova, *Russko-rumynskie literaturnye sviazi v pervoi polovine XIX veka*. Moscow: Nauka, 1966, pp. 42–50.

[314] Gordlevskii, V. A. "Kto takoi Kirdzhali?" In S. I. Vavilov et al., eds., *A. S. Pushkin, 1799–1949: Materialy iubileinykh torzhestv*. Moscow: Akademiia Nauk SSSR, 1951, pp. 261–81.

[315] Iazvitskii, V. "Kto byl Kirdzhali, geroi povesti Pushkina?," *Golos minuvshego*, 1919, No. 1–4: 45–60.

[316] Kodjak, Andrej, and Lorraine Wynne. "Puškin's 'Kirdžali': An Informational Model," *Russian Literature*, 7, No. 1 (1979): 44–66.

[317] Koroban, V. "Motivy moldavskikh ballad v povesti Pushkina 'Kirdzhali,'" *Oktiabr'* (Kishinev), 1956, No. 8: 85–88.

[318] Oganian, L. N. "Novye arkhivnye materialy o geroe povesti A. S. Pushkina 'Kirdzhali,'" *Pushkin na iuge*, Trudy pushkinskikh konferentsii Kishineva i Odessy, 1958, pp. 37–56.

[319] Oksenov, I. A. "Kirdzhali." In Oksenov, ed., *Pushkin: 1834 god*. Leningrad: Pushkinskoe obshchestvo, 1934, pp. 50–64.

[320] Trubetskoi, B. "Novye arkhivnye materialy o 'Kirdzhali,'" *Literaturnoe nasledstvo*, 58 (1952): 333–37.

[321] ———. *Pushkin v Moldavii*. Kishinev: Kartia Moldoveniaske, 1976, pp. 309–16.

Maria Shoning (*Maria Schoning*; fragment)

[322] Iakubovich, D. "*Maria Shoning* kak etap istoriko-sotsial'nogo romana Pushkina," *Zven'ia*, 3–4 (1934): 146–67.

"My provodili vecher na dache u kniagini D." ("We Were Spending the Evening at Princess D.'s Dacha"; fragment)

[323] Bikerman, I. "Kto takoi Vershnev?," *Pushkin i ego sovremenniki*, 19–20 (1914): 49–55.

[324] Gillel'son, M. I. "Pushkin v ital'ianskom izdanii dnevnika D. F. Fikel'mon," *Vremennik Pushkinskoi komissii*, 1967–1968 (published 1970): 14–32.

"Na uglu malen'koi ploshchadi" ("In the Corner of a Small Square"; fragment). See entries under Gosti s"ezzhalis' na dachu."

"Pikovaia dama" ("The Queen of Spades")

[325] Alekseev, M. P. "Pushkin i nauka ego vremeni." In Alekseev, *Pushkin: Sravnitel'no-istoricheskie issledovaniia*. Leningrad: Nauka, 1972, pp. 95–110.

[326] Al'tman, M. S. "O sobstvennykh imenakh v proizvedeniiakh Pushkina," *Uchenye zapiski Gor'kovskogo universiteta, Seriia istoriko-filologicheskaia*, 72 (1964): 390–91.

[327] Belousov, R. "Siluet 'pikovoi damy' (N. P. Golitsynoi)." In Belousov, *Iz rodoslovnoi geroev knig*. Moscow: Sovetskaia Rossiia, 1974, pp. 233–38.

[328] Bem, A. L. "*Faust* v tvorchestve Pushkina," *Slavia*, 13 (1934–35), 390–94.

[329] ———. "'Pikovaia dama' v tvorchestve Dostoevskogo." In Bem, ed., *O Dostoevskom: Sbornik statei*. Vol. 3. Prague: Svoboda, 1936, pp. 37–81.

[330] Bitsilli, P. "Zametki o Pushkine, II: Simvolika 'Pikovoi damy,'" *Slavia*, 11 (1932): 557–60.

[331] Bobrova, E. I. "Perevod P. Merime 'Pikovoi damy' (Avtograficheskaia rukopis')," *Pushkin: Issledovaniia i materialy*, 2 (1958): 354–61.

[332] Briggs, A. D. P. "'Pikovaya dama' and 'Taman'': Questions of Kinship," *Journal of Russian Studies*, 37 (1979): 13–20.

[333] Brzoza, Halina. "Dualizm immanentnoi mirovozzrencheskoi sistemy 'Pikovoi damy' A. Pushkina." In Bohdan Galster, ed., *O poetyce Aleksandra Puszkina*. Poznan: Uniwersytet im. Adama Mickiewicza, 1975, pp. 83–100.

[334] Burgin, Diana L. "The Mystery of 'Pikovaja dama': A New Interpretation." In Joachim Baer and Norman W. Ingham, eds., *Mnemozina: Studia litteraria russica in honorem V. Setchkarev*. Munich: W. Fink, 1974, pp. 46–56.

[335] Chernyshev, V. I. "Temnye slova v russkom iazyke." In I. I. Meshchaninov, ed., *Akademiku N. Ia. Marru*. Moscow: Akademiia Nauk SSSR, 1935, pp. 393–407.

[336] Chkhaidze, L. V. "O real'nom znachenii motiva trekh kart v 'Pikovoi dame,'" *Pushkin: Issledovaniia i materialy*, 3 (1960): 455–60.

[337] ———. "Pometki Pushkina na pis'me k nemu A. P. Pleshcheeva (Eshche o real'nom znachenii motiva trekh kart v 'Pikovoi dame')," *Vremennik Pushkinskoi komissii*, 1971 (published 1973): 82–88.

[338] Clayton, J. Douglas. "'Spader Dame,' 'Pique-Dame,' and 'Pikovaia dama': A German Source for Pushkin?," *Germano-Slavica*, 1974, No. 4: 5–10.

[339] Egunov, A. N. "Nemetskaia 'Pikovaia dama,'" *Vremennik Pushkinskoi komissii*, 1967–68 (published 1970): 111–15.

[340] Falchikov, M. "The Outsider and the Number Game: Some Observations on 'Pikovaia dama,'" *Essays in Poetics* (Keele), 2, No. 2 (1977): 96–106.

[341] Faletti, Heidi E. "Remarks on Style as Manifestation of Narrative Technique in 'Pikovaia dama,'" *Canadian-American Slavic Studies*, 11 (1977): 114–33.

[342] Gengel', M. A. "K izucheniiu leksiki Pushkina (Oboznachenie vremeni v 'Pikovoi dame')," *Uchenye zapiski Permskogo pedagogicheskogo instituta*, 2 (1937): 65–73.

[343] Gershenzon, M. O., "'Pikovaia dama.'" In [1], listed above, Vol. 4, pp. 328–34.

[344] Gide, André. "Préface à la 'Dame de Pique.'" In Gide, *Oeuvres complètes*. Ed. L. Martin-Chauffier. Vol. 11. Bruges: NRF, 1936, pp. 139–42.

[345] Gregg, Richard A. "Balzac and the Women in 'The Queen of Spades,'" *Slavic and East European Journal*, 10, No. 3 (1966): 279–82.

[346] Gribushin, I. I. "Iz nabliudenii nad tekstami Pushkina. 2: Vyigrysh na troiku i semerku do 'Pikovoi damy,'" *Vremennik Pushkinskoi komissii*, 1973 (published 1975): 85–89.

[347] Grossman, L. P. "'Pikovaia dama' i novella Ren'e." In Grossman, *Ot Pushkina do Bloka: Etiudy i portrety*. Moscow: Sovremennye problemy, 1926, pp. 65–72.

[348] ———. "Ustnaia novella Pushkina." In Grossman, *Etiudy o Pushkine*. Moscow: L. D. Frenkel', 1923, pp. 77–113.

[349] Iakubovich, D. "Literaturnyi fon 'Pikovoi damy' (Diukanzh, Fan-der-Vel'de.)," *Literaturnyi sovremennik*, 1935, No. 1: 206–12.

[350] ———. "O 'Pikovoi dame.'" In Iakubovich, *Pushkin: 1833 god*. Leningrad: Pushkinskoe obshchestvo, 1933, pp. 57–68.

[351] ———. "'Pikovaia dama.'" In A. S. Pushkin, *Pikovaia dama*. Leningrad: Khudozhestvennaia literatura, 1936, pp. 51–70.

[352] Kalushin, M. "Rabota Pushkina nad 'Pikovoi damoi.'" In *Pikovaia dama*. Opera P. I. Chaikovskogo. Leningrad: Iskusstvo, 1938, pp. 5–33.

[353] Kashin, N. "Po povodu 'Pikovoi damy,'" *Pushkin i ego sovremenniki*, 31–32 (1927): 25–34.

[354] Khodasevich, V. "'Pikovaia dama' A. S. Pushkina i povest' V. Titova 'Uedinennyi domik na Vasil'evskom.'" In Khodasevich, *Stat'i o russkoi poezii*. Petrograd: Epokha, 1922, pp. 97–106.

[355] Kodjak, Andrej. "'The Queen of Spades' in the Context of the Faust Legend." In Andrej Kodjak and Kiril Taranovsky, eds., *Alexander Puškin: A Symposium on the 175th Anniversary of His Birth*. New York: New York Univ. Press, 1976, pp. 87–118.

[356] Kogan, L. "Pushkin v perevodakh Merime ('Pikovaia dama')," *Pushkin: Vremennik Pushkinskoi komissii*, 4–5 (1939): 331–56.

[357] Labriolle, F. de. "Le 'Secret des trois cartes' dans la 'Dame de Pique' de Pushkin," *Canadian Slavonic Papers*, 11, No. 2 (1969): 261–71.

[358] Leighton, Lauren G. "Gematria in 'The Queen of Spades': A Decembrist Puzzle," *Slavic and East European Journal*, 21, No. 4 (1977): 455–69.

[359] ———. "Numbers and Numerology in 'The Queen of Spades,'" *Canadian Slavonic Papers*, 19, No. 4 (1977): 417–43.

[360] Lerner, N. O. "Istoriia 'Pikovoi damy.'" In Lerner, *Rasskazy o Pushkine*. Leningrad: Priboi, 1929, pp. 132–64.

[361] ———. "Original 'Pikovoi damy' (Kn. N. P. Golitsyna, urozhdennaia gr. Chernysheva)," *Stolitsa i usad'ba*, 1916, No. 52: 11–13.

[362] Lotman, Iu. M. "Tema kart i kartochnoi igry v russkoi literature nachala XIX veka," *Trudy po znakovym sistemam*, Vol. 7, Uchenye zapiski Tartuskogo gos. univ-a im. P. Stuchki, 394 (1975): 120–44.

[363] ———. "The Theme of Cards and the Card Game in XIXth Century Russian Literature," *PTL: A Journal for Descriptive Poetics and Theory*, 3, No. 3 (1978): 455–92.

[364] Manuilov, V. A. "'Pikovaia dama' A. S. Pushkina." In *Pikovaia dama*. Opera P. I. Chaikovskogo. Leningrad: Gos. Akademicheskii teatr opery i baleta im S. M. Kirova, 1935, pp. 89–117.

[365] Mikhailova, N. I. "Povestvovatel'naia struktura 'Pikovoi damy' (K izucheniiu tipov povestvovaniia v proze A. S. Pushkina)," *Vestnik Moskovskogo Universiteta, Seriia filologicheskaia*, 29, No. 3 (1974): 10–19.

[366] Murav'eva, O. S. "Fantastika v povesti Pushkina 'Pikovaia dama,'" *Pushkin: Issledovaniia i materialy*, 8 (1978): 62–69.

[367] Petrunina, N. N. "Pushkin i traditsiia volshebno-skazochnogo povestvovaniia (K poetike 'Pikovoi damy')," *Russkaia Literatura*, 23, No. 3 (1980): 30–50.

[368] Poddubnaia, R. "O poetike 'Pikovoi damy.'" In Bohdan Galster, ed., *O poetyce Aleksandra Puszkina*. Poznan: Uniwersytet im. Adama Mickiewicza, 1975, pp. 43–66.

[369] Poliakova, E. "Real'nost' i fantastika 'Pikovoi damy.'" In S. Mashinskii, ed., *V mire Pushkina: Sbornik statei*. Moscow: Sovetskii pisatel', 1974, pp. 373–412.

[370] Rabkina, N. A. "Istoricheskii prototip 'Pikovoi damy,'" *Voprosy istorii*, 43, No. 1 (1968): 213–16.

[371] Roberts, Carolyn. "Puškin's 'Pikovaja dama' and the Opera Libretto," *Canadian Review of Comparative Literature*, 6, No. 1 (1979): 9–26.

[372] Rosen, Nathan. "The Magic Cards in 'The Queen of Spades,'" *Slavic and East European Journal*, 19, No. 3 (1975): 255–75.

[373] ———. "The Magic Cards: A Correction," *Slavic and East European Journal*, 21, No. 2 (1977): 301–2.

[374] Schwartz, Murray M., and Albert Schwartz. "'The Queen of Spades': A Psychoanalytic Interpretation," *Texas Studies in Literature and Language*, 17 (1975): 275–88.

[375] Sharypkin, D. M. "'Pikovaia dama' i povest' Marmontelia 'Okno,'" *Vremennik Pushkinskoi komissii*, 1974 (published 1977): 139–42.

[376] ———. "Vokrug 'Pikovoi damy,'" *Vremennik Pushkinskoi komissii*, 1972 (published 1974): 128–38.

[377] Shaw, Joseph T. "The 'Conclusion' of Pushkin's 'Queen of Spades.'" In Zbigniew Folejewski et al., eds., *Studies in Russian and Polish Literature in Honor of Wacław Lednicki*. The Hague: Mouton, 1962, pp. 114–26.

[378] Slonimskii, A. L. "O kompozitsii 'Pikovoi damy.'" In Slonimskii, *Pushkinskii sbornik pamiati Professora S. A. Vengerova*. Moscow: Gos. izd., 1923, pp. 171–80.

[379] Tamarchenko, N. D. "O poetike 'Pikovoi damy' A. S. Pushkina," *Voprosy teorii i istorii literatury*. Uchenye zapiski Kazanskogo gos. ped. inst.-a, 72 (1971): 45–62.

[380] ———. "O zhanrovoi obshchnosti 'Pikovoi damy' A. S. Pushkina i *Prestupleniia i nakazaniia* F. M. Dostoevskogo," *XXVI Gertsenovskie chteniia: Literaturovedenie. Nauchnye doklady*. Leningrad: Leningradskii gos. ped. inst. im. A. I. Gertsena, 1973, pp. 44–49.

[381] ———. "'Pikovaia dama' A. S. Pushkina i 'neistovaia' literatura," *XXIII Gertsenovskie chteniia: Filologicheskie nauki*, Leningradskii gos. ped. inst. im. A. I. Gertsena, 1970, pp. 49–50.

[382] Tomashevskii, B. V. "Ritm prozy ('Pikovaia dama')." In Tomashevskii, *O stikhe: stat'i*. Leningrad: Priboi, 1929, pp. 254–318.

[383] Vinogradov, V. V. "Stil' 'Pikovoi damy,'" *Pushkin: Vremennik Pushkinskoi komissii*, 2 (1936): 74–147.

[384] Virolainen, M. N. "Ironiia v povesti Pushkina 'Pikovaia dama,'"

Problemy pushkinovedeniia, Leningradskii gos. ped. inst. im. A. I. Gertsena, 1975, pp. 169–75.

[385] Weber, Harry B. "'Pikovaja dama': A Case for Freemasonry in Russian Literature," *Slavic and East European Journal*, 12, No. 4 (1968): 435–47.

[386] Zapadov, A. "Chudo 'Pikovoi damy.'" In Zapadov, *V glubine stroki*. 2d rev. ed. Moscow: Sovetskii pisatel', 1975, pp. 45–72.

Povesti pokoinogo Ivana Petrovicha Belkina (*The Tales of the Late Ivan Petrovich Belkin*)

[387] Abakumov, S. I. "Iz nabliudenii nad iazykom *Povestei Belkina.*" In K. A. Alaverdov, ed., *Stil' i iazyk A. S. Pushkina.* Moscow: Uchpedgiz, 1937, pp. 66–89.

[388] Bel'kind, V. S. "Eshche raz o 'zagadke' I. P. Belkina," *Problemy pushkinovedeniia*, Leningradskii gos. ped. inst. im. A. I. Gertsena, 1975, pp. 55–58.

[389] ———. "Printsipy tsiklizatsii v *Povestiakh Belkina* A. S. Pushkina," *Voprosy siuzhetoslozheniia: Sbornik statei*, 3 (1974): 118–28.

[390] Bem, A. L. "Boldinskaia osen'." In Bem, *O Pushkine: Stat'i.* Uzhgorod: Pis'mena, 1937, pp. 98–103.

[391] Berkovskii, N. Ia. "O *Povestiakh Belkina* (Pushkin 30-kh godov i voprosy narodnosti i realizma)." In Berkovskii, *Stat'i o literature.* Moscow: GIKhL, 1962, pp. 242–356.

[392] Bethea, David M., and Sergei Davydov. "Pushkin's Saturnine Cupid: The Poetics of Parody in *The Tales of Belkin,*" *PMLA*, 96, No. 1 (1981): 8–21.

[393] Blagoi, D. D. "*Povesti Belkina* ('Vystrel,' 'Stantsionnyi smotritel''')." In Blagoi, *Ot Kantemira do nashikh dnei.* Vol. 2. Moscow: Khudozhestvennaia literatura, 1973, pp. 191–212.

[394] Brun-Zejmis, Julia. "*Malen'kie tragedii* and *Povesti Belkina*: Western Idolatry and Puškinian Parodies," *Russian Language Journal*, 32, No. 111 (1978): 65–75.

[395] Eikhenbaum, B. M. "Boldinskie pobasenki Pushkina," *Zhizn' iskusstva*, 1919, No. 316–17: 2, and No. 318: 2.

[396] Gippius, V. V. "*Povesti Belkina.*" In Gippius, *Ot Pushkina do Bloka.* Moscow: Nauka, 1966, pp. 7–45.

[397] Gregg, Richard A. "A Scapegoat for All Seasons: The Unity and the Shape of *The Tales of Belkin,*" *Slavic Review*, 30, No. 4 (1971), 748–61.

[398] Gukasova, A. G. *'Povesti Belkina' A. S. Pushkina.* Moscow: Akademiia Pedagogicheskikh Nauk RSFSR, 1949.

[399] Iakubovich, D. "*Povesti Belkina.*" In A. S. Pushkin, *Povesti Belkina.* Leningrad: Khudozhestvennaia literatura, 1936, pp. 119–48.

[400] ———. "Predislovie k *Povestiam Belkina* i povestvovatel'nye priemy Val'ter Skotta." In N. V. Iakovlev, *Pushkin v mirovoi literature: Sbornik statei.* Leningrad: Gos. izd., 1926, pp. 160–87, 376–83.

[401] ———. "Reministsenzii iz Val'ter Skotta v *Povestiakh Belkina,*" *Pushkin i ego sovremenniki,* 37 (1928): 100–118.

[402] Iskoz, A. S. [Dolinin]. "*Povesti Belkina.*" In [1], listed above, Vol. 4, pp. 184–200.

[403] Kodjak, Andrej. *Pushkin's I. P. Belkin.* Columbus, Ohio: Slavica, 1979.

[404] ———. "Shifr Pushkina," *Novyi zhurnal,* 101 (1970), 80–94.

[405] Liubovich, N. "*Povesti Belkina* kak polemicheskii etap v razvitii pushkinskoi prozy," *Novyi mir,* 1937, No. 2: 260–74.

[406] Makogonenko, G. "O *Povestiakh Belkina* A. S. Pushkina." In A. S. Pushkin, *Povesti Belkina.* Leningrad: Khudozhestvennaia literatura, 1974, pp. 3–24.

[407] Mikhailova, N. I. "Boldinskie povesti Pushkina i parodii Senkovskogo," *Boldinskie chteniia,* Volgo-Viatskoe knizhnoe izd., 1977, pp. 144–52.

[408] Prokudin, S. V. "K voprosu o povestvovatel'noi strukture *Povestei Belkina,*" *Po zakonam zhanra,* Tambovskii gos. ped. inst., 1975, pp. 76–91.

[409] Sazonova, S. "Zanimatel'nost' kak khudozhestvennyi priem v *Povestiakh Belkina,*" *Pod''em,* 1975, No. 5: 123–27.

[410] Shvartsband, S. M. "Istoriia odnoi mistifikatsii (K voprosu o sushchnosti obraza I. P. Belkina)," *Voprosy russkoi, sovetskoi i zarubezhnoi literatury,* Nauchnye trudy Novosibirskogo gos. ped. inst.-a, 65 (1971): 73–86.

[411] ———. "Zhanrovaia priroda *Povestei Belkina* A. S. Pushkina (Sootnoshenie siuzheta, stilia i zhanra)," *Voprosy siuzhetoslozheniia: Sbornik statei,* 3 (1974): 129–42.

[412] Tudorovskaia, E. A. "Vremia *Povestei Belkina,*" *Voprosy literatury i fol'klora,* Izd. Voronezhskogo Univ.-a, 1973, pp. 220–23.

[413] Unbegaun, B. O. "Introduction." In A. S. Pushkin, *The Tales of the Late Ivan Petrovich Belkin.* Oxford: Blackwell, 1947, pp. xi–xxxiii.

[414] Uzin, V. S. *O 'Povestiakh Belkina': Iz kommentariev chitatelia.* Petrograd: Akvilon, 1924.

[415] Van der Eng, Jan, A. G. F. van Holk, and Jan M. Meijer. *'The Tales of Belkin' by A. S. Puškin.* Dutch Studies in Russian Literature, No. 1. The Hague: Mouton, 1968.

[416] Varneke, V. "Postroenie *Povestei Belkina,*" *Pushkin i ego sovremenniki,* 38–39 (1930): 162–68.

[417] Ward, Dennis. "The Structure of Pushkin's *Tales of Belkin,*" *Slavonic and East European Review,* 33, No. 81 (1955): 516–27.

Individual tales in *Povesti Belkina*

"Baryshnia-krest'ianka" ("The Squire's Daughter")

[418] Al'tman, M. S. "'Baryshnia-krest'ianka' (Pushkin i Karamzin)," *Slavia*, 10 (1931): 782–92.

[419] Magazanik, E. "Dve Lizy: Krest'ianka-baryshnia i baryshnia-krest'ianka," *Trudy Samarkandskogo gos. universiteta im. Navoi*, n.s., 200 (1972): 47–58.

[420] Shelgunova, L. M. "'Esli-koli' v povesti 'Baryshnia-krest'ianka,'" *Russkaia rech'*, 1971, No. 2: 33–37.

[421] Shelgunova, L. M. "Iz nabliudenii nad iazykom povesti A. S. Pushkina 'Baryshnia-krest'ianka' (Khudoshestvennaia znachimost' prilagatel'nykh, oboznachaiushchikh tsvet)," *Problemy iazyka i stilia v literature*, Volgogradskii ped. inst. im. A. S. Serafimovicha, 1975, pp. 158–71.

[422] Speranskii, M. N. *"Baryshnia-krest'ianka"* Pushkina i *"Urok liubvi"* g-zhi Montol'e. Kharkov: [publ.?], 1910.

"Grobovshchik" ("The Undertaker")

[423] Bocharov, S. G. "O smysle 'Grobovshchika' (K probleme interpretatsii proizvedeniia)," *Kontekst, 1973: Literaturno-teoreticheskie issledovaniia*, 1974, pp. 196–230.

"Metel'" ("The Blizzard")

[424] Gershenzon, M. O. "Sny Pushkina." In Gershenzon, *Stat'i o Pushkine*. Moscow: Academia, 1926, pp. 97–98.

[425] Lednicki, Wacław. "Bits of Table Talk on Pushkin. III: 'The Snowstorm,'" *American Slavic and East European Review*, 4 (1947): 110–33. Reprinted in [53], listed above.

[426] Vinogradov, V. V. "Stil' i kompozitsiia povesti Pushkina 'Metel',''" *Kniga sporit s fil'mom*, "Mosfil'm," 7 (1973): 244–64.

[427] Vol'pert, L. I. "Pushkin i Lashosse (O siuzhetnom motive 'Meteli')," *Vremennik Pushkinskoi komissii*, 1975 (published 1979): 119–21.

"Stantsionnyi smotritel'" ("The Stationmaster")

[428] Al'tman, M. S. "Bludnaia doch' (*Unizhennye i oskorblennye* i 'Stantsionnyi smotritel'')," *Slavia*, 14 (1937): 12–30.

[429] Bel'kind, V. S. "Obraz 'malen'kogo cheloveka' u Pushkina i Dostoevskogo (Samson Vyrin i Makar Devushkin)," *Pushkinskii sbornik*, Pskovskii gos. ped. inst. im S. M. Kirova, 1968, pp. 140–47.

[430] Bocharov, S. G. "Pushkin i Gogol' ('Stantsionnyi smotritel'' i 'Shinel'')." In N. L. Stepanov et al., eds., *Problemy tipologii russkogo realizma*. Moscow: Nauka, 1969, pp. 210–40.

[431] Little, Edmund. "The Peasant and the Stationmaster: A Question of Realism," *Journal of Russian Studies*, Vol. 38 (1979): 23–31.

[432] Savvin, N. A. "'Stantsionnyi smotritel'" A. Pushkina," *Russkii iazyk v sovetskoi shkole*, 1930, No. 1: 63–66.

[433] Shaw, J. Thomas. "Puškin's 'The Stationmaster' and the New Testament Parable," *Slavic and East European Journal*, 21, No. 1 (1977): 3–29.

[434] Vinogradov, V. V. "K izucheniiu iazyka i stilia pushkinskoi prozy (Rabota Pushkina nad povest'iu 'Stantsionnyi smotritel'')," *Russkii iazyk v shkole*, 1949, No. 3: 18–32.

"Vystrel" ("The Shot")

[435] Busch, Ulrich. "Puškin und Sil'vio (Zur Deutung von 'Vystrel'; eine Studie über Puškins Erzählkunst)." In M. Braun and E. Koschmieder, eds., *Slawistische Studien zum V. Internationalen Slawistenkongress in Sofia, 1963*. Göttingen: Vandenhoeck & Ruprecht, 1963, pp. 401–25.

[436] Grossman, L. P. "Istoricheskii fon 'Vystrela.'" In Grossman, *Stat'i o Pushkine*. Chicago: Russian Language Specialties, 1968, pp. 203–35. Originally published in Moscow in 1930.

[437] Kodjak, Andrej. "O povesti Pushkina 'Vystrel,'" *Mosty*, 15 (1970): 190–212.

[438] Lerner, N. O. "Pushkinologicheskie etiudy. IX: K genezisu 'Vystrela,'" *Zven'ia*, 5 (1935): 125–33.

[439] Petrovskii, M. "Morfologiia pushkinskogo 'Vystrela.'" In V. Briusov, ed., *Problemy poetiki*. Moscow: Zemlia i fabrika, 1925, pp. 173–204.

[440] Poddubnaia, R. N. "Geroi i ego literaturnoe razvitie (Otrazhenie 'Vystrela' Pushkina v tvorchestve Dostoevskogo)." In G. M. Fridlender, ed., *Dostoevskii: Materialy i issledovaniia*. Vol. 3. Leningrad: Nauka, 1978, pp. 54–66.

[441] Reformatskii, A. A. *Opyt analiza novellisticheskoi kompozitsii*. Vol. 1. Moscow: Opoiaz, 1922.

[442] Shaw, J. Thomas. "Puškin's 'The Shot,'" *Indiana Slavic Studies*, Indiana Univ. Publications, Russian and East European Series, 28 (1963): 113–29.

Roman na kavkazkikh vodakh (A Novel at a Caucasian Spa; fragment)

[443] Izmailov, N. V. "*Roman na kavkazkikh vodakh*: Nevypolnennyi zamysel Pushkina," *Pushkin i ego sovremenniki*, 37 (1928): 68–99.

Roman v pis'makh (A Novel in Letters; fragment)

[444] Lotman, Iu. M. "Tri zametki k pushkinskim tekstam: 1," *Vremennik Pushkinskoi komissii*, 1974 (published 1977): 88–89.

[445] Vol'pert, L. I. "Pushkin i Shoderlo de Laklo (Na puti k *Romanu v pis'makh*)," *Pushkinskii sbornik*, Uchenye zapiski Leningradskogo gos. ped. inst.-a im. A. I. Gertsena, 483 (1972): 84–114.

Roslavlev (unfinished)

[446] Filippova, N. "Zakonchen li pushkinskii *Roslavlev*?," *Russkaia literatura*, 1962, No. 1: 55–59.
[447] Glukhov, V. I. "O tvorcheskom zamysle povesti Pushkina *Roslavlev*," *Nauchnye doklady vysshei shkoly: Filologicheskie nauki*, 1962, No. 1: 98–107.
[448] Grushkin, A. I. "*Roslavlev*," *Pushkin: Vremennik Pushkinskoi komissii*, 6 (1941): 322–37.
[449] Gukovskii, G. A. "Ob istochnike *Roslavleva*," *Pushkin: Vremennik Pushkinskoi komissii*, 4–5 (1939): 477–79.
[450] Tomashevskii, B. V. "Zametki o Pushkine. II: 'Kinzhal' i mm-e de Staël," *Pushkin i ego sovremenniki*, 36 (1923): 82–95.
[451] Vengerov, S. A. "Russkaia Sharlotta Korde." In [1], listed above, Vol. 4, pp. 555–60.

Russkii Pelam (*A Russian Pelham*; fragment)

[452] Annenkov, N. V. "Literaturnye proekty A. S. Pushkina. Plany sotsial'nogo romana i fantasticheskoi dramy," *Vestnik Evropy*, 16, No. 7 (1881): 29–60.
[453] Kazantsev, P. M. "K izucheniiu *Russkogo Pelama* A. S. Pushkina," *Vremennik Pushkinskoi komissii*, 1964 (published 1967): 21–33.
[454] Povarin, S. I. "*Russkii Pelam* A. S. Pushkina," *Pamiati A. S. Pushkina: Sbornik statei prepodavatelei i slushatelei Istoriko-filologicheskogo fakul'teta Sankt-Peterburgskogo universiteta*, Zapiski Istoriko-filologicheskogo fakul'teta, 57 (1900): 329–50.
[455] Shesterikov, S. P. "Odna iz vospetykh Pushkinym." In M. P. Alekseev, ed., *Pushkin: Stat'i i materialy*. Vol. 1. Odessa: Odesskii dom uchenykh, 1925, pp. 32–46.

"Uchast' moia reshena" ("My Fate Is Sealed"; fragment)

[456] Borovskii, Ia. M. "K tekstu nabroska 'Uchast' moia reshena'," *Vremennik Pushkinskoi komissii*, 1973 (published 1975): 77.

"Uedinennyi domik na Vasil'evskom" ("The Lonely Cottage on Vasilev Island"; apocryphal)

[457] Akhmatova, A. A. "Neizdannye zametki Anny Akhmatovoi o Pushkine" (comp. and ed. E. G. Gershtein), *Voprosy literatury*, 1970, No. 1: 195–206.
[458] ———. "Pushkin i Nevskoe vzmor'e" (ed. E. G. Gershtein), *Literaturnaia gazeta*, 1969, No. 23: 7.
[459] Brodskii, N. "Novoe o Pushkine," *Golos minuvshego*, 1913, No. 4: 270–75.
[460] Khodasevich, V. "'Pikovaia dama' A. S. Pushkina i povest' V. Titova 'Uedinennyi domik na Vasil'evskom.'" In Khodasevich, *Stat'i o russkoi poezii*. Petrograd: Epokha, 1922, pp. 97–106.

[461] Kodjak, Andrej. "Ustnaia rech' Pushkina v zapisi Titova." In *American Contributions to the Seventh International Congress of Slavists* (Warsaw, Aug. 21–27, 1973), Vol. 2: *Literature and Folklore*. Ed. Victor Terras. The Hague: Mouton, 1973, pp. 321–38.

[462] Lerner, N. O. "Zabytaia povest' Pushkina," *Severnye zapiski*, 1913, No. 1: 184–88.

[463] Phillips, Delbert. "'Uedinennyj domik na Vasil'evskom (ostrove)': Puškin and the Veiled Supernatural," *Russian Language Journal*, 32, No. 112 (1978): 79–87.

[464] Pisnaia, N. N. "Fabula 'Uedinennogo domika na Vasil'evskom,'" *Pushkin i ego sovremenniki*, 31–32 (1927): 19–24.

[465] Shchegolev, P. E. "'Uedinennyi domik na Vasil'evskom': Rasskaz A. S. Pushkina, zapisannyi V. P. Titovym," *Den'*, 1912, No. 81–83: 22–24.

[466] Smirnov, I. P. "'Uedinennyi domik na Vasil'evskom' i 'Povest' o Savve Grudtsyne,'" *Pushkin: Issledovaniia i materialy*, 9 (1979): 207–14.

[467] Stepanov, N. L. "Povest', rasskazannaia Pushkinym." In Stepanov, *Poety i prozaiki*. Moscow: Khudozhestvennaia literatura, 1966, pp. 125–38.

[468] Zinger, L. "Sud'ba odnogo ustnogo rasskaza," *Voprosy literatury*, 1979, No. 4: 203–28.

"Vliublennyi bes" ("A Devil in Love"; outline)

[469] Oksman, Iu. G. "Vosstanovim li plan 'Vliublennogo besa'?" In B. L. Modzalevskii et al., ed., *Atenei: Istoriko-literaturnyi vremennik*. Vol. 1–2. Leningrad: Atenei, 1924, pp. 166–68.

[470] Tsiavlovskaia, T. "'Vliublennyi bes' (Neosushchestvlennyi zamysel Pushkina)," *Pushkin: Issledovaniia i materialy*, 3 (1960): 101–30.

"V nachale 1812 polk nash stoial" ("At the Beginning of 1812 Our Regiment Was Stationed"; fragment)

[471] Bondi, S. "Nachalo povesti." In Bondi, *Novye stranitsy Pushkina*. Moscow: Mir, 1931, pp. 104–8.

"Zapiski molodogo cheloveka" ("Notes of a Young Man"; fragment)

[472] Oksman, Iu. G. "Povest' o praporshchike Chernigovskogo polka (Neizvestnyi zamysel Pushkina)," *Zvezda*, 1930, No. 7: 217–20.

Other Frequently Cited Sources

[473] Bartenev, P. I. *Rasskazy o Pushkine, zapisannye so slov ego druzei P. I. Bartenevym v 1851–1860 godakh*. Ed. M. A. Tsiavlovskii. Leningrad: M. & S. Sabashnikov, 1925.

[474] Bestuzhev-Marlinskii, A. A. *Sochineniia.* Vol. 1. Moscow: GIKhL, 1958.

[475] Dostoevskii, F. M. *Polnoe sobranie sochinenii.* 30 vols. Leningrad: Nauka, 1973–.

[476] Dymshits, A., ed. *Pushkin v vospominaniiakh sovremennikov.* Leningrad: GIKhL, 1950.

[477] Gogol', N. V. *Polnoe sobranie sochinenii.* 14 vols. Moscow: Akademiia Nauk SSSR, 1937–52.

[478] Irving, Washington. *The Works of Washington Irving.* Vols. 1 and 2. Philadelphia: Lea & Blanchard, 1840.

[479] Modzalevskii, B. L. "Biblioteka A. S. Pushkina: Bibliograficheskoe opisanie," *Pushkin i ego sovremenniki,* 9–10 (1910): i–xix, 1–442.

[480] Nodier, Charles. *Oeuvres de Charles Nodier.* Vol. 2. Geneva: Slatkine Reprints, 1968. Originally published in Paris in 1832.

[481] *Polnoe sobranie russikh poslovits i pogovorok, raspolozhennoe po azbuchnomu poriadku.* St. Petersburg: Tip. Karla Kraia, 1822.

[482] Saitov, V. I., ed. *Ostaf'evskii arkhiv kniazei Viazemskikh.* Vols. 2 and 3. St. Petersburg: M. M. Stasiulevich, 1899.

[483] Scott, Sir Walter. *The Waverley Novels.* 25 vols. Edinburgh: A. & C. Black, [1829].

[484] Vatsuro, V. E., et al., comps. *A. S. Pushkin v vospominaniiakh sovremennikov.* 2 vols. Moscow: Khudozhestvennaia literatura, 1974.

[485] Veresaev, V. [Smidovich]. *Pushkin v zhizni.* 6th rev. ed. Vols. 1 and 2. Moscow: Sovetskii pisatel', 1936.

[486] Viazemskii, P. A. *Polnoe sobranie sochinenii.* Ed. S. D. Sheremetev. 12 vols. St. Petersburg: M. M. Stasiulevich, 1878–86.

[487] ———. *Staraia zapisnaia knizhka.* Ed. L. Ginzburg. Leningrad: Izd. pisatelei, 1929.

Index

Index